sex among the ʀabble

sex among the rabble

AN INTIMATE HISTORY OF GENDER & POWER

IN THE AGE OF REVOLUTION, PHILADELPHIA,

1730–1830   CLARE A. LYONS

Published for the OMOHUNDRO INSTITUTE

OF EARLY AMERICAN HISTORY AND CULTURE,

Williamsburg, Virginia, by the UNIVERSITY OF

NORTH CAROLINA PRESS, Chapel Hill

The Omohundro Institute of Early American History and Culture is sponsored jointly by the College of William and Mary and the Colonial Williamsburg Foundation. On November 15, 1996, the Institute adopted the present name in honor of a bequest from Malvern H. Omohundro, Jr.

© 2006
The University of North Carolina Press
Set in Scala by Keystone Typesetting, Inc.
Manufactured in the United States of America
Library of Congress Cataloging-in-Publication Data
Lyons, Clare A.
Sex among the rabble : an intimate history of gender
and power in the age of revolution, Philadelphia,
1730–1830 / Clare A. Lyons.
    p. cm.
Includes bibliographical references and index.
ISBN-13: 978-0-8078-3004-8 (cloth: alk. paper)
ISBN-10: 0-8078-3004-6 (cloth: alk. paper)
ISBN-13: 978-0-8078-5675-8 (pbk.: alk. paper)
ISBN-10: 0-8078-5675-4 (pbk.: alk. paper)
1. Sex—Pennsylvania—Philadelphia—History.
2. Sex role—Pennsylvania—Philadelphia—History.
3. Marginality, Social—Pennsylvania—Philadelphia—
History. I. Omohundro Institute of Early American
History & Culture. II. Title.
HQ18.U5L96   2006
306.7'09748'1109033—dc22   2005020668

This book received indirect support from an
unrestricted book publications grant awarded to
the Institute by the L. J. Skaggs and Mary C. Skaggs
Foundation of Oakland, California.

cloth   10 09 08 07 06   5 4 3 2 1
paper   10 09 08 07 06   5 4 3 2

For my Parents,
Beverly Lyons (née Pagano)
and Cornelius P. Lyons,
with Love and Gratitude . . .

CONTENTS

ILLUSTRATIONS AND TABLES

ABBREVIATIONS AND SHORT TITLES

AAS

    American Antiquarian Society, Worcester, Massachusetts

APS

    American Philosophical Society, Philadelphia

AWM

    American Weekly Mercury

CCAP

    City and County Archives of Philadelphia

DOD

    Guardians of the Poor, Almshouse Daily Occurrence Docket, 1789–1825, CCAP

FHL

    Friends Historical Library of Swarthmore College

FJ

    Freeman's Journal

Gloria Dei, Marriages

    Old Swedes (Gloria Dei) Church, Baptisms and Marriages, vols. I–IV, 1750–1825, HSP

GPCB

    Guardians of the Poor, Cases Referred to the Committee Upon Bastardy, 1821–1826, CCAP

GPM

    Guardians of the Poor, Minutes, 1788–1830, CCAP

GPSD

    Guardians of the Poor, Solicitor's Docket, 1822–1828, John M. Scott, Solicitor, HSP

HSP

    Historical Society of Pennsylvania, Philadelphia

IG

    Independent Gazetteer

LCP

Library Company of Philadelphia

MCD

Mayor's Court, Docket, 1759–1771, HSP; 1779–1830, CCAP

MSM

Magdalen Society of Philadelphia, Minutes of the Board of Managers.
1800–1825, HSP

OP, Bonds

Overseers of the Poor, Memorandum Book, Bonds of Indemnity,
1755–1787, HSP

OPM

Overseers of the Poor, Minutes, 1768–1787, CCAP

PC

Pennsylvania Chronicle

PDP

Pennsylvania Supreme Court, Pennsylvania Divorce Papers, 1785–1815,
PSA

PEP

Pennsylvania Evening Post

PFT

Prisoners for Trial, Philadelphia County Prison, Docket, 1790–1830,
CCAP

PG

Pennsylvania Gazette

PH

Pennsylvania Herald

PHS

Presbyterian Historical Society, Philadelphia

PJ

Pennsylvania Journal

PL

Pennsylvania Ledger

PM

Pennsylvania Mercury

PMHB

Pennsylvania Magazine of History and Biography

PP

Pennsylvania Packet

PSA

Pennsylvania State Archives, Harrisburg

PWMM

Society of Friends, Philadelphia Women's Monthly Meeting, Minutes, 1760–1780, FHL

QSD

Court of Quarter Sessions, Docket, Philadelphia County, 1753–1785, HSP; 1786–1830, CCAP

WMQ

William and Mary Quarterly

INTRODUCTION

This book explores power in an early American city. It investigates the sexual culture created in Philadelphia and the intimate history of its people. Cultural understandings of sexuality were central to establishing, regulating, and contesting social hierarchies from early colonial days through the Revolutionary era and into the nineteenth century. The study of sexuality provides a rich entry point to explore power relations between men and women, whites and blacks, and the better and lower sorts during the formative years of the new nation.

The reader is asked to re-envision early Philadelphia. Images of chaste Quakers in an orderly city need to be replaced with a vision of a small but growing, heterogeneous, frequently raucous colonial city that permitted a wide array of sexual expression. During the middle of the eighteenth century, Philadelphians created a vibrant pleasure culture and made nonmarital sexual indulgence a part of it. They fashioned a malleable gender system, which entertained increasing assertions of female autonomy as the century wore on. Following the Revolution the pleasure culture grew, and more Philadelphians engaged in casual sexual relations. Sex commerce expanded, illegitimacy increased, and adulterous liaisons became more common, as did serial relationships. Across a broad spectrum, men and women adopted expansive sexual lives independent of marriage, and they crossed all social boundaries to do so. The expanding sexual possibilities of the late eighteenth century reflected new ideas of the proper power relations between men and women and between social classes.

In the early nineteenth century these heterogeneous possibilities would be foreclosed by the reconstruction of the gender system and new efforts to police sexuality. The city's emerging middle class promoted new notions of normal male and female sexuality to circumscribe behavior and restrict legitimate sexual practice. This study explores that profound transformation, why it occurred and what role it played in negotiating power relations in the new nation. Redefining and regulating sexuality could constrain the autonomy of the individual, strengthen the institution of the family, and thus bolster the stability of society.

Eighteenth-century Philadelphians, like Europeans, lived through the tumultuous times of the Enlightenment. The changes in gender, sex, and power in Philadelphia were part of this larger transformation in worldview. Early modern Europeans fundamentally altered their beliefs in the cosmological and natural world order, creating a cascading series of problems and possibilities for the organization of society and the fulfillment of the individual. Scientific rationalism overturned the belief in a fixed, hierarchical world order, replacing it with a dynamic model of the cosmos and human society. The belief that man was a rational agent meant that humanity could shape its own destiny and perfect human society. This sea change in worldview undermined existing social and political organization, challenging both the gender hierarchy and the political order.

The Enlightenment's reconsideration of the relationship of the individual to the political state led to the creation of the first modern democratic republics. Europeans, Euro-Americans, and African-Americans put the experimental philosophies that heralded individual liberty and self-governance into practice. New republics in the United States, France, and Haiti broke down traditional hierarchies and reconstituted societies, and competing groups struggled to assert their own rights and contain those of others.

The gender system was transformed as well. Before the eighteenth century, gender was primarily performative, enacted through dress and deportment; gender was not understood as essential biological difference. Gender was one among many ordained and fixed hierarchical relationships that ordered society. Men and women both were believed to be naturally lusty, and women to be especially vulnerable to sexual temptation. The Enlightenment undermined the belief in such natural hierarchies and upset the basis for woman's subordination to man. A new conceptual framework would be necessary if the gender hierarchy was to be maintained. The response, developed over the eighteenth century, was to reconceptualize gender by positing radical differences between men and women and fixing them in the anatomical body. The creation of binary opposite gendered sexualities was at the core of this new gender system. By the early nineteenth century, gendered sexualities had quelled the subversive possibilities implicit in this new world order.[1]

---

1. On the performative nature of gender, see Judith Butler, *Gender Trouble: Feminism and the Subversion of Identity* (New York, 1990). On gender as performative in early modern Britain, see Anthony Fletcher, *Gender, Sex, and Subordination in England, 1500–1800* (New Haven, Conn., 1995); George Haggarty, *Men in Love: Masculinity and Sexuality in the Eighteenth Century* (New York, 1999); Alan Bray and Michel Rey, "The Body of the Friend: Continuity and Change in Masculine Friendship in the Seventeenth Century," in Tim Hitchcock and Michèle Cohen, eds., *English Masculinities,*

This work studies how Philadelphians fashioned their society through these transformations and how this reconceived worldview altered the relationship of gender and sex to power and social control. It considers how these intellectual developments affected the dispossessed: especially women and African-Americans of the lower orders. More fundamentally, it explores how gender—as a system used to organize and regulate power—operated during these profound transformations.[2]

This study begins in the eighteenth century when European colonists nurtured their young colony as the traditional bases of society came under attack. By the late colonial period Philadelphians were renegotiating the power relations between men and women, as the conceptual underpinnings of female subordination to men eroded. The creation of the Revolutionary Republic forced Philadelphians to address the questions of women's status raised by the Enlightenment. The Revolution both instigated a conservative reaction to the changes already under way and legitimized challenges to male dominance. Women exercised new levels of sexual independence, acting to achieve self-fulfillment and undermining patriarchal authority. Members of the city's lower classes fashioned a moral code that allowed for serial nonmarital monogamy, self-divorce, and boisterous, bawdy, and public heterosocial sex play; and some couples boldly crossed the color line to establish intimate relationships, claiming a right to personal happiness not circumscribed by the racist notions circulating around them.

In the early nineteenth century, women were granted intellectual competency in exchange for the acceptance of a new, inert female sexuality. That com-

1660–1800 (London, 1999), 65–84; David Lorenzo Boyd and Ruth Mazo Karras, "The Interrogation of a Male Transvestite Prostitute in Fourteenth-Century London," *GLQ: A Journal of Gay and Lesbian Studies,* I (1993–1995), 459–465. On gender, science, and anatomy, see Carolyn Merchant, *The Death of Nature: Women, Ecology, and the Scientific Revolution* (San Francisco, 1980); Ludmilla Jordanova, *Sexual Visions: Images of Gender in Science and Medicine between the Eighteenth and Twentieth Centuries* (Madison, Wis., 1989); Jordanova, *Nature Displayed: Gender, Science, and Medicine, 1760–1820* (New York, 1999); Londa Schiebinger, *Nature's Body: Gender in the Making of Modern Science* (Boston, 1993); Schiebinger, *The Mind Has No Sex? Women in the Origins of Modern Science* (Cambridge, Mass., 1989); Thomas Laqueur, *Making Sex: Body and Gender from the Greeks to Freud* (Cambridge, 1990).

2. Joan W. Scott, "Gender: A Useful Category of Historical Analysis," *American Historical Review,* XCI (1986), 1053–1075.

promise foreclosed the latent equality embodied in Enlightenment thought and delegitimated the expressions of individual autonomy embraced by many Philadelphia women in the early new nation. The threats to social stability implicit in women's equality were countered by a new gender system built on sexuality, promoted by patriot leaders and the emerging middle class. The basis of women's subordination to men was recast, based on her essentialized inert sexuality in opposition to the virile male, who exercised sexual agency through the use of reason. This reconstruction was accomplished by inscribing sexual deviance onto women of the lower classes and women of color. By increasingly associating licentious sexuality with these already stigmatized groups, Philadelphia's journalists, reformers, and legal authorities delegitimated a wide range of nonmarital sexual practices. Ascribing licentious sexuality to the women of the rabble also promoted the belief that normal women experienced only tepid sexual desire expressed through marital monogamy.

This work seeks to contribute to the understanding of early American history in several ways. First, it uncovers and documents patterns of sexual behavior, and their corresponding moral codes, embraced by the most diverse community of colonial British North America and the early national United States. Some of these were rooted in religious doctrines, others were based on plebeian and ethnic traditions, and still others were seemingly creations of the Revolutionary era. Further, it explores the conflict between these sexual practices and the creation of the republican state, with its attendant national morality.

Second, this work begins to fill a crucial gap in the history of sexuality in America, by exploring the transformation of the colonial constructions and regulation of sexuality into the nineteenth-century gender system. Historical understanding of the role of sexuality in structuring and contesting power relations has been concentrated in either the colonial context or the nineteenth century. Little scholarship has engaged with the transformation from one to the other of these two conceptualizations of sexual desire and their systems of sexual regulation. By examining this transitional period, when the modern American sexual system was created, this work explains how class and racial divisions were used to constitute new constructions of sexuality that became the foundation for gender. The reconstruction of normative female sexuality cast the lustful woman as deviant. By enacting policing mechanisms that highlighted the nonmarital sexual behavior of African-Americans and the lower sorts, Philadelphians created the appearance of licentiousness of the rabble and restraint of the middle classes. Recasting normal female sexuality as reserved would also place responsibility for sexual transgression on women, thereby masking male sexual privilege, and codify the sexual vulnerability of nonelite women.[3]

This study simultaneously illuminates how the gendering of sexuality in the new nation helped perpetuate subordination of African-Americans as slavery receded. Enormous change in ideas about race and the status of African-Americans flourished in the middle and northern colonies. Pennsylvania dismantled slavery following the American Revolution, and Philadelphia was the first major city to grapple with negotiating freedom with a substantial population of freedmen and women after the Revolution. Here sexuality played an important role in early race relations. White Philadelphians' racialized constructions of sexuality became important tools in reconstituting racial oppression without slavery. The new, highly gendered construction of sexuality denied normative sexuality to African-American women, highlighting instead race-based distinctions in sexual character. In exploring Philadelphia, this study contributes to a growing body of literature on how race and gender worked together to configure social structures and deploy power in early America.[4]

3. On colonial sexuality, see Laurel Thatcher Ulrich, *Good Wives: Image and Reality in the Lives of Women in Northern New England, 1650–1750* (New York, 1980); Roger Thompson, *Sex in Middlesex: Popular Mores in a Massachusetts County, 1649–1699* (Amherst, Mass., 1986); Cornelia Hughes Dayton, *Women before the Bar: Gender, Law, and Society in Connecticut, 1710–1790* (Chapel Hill, N.C., 1995). On the nineteenth century, see Nancy F. Cott, "Passionlessness: An Interpretation of Victorian Sexual Ideology, 1790–1850," *Signs,* IV (1978), 219–236; Christine Stansell, *City of Women: Sex and Class in New York, 1789–1860* (Urbana, Ill., 1982); Michael Grossberg, *Governing the Hearth: Law and the Family in Nineteenth-Century America* (Chapel Hill, N.C., 1985); Patricia Cline Cohen, *The Murder of Helen Jewett: The Life and Death of a Prostitute in Nineteenth-Century New York* (New York, 1998); Martha Hodes, *White Women, Black Men: Illicit Sex in the Nineteenth-Century South* (New Haven, Conn., 1997); Karen Lystra, *Searching the Heart: Women, Men, and Romantic Love in Nineteenth-Century America* (New York, 1989).

4. Pennsylvania's Gradual Abolition Act became law in 1780. Gary B. Nash, *Forging Freedom: The Formation of Philadelphia's Black Community, 1720–1840* (Cambridge, Mass., 1988); Nash and Jean R. Soderlund, *Freedom by Degrees: Emancipation in Pennsylvania and Its Aftermath* (New York, 1991); W. Jeffrey Bolster, *Black Jacks: African American Seamen in the Age of Sail* (Cambridge, Mass., 1997). On race, sex, gender, and power in other regions, see Kathleen M. Brown, *Good Wives, Nasty Wenches, and Anxious Patriarchs: Gender, Race, and Power in Colonial Virginia* (Chapel Hill, N.C., 1996); Kirsten Fischer, *Suspect Relations: Sex, Race, and Resistance in Colonial North Carolina* (Ith-

Finally, the focus on sexuality demonstrates that restructuring gender relations was integral to reconstituting social hierarchies in the new Republic. Viewing the period of the American Revolution through the lens of sexuality, one sees that gender relations were unstable and patriarchy was contested. In Philadelphia there was more "gender trouble" brewing than historians have previously imagined.[5]

Unlike the older New England colonies to the north and Chesapeake colonies to the south, Philadelphia had no lengthy history of local gender traditions to serve as ballast in these tumultuous times. Gender relations thus were particularly volatile, and women's assertions of self-determination were aided by this void. New England, by contrast, had its seventeenth-century past as "a little commonwealth," centered on patriarchal families supported by the Congregational Church. The seventeenth-century Chesapeake had weathered a period of gender instability but had by the early eighteenth century solidified its social structure through the establishment of the patriarchal planter elite. Gender had been instrumental in generating the twin pillars of the social structure: racially based hereditary slavery and female subordination to men through a tightly controlled system of marriage. In each region, these seventeenth-century experiences gave rise to a particular gender culture that influenced their interaction with eighteenth-century intellectual and political forces. Philadelphia, as the capital city of a colony forged in the eighteenth century, presents a different history of gender, sex, and power in early America.[6]

Eighteenth-century Philadelphia was the most ethnically diverse city in British North America. Its English majority lived side by side with Scots, Welsh, German, Scotch-Irish, African, and African-Caribbean people as well as a smattering of French, Spanish, and Portuguese, to make it extraordinarily var-

---

aca, N.Y., 2002); Sharon Block, "Lines of Color, Sex, and Service: Comparative Sexual Coercion in Early America," in Martha Hodes, ed., *Sex, Love, Race: Crossing Boundaries in North American History* (New York, 1999), 141–163.

5. "Gender trouble" is Judith Butler's term, referring to moments when the attributes associated with male and female gender are disrupted and thus gender is revealed as purely a social creation; see Butler, *Gender Trouble*.

6. The history of gender relations in both regions was contested and dynamic and was not a static system over the course of the seventeenth and eighteenth centuries. But, in comparison to the frontier upstart colony of Pennsylvania, Massachusetts and Virginia in particular had colonial traditions to draw upon as they faced the new world order created in the eighteenth century. The literature on gender in colonial America is vast. For some of the most important works on New England, see John Demos, *A Little*

iegated. By the 1790s Philadelphia boasted the largest free African-American community in the new nation. Most of Philadelphia's eighteenth-century growth depended on immigration, bringing a steady flow of newcomers. Philadelphians maintained their links to European culture through the city's maritime connections. Mariners shipped out from the largest shipping center of the region and landed in the port for short stays from abroad, immigrants arrived and mixed with the city's population, and the city's elite traveled periodically to England and Europe for leisure, business, and education. By the time of the Revolution Philadelphia was the largest city in British North America and would remain the economic and political center of the new nation. It was intellectually rich, boasting the nation's first libraries, medical schools, and philosophical societies, and was a locus of innovative political thought. From midcentury on, Philadelphia was also at the leading edge of economic development, first through mercantile expansion and in the early nineteenth century as a capitalist market economy. The city developed modern economic classes, creating tensions and conflicts as Philadelphians negotiated new market relations. Philadelphia was both an eighteenth-century European city that experienced similar patterns in sexual behavior and a place where European notions met American social, political, and economic imperatives and mixed to create new political uses of sexuality.[7]

Recovering the historical experience of sexuality poses particular difficulties. Few people wrote about their sexual experiences. Yet sexual intimacy was

Commonwealth: Family Life in Plymouth Colony (New York, 1970); Ulrich, _Good Wives;_ Carol F. Karlsen, _The Devil in the Shape of a Woman: Witchcraft in Colonial New England_ (New York, 1987); Dayton, _Women before the Bar;_ Elizabeth Reis, _Damned Women: Sinners and Witches in Puritan New England_ (Ithaca, N.Y., 1997); Jane Kamensky, _Governing the Tongue: The Politics of Speech in Early New England_ (New York, 1997). On the Chesapeake: Lois Green Carr and Lorena S. Walsh, "The Planter's Wife: The Experience of White Women in Seventeenth-Century Maryland," _WMQ,_ 3d Ser., XXXVI (1977), 542–571; Brown, _Good Wives, Nasty Wenches;_ Fischer, _Suspect Relations._ On both regions: Mary Beth Norton, _Founding Mothers and Fathers: Gendered Power and the Forming of American Society_ (New York, 1996).

7. Susan E. Klepp, "Demography in Early Philadelphia, 1690–1860," in Klepp, ed., _Symposium on the Demographic History of the Philadelphia Region, 1600–1860,_ APS, _Proceedings,_ CXXXIII, no. 2 (June 1989), 85–111; Thomas M. Doerflinger, _A Vigorous Spirit of Enterprise: Merchants and Economic Development in Revolutionary Philadelphia_ (Chapel Hill, N.C., 1986); Eric Foner, _Tom Paine and Revolutionary America_ (New York,

nearly universal and often reflected the tenor of a relationship, whether affection, appreciation, and respect, or control and domination. Sexual behavior, like any other fundamental human experience, has no fixed meaning. To write a history of sexuality one must perform an act of cultural translation by recovering and explaining the meanings attached to familiar behaviors. This study interweaves two story lines to accomplish that: it explores sexual behavior left in the historical record, and it analyzes the meanings, often various and in conflict, associated with those behaviors.

Traditional social history techniques join with cultural history discourse analysis to create a full account of the sexual terrain in Philadelphia. The two major sources are documentation of sexual behavior within Philadelphia and popular print material produced or available there. Court, church, and social agency records help reconstruct case histories of illegitimacy to illustrate changing patterns of behavior from the 1760s through the 1820s and allow a similar analysis of the women arrested for prostitution and of those admitted to the Magdalen Asylum, 1790–1820. The history of self-divorce is constructed through newspaper advertisements (1726–1785), and formal divorce through legal records (1785–1815). Popular print sources include almanacs, broadsides, songsters, jestbooks, crime pamphlet literature, and popular imported books, which uncover the ways popular culture reflected concerns about gender and sexuality and simultaneously constructed sexual types. This methodology illuminates the interplay between sexual behavior and the cultural construction of early American understandings of sexuality and how

1976); David S. Shields, *Civil Tongues and Polite Letters in British America* (Chapel Hill, N.C., 1997); Billy G. Smith, *The "Lower Sort": Philadelphia's Laboring People, 1750–1800* (Ithaca, N.Y., 1990); Ronald Schultz, *The Republic of Labor: Philadelphia Artisans and the Politics of Class, 1720–1830* (New York, 1993).

On sexuality in Britain, see Paul-Gabriel Boucé, ed., *Sexuality in Eighteenth Century Britain* (Manchester, 1982); G. S. Rousseau and Roy Porter, eds., *Sexual Underworlds of the Enlightenment* (Manchester, 1987); Porter and Lesley Hall, *The Facts of Life: The Creation of Sexual Knowledge in Britain, 1650–1950* (New Haven, Conn., 1995); John R. Gillis, *For Better, for Worse: British Marriages, 1600 to the Present* (Oxford, 1985); Alan Macfarlane, *Marriage and Love in England: Modes of Reproduction, 1300–1840* (Oxford, 1986); Lawrence Stone, *The Family, Sex, and Marriage in England, 1500–1800* (New York, 1977); Randolph Trumbach, *Sex and the Gender Revolution*, I, *Heterosexuality and the Third Gender in Enlightenment London* (Chicago, 1998); Thomas DiPiero and Pat Gill, eds., *Illicit Sex: Identity Politics in Early Modern Culture* (Athens, Ga., 1997).

print culture participated in the contests over power, authority, and sex in the City of Brotherly Love.

The terms *gender, sex,* and *sexuality* have undergone substantial rethinking in the last twenty years and may require clarification. I use *gender* to mean the set of beliefs and ideas ascribed to the social categories man and woman. *Sex* refers to erotic desire and erotic bodily practice. I assume neither a fixed biological basis for gender nor a transhistorical notion of sexual desire, but instead consider how eighteenth- and nineteenth-century Philadelphians conceptualized their bodies, desires, and significant social categories. *Sexuality* has also evolved in recent years as a historical concept. The debates on the historical emergence of sexuality and sexual identity are too extensive to recite here. But sexuality, if it is defined as a recognized core attribute of the individual self, was an invention in Western culture at some point during the transformations discussed in this book and was tied to both the emergence of normative heterosexuality and the invention of a rigidly bounded inert definition of female sexuality.[8]

This study begins with an examination of the sexual terrain of colonial and Revolutionary Philadelphia. Chapter 1 explores the gender culture, probing the dynamics of marriage through self-divorce and popular representations of marriage. Chapter 2 investigates the development of the urban pleasure culture and examines bastardy and prostitution. Chapter 3 scrutinizes the discourse on sexuality present in popular print—the eroticization of print culture in an expanding multiclass, mixed-gender reading public—and analyzes the discursive work of representations by reading them against the actual sexual behavior of the men and women of the city.

Part II addresses sexuality in the era of democratic revolutions (1780–1800). Chapter 4 reveals the blossoming of a heterogeneous, dynamic, but contested sexual culture and examines the class and racial dynamics at work as

8. The scholarly consensus once was that the concept of sexuality and the creation of sexual identities were products of the nineteenth century. Modern scholarship on gender and sexuality in the eighteenth century suggests that the development of sexuality as an attribute of the individual and sexual identity as a core aspect of the self should be understood as stages in a longer process that began in the eighteenth century. See Haggarty, *Men in Love;* Clare A. Lyons, "Mapping an Atlantic Sexual Culture: Homoeroticism in Eighteenth-Century Philadelphia," *WMQ,* 3d Ser., LX (2003), 119–154; David M. Halperin, "Forgetting Foucault: Acts, Identities, and the History of Sexuality," *Representations,* LXIII (1998), 93–120.

the centrifugal forces of revolution faced the political needs of a new nation. Chapter 5 explores the political dynamics as these same forces interact with the independent sexual behavior of some women in the early Republic, the gender politics between men and women engaging in nonmarital sexual behavior, and the role of sexuality in the Revolutionary debate on women's status in the new Republic.

The concluding section, Part III, focuses on the three successive waves of assault against the expansive sexual culture in the early nineteenth century. Chapter 6 analyzes the cultural reinterpretation of nonmarital sexuality in popular print. Chapter 7 presents Philadelphia's efforts to reform the sexual habits of its citizens through benevolent means. Chapter 8 explores the move to compel sexual conformity through punitive public policy. This final section of the book demonstrates how the establishment of the middle-class gender system normalized sex and created the illusion of deviancy among the rabble to explain and thus justify the subordinate status of nonelite women, African-Americans, and the lower classes in antebellum America.

PART I

THE SEXUAL TERRAIN OF
COLONIAL AND REVOLUTIONARY
PHILADELPHIA

In 1762 John Studham, a Philadelphia mariner, fathered an illegitimate child with Rebecca Holland. When the child was four months old, Studham posted bond with the city's Overseers of the Poor to guarantee that he would support the child. His relationship with Holland was fleeting and did not persist beyond the birth of their child. In 1767 Studham's subsequent marriage to Ann Studham was also ending, at her insistence, when she left John. This short, intimate history reveals that, over the course of five years, John Studham entered and left at least two intimate relationships, his wife Ann separating herself from him to make a new start and Rebecca Holland bearing a child she would raise without its father's active involvement.[1]

Mariner John Goggin's and his wife Catherine Bryan's intimate relationships were equally turbulent and complex. In January 1764 John took out an advertisement in the *Pennsylvania Gazette* stating the terms of his self-divorce from Catherine, severing the economic ties of husband and wife and warning the public to treat her no longer as his dependent. The couple had sworn the termination of their marriage before witnesses, and each had renounced marital claims upon the other. John claimed that he had been "obliged" to "discharge the said Catherine from him" because Catherine had been "guilty of divers Misdeameanors." Twelve months later Catherine delivered an illegitimate child fathered by an unidentified African-American Philadelphian. We know nothing about the nature of the relationship that produced this child, nor whether Catherine's relationship with its father prompted the termination of her marriage. We know only that Catherine was pregnant with this child three months after John ran his ad and that John claimed his wife had "notoriously abandoned herself to a lewd and dissolute Course of Life"

---

1. OP, Bonds, Nov. 11, 1762; *PJ*, Dec. 10, 1767.

for many years when he petitioned the Provincial Assembly for a divorce in 1766.[2]

What are we to make of the sexual experiences of the Goggins and the Studhams? How can we begin to understand their choices to engage in sexual relations that produced illegitimate children, to leave a husband or wife for a new mate or no mate at all, or to engage in sexual relationships across the colonial color line? What did these choices mean to them and to the community around them? What were their understandings about male and female sexuality, and the relationship of sexual behavior to family formation? What were the culturally accepted practices of sexuality in early Philadelphia? And how did these choices reflect the acceptance, rejection, or negotiation of the power relations between men and women, whites and blacks, or the highborn and lower sorts in eighteenth-century society?

We will grapple with these questions in Part I. Chapter 1 explores the gender culture of colonial Philadelphia by examining marriage and self-divorce. Marriage was the linchpin of the early modern gender system in England and its North American colonies. For most colonists marriage structured the relationship between men and women and established the expected patterns of sexual behavior. The stability of the early modern gender system, and by extension, society in general, rested on the faithful performance of gender roles by husbands and wives in marriage. The content of these roles flowed from a belief in the natural superiority of men over women, embodied in the patriarchal family.[3] The husband, as patriarch, was the head of his family and was granted control and responsibility for his dependents: his wife, his children, his servants, and in British North America his slaves. Because marriage granted the husband control of his wife's body, marriage is fundamental to understanding how gender, power, and sexuality operated in Philadelphia. Analyzing marital unions that did not hold allows us to probe the power struggles and grievances between men and women and explore the strength of eighteenth-century marriage bonds. The practice of self-divorce through elopement advertisements and the cultural representations of marriage in popular print suggest that gender relations were unstable and patriarchy was

2. *PG*, Jan. 12, 1764; *Pennsylvania Archives*, 8th Ser. ([Harrisburg], 1931–1935), VII, 5841. John Goggin was the first person to request a divorce in colonial Pennsylvania; his request was denied.

3. Anthony Fletcher, *Gender, Sex, and Subordination in England, 1500–1800* (New Haven, Conn., 1995); Carole Pateman, *The Sexual Contract* (Stanford, Calif., 1988), 19–38, 85–92.

contested. This gender culture would have serious implications for the relationship of sexuality to marriage as the century wore on.

The marital gender system provides the context for understanding nonmarital sexuality in Chapters 2 and 3. We will examine what Philadelphians called "bastardy," meaning begetting and bearing children outside recognizable families or long-term relationships, and the other forms of nonmarital sexual practices that flourished in the pleasure culture of the 1760s, in Chapter 2. In Chapter 3 we will explore the ideas about sexuality expressed in Philadelphia's popular print culture. We shall find that the Studhams and the Goggins were not deviant members of their communities and that their choices were comprehensible to their neighbors. The behaviors they exemplify will open a window into an intimate world, allowing us to understand the evolving power relations of colonial and Revolutionary Philadelphia.

CHAPTER I

A Springboard to Revolution

Runaway Wives and Self-Divorce

WHEREAS Elizabeth the Wife of John Crede, of Buckingham Township, Bucks County, may probably run me in Debt: This is therefore to inform all Persons not to give her Credit on my Account; for I will not pay any Debts she may contract, we having separated from each other, by Consent, now 20 years.

　[*PG*, June 2, 1743]

Freedhold, Monmouth county, East New-Jersey, Jan. 25, 1768
Whereas ELEANOR, Wife of the Subscriber, hath eloped from him, and run him considerably in Debt, besides pilfering from him a valuable Sum of Money, and sundry Effects of Value, and continues to strole about the Country, with a certain red haired Highland Tinker, who calls himself JOHN M'DONALL . . . and passes for his Wife; and as he has Reason to fear she will run him yet farther in Debt, takes this Method of requesting all Persons, not to trust her on his Account, for he will pay no Debts of her contracting, after the Date hereof. WILLIAM ORCHARD

　[*PG*, March 10, 1768]

WHEREAS *Hannah Joyce* (whose maiden name was *Turner*) the wife of *Peter Joyce Fitzgerald,* hath eloped from her said husband, and lives in a scandalous manner with another man, named *Richard Stagtham Thomas,* Brass Founder, with whom she has attempted a marriage before the Swedish Minister—These are to warn all persons not to harbour her in such a scandalous manner, nor to credit her on my account, for I will pay no debt of her contracting from the date hereof.

　June 2, 1772　PETER JOYCE FITZGERALD
　[*PG*, June 4, 1772]

Advertisements for "eloped" or runaway wives, such as for Elizabeth, Eleanor, and Hannah, regularly appeared in Philadelphia's colonial newspapers. They declared the departure of a wife and notified the public that her husband had, therefore, severed his economic ties to her. Like Eleanor Orchard, who left her husband for her "red haired Highland Tinker," such wives had reputedly permanently abandoned their marriages. These advertisements document one customary practice of self-divorce popular in the eighteenth century and provide a rare opportunity to evaluate the nature of marital discord in colonial America, where legal divorce was difficult to obtain. Most eighteenth-century marriages were probably mutually beneficial and possibly rewarding. Certainly, the majority did last until the death of a spouse. Those that did not allow us to probe into areas of contestation and disagreement over power relations in marriage and provide an entry point into the gender culture of eighteenth-century Philadelphia.

In Philadelphia, runaway wife advertisements were used throughout the century and were an effective means of marital dissolution, recognized and respected by the community at large. In the English-language newspapers, 841 husbands advertised their wives between 1726, when the *American Weekly Mercury* printed the first self-divorce notice from a Pennsylvania press (placed by a Philadelphia carpenter), and 1786, the first year absolute divorce with a right to remarry was available to Pennsylvania citizens. Half of these advertised the marital dissolution of Philadelphia couples, and the other half, of couples from the surrounding Pennsylvania counties and the bordering areas of Delaware and New Jersey that used the Philadelphia press.[1] But newspaper

1. Advertisements were culled from the twelve English-language newspapers printed in Philadelphia from the first newspaper in 1719 through 1786. An additional 26 advertisements, 1787–1800, were taken from *PG* and are used in this database, producing a total of 867 advertisements for analysis (439 from Philadelphia, 428 from the surrounding region). First ad, *AWM*, Nov. 3, 1726, Joseph and Catharine Wood.

Of all the ads, 92 percent (801) explicitly declared the wife's departure; the other ads terminated the couple's economic unity without presenting a cause. In only 1 percent of the advertisements did the couple reconcile, the wife return, and the husband revoke his first proclamation.

The geography of rural runaway wife advertisements followed agricultural settlement, radiating out from the city of Philadelphia and along the region's waterways. During the 1730s and 1740s they advertised women from the Pennsylvania counties surrounding the city (Bucks, Chester, Philadelphia, and Lancaster up the Susquehanna River) and from settlements up and down the Delaware River. By the 1760s advertisements included women from the next ring of settlement and up to Cumberland County and Trenton, New Jersey. A handful of ads were submitted by men from as far away as Maryland, Virginia, and New York.

I indicate the geographic location of self-divorcing couples when it has bearing on interpretation and is not obvious from the text.

advertisements were only one form of notice used in self-divorce. Other methods included "crying" a wife throughout the town or posting notices around the neighborhood, declaring a wife had eloped and proclaiming the termination of the marriage. (Evidence of these self-divorces is lost to us.) The prevalence of newspaper advertisements declaring self-divorce demonstrates that for many segments of eighteenth-century society marriage did not have to be permanent. For these couples and the community that countenanced their behavior, marriage was not tightly bound for life; marital bonds could be broken.[2]

Marital dissolution through newspaper advertisement had its roots in seventeenth- and eighteenth-century English and Welsh plebeian practices of self-marriage and self-divorce. Legal divorce was unavailable to all but the nobility under English law until the mid-nineteenth century, but English men and women worked around the absolute ban on divorce through locally recognized protocols for self-divorce. The most famous form of self-divorce was wife sale, whereby a husband transferred guardianship of his wife to another man through a ritualized "sale" for a nominal sum. The rite was public, with the wife's consent, after a private agreement between the departing husband and the newly forming couple. Philadelphians shied away from public wife sale. As practiced in England, it required bringing a wife to market with a noose around her neck and engaging in a ritualized mock sale to her new husband. One imagines that this rite was too close to the actual sale of Africans into slavery in Philadelphia's markets to retain its central tenets of con-

2. Posting written notice of runaway wives was still being practiced in the late 1760s, long after newspapers had become a reliable means of public communication; see, for example: *PG*, Jan. 15, 1767, Jane and Charles Tennent, in Philadelphia; *PJ*, May 19, 1768, Ruth and John Corwine, in Amwell, western New Jersey; *PJ*, Feb. 9, 1748, Mary and Joseph Zans, for oral notice.

Approximately 2 percent of Philadelphia's married couples advertised a wife from the 1740s through the 1780s, based on my estimate that three-quarters of Philadelphians married at some point in their lives. Household composition analysis done by historians Carole Shammas and Karin Wulf for pre-Revolutionary Philadelphia indicates at least one-quarter of the city's adult female population was unmarried. Karin Wulf, *Not All Wives: Women of Colonial Philadelphia* (Ithaca, N.Y., 2000) (I used tables 3.2 and 3.3, pp. 94–95); Carole Shammas, "The Female Social Structure of Philadelphia in 1775," *PMHB*, CVII (1983), 69–83 (I used table 1, p. 71).

For a study that examines elopements throughout British North America, see Kirsten Sword, "Wayward Wives, Runaway Slaves, and the Limits of Patriarchal Authority in Early America" (Ph.D. diss., Harvard University, 2002).

sent and mutual agreement. But other forms of self-divorce, such as the returning of wedding rings accompanied by declarations of marital dissolution by both parties and the less sensational practice of newspaper advertisement, were adopted by Pennsylvania colonists to adjudicate marital dissolution. In a strict legal sense divorce was not possible in colonial Pennsylvania, and yet these newspaper advertisements demonstrate that many colonists believed that ending a marriage was acceptable, even advantageous and just, under certain circumstances.[3]

The language of these ads drew upon English common law traditions to sever a husband's financial responsibility for his wife. To this end they incorporated two elements necessary to dismantle the fundamental economic relationship that underlay marriage. Under English common law a wife had the right to a husband's financial support, and a husband the obligation to support her. A couple could separate and live apart, but a husband's financial obligation to his wife continued. This obligation was discharged, however, if his wife eloped from him: she lost her claim to his maintenance and to her dower right on his estate upon his death. By placing an advertisement claiming one's wife had eloped, especially one that stood unchallenged, a husband could assert that he was free of his financial obligations to his wife. Equally important, these ads allowed a husband to terminate the customary practice of his wife's

3. I have found only one instance of the public transfer of a wife from one husband to another, and this occurred before an unsuspecting minister (Gloria Dei, Marriages, II, June 1796). For examples of self-divorce advertisements in London newspapers, see *Daily Advertiser* (London) for 1743: Jan. 4, 5, 20, June 2, 11, 13, 15, 20, 27.

Marriage was largely unregulated in early modern England until the passage of the Hardwicke Marriage Act in 1753 (26 Geo. II, c. 37), which required the consent of parents for youth under twenty-one and made all marriage not performed by regular clergy, after proper notice, null and void. Estimates of the number of English common law, or irregular, marriages range from John Gillis's 20–30 percent to the more conservative estimate of Lawrence Stone. E. P. Thompson, *Customs in Common: Studies in Traditional Popular Culture* (New York, 1993), esp. chap. 7, "The Sale of Wives," 404–462; Samuel Pyeatt Menefee, *Wives for Sale: An Ethnographic Study of British Popular Divorce* (New York, 1981); John R. Gillis, *For Better, for Worse: British Marriages, 1600 to the Present* (Oxford, 1985), 9–105 (on marriage before 1753), 209–219 (on self-divorce); Alan Macfarlane, *Marriage and Love in England: Modes of Reproduction, 1300–1840* (Oxford, 1986), 223–230 (on the constraints on legal divorce); Lawrence Stone, *The Family, Sex, and Marriage in England, 1500–1800* (New York, 1977), 31–37 (on marriage), 40 (divorce); Stone, *Road to Divorce: England, 1530–1987* (Oxford, 1990), 21, 141–148 (self-divorce), 51–120 (marriage), 121–127 (on Hardwicke Marriage Act).

doing business and accruing debts in his name. The intention of these self-divorces through advertisement was to sever the economic ties that bound husband and wife and allow each to establish new relationships. For many Philadelphians self-divorce was a legitimate means to completely terminate a marriage. Many, like Hannah Joyce, considered themselves free to remarry, as her attempt to do so at Philadelphia's Gloria Dei church attests.[4]

Self-divorce was an accepted, customary practice, but establishing what constituted a legitimate grievance warranting self-divorce was fluid and contested. The public proclamation of the cause for divorce relied on a delicate dialectic: articulating an acceptable cause and yet framing that grievance in ways that promoted a particular gendered interpretation of proper power relations in marriage. Over the course of the eighteenth century what could be plausibly and publicly asserted as a marital grievance changed. Men and women competed to extend the boundaries of legitimate cause for self-divorce by expanding the forms of inexcusable spousal behavior, usually in ways that garnered more legitimate power for their own positions as husbands or wives. In doing so, they loosened the bonds of marriage and promoted values gaining ground in eighteenth-century society: self-determination, personal satisfaction, and individual choice. Such values, when applied to women, were antithetical to the central concept of the marital union: the merging of two persons into one, with the ultimate power and authority residing with the husband. By the 1760s self-divorce became a way for some women to exercise a greater degree of self-determination and legitimate the desire to achieve personal happiness. For all Philadelphians it was a way to view and

4. Macfarlane, *Marriage and Love in England,* 228–229 (on dower and elopement). Absolute divorce by law was available in colonial Pennsylvania only in cases of incestuous marriage. Divorce from bed and board, without the right to remarry, could be granted by the governor where a spouse had been convicted of rape, sodomy, bestiality, or bigamy. There was, however, no mechanism to use these limited grounds, and no divorce petitions were sent to the governor before the mid-1760s.

In 1766 John Goggin was the first to petition for a divorce. He was among six Pennsylvanians to attempt divorce through an act of assembly in Pennsylvania between 1766 and 1773, when the Privy Council in England disallowed divorce through colonial assemblies, after allowing only one divorce in colonial Pennsylvania. The next attempts at legal divorce were initiated in 1777 after Pennsylvania's break with England. Thomas R. Meehan, "'Not Made out of Levity': Evolution of Divorce in Early Pennsylvania," *PMHB,* XCII (1968), 441–464; James T. Mitchell, Henry Flanders, et al., comps., *The Statutes at Large of Pennsylvania* (Harrisburg, 1896–1915), II, chaps. 3, 4, 5, esp. pp. 7–9.

Means to sever economic ties however as to unsure allowing to the allow in a establish new relationship

personal satisfaction & individual choice was stressed in 18th century

consider the power plays between husbands and wives that were enacted in the public press.

Self-Divorce and the Colonial Gender Culture

We have long known that husbands in eighteenth-century British North America used marital desertion to end marriages they found unsatisfying. They did so in Philadelphia, and probably more frequently than wives "eloped." Cases of deserted wives litter the account books of the Philadelphia Overseers of the Poor, the agency responsible for aiding those in need. But what is particularly striking in the phenomenon of runaway wife advertisements is the steady use of a form of marital dissolution apparently initiated or agreed to by wives. The ads assert that wives left their husbands. As such, they suggest that husbands' patriarchal rights underpinning the laws of marriage were not universally accepted as the proper, or only, structure for power relations between men and women. But how sure can we be that husbands wrote truthfully when they claimed their wives had departed? Why couldn't a man simply leave his wife, advertise that she had eloped, and be free of her?[5]

Three supporting systems of possible intervention prevented husbands from easily falsifying the facts. First, by midcentury some newspaper editors were unwilling to place such ads without a certificate from a magistrate supporting the husband's claims. Benjamin Franklin printed the policy of his *Pennsylvania Gazette* as an addendum to one ad in 1748:

> N.B. No Advertisements of elopements will hereafter be inserted in this paper, but such as shall come to the press accompanied with a certificate from some Magistrate, that there is good cause for such publication.[6]

5. Deserted wives appear in all extant eighteenth-century records kept by the Overseers and Guardians of the Poor (the Overseers of the Poor changed their name to the Guardians of the Poor after the Revolution). The Overseers of the Poor were charged with enforcing marital support and child support and provided aid to those in need though small pensions and supplies. They also operated the almshouse after it opened in 1767. Women seeking enforced, mandatory support from their husbands appear in the Overseers' minutes, and those whose husbands were poor or had abandoned them and left the region (and were therefore out of the Overseers' reach) are recorded receiving public aid or taking refuge in the almshouse. For desertion in the early nineteenth century, see Merril D. Smith, " 'Whers Gone to She Knows Not': Desertion and Widowhood in Early Pennsylvania," in Larry D. Eldridge, ed., *Women and Freedom in Early America* (New York, 1997), 211–228.

6. *PG,* June 16, 1748.

Second, if a wife had not eloped but had been deserted by her husband, she could appeal to the local Overseers of the Poor to compel her husband to provide her with support. When mariner Thomas Dunbar advertised his wife, Rebecca, to sever their connection in 1760, Rebecca immediately turned to the Overseers. One week later Thomas had given his bond to the Overseers guaranteeing his financial support of his wife. The couple could separate and live as they chose, but, unless Rebecca had eloped, she still had a right to support, and Thomas was legally obliged to fulfill his financial responsibilities as her husband. Twenty years later, in 1781, when William Calvery falsely asserted his wife's elopement in the city's papers, he soon found himself facing legal action by the Overseers to seize his property for his wife's support.[7]

The Overseers of the Poor were responsible for securing support for all deserted wives and abandoned children, and their first recourse was to intervene to force husbands to meet their obligations. Wives unjustly declared elopers could, and did, turn to the Overseers to enforce their rights. But this seldom occurred. Cases of deserted wives occupy a persistent place in the records of the Philadelphia Overseers (and later the Guardians) of the Poor throughout the century. But these couples were rarely the same ones who practiced self-divorce through the city's newspapers. A fairly complete set of records of the Overseers exists from midcentury until the British occupation of Philadelphia in 1777. During this period Rebecca Dunbar and Margaret Alexander were the only advertised wives who responded to their husbands' pronouncements by enlisting the Overseers to enforce their marital rights. (A full record of the Overseers' actions on behalf of deserted wives would probably reveal a few other wives who had not in fact eloped, but had been deserted.) But the small number of cases where advertised wives took the path used by scores of deserted wives, using the Overseers to challenge their husband's assertion that they had eloped, suggests that most of them had indeed left their husband and ended their marriage.[8]

7. *PG*, July 31, 1760, Rebecca and Thomas Dunbar; OP, Bonds, and OPM, Aug. 7, 1760. See also *PJ*, Apr. 21, 1779, Margaret and John Alexander, and OPM, Apr. 22, 1779; *PJ*, Mar. 28, 1781, Mary and William Calvery, and OPM, Jan. 31, Feb. 7, 1782.

8. Records of the Overseers of the Poor that survive include the Bond Book, which records entries from 1755 through 1770 (and again from 1780 through 1787); the Minutes from 1767 until British occupation of the city in 1777; and a cache of orders for support from the mayor to the Overseers that includes cases of marital desertion have survived for 1750/1. Evidence from the early 1780s confirms that only a small number

The third and most dynamic system of intervention to ferret out false accusations of wives' elopements was the published responses of the wives themselves. Wives countered their husbands' interpretation of events by placing responding advertisements in 5 percent of the cases. These ads began appearing in the 1740s and increased after 1760. In all, forty-one wives took to the public presses to present their rendition of events. The overwhelming majority of these responses did not deny that the wife had left her husband but did dispute that their actions could be characterized as "elopement." They claimed instead that their actions were justified under the circumstances. The fact that only two wives claimed that they still resided with their spouses suggests a fundamental truth within these ads: wives did take an active part in self-divorce in colonial and Revolutionary Philadelphia. Many wives took the initiative to leave their marriages. Others left only when they believed they had no other choice and were driven from their homes, often by abusive husbands. In both circumstances wives participated in defining acceptable and unacceptable behavior within a marriage. They made these judgments when they left their marriage, and their decisions were broadcast throughout the community in the newspapers and when they responded to their husbands' ads by appealing to public justice.[9]

The wives' responses indicate that early in the century wives believed that they needed to carefully script their self-presentation in the press, presenting proper deference both to wifely submission and to the community's collective will and judgment. But after midcentury wives took a more active and open role in defining acceptable and unacceptable marital situations and husbands' conduct, and their responses in the public press increasingly and openly assaulted husbands' patriarchal prerogatives as the century wore on. By the

---

of women contested the truthfulness of their husband's claim of elopement by seeking intervention by the Overseers. During the first three years of the decade, when forty-five Philadelphia husbands placed wife elopement ads, only two wives challenged their husband's claim and brought their cases to the Overseers to compel their husband's financial support. Overseers of the Poor records are complete for this period. See OPM, 1780–1782, and OP, Bonds.

9. Each advertisement usually ran for several weeks, making runaway wife ads a constant presence in colonial newspapers. The data used here are all runaway wife advertisements from the first ad in 1726 through 1786, 841 in total. Of the published responses, 46 percent were from Philadelphia wives, and 54 percent were from wives living in the surrounding region.

1760s wives' counterclaims often attacked those prerogatives in the physical control of wives, economic control of family resources, and exclusive access to wives' bodies.

Self-divorce was widespread, accepted as legitimate by the city's artisans and laboring classes. Men who advertised the dissolution of their marriages in the city's newspapers were drawn overwhelmingly from the lower and middling occupations. The majority, 62 percent, were from the city's lower laboring classes: the mariners, laborers, and lower craftsmen like tailors, cordwainers, and coopers. (Men from these occupations accounted for approximately half of the city's male workforce in the late colonial period.) A full one-quarter of the men with known occupations were mariners. The family lives of mariners are often difficult to document, but in this instance their periodic voyages away from the city made clarification of their wives' economic status an important matter. During their absences mariners were unable to intercede to stop their former wives from accruing debts on their behalf. Advertising the end of a marriage was an important safeguard against debt, economic ruin, and possible imprisonment in debtor's jail.[10]

Husbands who occupied middling occupational status accounted for 36 percent of the advertisers with known occupations. Drawn from the lower middling ranks on up to the top of the middle strata, they were butchers, bakers, house carpenters, bricklayers, saddlers, glovemakers, perukemakers, stonemasons, brass founders, tobacconists, distillers, shopkeepers, and sea captains. The artisans, craftsmen, and shopkeepers of the middling ranks

10. Men placing self-divorce ads from the laboring classes included a wide range of occupations, among them peddler, plasterer, tobacco spinner, staymaker, joiner, netmaker, miner, chimney sweep, cutter, and unspecified journeyman. Occupations were established for 116 of the 439 Philadelphians who advertised their wives. The data are more complete for the colonial and Revolutionary era, when one-third of the occupations are known (33 percent). The proportion of known occupations drops for the last two decades of the century to slightly more than 13 percent. I used the occupational classification scheme developed by Billy G. Smith, The "Lower Sort": Philadelphia's Laboring People, 1750–1800 (Ithaca, N.Y., 1990).

I analyze occupational status rather than personal wealth for two reasons. First, many of the advertisements give the husband's occupation for the colonial era, when tax records are not available. Second, occupation was more significant in establishing a man's social standing in colonial society than was personal wealth. A highly successful artisan, for instance, rarely attained the elite social standing of an educated gentleman, despite his wealth. On the danger of debt, see, for example, John Hood, who wrote his advertisement from the Philadelphia jail. PG, Oct. 20, 1768, Rebecca and John Hood.

spanned a wide range of personal wealth, sometimes considerable. It was rare, however, for men of the elite occupations, the clergymen, lawyers, merchants, and "gentlemen," to practice self-divorce through the press.[11]

Self-divorce was practiced by all European ethnic groups. The majority practicing self-divorce were English, the ethnic majority of the city. Scots, Germans, and Irish also practiced self-divorce in significant numbers, again roughly consistent with their representation in the population. Members of the city's smaller ethnic groups also placed such ads, including some French- men, Swedes, and Italians. The exception to this widespread use of self- divorce was, of course, the region's African-Americans. As slaves, they were denied the right to full legal marriage. While African-Americans held in slav- ery certainly established customary marriages and divorce procedures, the society around them refused to grant them the privileges and responsibilities of marriage that these newspaper advertisements were designed to curtail. No African-Americans placed runaway wife advertisements until the passage of the Pennsylvania Gradual Abolition Act of 1780.[12]

In many of the self-divorces we have no way of knowing what circum- stances induced a wife to end her marriage. The advertisements simply de- clare her departure and the termination of the marital financial union. These skeletal ads attest to the fact that these wives perceived that they could leave a marriage they viewed as untenable and that they exercised that option. The ads that do include detailed accounts of the circumstances of a wife's departure *may* tell us what happened. In many cases the facts presented would have been authenticated or found blatantly untrue by the local community of readers, who would often know the circumstances of the marital rupture. The detailed

11. The hatter Samuel Pennock, for example, was rated in the top eightieth percen- tile of the city's taxable residents in 1772, the year he advertised his wife (1772 Provincial Tax List, CCAP; *PG*, Aug. 3, 1774, Martha and Samuel Pennock). The one merchant known to have advertised his wife was assessed for taxation at the middle rank of those taxable, not among the economic elite, and there were two artisans whose wealth placed them among the city's wealthiest men (both cases occurring during the tur- bulent early 1780s).

12. Ethnicity of Philadelphia husbands placing elopement advertisements by per- centage: English, 54; German, 13; Scots, 13; Irish, 12; French, 4; Welsh, 2.5; Swedish, 1; Italian, 0.5. Ethnicity was established by analyzing the surnames of those who adver- tised their wives and thus must be taken only as approximations. Charles Biley, a Philadelphia blacksmith, was the first African-American to place a runaway wife adver- tisement in a Philadelphia newspaper (*PEP*, Oct. 28, 1780), immediately after the passage of Pennsylvania's Gradual Abolition Act of 1780.

ads may, therefore, fairly accurately represent the husbands' interpretation of events. They certainly presented an accepted script of what eighteenth-century men from the mid-Atlantic region expected in terminating marriages. They shaped their advertisements to present an implicit indictment of their wife's failure to fulfill the fundamental tenets of a wife's role in marriage. Broadcasting her departure, in and of itself, implied a wife's repudiation of her role as the dutiful, constant helpmeet.

One typical scenario husbands presented was a wife's utter refusal to remain within her husband's household. Husbands wrote that their wives "refused to Cohabit" with them or "absolutely refused to live any longer" with them. Shipwright Joseph Hulings, whose wife "has refused to live with him any longer," might have been a particularly difficult man to live with. Eight years later his female servant went before the bar to have her term of service canceled because of Hulings's abuse, and the court released her.[13]

Occasionally a husband presented the details of a wife's resolute rejection of him. In 1746, for example, Johanna Holder left her millwright husband, John, when he moved the household from Trenton, New Jersey, to Darby in Chester County. When John moved to Darby, Johanna moved to Philadelphia, and, according to John, "hath refused to come and live with her said Husband, notwithstanding his repeated Solicitations and suitable Provision made for her Removal." When John sought her out in Philadelphia, she rebuffed "his earnest Invitation" to reconcile and "refus'd to go home with him." Johanna chose to put more distance between herself and John. She left Philadelphia after this meeting and returned to Trenton, taking their child with her against her husband's wishes. Holder was more forthcoming than many husbands in narrating the details of a wife's rejection, but there must have been many such stories behind the husband's bland statements that his former partner "refuses my bed and board."[14]

Throughout the eighteenth century, husbands' ads criticized their wives for failing to fulfill their roles as mothers. They asserted the primacy of their wives' child-rearing responsibilities and claimed an additional harm when their wives left children behind as they abandoned their marriage. John Lee

13. *AWM*, Nov. 3, 1726, Catherine and Joseph Wood (Philadelphia); *PJ*, Dec. 13, 1775, Agnes and John Forsythe; *PG*, Feb. 19, 1756, Elizabeth and Joseph Hulings (Philadelphia), and QSD, March session 1764.

14. *PG*, Apr. 10, 1746, Johanna and John Holder; *PC*, Jan. 17, 1744, Susanna and Peter Cline (Philadelphia).

indicted his wife for "leaving him four small Children to provide for." Casper Hoffman thought it important to elaborate that his wife Elizabeth "hath Eloped from her Husband the second Day of February last [five months earlier], and left on his Hands two Children, one of five Years, and the other two Years of Age." Matthew Wood felt the loss of his wife's labor in child rearing when Rebecca had eloped, "leaving him with five small Children to take care of." In other instances the charge of child abandonment was made as an indictment against the wife's womanhood. Husbands suggested that their wives had acted unnaturally when they privileged their own well-being over a woman's duty to tend to her children. As corroborating evidence of his wife's bad character, Bryan Kennedy began his ad proclaiming that his wife had "left her Child of 21 months old with him." A mother who would leave her infant babe was, Kennedy asserted, self-indulgent and could easily be believed to be "loose" and "disorderly." For Adam Gayler of the Northern Liberties little more need be said than that Elizabeth "hath Eloped from her said Husband, and left her Sucking Babe." Many of the wives who left children behind must have faced a heart-wrenching decision to assert their own interests over the possible well-being of their children. Taking children with them, as Johanna Holder did, also violated husbands' patriarchal prerogatives and could be perceived as equally insubordinate and rebellious behavior.[15]

Another circumstance husbands occasionally presented was that their wives had left them to establish a new conjugal union. At the time John Lee advertised his wife, Joan, in 1739, she had been gone for three years and had established a relationship with a new man that had produced a child. Perhaps the news of the new couple's child prompted John Lee to formalize their self-divorce. Ruth Horn was "pretty far gone with Child" when she "went away with one John Hewet," who one suspects was the father of her child. In these instances women were practicing a form of serial monogamy, moving from

15. *PG*, Apr. 19, 1739, Joan and John Lee; *PJ*, June 28, 1759, Elizabeth and Casper Hoffman (Philadelphia); *AWM*, June 10, 1742, Rebecca and Matthew Wood; *PG*, Aug. 29, 1745, Bryan and Judith Kennedy (Philadelphia); *AWM*, Aug. 19, 1736, Elizabeth and Adam Gayler (Philadelphia). Husbands continued to cite their wife's abandonment of the couple's children to suggest the wife's culpability in terminating the marriage throughout the century. For examples in the latter half of the eighteenth century, see *PJ*, Jan. 26, 1758, Elizabeth and Jonathan Worrel; *PJ*, May 19, 1768, Ruth and John Corwin; *PEP*, Jan. 13, 1776, Honor and Edward Powers (Philadelphia); *PJ*, May 15, 1776, Christiana and Godfry Weltzell (Philadelphia); *PEP*, Jan. 27, 1778, Susannah and William Brooks.

one conjugal unit to another. Sometimes accusations of infidelity were less specific, stating only that she "hath eloped from him, and lives in a very disorderly manner," as John Hickey claimed of his wife, Mary, or when Bryan Kennedy asserted that his wife, Judith, "leads a loose, disorderly Life," living separate from him in Philadelphia. But husbands' claims that their wives had left them to pursue relationships with other men were fairly unusual early-to-midcentury, occurring in fewer than 9 percent of the ads from 1726 to 1760.[16]

The most common detail husbands' self-divorce ads presented was that their wives left with some of the property from the marital union and went their merry way. They often took "sundry goods" or "wearing apparel" but sometimes took considerable property in household goods, furniture, trade inventory, money, or financial bonds. Catherine, wife of Philadelphia carpenter Joseph Wood, the first wife advertised in the Philadelphia press, sold some of the couple's property before she left and took more of it with her when she removed to her daughter's house outside the region in 1726. Wood, like most husbands, recorded her appropriation of "his goods" but did not call for either the return of those goods or for her arrest for theft. He simply hoped to stop all further economic dealings with Catherine and to withdraw her ability to draw credit on his account.[17]

In a technical legal sense the property these women appropriated was often their husband's. The fruits of a wife's labor were the property of her husband. But the consistent pattern of wives' taking some goods, and husbands' acquiescing to their wives' assertion of a just claim to this property, suggests that another understanding about marital property was operating here. While husbands used terms such as "confiscated," "imbezled," "carried off," or "taken" to describe their wives' actions, only rarely did they seek to recover this property. Instead, they tacitly agreed that their wives had a right to some of the marital property upon the termination of the marriage. These wives were laying claim to part of their economic contribution to the marriage. In a sense they were taking a portion of the dower they would never inherit from these marriages because they had left their husband. By letting a wife who

16. *PG*, Apr. 19, 1739, Joan and John Lee; *PG*, Apr. 5, 1759, Ruth and William Horn; *PJ*, July 31, 1755, Mary and John Hickey (Philadelphia); *PG*, Aug. 29, 1745, Judith and Bryan Kennedy (Philadelphia). Sexual misbehavior of a wife was presented in 8 percent of the advertisements placed by Philadelphia husbands between 1726 and 1760, and in 9 percent from the surrounding region in this era.

17. *AWM*, Nov. 3, 1726, Catherine and Joseph Wood.

took property go unmolested by the law, a husband granted her a small economic portion of the marital property at the end of their marriage, perhaps clearing the economic slate of any future claims she might make upon his estate.[18]

A division of property was a standard part of marital separations for couples who parted by mutual agreement (not by elopement advertisement). Michael MaGraw, for example, submitted a public notice expressing the terms of his separation from his wife, Ann, in the *Pennsylvania Journal* in 1775, explaining that they

> have mutually agreed to live separate and apart from each other; and in consideration of my having given her divers Articles of Household Furniture, she has agreed to work for her own subsistence, and has released me from all demands on that account. I therefore request, That no persons give her credit on my account, as I will pay no debt of her contracting since our separation.[19]

Michael agreed to give Ann part of their marital property, and she agreed to relinquish her claims on Michael for support. Ann was to be her own financial agent, responsible for her own upkeep. John and Mary Fenby had apparently made similar arrangements thirty years earlier when this Philadelphia porter and his wife parted ways. Like Michael MaGraw, John Fenby needed to notify the public that he was no longer financially responsible for his wife. John,

18. See, for example, *PJ*, Aug. 14, 1755, Ann and Richard Venable (Philadelphia); *PJ*, Sept. 20, 1759, Jean and Robert Robson (Philadelphia); *PJ*, Sept. 2, 1762, Ann and William Meek (Philadelphia); *PJ*, July 28, 1763, Sarah and John Andraw (Philadelphia); *PJ*, July 9, 1767, Bridget and Richard Sweetman (Philadelphia).

In only four cases did a husband solicit the aid of the public in securing his wife in jail. In three of these cases the wife had left with her paramour, and the husband charged the public to secure both parties to recover his property. In the fourth case the wife departed seated on his mare, and he sought its return. The overwhelming majority of husbands did not seek their wife's return or punishment. *PG*, Apr. 5, 1759, Ruth and William Horn; *PJ*, Feb. 19, 1751, John and Gerteret Beesely; *PC*, Dec. 30, 1771, Elizabeth and Henry Haeny (Philadelphia); *PJ*, Oct. 13, 1779, Ann and John M'Cree (Philadelphia). John M'Cree had also placed an earlier ad in 1776, not offering a reward, when his wife left on foot (*PG*, July 31, 1776).

19. *PJ*, Mar. 9, 1775, Ann and Michael MaGraw (Philadelphia). Couples like the MaGraws, who separated by mutual agreement and did not write elopement ads, were not counted as cases of self-divorce through runaway wife advertisement.

however, chose not to make his separation agreement public but ran a brief elopement ad at the end of July 1746. Mary Fenby placed her own ad the following week clarifying the marital dissolution. According to Mary, John had run his ad claiming elopement, "tho' 'tis well known, they parted by Consent, and agreed to divide their Goods." Mary went on to protest that John had not as yet "fully" fulfilled his part of the bargain, "but detains her Bed and Wedding Ring." Furthermore, "as she neither has, nor desires to run him in Debt, believing her own Credit to be full as good as his; so she desires no one would trust him on her Account, for neither will she pay any Debts of his contraction." Mary clearly understood their financial relationship had been one of mutual participation requiring shared rewards, and she saw herself as an important economic actor in her own right.[20]

Division of property was vital to Timothy and Catherine Kavanaugh's separation agreement, including a portion of his lands. The couple separated twice, and both times a division of property was part of their arrangement. According to Timothy, the couple first "parted on a private agreement," and Catherine departed with "sundry of my goods and property." Several years later Catherine returned, and the couple reconciled for a period before separating again. This time they had their agreement witnessed and recorded by a justice of the peace and finalized their economic relationship by Timothy's selling his "lands and property" in order to "deliver to her such a share of my estate, in money."[21]

This custom of the wife's receiving a share of the marital property when a marriage ended by mutual consent was embraced by wives who left their marriages under less amicable circumstances. Eloped wives expected their economic share and understood that they acted justly when they took property with them. When couples in the eighteenth-century mid-Atlantic recognized a woman's right to property in self-divorce, they were acting in concert with contemporaneous plebeian customs in England and Wales and in accordance with divorces in Scotland, where spouses were expected to return property brought into a marriage to its premarriage owner and to divide their marital goods. On this point most Philadelphia husbands and wives agreed: a wife deserved a portion of the couple's economic resources when a marriage ended. English common law in force in Pennsylvania gave a husband legal ownership of all property generated by husband and wife during their marriage, but many couples of the nonelite classes followed those other traditions

20. *PG*, July 31, Aug. 7, 1746, Mary and John Fenby.
21. *PG*, Aug. 17, 1774, Catherine and Timothy Kavanaugh.

that granted wives some economic standing and recognized their important economic contributions to the family economy.[22]

An important support for women's claims to marital property at the end of a marriage was the customary economic roles granted to wives during the marriage. Colonial women were often economic partners in marriages based on mutual dependence. Self-divorce advertisements are filled with references to the kinds of economic transactions wives routinely performed. While English common law placed all married women within their husband's coverture, thereby denying wives independent ability to own property, make contracts, and undertake financial obligations, colonial wives often made economic contracts as their husband's agent. Wives bought and sold goods, extended credit, and accepted payment against debts owed to their husband. A wife might even assign bonds or be involved in settling the estate of a deceased neighbor for whom her husband stood as executor. Eighteenth-century economic relations were based on this exchange of debt and credit, little business was done on a cash-and-carry basis, and accounts were settled periodically. Wives, particularly in the developing mercantile economy of Philadelphia, customarily participated in these exchanges.

Coverture

Wives used the legal doctrine of necessity that allowed them to undertake financial agreements (sales and debts) that were necessary for the running of their households or that were customary to a wife of her position. Thus, for example, the wife of a cordwainer or tailor who normally made purchases or accepted payment for her husband's wares had through accepted practice established her right to do so in the future unless expressly prohibited by her husband. In Philadelphia, where it was common for an artisan's wife to assist him in his business and where 20 percent of men made their livelihood through seafaring, it was common practice to accept a wife's word in her husband's stead in business matters. Unless husbands warned their neighbors not to treat their wives as their economic agents, neighbors would do business with their wives. John Holder worried that his wife, Johanna, who refused to live with him, could continue accepting payments of money due him or sell his goods for her own benefit if he did not publicly terminate her customary business practices:

> This is therefore to caution all Persons not to give her Credit on his Account, for he is determined henceforth to pay no Debts of her Contracting:

22. Gillis, *For Better, for Worse*, 209–219; Stone, *Road to Divorce*, 5–6, 80–81; Leah Leneman, *Alienated Affections: The Scottish Experience of Divorce and Separation, 1684–1830* (Edinburgh, 1998), 6–11.

And they are hereby farther caution'd not to buy or receive any Household Goods of the said Johanna, without express License from her Husband, not to pay her any Money due by any Contract with him.

James M'Ginnis was less detailed but nevertheless quite clear when he wrote that "he is determined neither to pay any debts of her contracting, or allow her transactions of his business to have the least validity, from this third day of January, 1772."[23]

Eighteenth-century women of the mid-Atlantic region probably had myriad reasons for leaving their husbands. But they all shared one thing: they lived in an economic and cultural environment that made leaving a marriage possible, if sometimes difficult. Elopement advertisements reflect a fundamental economic reality of eighteenth-century gender relations in Philadelphia and the surrounding farming communities. By the middle third of the eighteenth century, women were significant economic actors. Both the agricultural and urban economies relied on women's productive labor to function smoothly and profitably. Women's labor, with its opportunity for female self-support, moderated the patriarchal power of men over women in marriage, despite the law of coverture, which encouraged women's economic subordination to their husbands. More than bravado lay behind a wife's claim that her "credit was as good as his." The growth of the market economy had created spaces for female economic self-sufficiency through women's involvement in the urban market for labor and goods and the agricultural production and marketing of women's wares. Such statements were testimonials that women were aware of their economic value.[24]

23. *PG*, Apr. 10, 1746, Johanna and John Holder; *PC*, Jan. 6, 1772, Ann Delap and James M'Ginnis. M'Ginnis did not refer to Ann Delap as his wife, although she appears to have enjoyed the customary role as his spouse.
    See also Marylynn Salmon, *Women and the Law of Property in Early America* (Chapel Hill, N.C., 1986), 42–57 (on doctrine of necessity); Smith, *"Lower Sort,"* 214 (on customary practices). The expectation that wives would be economic actors was enhanced by the establishment of feme sole trader status for the wives of mariners and others whose husband's trade necessitated their absence. Feme sole status allowed them full control over their own financial dealings. This act was passed by the Assembly in 1718. Mitchell, Flanders, et al., comps., *Statutes at Large*, III, 99–100.

24. Joan M. Jensen, *Loosening the Bonds: Mid-Atlantic Farm Women, 1750–1850* (New Haven, Conn., 1986); Paul G. E. Clemens and Lucy Simler, "Rural Labor and the Farm Household in Chester County, Pennsylvania, 1750–1820," in Stephen Innes, ed., *Work and Labor in Early America* (Chapel Hill, N.C., 1988); Mary M. Schweitzer, *Custom and*

Mid-Atlantic farm women were often deeply involved in the growing market relations, from the production and sale of textiles, poultry, and dairy goods to selling their labor for wages or goods as young unmarried women.[25] They developed economic skills that could be applied outside the household economy and came to see themselves as capable economic agents. Women who had grown up selling their skills and labor and who as farm wives sold goods produced with their own hands and regularly made economic bargains were equipped to provide for their own subsistence and could envision that possibility. Most farm women probably understood their economic competency as consistent with their roles as wives and mothers. But those saddled with intolerable husbands found that their economic skills and labor value made it possible to trade their current lot for a less certain but perhaps more promising future down the road.

Women who left rural marriages sometimes moved in with nearby kin and contributed their labor to those households in return for household membership. Others relocated to another rural community to find a new mate—or with a new mate in tow. But the option mentioned most often by abandoned husbands was that their wives had left the countryside for the city. By relocating to Philadelphia a woman could create a new identity, become a self-supporting individual, and perhaps find a new mate.

The urban economy made living as an unmarried independent woman viable. The city could be attractive to women who left their husbands, both those from the farming hinterland and those who lived there. By eighteenth-century standards Philadelphia offered extensive opportunities for female economic self-sufficiency. Employment opportunities in domestic service increased dramatically during the second half of the eighteenth century, as Philadelphians relied less on indentured servants for such labor. Demand for paid domestic labor was also driven by rising standards of domestic comfort and display, fueled by growing consumerism and a desire to demonstrate social status. Employing women in one's home to help with household labor became common.[26]

_____

Contract: Household, Government, and the Economy in Colonial Pennsylvania (New York, 1987); Lisa Wilson, *Life after Death: Widows in Pennsylvania, 1750–1850* (Philadelphia, 1992); Wulf, *Not All Wives*.

25. Jensen, *Loosening the Bonds;* Judith A. Ridner, " 'To Have a Sufficient Maintenance': Women and the Economics of Freedom in Frontier Pennsylvania, 1750–1800," in Eldridge, ed., *Women and Freedom in Early America*, 167–190.

26. By 1775, 38 percent of households in wealthy Chestnut Ward hired domestic

Other women established trades in specific domestic skills such as white-washing, nursing, midwifery, and mortuary work or opened boardinghouses. Unlike the farming household economy, which functioned best with both male and female labor, domestic employment provided a livelihood for women in Philadelphia outside the marriage partnership. The urban economy also provided opportunities in retailing of goods, food, and drink. Female proprietors accounted for as many as half of the city's retail establishments and for one-fourth of its taverns (although these tended to be smaller than those owned by men). Women operated small corner grogshops and neighborhood taverns. They worked as hucksters up and down the city streets selling the daily leftovers of fresh food and baked goods from the city's markets. They were successful shopkeepers, selling everything from dry goods to liquors, cloth, and books. A woman could enter into these businesses with a little capital (perhaps removed from her marital home in flight), personal skills in networking, and a lot of hard work. A significant number of women relied on these strategies for their own support.[27]

Unmarried women were a sizable part of the Philadelphia population, and female-headed households accounted for between 12 and 20 percent of all households during the late colonial period. By the 1770s more than one-third of the city's adult female population were unmarried and living in the households of nonrelatives. Some never married, despite a sex ratio that gave men a slight numerical edge; others were widows who chose not to remarry; and some had separated from their husbands, choosing instead to live independently. These adult women had made economic places for themselves outside their natal households without establishing marital households.[28]

The economics of marriage for the majority of the city's families, those of

---

laborers; in the more modest neighborhood of East Mulberry Ward, 15–20 percent of households did, most of them adult women. See Wulf, *Not All Wives*, 130–146.

27. Wulf, *Not All Wives*, 130–148 (on female trades). On indentured servants, see Sharon V. Salinger, " 'Send No More Women': Female Servants in Eighteenth Century Philadelphia," *PMHB*, CVII (1983), 29–48; Salinger, *"To Serve Well and Faithfully": Labor and Indentured Servants in Pennsylvania, 1682–1800* (New York, 1987). On female retailing, see Patricia Cleary, " 'She Will Be in the Shop': Women's Sphere of Trade in Eighteenth-Century Philadelphia and New York," *PMHB*, CXIX (1995), 181–202; Peter Thompson, *Rum Punch and Revolution: Taverngoing and Public Life in Eighteenth-Century Philadelphia* (Philadelphia, 1999).

28. Wulf, *Not All Wives*, 93–94 (on female-headed households). Wulf demonstrates that the life cycle of many urban women included long periods outside marriage.

the laboring classes, also encouraged women's involvement in wage labor. Low wages and the seasonal employment of laboring men compelled both husbands and their wives to seek employment. It was not unusual for wives to work in domestic employment while their husbands sought work where they could. Couples like Mary Ann and John Harrison were typical. Mary Ann had taken up a place as a domestic outside the city while John waited for work in the maritime trades. While economic necessity was probably more important than individualistic impulse in propelling wives of the lower classes into the paid workforce, their employment lessened their economic dependence on husbands.[29]

Wives of laboring men often hung on at the edges of poverty as husbands struggled to secure steady employment or gave up completely and deserted their wives. John Badder came and went with the seasons, bringing his wife and child only "two pair of shoes each, and one yard and three quarters of lincey, and twenty shillings in money" in the course of two years. Women working in domestic employment could expect to earn only about half what their husbands earned when fully employed. But, when that husband proved unsatisfactory, a wife could "hire to work" as Elizabeth Badder did to support herself and child, and survive on her own. Occupational segregation by gender and the gender bias in wages made single existence a challenge for all but elite women, but the urban environment did provide economic opportunities for women to opt out of marriage. Market forces of this port city had, by the middle of the eighteenth century, undermined the ability of many husbands to fully support their wives, but they had also eroded their wives' need to subordinate themselves to their husbands' will for economic survival.[30]

In concert with economic forces, competing gender discourses also undermined husbands' abilities to claim absolute patriarchal authority successfully. English, Welsh, Scots, Irish, and German Philadelphians each brought particular beliefs about marriage and sexual behavior to their intimate lives, creating a complex cultural environment. English and Welsh plebeian traditions granted men and women more latitude to enter and end marriages than English law allowed. Self-marriage and self-divorce were regulated by local custom and the prevailing belief among the plebeian classes that marriage was

29. *PG*, Oct. 9, 1776, Mary Ann and John Harrison; Smith, *The "Lower Sort."*
30. *PG*, June 16, 1768, Elizabeth and John Badder. On the emergence of urban poverty among men of the laboring classes in the 1760s and 1770s, see Gary B. Nash, "Poverty and Poor Relief in Pre-Revolutionary Philadelphia," *WMQ*, 3d Ser., XXXIII (1976), 3–30; Nash, *The Urban Crucible: The Northern Seaports and the Origins of the American Revolution* (Cambridge, Mass., 1979).

a civil contract between two individuals formed through their consent and could be rescinded by mutual release of the marital ties by husband and wife. For many, female sexuality was not absolutely contained within lifelong marriage as the law directed.[31]

Scots who immigrated to eighteenth-century Philadelphia brought a strong tradition of marriage based on simple consent and a legally sanctioned tradition of full divorce. Because marriage could be entered into and also terminated at will, Scottish law granted women greater control of their sexuality and created more fluid power relations between men and women in marriage. Celtic Irish tradition and practice placed little importance on the conjugal family unit and did not attempt to control female sexuality through marriage. Before the Cromwellian conquest and the imposition of English law, the Irish embraced self-marriage, self-divorce, and remarriage and allowed legitimate cohabitation. Because Irish social organization before the English conquest was based on clan affiliation rather than the conjugal family, creation of the conjugal unit through marriage was not highly regulated. Exclusive and permanent rights to a woman's body in marriage were not part of the Irish Celtic gender system. Irish men and women who immigrated to eighteenth-century Philadelphia left a society where these traditions, and the Irish Christian marriage practices of Catholicism, had been illegal since the mid-sixteenth century. Many had cultivated a subversive disregard for the English legal dictates on marriage and divorce. Couples like Mary and Robert Mitchell drew on those traditions when they terminated their marriage through self-divorce upon arrival on American soil. Other ethnic groups embraced traditions that accentuated the importance of marriage bonds and sexual constancy in marriage. The city's German population immigrated from a society where marriage was tightly bound, fidelity expected, and divorce impossible. In the wake of the Protestant Reformation marriage gained importance as the central organizing system of German society, and older forms of self-divorce were frowned upon.[32]

31. These customs operated outside statutory law but were generally recognized as legitimate and allowed to operate unimpeded until the passage of the Hardwicke Marriage Act in 1753.

32. *PC*, July 26, 1773, Mary and Robert Mitchell; Isabel V. Hull, *Sexuality, State, and Civil Society in Germany, 1700–1815* (Ithaca, N.Y., 1996), 17–34. Early modern Scotland followed medieval canon law traditions concerning marriage. Scots had enjoyed the right to divorce in cases of adultery or desertion with the right to remarry since the sixteenth century. Under Scottish law a full legal marriage was enacted by the mutual agreement of a man (over age fourteen) and a woman (over age twelve) and the sub-

Pennsylvania Quakers also contributed. Quaker religious teachings professed equalitarian marriages, competing with prevailing English legal understandings that marital authority resided with husbands. Quakers believed in gender equality of the soul and women's equal place in religious organization and practice. Quaker founders George Fox and his wife, Margaret Fell, had taught that gender relations in marriage before the Fall from grace were pure and free from gender hierarchy and female submission. Quakers advocated a marriage union of two equal "helpsmeet" partners, striving to recreate prelapsarian gender relations. Within Quaker theology, male superiority and domination within marriage were viewed as a punishment meted out to both men and women for the Fall. The goal of marriage was to return to this untainted equal partnership.[33]

Puritan as well

Colonial Pennsylvania's marriage law allowed the colony's diverse cultural groups to follow their own traditions. Although Pennsylvania was an English colony, the Quaker commitment to freedom of conscience led the colony to adopt laws that left marriage largely unregulated. In England the emerging middle classes led a campaign to delegitimate the customs of self-marriage and self-divorce. Regularized, state-sanctioned marriage codifying patriarchal dictates of the common law became a hallmark of middle-class legitimacy and the law of the land after 1753. In Pennsylvania, by contrast, the form and content of marriage, as enacted in 1701 and amended in 1730, remained a personal choice. The law spelled out the procedures couples were to follow to marry, but they could be discarded if the couple married within the religious organization of their membership. According to Quaker beliefs the state could not intercede in an individual's chosen religious beliefs or practice. The marriage law could easily be sidestepped, and thus the door was open to irregular

---

sequent consummation of their vows. Unlike England, where such unsolemnized exchanges of vows, while recognized, conferred no property rights, these marriages in Scotland conferred upon husband and wife complete property rights of full marriage. Marriage could be entered into and ended without church or state endorsement. In England marriages so constituted were recognized as valid until the mid-eighteenth century but carried no property rights. After 1753 such irregular marriages, very popular among the plebeian classes, were deemed invalid and illegal. See Stone, *Road to Divorce*, 5–6, 80–81; Leneman, *Alienated Affections*, 6–11; Anne Laurence, "The Cradle to the Grave: English Observation of Irish Social Customs in the Seventeenth Century," *Seventeenth Century*, III (1988), 63–84. Pennsylvanians adopted a tenet of Scottish divorce law when they included a four-year absence as a legal cause of action for divorce in the state's first divorce law in 1785.

33. Wulf, *Not All Wives*, chap. 2, "Elizabeth Norris's Reign: Religion and Self," 53–75.

marriages. Pennsylvania's colonial leadership embraced the concept of the primacy of free will in marriage, even as it hoped that will would be guided by God. Marriage became a private and religious matter, and couples married in their homes, in churches, and by simple exchange of vows. Some simply set up housekeeping together and by fulfilling the roles of husband and wife established themselves as a married pair. Without tightly regulated marriage, Pennsylvanians were free to practice a whole host of marriage rites that expressed their particular beliefs concerning proper gender relations.[34]

This rich but complex cultural environment meant that Philadelphians navigated matrimonial waters and sexual relationships with distinct and contradictory understandings of proper power relations between men and women in marriage, and the expected relationship of marriage to the control of female sexuality. Ethnic traditions and beliefs contributed to the fluid and dynamic nature of Philadelphia's gender culture but often operated below the surface of public discourse. The Quaker ideal that God ordained equality between men and women in marriage created a strong counterdiscourse to the English belief in the natural superiority of husbands. Both ideas circulated widely and competed for supremacy in eighteenth-century Pennsylvania.

34. Mitchell, Flanders, et al., comps., *Statutes at Large*, II, 21–23 (the law as proposed in 1700), 161–162 (as enacted in 1701), IV, 152–154, A Supplement to the Act entitled "An Act for Preventing Clandestine Marriages." For discussion of eighteenth-century campaigns against clandestine and irregular marriages and their culmination in the 1753 Hardwicke Marriage Act, see Stone, *Road to Divorce*, 121–127; Gillis, *For Better, for Worse*, 135–142.

Stated procedures in Pennsylvania included consulting parents (and after 1730 securing parental permission), establishing that one was free of the impediments to marriage (such as labor status as indentured servant or slave, or a prior marriage), posting notice of intent to marry, and exchanging vows.

For self-divorcing couples who were not legally married but cohabited as man and wife, see *PJ*, Aug. 2, 1770, Ann White and John Power (Philadelphia); *PJ*, June 17, 1756, Mary Read and Thomas Evans (Philadelphia); *PL*, Nov. 11, 1775, John Hetherington and Isabel Craig; *PJ*, May 3, 1783, Elizabeth Canaga and William Nickson (Philadelphia). For instances of self-marriage: advertisement for runaway servant Rachel Pickerin, *PG*, Dec. 23, 1746; and Agnes Mackey, *PJ*, Apr. 21, 1748.

In the early nineteenth century Pennsylvania Chief Justice John Bannister Gibson believed self-marriage was widespread. In his opinion affirming the validity of common-law marriage he claimed that to fail to recognize common-law marriage would "bastardize" much of the population. Gibson's opinion, *Rodernbaugh vs. Sanks*, Pa. (2 Watts) (1833), 9.

Eighteenth-century popular culture reflected the contested power relations demonstrated in self-divorces and the cultural conflict over the proper gender relations in marriage. Newspapers and especially almanacs in Philadelphia during the first half of the century were full of humorous poems and anecdotes about marriage as a site of conflict between men and women. Produced cheaply and widely purchased by Philadelphians, almanacs in particular were an important locus of cultural production and were unique in colonial print culture. Unlike the bulk of reading material in Philadelphia, which was imported from England, almanacs were produced domestically. More than any other print source, colonial almanacs were a local cultural production. In creating almanacs, Philadelphia editors selected material from English sources and composed locally oriented pieces. Almanacs were standard purchases for colonial readers, eclipsed by only Bibles and primers. Benjamin Franklin was printing ten thousand almanacs a year by the late 1740s, and he was only one of four printers producing almanacs in the city.[35]

The humor in these almanacs is the closest source we have to the gibes and jokes of colonists. Depictions of marriage as primarily a place of conflict were prevalent and demonstrate that power struggles between husband and wife resonated with a much broader population than those who left their marriages. Almanac ditties such as the one that topped the March calendar for *The American Almanac for 1729* suggested that marriage had its dark side and might not be such a happy place.

March
Nick slighted Women, Marriage he decry'd;
To which his Friend *Tom* waggishly reply'd,
In Marriage are two happy Days allow'd,
A Wife in Wedding-Sheets and in a Shrowd,
How can the marriage State then be accurs'd,
Since the last Day's as happy as the First?[36]

35. These printers took on printing jobs for several almanac producer-editors as well as publishing their own almanacs. The ten-thousand figure is from 1748, when Franklin took a full accounting of his printing-bookselling business in preparation for selling his share to his former partner David Hall. The four printers were Franklin, William Bradford, Isaiah Warner, and Anthony Armbruster. James N. Green, "The Book Trade in the Middle Colonies," in Hugh Amory and David D. Hall, eds., *A History of the Book in America*, I, *The Colonial Book in the Atlantic World* (New York, 2000), 278.

36. Titan Leeds, *The American Almanack for . . . 1729* (Philadelphia: Keimer, 1728).

Men tempted into marriage by the promise of sexual fulfillment in conjugal intimacy could soon come to regret their choice. As an almanac ditty suggested in 1734, once men married, they longed for a way out:

Wedlock, as old Men note, hath likened been,
Unto a public Crowd or common Rout;
Where those that are without would fain get in,
And those that are within would fain to get out.[37]

During the first half of the eighteenth century, representations of gender conflict were situated almost exclusively in a marital setting. The battle between the sexes was between husband and wife and was quite appealing to colonial readers. In almanacs printed in Philadelphia and marketed throughout the region, depictions of heated marital conflict and gibes at erring wives began appearing in the late 1720s. Gender conflict in marriage became a staple of almanacs produced in the 1730s and persisted unchallenged as the most common reference point for gender relations until the 1760s.[38]

The popularity of marital conflict can be seen most clearly in the editorial decisions of young Benjamin Franklin. Although Franklin's almanac was not the first to publish anecdotes bemoaning the difficulties of marriage, the theme came to dominate the humorous pieces it published during the 1730s, 1740s, and 1750s. Franklin opened his first edition of *Poor Richard's Almanac* with a ditty above the January calendar that decried the impossibility of finding a faultless bride. A husband's instruction would be required to fashion such a wife, because, the punch line quipped, no such wives were "ready made." Half the narrative (noncalendar) text here depicted conflict between husband and wife. Franklin closed with a December rhyme bemoaning the hardships inflicted on a husband by a self-indulgent wife.

She that will eat her breakfast in her bed,
And spend the morn in dressing of her head,
And sit at dinner like a maiden bride,

37. Richard Saunders [Benjamin Franklin], *Poor Richard . . . An Almanack for . . . 1734* (Philadelphia: Franklin, 1733).

38. My argument here is based on a content analysis of all almanacs printed in Philadelphia during the eighteenth century. Cornelia Hughes Dayton noted a similar trend in popular culture in New England: "Satire and Sensationalism: The Emergence of Misogyny in Mid-Eighteenth Century New England Newspapers and Almanacs," paper presented to the New England Seminar of the American Antiquarian Society, Worcester, Mass., Nov. 15, 1991.

And talk of nothing all day but of pride;
God in his mercy may do much to save her,
But what a case is he in that shall have her.

Franklin had presented a theme his audience found compelling, and he used it to build his readership.[39]

In the following year Franklin strengthened the emotional charge of the marital conflict by bringing in an oppositional voice, Poor Richard's wife, "Mrs. Bridget Saunders." By creating a narrative fiction of gender conflict between the narrator and his wife, Franklin hoped to draw readers more deeply into the material. Male and female readers each had a character to relate to as they read through the tumultuous battle of the sexes within the almanac's pages. Bridget's first piece was a response to the December poem of the preceding year that had complained of wifely faults. The paired poems also delineated the classic faults early-eighteenth-century Pennsylvanians associated with failing marriages and deficient husbands and wives: drunken, neglectful husbands and useless, nonproductive wives.

December
By Mrs. Bridget Saunders, my Dutchess, in Answer to the December Verses of Last Year.

He that for sake of Drink neglects his Trade,
And spends each Night in Taverns till 'tis late,
And rises when the Sun is four hours high,
And ne'er regards his starving Family:
God in his Mercy may do much to save him.
But, woe to the poor Wife, whose Lot it is to have him.

The two pieces bridged the readers' interest from one year to the next and promised more observations of this marital spat in the future.[40]

39. Saunders [Franklin], *Poor Richard for 1733* (1732). Franklin's almanac continued to target marriage as a topic for humorous attacks during the 1750s, but the tone had softened somewhat. The most violent conflict-ridden material was printed in the 1730s and 1740s. Franklin's own aspirations to enter elite polite society probably encouraged him to moderate his earlier overtly antiwoman material. Such direct attacks on women were, after midcentury, not genteel for a man of such upwardly mobile class aspirations.

40. Ibid., *1734* (1733). Franklin later used these same techniques in his Busy Body series in his *PG* to work the theme of gender conflict.

Bridget Saunders's role and marital conflict increased in subsequent editions of *Poor Richard's Almanac*. By 1738 gender conflict had become Franklin's signature theme. Bringing in a woman's voice might have been what allowed Franklin to print the most virulent antiwoman pieces published in early colonial Pennsylvania almanacs. Franklin played angry antiwoman ditties off against endearing depictions of a bumbling Bridget Saunders. In 1738, for instance, Bridget intercepts the almanac text on the way to the printer "to see if he had not been flinging some of his old Skitts at me," and secretly rewrites the customary editor's preface. Bridget declared, "I had a Design to make some other Corrections; and particularly to change some of the Verses that I don't very well like; but I have just now unluckily broke my Spectacles; which obliges me to give it [to] you as it is." Wives, it appears, would object to the filler content. Having warned the reader, in this humorous way, that women might object to the almanac content, Franklin then follows with a poem in which a husband advised a doctor to kill his wife:

> *Dick's* Wife was sick, and pox'd the Doctor's Skill,
> Who differ'd how to cure th' inveterate Ill.
> Purging the one prescrib'd. No, quoth another,
> That will do neither Good nor Harm, my Brother.
> *Bleeding's the only Way;* 'twas quick reply'd,
> That's certain Death;—But e'en let *Dick* decide.
> *Ise no great skill,* quo' Richard, *by the Rood;*
> *But I think Bleeding's like to do most good.*[41]

Some of this humor was based on reciprocal gender animosity. Marital trouble begins, almanac ditties suggested, when men or women fail to fulfill their proper roles. As Franklin put it:

> Ill thrives that hapless Family that shows
> A Cock that's silent, and a Hen that crows:
> I know not which lives more unnatural Lives,
> Obeying Husbands, or commanding Wives.[42]

But in almanac humor it was almost always willful wives who undermined proper gender relations in marriage, leading to unhappiness. Reflecting the perspective of the male authors and editors, marital conflict was a woman's fault. Almanacs complained of the sins of women's sharp tongues and strong

41. Ibid., *1738* (1737).
42. Ibid., *1734* (1733).

wills, "For ne'er heard I of Woman good or ill, / But always loved best, her own sweet Will." They warned that a husband could be saddled with a wife who would thwart his desires at every turn. The most persistent charge leveled against erring wives was that willful wives would reject the subservience due their husbands by their aggressive or unrelenting speech. "The Hen that Crows" was spoken of as "prattling Women" who "are despis'd" and "Scolds" whose husbands seek refuge from their wives' incessant speech.[43] Wives' speech could be so annoying that going deaf could provide comic relief:

> On his late Deafness
> Deaf, giddy, helpless, left alone,
> To all my Friends a Burthen grown,
> No more I hear a great Church Bell,
> Than if it rang out for my Knell:
> At Thunder now no more I start,
> Than at the whispering of a Fart,
> Nay, what's incredible, alack!
> I hardly hear my *Bridget's* Clack.[44]

Almanacs told stories of what women who refused to submit to their husband's will might expect. Wives' unruly tongues could be countered by a husband's strong arms. In one witty struggle the husband corrects his wife with a beating and threatens more of the same should she not submit:

> *Sam's* Wife provok'd him once; he broke her Crown,
> The Surgeon's Bill amounted to Five Pound;
> *This Blow* (she brags) *has cost my Husband dear,*
> *He'll ne'er strike more. Sam* chanc'd to over-hear.
> Therefore before his Wife the Bill he pays,
> And to the Surgeon in her Hearing says:
> *Doctor, you charge Five Pound, here e'en take Ten;*
> *My Wife may chance to want your Help again.*[45]

Humor might soften the blow of force directed at wives in these sayings and ditties, but the assertion of an ever-present male threat was there nonetheless. We know from newspaper reports and court records that men's physical

43. Leeds, *Almanack for 1729* (1728); Saunders [Franklin], *Poor Richard for 1733* (1732), *1743* (1742); William Ball, *New-Jersey Almanack for . . . 1745* (Philadelphia: Bradford, 1744).

44. Saunders [Franklin], *Poor Richard for 1739* (1738).

45. Ibid., *1736* (1735).

power over their wives was not absolute in eighteenth-century Philadelphia, despite these claims to the contrary. But men resisted this reality and sought to assert their dominance through the circulation of jokes such as these.

Mid-Atlantic readers were steeped in these images of domestic conflict, which were an important part of the context through which men and women read and interpreted runaway wife ads. Vocal wives who proclaimed their just reasons for departing from their marriages spoke in opposition to representations that reduced their claims of hardships to the ravings of obstreperous, unruly wives. Wives who eloped from their husbands had certainly rejected the proper gender relations prescribed by popular print culture. While these ditties would have been funny to both men and women because they openly aired the tensions surrounding power relations in marriage, the lessons of gender deviance were aimed at women. Almanacs and newspapers printed the jokes of their culture, but they also waged a cultural assault on women's independence from a man's perspective. The *American Almanac* summed up the proper relationship of man and wife in its February 1733 rhyme:

February
A Wife's Mans Partner, and has Right to share
In's greatest Fortunes or his meanest Fare,
Satisfy'd in's Misfortunes she ought to be,
Both are by marriage plac'd in one Degree,
Both the same Flesh, when made each other's Mate,
And both united in the self-same State;
But Man has title to the upper Hand,
All Wymen may ask, but Man should command.[46]

Marriage was a partnership, but one in which a wife joined her husband's life and was to follow his lead. When push came to shove, the "man should command."

Popular representations of gender and marriage produced in Philadelphia during the first half of the eighteenth century presented marriage as a site of everyday conflict. Almanac editors tended to side with husbands and propose that adherence to patriarchal power relations in marriage was the antidote. But other forces militated against their success. The economic options available to women in the city, the religious support for equalitarian marriage (particularly

46. Leeds, *American Almanack for 1733* (Philadelphia: Bradford, 1732).

in Quaker theology and practice), and the cultural traditions of Scottish, Irish, and other immigrant groups that embraced free choice in marriage and divorce by mutual consent—all undermined the logic of patriarchal marriage as the natural gender order. The proliferation of these same popular cultural representations of gender conflict in early modern England has been interpreted as evidence of anxiety over the stability of patriarchal marriage as the bedrock of the gender system. Cast into the multiethnic, multicultural environment of early Philadelphia, these representations suggest, not an anxiety over the stability of the patriarchal gender order, but rather the inability—or difficulty—of establishing it at all. The seeds of patriarchal marriage had not taken firm root in colonial Philadelphia. The gender culture of midcentury Philadelphia instead allowed for negotiation and struggle between men and women over the distribution of power and authority in marriage: here women had relatively wide options outside marriage by eighteenth-century standards and thus more power to negotiate within marriage.[47]

what undermined patriarchal marriage ↓ gender conflict ↓ not anxiety over natural order just inability of establishing in Phila.

Self-Divorce and the Power Plays of Marriage after Midcentury

This unsteady ground made way for more direct challenges to male authority and assertions of female will after midcentury. By the 1760s wives openly critiqued their husbands' behavior, and some replaced them by establishing sexual relationships with men they found more satisfactory. The gender culture Philadelphians had created facilitated women's ability and willingness to evaluate their marriages, fostered weak patriarchal control of female sexuality, and influenced the development of a sexual culture in which female sexuality was not rigidly tied to lifelong monogamous marriage.

When wives spoke for themselves and placed newspaper advertisements in response to their husbands', they asserted their understanding of unacceptable behavior in a marriage and displayed the self-presentation they believed was expected in a wronged wife. Colonial wives' grievances focused on their husbands' economic misbehavior or physical abuse. They generally framed their public declarations deferentially, presenting themselves as bowing to community norms of proper husbandly behavior. They stated their grievances

47. Anthony Fletcher, *Gender, Sex, and Subordination in England, 1500–1800* (New Haven, Conn., 1995), chap. 1, "Prologue: Men's Dilemmas," 3–29. Fletcher and others have analyzed this discursive development of sixteenth- and seventeenth-century England. Much of this material continued to enjoy a broad circulation through reprints and rewritings during the eighteenth century.

through surrogates or scripted them to reflect proper wifely subservience. Christian Douglass's advertisement was typical of these early responses. Christian did not make her case herself but relied instead on the collective voices of four neighboring women. Francis Alison, Elizabeth Parmelea, Lydia Ashton, and Margaret Thomas wrote on Christian's behalf, vouching that she had not eloped, but was confined to bed:

> We whose Names are under written, do certify, that if by that Name be understood a certain Christian, the Wife of James Douglass, of this City, Stone cutter, we believe that she never eloped from her said Husband, but has been confined mostly to her Bed since the 22d of this Instant.[48]

These women were privy to the intimate details of Christian's seclusion during the previous week, but they refrained from divulging those details for public consumption. The list of female names suggests that Christian was recovering from childbirth, illness, or physical abuse with the aid of these women. But it was enough to assert that Christian was "confined" to her bed and leave the reader to imagine the most plausible reasons for her disappearance from public view.[49]

After midcentury, and especially after 1760, the frequency and character of wives' responses began to change. In the 1760s, 1770s, and 1780s the proportion of wives who rebutted their husband's interpretation of their marital rupture nearly doubled. These ads took on a new, openly confrontational tone. Jane Tennent, for instance, stated that she printed her advertisement "in order to do myself Justice, and set the Matter in a clear light to the Public," and Mary Meyer wrote that her husband's advertisement "obliges me to take this method of arraigning him at the bar of the candid public, hoping that his feared conscience will convict him of several facts." These wives asked their peers to examine the particulars of their cases, evaluate the merits, and endorse the negative judgment implicit in a wife's departure. Rather than appealing to an accepted common ground that all would agree the erring husbands had transgressed, these wives expanded the boundaries of unacceptable hus-

48. *PG*, Dec. 6, 1759, Christian and James Douglass; James Douglass's ad, *PG*, Nov. 29, 1759.

49. For eighteenth-century women's authority in the area of women's health and their role in local adjudication of disputes, see Laurel Thatcher Ulrich, *Good Wives: Image and Reality in the Lives of Women in Northern New England, 1650–1750* (New York, 1980); Ulrich, *A Midwife's Tale: The Life of Martha Ballard, Based on Her Diary, 1785–1812* (New York, 1990).

bandly behavior and asked their neighbors to join them in endorsing these new terms of what constituted abuse of power by their husbands.[50]

Wives often bolstered their cases by drawing on public knowledge of their own characters and domestic situations, as when Alice Herbert of Philadelphia was advertised by her husband Michael:

> I take this method to give a true state of the case between me and my husband, to convince the public what a brutish, malicious, scandalous fellow he is; for it is well known to all my neighbours and acquaintance, that I have behaved myself as becomes a good subject of our Sovereign Lord the King, and that I did, by all ways and means, endeavour to get a good honest livelihood, and I can, when called upon, get my neighbours, of sufficient credit, to testify the same, and that I am neither a whore, thief, or a drunkard; but it being my misfortune to marry so disagreeable a person as the said Michael Herbert is.[51]

Eighteenth-century wives, like their husbands, relied on their reputations to facilitate economic and personal relationships, and good character was especially important for women who had severed ties with their former husband.

The most common justification wives put forth to explain departing from their marriage was physical abuse. Their public revelations that domestic violence caused their marital rupture asserted that there were limits to the level of force a husband could use in exercising his patriarchal right to correct and control his wife. Before midcentury, wives relied upon community norms that defined the boundary that separated a husband's legitimate use of physical force from intolerable violence. They produced evidence that other authorities had also determined that their husbands had overstepped those boundaries, and characterized their husbands' actions as life-threatening.

During the 1740s wives' narratives of domestic abuse incorporated an air of wifely submission and long-suffering patience. They shied away from specific descriptions and appealed instead to a standard of life-threatening abuse that no wife was expected to endure. Hannah Willock's 1743 ad, for instance, stated only that she "was obliged in Safety of her Life, to leave her said Husband, because of his Threats and cruel Abuses for some Time past." Hannah had left only after the couple had agreed to separate and had penned a separation

---

50. *PG*, Jan. 1, Feb. 5, 1767, Charles and Jane Tennent; *PJ*, Aug. 18, 1773, Thomas and Mary Meyer. Between 1726 and 1759, 8 of the 249 wives placed responding ads; from 1760 to 1787, 33 of the 592 wives placed responding ads.

51. *PC*, Aug. 22, 1768, Michael and Alice Herbert.

agreement. Demonstrating proper female deference, Hannah did not write the ad herself, but enlisted a male surrogate, "Richard Bright, Master of Arms to the Ship *Wilmington*." Jane Dorsius in 1748 also made her case through a male voice, her father, Derrick Hogeland. He wrote that he had taken Jane and her children into his care "after a long Series of ill Usage patiently borne by the said Jane." Only after Jane had been left for several days without anything "to subsist on" had Hogeland "fetch'd them home."[52]

Elizabeth Dunlap also claimed her husband, James, had violated the standard of life-threatening violence when she placed her ad in 1742. She had been "obliged in safety of her life to leave her said Husband because of his threats and cruel abuses for several years past repeatedly offered and done to her, and that she went no farther than to her father's House." She had left, but not eloped: she had fled in fear for her life. What was at stake here, beyond Elizabeth's and James's personal reputations, was Elizabeth's culpability as an "eloped" wife. If she had eloped, she would have lost her dower rights, which she intended to enforce:

> The said James Dunlap having a considerable estate in lands in said county, which the said Elizabeth is informed he intends to sell as soon as he can, she therefore thought proper to give this notice to any person or persons that may offer to buy, that she will not join in the sale of any part of said lands, but that she intends to claim her thirds (or right of dower) of and in all the lands the said James Dunlap has been seized and possessed of since their intermarriage, whosoever may purchase the same.

Elizabeth's ad gave notice that a sale of these lands without her consent would bring a legal challenge.[53]

Wives' responding advertisements reveal the typical recourses available to them. A wife whose husband had exceeded acceptable corrective force was expected to seek community intervention. She should, like Mary Dicks, enlist the aid of her family. If familial intervention did not temper her husband's actions, she was to call on the local justice of the peace or magistrate to "bind him to the Peace." When those steps failed to restrain a husband's violence and reconcile the couple, a wife's decision to abandon her marriage was generally understood as legitimate. Mary Dicks was acutely aware of the impor-

52. *AWM*, June 16, 1743, Alexander and Hannah Willock; *PG*, June 16, 1748, Peter Henry and Jane Dorsius.

53. *PG*, June 17, 1742.

tance of these steps when she wrote her advertisement explaining her circumstances. She included all the necessary elements, beginning with the nature of the abuse: "That on the 17th Day of December, 1761, my Husband John Dicks did beat and abuse me his Wife very much, and threatened to shoot me divers Times." The next day she sought aid and intervention from her family nearby: "On the 18th I went to my Brother and Sisters, about one Mile and an Half from Chester [her home], and acquainted them of the Affair; my Brother and I returned to Chester immediately, where he, in his desperate Humour, shut the Door, and would not suffer me to enter my own House." Despite her brother's intervention, the abuse continued, and Mary was "obliged of late to bind him to the Peace, being in Danger of my Life." Mary, contrary to her husband's claims, had not eloped, but was instead the victim of a violent husband, as judged by herself, her family, and finally the community at large through the justice of the peace.[54]

Philadelphian Rebecca Hood had also first turned to the city's justice of the peace to halt the excessive violence of her husband before leaving him. When a husband's physical violence toward his wife overstepped her understanding of his prerogative to correct her, she could initiate legal action against him by swearing an oath before her local justice of the peace recounting the violence she had endured and indicating that she feared for her personal safety. The justice of the peace would investigate the allegations and, finding them true, would then require the husband to post a monetary bond guaranteeing his future good behavior toward his wife and to secure additional bonds from two other men of property on his behalf. The seriousness of this offense was reflected in the sizable bonds required of husbands deemed especially violent. Patrick Motley, for example, was required to produce a bond of two hundred pounds and two bonds worth one hundred pounds each from two "good Freeholders" in 1768 when his order was recorded by the city's Mayor's Court. Motley's bonds were double the amount typical for most offenses at the time. High monetary bonds might also, however, discourage a wife's use of the law, as her own financial well-being was intricately tied to her husband's. This early American version of a temporary restraining order was backed by the financial threat of the forfeiture of these bonds. If a husband persisted in his abuse, the court would collect on the bond and could, at the wife's request, establish a court-ordered separate maintenance for her, allowing

54. *PG*, Jan. 14, 21, 1762, Mary and John Dicks.

her to live apart from her husband but requiring him to provide her financial support.[55]

This system was just what Rebecca Hood referred to when she explained, "The true Cause of her leaving him [John Hood] was his cruel, barbarous and unparalleled Treatment of her at sundry Times; whereby she was put in Danger of her Life, as was made appear before one of His Majesty's Justices of the Peace for the County of Philadelphia, and perhaps will more fully appear at the next General Session of the Peace." A husband could dispute his wife's claims at the quarterly court sessions, but John, like most husbands, chose not to.[56]

The justice of the peace had some discretion to evaluate whether a wife was truly in danger, but legal authorities had a stake in confining husbands' exercise of power to behavior that validated husbands' position as the natural authority. When husbands abused that power by excessive physical violence, they undermined the legitimacy of the dominance granted to them as hus-

55. MCD, Patrick Motley, July 1, 1768. See also QSD, Mary and James Roberts, June 6, 1774. James Roberts was required to post bonds in the same amount to restrain his violence toward his wife.

On court-ordered separate maintenance, see, for example, Anna Maria and John Byser, MCD, January session, 1761. Anna Maria convinced the court that John's abuse warranted their intervention, and they ordered him to provide her with a weekly sum of 7s. 6d.

This legal procedure of posting bond was established in the earliest legal codes of Pennsylvania and maintained throughout the century. See Mitchell, Flanders, et al., comps., *Statutes at Large*, II, 23, An Act about Binding to the Peace (1700); James Parker, *Conductor Generalis; or, The Office, Duty, and Authority of Justices of the Peace* . . . (Philadelphia, 1764); A Gentleman of the Law, *The Conductor Generalis* . . . (Philadelphia, 1792), 336. The 1700 statute allowed a person to secure a bond to the peace when someone threatened to "wound, kill or destroy" or "do him any harm in person or estate." The justice of the peace manual expressly states that this statute may be used by a wife against her husband: "All persons . . . have the right to demand surety of the peace, and it is certain, a *wife* may demand it against her husband, threatening to beat her outrageously, and that a *husband* also may have it against his wife" (*Conductor Generalis* [1792], 336). Typical bond requirements for other offenses, such as disorderly behavior or keeping a disorderly house, and typical bonds guaranteeing court appearances, ranged from twenty-five pounds to one hundred pounds during this period.

56. *PG*, July 5, 12, 1759, Rebecca and John Hood. The Hoods did not appear before the Court of Quarter Sessions or the Mayor's Court. See also *PG*, Nov. 24, 1784, Ann and Obed Hudson. The Hudsons lived in western New Jersey, where Ann "was obliged to swear the peace against" Obed, who was then required "to give bonds, with sufficient security for his good behavior."

bands. Justices followed community standards of acceptable and unacceptable physical force. These standards were constructed and reinforced through systems of community justice such as newspaper proclamation and community intervention "to bind" abusive husbands "to the peace." Wives, especially after midcentury, played a vital part in defining unacceptable violence and policing it.[57]

Sometimes women took policing into their own hands, as in Chester County in 1735. The *Pennsylvania Gazette* reported that a group of women who had observed a man "being unreasonably abusive to his Wife upon some trifling Occasion" at a public sale intervened to pass judgment and punish him for his offense. They "form'd themselves into a Court, and order'd him to be apprehended by their Officers and brought to Tryal." Having found him guilty, they "duck'd" him in a nearby pond and cut off half his hair and beard. This crowd of women insulted the offender's masculinity by inflicting ducking, traditionally reserved for women, and emasculating him by shearing his locks and beard. These punishments announced his failure to exercise proper male authority. A crowd enjoyed this impromptu judicial act, witnessing the humiliation possible when a husband exceeded his customary authority. News of this female court's intervention quickly spread through the press to readers throughout the region.[58]

Such direct actions to police community norms were probably regular occurrences, but many of them might not have been as spectacular as this apparently spontaneous collective recognition. In England such instances were often the culmination of a longer period of surveillance and growing concern over unacceptable behavior. We don't know whether this Chester husband became the target of his neighborhood wives because of repeated instances of domestic abuse. But it is clear that these women shared an understanding of unacceptable treatment of a wife and that they could act upon it when that standard was violated. Their men too demonstrated support of such community policing by gathering as spectators without interrupting the proceedings.

Just as justices saw the value of limiting husbands' physical violence, male neighbors sometimes saw it in their interest to intervene in husbands' use of

57. For a discussion of the use of bonds to inhibit domestic violence in early-nineteenth-century Baltimore, see Stephanie Cole, "Keeping the Peace: Domestic Assault and Private Prosecution in Antebellum Baltimore," in Christine Daniels and Michael V. Kennedy, eds., *Over the Threshold: Intimate Violence in Early America* (New York, 1999), 148–172.

58. *PG*, Apr. 17, 1735.

excessive force against their wives. The *Pennsylvania Journal* reported just such an instance in 1752.

> We hear from Elizabeth-Town, that an odd Sect of People have lately appeared there, who go under the Denomination of Regulators; there are near a Dozen of them, who dress themselves in Women's Cloaths, and painting their Faces, go in the Evening to the Houses of such as are reported to have beat their Wives; where one of them entering in first, seizes the Delinquent, while the rest follow, strip him, turn up his Posteriors, and flog him with Rods most severely, crying out all the Time, Wo to the men that beat their Wives;—It seems that several Persons in that Borough, (and 'tis said some very deservedly) have undergone the Discipline, to the no small Terror of others, who are any Way conscious of deserving the same Punishment.

Thus, in a gender reversal, men dressed as women to police the behavior of other men. Men's cross-dressing symbolically demonstrated the danger to the gender hierarchy that excessive wife abuse held: if men did not justly use the power granted by law and custom, wives might justly claim the prerogatives of resistance and rebellion. Dressing as women reminded the community of this possibility and demonstrated men's solidarity with their wives in community policing. These mid-Atlantic colonists had adapted and refined traditions of what E. P. Thompson has termed "rough music" to adjudicate local public justice. These customs did provide a measure of protection against extreme domestic violence, but they simultaneously acknowledged and reinforced the legitimacy of patriarchal gender relations and husbands' authority by setting limits on its outermost boundaries. The escalation of vocal protests by abused wives as the eighteenth century wore on attests to women's attempts, with some success, to constrict the accepted levels of physical force granted to husbands.[59]

By the 1750s abused wives' deferential scripts had given way to outraged advertisements that often specified the details of abuse. Lydia Rue's rendition, in 1748, was typical of the developing narrative trend of wives who refused to suffer spousal abuse. She began her ad much as previous wives did, explaining that she had departed "after a long and series of Ill-usage patiently borne." But she then presented the particular abuses she had suffered. Her husband had

59. This incident occurred in Elizabeth Town, New Jersey (*PJ*, Dec. 26, 1752). For British customs, see Thompson, *Customs in Common*, chap. 8, "Rough Music," 467–538; Anna Clark, *The Struggle for the Breeches: Gender and the Making of the British Working Class* (Berkeley, Calif., 1995), 73–87.

left her alone in her Philadelphia home for several days with "nothing to subsist on" following childbirth, "not being a Month brought to Bed." He returned "home in a frightful Manner and lock'd her out of Doors" and denied her and her child support. When she returned from her neighbor's refuge the next day, he was out selling off the couple's goods; and, when he returned, "he told her 'If she would not go she might stay there and starve to Death.'" Finally, she suffered the indignity of being denied access to her own home by a man stationed at her doorstep by her husband to bar her entry "whilst he went and published an Elopement." Lydia Rue was driven from her Philadelphia home by her abusive husband, but she did not demurely submit. Her ad vilified her husband to his neighbors by detailing his cruel treatment of her, the mother of his newborn child.[60]

Like Lydia Rue, Mary Blum of the Northern Liberties also complained of persistent physical abuse with periods of material want and sporadic desertion. Mary, too, exposed her husband as "a man of a vile behavior" and threatened to "give a more full description of him, to caution the public against such a villain," including "several scandalous circumstances [that] can be proved against him" if he continued "to spread false reports of me." These women had rejected the public presentation of wifely submission for one of equal justice in their marital disputes. They publicly announced resistance to absolute male power in marriage and asserted that they, as the affected individuals, could determine when husbands had overstepped the legitimate exercise of authority.[61]

In these ads from midcentury through the Revolution, wives participated directly as individuals to establish the limits of husbands' authority and use of force. Detailing the abuse they had endured, they renegotiated the boundary of unacceptable physical force, believing that these indignities revealed behavior beyond what a husband should be allowed to force his wife to endure. They wrote of experiences like Barbara Arndorff's of being tied up in a "hog-stye" and then "abused . . . in a barbarous manner," accompanied by threats that "he would break my limbs." Barbara detailed scenes of abuse within her home and others where violence occurred outdoors in public. She closed her ad with the retort that her "credit is full as good as his" and that she "will pay no debts of his contracting." Mary Thomas described being "very much terrified" when her husband demanded she leave, threatening her "with a couple of hickory rods,

60. John and Lydia Rue were Philadelphia residents in 1748 when their marriage ended. *PJ*, Oct. 13, 1748, John and Lydia Rue.

61. *PJ*, Nov. 26, 1767, Peter and Mary Blum.

beating the table, and threatening with these at a terrible rate." Mary Meyer described scenes so frightening that "for several months I have been obliged to be hid." Her husband had repeatedly threatened her with "his loaded pistols," kept, she said, "to dispatch me." She described her husband's fits of rage: "He, with horrible oaths broke open every lock (tho' he had all the keys) destroyed and burnt my books, etc. and spent what cash he found, and mal-treated me."[62]

The physical abuse these wives complained of often took place within a power struggle over a husband's dominance and a wife's submission to his will. John Arndorff's abuse was designed to elicit a confession of adultery from his wife, Isaiah Thomas's brandishing of the hickory rods was done to secure a promise that his wife would not visit her father's or neighbors' homes, and Thomas Meyer's mortal threats punctuated a conflict over property from his wife's previous marriage.

By publicizing their outrage, wives challenged the legitimacy of a husband's use of brute force to secure masculine authority in marriage. These wives used public exposure of their husbands' violence to redraw the line between corrective force and abuse. One isolated incident of physical abuse, unless life-threatening, was insufficient to warrant a wife's departure. But long-term physical abuse, especially when coupled with lack of material support, justified leaving one's husband. By the 1760s a husband who struck his wife or beat her "judiciously" with a switching branch for insubordination was within his rights. But one who put his wife in grave danger, or beat her in a "barbarous" or "tyranical" manner, or responded with violence despite repeated community intervention had overstepped that divide.

Wives who complained of their husbands' economic failures also became more assertive after midcentury. When wives criticized a husband's economic performance, they evaluated how well he fulfilled the central marital obligation and the basis of masculine authority in early America and found him wanting. Husbands' economic competence lay at the heart of a good eighteenth-century marriage. The central element of the marriage contract was a man's pledge to take his wife under his care, to provide support and protection in exchange for her voluntary submission to him. By law a woman gave up her economic self to her husband at marriage. A husband's economic incompetence or failure to

62. *PG*, Feb. 14, 1771, John and Barbara Arndorff (John had advertised Barbara in one of Philadelphia's German-language newspapers, and he followed up her ad in *PG* with a response of his own there, Feb. 28, 1771); *PG*, Aug. 27, 1767, Isaiah and Mary Thomas, and Isaiah Thomas's ad, *PG*, July 30, 1767; *PJ*, Aug. 18, 1773, Thomas and Mary Meyer, and Thomas Meyer's ad, *PG*, Dec. 9, 1772.

provide for a wife's subsistence was, in a sense, a failure to fulfill his marital obligations. This was the case, it will be recalled, when Jane Dorsius left her husband Peter in 1748. Her departure came only after enduring his "intemperance and extravagancy," during which time he had "squandered most of his substance" and had been forced to sell most of his possessions. Peter Dorsius's intemperance and economic mismanagement had cost him his ministerial office and led the local magistrate to take control of his estate for his family's benefit. Despite this intervention, Peter continued to liquidate his remaining assets. Jane, left with "nothing to subsist on," was justified, her appeal contended, in going to live with her father. Jane, like the abused wives early in the century, carefully presented her case to demonstrate that she was not alone in her critique of Peter's economic failing. Rather than assert her right independently, she left her husband only after the broader community had passed judgment and Peter had failed to change his ways.[63]

Later in the century wives such as Lydia Anderson asserted that they could evaluate their husbands' economic competency and pass judgment independently if they found them woefully inadequate. Lydia's ad, in 1763, exudes her confidence that she can enlist the public's support in her assertion that William Anderson's actions justified their separation:

These are to let the Public know the Reason I live separate from him is this, that in about three Years he spent near Three Hundred Pounds of my Estate, and was never sober one Week in the Whole time; so let this be a Warning, that my Estate shall pay no more for him after this Date.[64]

In a reversal of husbands' attacks on self-divorcing women's mothering, some wives after 1760 played up their roles as protective mothers to challenge their husbands' financial authority. When a husband had misused property his wife brought to the marriage from a former husband's estate, her ad was often particularly irate. These wives asserted that their actions to separate themselves from their husbands were necessary to protect their children's well-being. Mary Baily charged her husband with "embezzling the estate of JOHN CAMPBELL," her late husband, and reminded the public that Campbell's

63. *PG*, June 16, 1748, Jane and Peter Henry Dorsius. See also, for example, Louise and William Leddel, *PG*, Jan. 23, 1753. William allegedly spent £450 sterling of Louise's money. For an example of wives' evaluating husbands' economic competency in New England, see Cornelia Hughes Dayton, "Scrutinizing Yeoman Competency: Contests over Legal Guardianship in Early New England," paper presented at the Annual Meeting of the American Historical Association, January 2001.

64. *PG*, Nov. 17, 1763, Lydia and William Anderson.

assets were for the use of his children. Sophia Conner's charges were more expansive. She began by chastising her husband for placing his ad: "Edward Conner has, in a most scandalous and shameful Manner, misrepresented and cried me down in the public Papers, as a strolling worthless Woman." Edward Conner had indeed claimed that Sophia "has strolled from Place to Place these four years past, and run me in Debt." According to Sophia, however, it was Edward's economic failures that forced Sophia to fend for herself.

> I therefore, Sophia, Wife of Edward Conner, of the Northern Liberties, take this Opportunity to inform the Public, that I have these 8 years past, suffered and lost by this tyranical Husband an Abundance. As for his calling me a Stroller, all them that know me, can testify that his wretched Behavior has, in a Manner, drove me to it; for when he had run all through what he conveniently could come at, of what my former Husband left to me and my Chi[ld]ren, he left me destitute of all Manner of Subsistance, then I was obliged to shift for myself.

Edward would not leave Sophia to her own resources but returned to her periodically to make use of the property she had procured through charity and family resources. He had a husband's legal claim to the goods and money she procured, but, if Sophia could sever their marital ties and protect her own economic reputation, she could be clear of him.[65]

By the 1760s a new attack on the patriarchal prerogatives of husbands had appeared in the city's newspapers alongside wives' condemnatory responses. Wives' sexual behavior emerged as a fundamental issue in terminating marriages. After 1760, wives' sexual independence, often embodied in a liaison with a new partner, became the most common cause cited for ending a marriage. The frequency with which wives' sexual infidelity and their actions to establish a new relationship were specified as the cause for the marital breakup rose dramatically, especially for couples self-divorcing in the city of Philadelphia. During the 1760s a full 37 percent of self-divorce advertisements placed by Philadelphia husbands mention the sexual misbehavior of their wives. Between 1760 and 1790, 30 percent of Philadelphia's elopement ads included claims of a wife's infidelity, against only 8 percent in the 1720s–1750s. Assertions of sexual misbehavior also rose in the greater Philadelphia region, but to a smaller degree. For couples living outside the city, 18 percent of husbands' ads between 1760 and 1790 referred to wives' sexual misbe-

65. *PJ*, July 28, 1773, Mary and William Baily (Philadelphia); *PG*, Feb. 5, 26, 1767, Sophia and Edward Conner (Philadelphia).

havior. Whereas economic disagreements and husbands' physical abuse were the most common complaints in the marital ruptures of the colonial era, wives' pursuit of another relationship became the most common cause for the rest of the eighteenth century. For Philadelphians, sexual behavior became the central issue expressed by self-divorcing men and women.[66]

The wives of seafaring men allegedly committed "adultery" or "very disorderly behavior" while their husbands were away at sea. Their husbands posted ads severing their marital ties once they returned to Philadelphia, asserting, as John Ross did, that his wife's "conduct during my absence the two last voyages beyond sea, has justly forfeited all my future connection with, or regard for her." Other women left their husbands and the city with a new man in tow. Mary McKinley left her husband in Philadelphia and was reputedly living "with another man near Lancaster" when her husband advertised her from Philadelphia in 1764; and Ann White left in the company of a former lodger whom her husband suspected had become her lover. Still other women moved in with men elsewhere in the city. Some husbands made general claims against their wives' sexual fidelity, such as Jacob Johnson's assertion that his wife "behaved to me her Husband in a base and wicked Manner, by keeping Company with other Men"; and Enoch James's description that "she has kept company for sometime past with a certain man who some call a cobler, lately come from Cuckold's Town, which I have reason to believe was one great cause of her eloping from me." But others, like William Douglass, made their accusations of adultery directly. Ann, his ad declared, had "eloped from my Bed, and been taken in Crim[inal] Con[versation]"—she had left her own home and been caught in the act of adultery.[67]

66. Decadal percentage figures for Philadelphia were: 1760s, 37; 1770s, 28; 1780s, 26. Those for the region were: 1760s, 17; 1770s, 20; 1780s, 17. Between 1726 and 1760 sexual misbehavior was raised in 8 percent of the Philadelphia cases and 9 percent for the greater region. Cases of unintentional bigamy, where a husband long thought dead returns and the couple dissolves the current union in favor of the original, were not counted as sexual misbehavior.

67. For mariners, see, for example, *PG*, May 1, 1766, Catherine and John Gree; *PG*, Sept. 23, 1773, Tacey and John Chatham; *PG*, Oct. 27, 1768, Sarah and John Ross; *PJ*, Aug. 2, 1770, Ann White and John Power; *PJ*, Nov. 8, 1764, Mary and William McKinley. For women who moved within the city, see, for example, *PJ*, July 18, 1771, Margaret and Bryan Ryan; *PP*, May 25, 1782, Martha and Walter Taylor; *PG*, May 23, 1765, Mary and Jacob Johnson; *PP*, July 11, 1774, Enoch James and Rachel James; *PEP*, May 18, 1775, Ann and William Douglass. There actually was a town called Cuckold in eighteenth-century Pennsylvania.

Some of the advertisements claiming a wife's sexual misbehavior were probably slander by perturbed and rejected husbands, exaggerating or falsifying their accounts of their wives' sexual misconduct. But it is also likely that other men who advertised their wives purposely omitted these intimate details to conceal the embarrassment of being cuckolded by their wives. Evidence from subsequent divorce petitions suggests this was the case. A handful of men sought legal divorce after they had self-divorced by newspaper advertisement, either by petitioning the Pennsylvania Assembly between 1766 and 1785 or by bringing suit after divorce was fully legalized in 1786.[68] In these cases husbands' newspaper advertisements were more likely to conceal their wives' sexual escapades than to expose them. But many of these husbands subsequently produced detailed accounts of their wives' infidelity in their divorce proceedings. When he ran his advertisement in 1768, George Keehmle, a Philadelphia surgeon-barber, simply stated that his wife had eloped and he would not pay any of her future debts. When he appealed to the Assembly for divorce, it was his wife's adultery that swayed them to his cause. John Goggin made no mention of his wife's cross-racial adultery in his self-divorce advertisement of 1764, stating only that his wife had been guilty of "diverse misdemeanors." But Goggin's wife gave birth to a "mulatto" child twelve months later, which was the grounds for his divorce petition. Men like Keehmle and Goggin might have had good reasons to withhold private information from the public presses. And those husbands who did lie when they claimed their wives had been unfaithful could expect to be challenged by their wives in print, as wives more aggressively defended themselves in print after 1760. So, while some men might have manufactured stories of their wives' infidelity, they were probably offset by others' reluctance to expose it.[69]

68. Only 11 of the 439 Philadelphia husbands who placed advertisements to self-divorce, from 1726 through 1786, ever filed for a legal divorce.

Sexual infidelity was not necessary to establish a legal divorce under the Pennsylvania Divorce Act of 1785. Noncohabitation for four years was legal grounds for a divorce.

69. George and Elizabeth Keehmle, *PG*, June 23, 1768, *Journals of the House of Representatives of the Commonwealth of Pennsylvania, Beginning . . . November, 1776 . . .* (Philadelphia, 1782–), Feb. 8, 1783; *PG*, Jan. 12, 1764, John and Catherine Goggin, *Pennsylvania Archives*, 8th Ser. ([Harrisburg], 1931–1935), VII, 1766, 5841. Note that George Keehmle had been granted a divorce in 1772 when he originally made his petition, but the crown had disallowed the action. There were eight wife reply ads before 1760 and thirty-three after.

The eight cuckolded husbands cases were Keehmle; Goggin; Mary and William Hurrie, *PP*, Nov. 29, 1773, *Journals*, June 13, 1781, 667; Elizabeth and James Martin, *PP*,

Those who presented general claims of a wife's sexual misconduct relied on their own reputation and general knowledge of the wife's behavior for their veracity. The specific and detailed information in other ads suggests that many of the allegations of sexual misconduct were probably based in fact. As in ads from earlier decades, much of this information was verifiable by the community at large, by neighbors, family, and friends. When John Green advertised his wife's elopement in 1774, he provided all the information necessary to substantiate his claims: "She went away with a certain JOHN TUCE a Taylor by Trade, who left his Wife in Philadelphia." Anyone who did business with Tuce or was acquainted with his abandoned wife would know exactly whom John Green was referring to, and that the woman by his side had just left her husband for Tuce's company. Even ads that identified a wife's new partner only by his trade often made the couple and their sexual liaison identifiable. When William Brooks published that his wife "cohabits with a certain man, a kind of smuggler and cordwainer," he was probably confident that their community of acquaintances would know whom he meant.[70]

Sexual misbehavior was now at the heart of marital conflict for more Philadelphians than in the past. Many of the women who left their marriages in the

---

July 16, 1778, *Journals*, Feb. 13, 1779, 312; Margaret and John Alexander, *PJ*, Apr. 21, 1779, *Journals*, Aug. 14, 1782, 653; Mary and Jacob Peck, *FJ*, Nov. 14, 1781, *Journals*, Aug. 17, 1782, 657; Sarah and Thomas Phillips, *PP*, Oct. 3, 1782, *Journals*, Aug. 29, 1782, 677; Ann and William Parker, *PP*, July 15, 1783, *Journals*, Sept. 3, 1783, 915.

In all eight cases, the husband failed to mention the wife's sexual infidelity in his advertisement but produced detailed evidence of adultery, or bastardy, in his divorce petition. In five of the cases the action for divorce was filed within a year and a half of the advertisement, suggesting that these husbands purposely did not expose their wife's sexual misbehavior. The cause of action for the divorce in the other three cases was abuse of the wife, desertion by the wife, and the husband's adultery.

This trend was similar in the era after divorce became legal. Three of the twenty-six husbands who advertised their wife's elopement in *PG* from 1787 to 1800 subsequently filed for a legal divorce. Two of these husbands omitted the wife's adultery, but the third proclaimed it in the press. Eleanor and Jacob Lightwood, *PG*, Aug. 15, 1787, PDP, filed 1797, depositions, 1805; Catharine and John Martin, *PG*, July 11, 1792, PDP, 1792; Sarah and John Knight, *PG*, Nov. 26, 1788. John Knight claimed he was prosecuting a libel for divorce in his advertisement but does not appear in the Pennsylvania divorce records.

70. *PG*, Jan. 19, 1774, Anne and John Green (Philadelphia); *PEP*, Jan. 27, 1778, Susannah and William Brooks (Philadelphia).

later part of the eighteenth century did so, at least in part, to establish new, more satisfactory relationships; other women were rejected by their husbands because of their sexual infidelity. The establishment of a new love interest, with the pursuit of personal self-fulfillment that this implied, had become an integral part of marital dissolution by the 1760s. Women seeking new men had become part of the expected script of self-divorce in pre-Revolutionary Philadelphia as well.

Philadelphia's wives had also expanded the role they would play in the public dismantling of marital unions. In the words of Lydia Mathew, wives now claimed a right "publicly to lay open . . . the treatment I have received" and "leave it with an impartial public and the neighborhood in which we live to judge." Mathew's words asserted her right to equal participation in the court of public opinion. But in fact she and the other eloped wives had already passed judgment by taking action to leave their husbands. These wives had transcended their early-eighteenth-century submissive deportment and asserted in its place the validity of their own judgments of their husbands' faults. In the public press wives had challenged their husbands' economic competence and authority, their right to compel submission to authority by force, and their exclusive control of access to their wives' bodies for sexual pleasure.[71]

In the 1760s, a decade before the American Revolution challenged the established political order, numerous Philadelphia wives had begun to challenge the patriarchal order by attacking subordination embedded in patriarchal marriage. Their assault was built upon the foundation of the city's fluid and contested colonial gender culture. By the 1760s, 1770s, and 1780s, self-divorce in the public press revealed new sexual practices and publicized the pursuit of happiness initiated by wives who left their marriages. Their actions raised perplexing questions about the proper ordering of society and the power to be granted to women—questions that would only be complicated by other developments in the sexual culture of the pre-Revolutionary city.

71. *PG*, Dec. 23, 1789, Joseph and Lydia Mathew.

CHAPTER 2

The Fruits of Nonmarital Unions

Sex in the Urban Pleasure Culture

The H A L F - J O E *changed*

A Butcher in one of our capital cities, in his seeking for cattle in the neigh-
bouring province, used frequently to put up at a certain tavern, where the
care the house fell upon a likely hired Maid; for whom the Butcher
conceived an amorous inclination: he tried various means to inveigle her to
his wishes, but found all his efforts in vain: About three years ago finding
her at her old quarters, he tempted her with a piece of gold, well known by
the name of a *Half-Joe:* The poor Girl was unable to resist the shining bait,
and consented to his desires. The next morning the Butcher going off early,
enquired for the master, and then asked him for the *Change of his Half-Joe,*
which he had given the Maid the night before for him to change; the master
answered he knew nothing of it, but immediately called the Maid, who
being greatly confused at such a question, and not chusing to own for what
purpose she had taken it, replied she had forgot, and directly returned it to
the Butcher, who accordingly paid the landlord, and went off. About 2 years
after the Butcher happened to travel that way again, and being at the same
tavern, he was not long seated before he found himself surrounded by the
constable and overseers of the poor, (the Girl in the interval being brought
to bed) who acquainted him that a burthen had been brought upon their
township, through his means, and he must defray all expences thereon
before he departed. This alarmed the Butcher in his turn; but to avoid
further trouble, he complied to pay all charges, and to give a good treat into
the bargain, which amounted in the whole to upwards of Forty Pounds. To
add a little to his mortification, the young Woman made her appearance
amongst the company, and with a sarcastic smile, acosted him, with these
words, *I hope, Sir, you have now got the Change for your Half-Joe.*[1]

In 1768 "The Half-Joe *Changed*" appeared in the *American Calend[a]r,* an
almanac known for the witty tales following the annual calendar. It was pub-

---

1. Philo Copernicus, *The American Calend[a]r; or, An Almanack for the Year 1768*
(Philadelphia: Bradford, 1767).

lished by William Bradford and sold at his London Coffee-House, near the Philadelphia waterfront, the first year after Philadelphians openly acknowledged and documented numerous cases of bastardy within their community. The merchants and sea captains who bought the almanac and the artisans who used it to chart their business accounts read the story knowing that bastardy had become somewhat common in their community. The protocol of intervention by the local Overseers of the Poor to secure child support was familiar enough to Philadelphia readers to provide the comic twist at the end of this story. One can imagine these men reading this tale aloud to one another as they drank their coffee and heard the news of the day at Bradford's coffeehouse, the communication hub for the mercantile community of Philadelphia.

The sexual encounter in this tale is portrayed in a light and humorous tone, where a man's lust for a particularly lovely maid might understandably lead him to seek sexual intimacy outside either courtship or marriage. But, should he engage in trickery to treat her unfairly, he would likely end up the butt of the joke. The maid in this tale is also depicted as acting reasonably, resisting the butcher's advances, then succumbing to the temptation of the gold coin and willingly engaging in the sexual union. However, once she is pregnant and conned out of her payment, the community of men comes to her aid and demands that the butcher provide for the support of this child. The maid, unabashed, confronts him and boldly stakes her claim.

The account in "The Half-Joe *Changed*" was remarkably similar to the real-life situation that men and women of Philadelphia encountered when they bore children outside permanent relationships in the 1760s and 1770s. The lessons conveyed by it were the same lessons embodied in the city's regulation of bastardy through the Overseers of the Poor. Like the butcher, the Philadelphia men were held financially accountable for their offspring; like the tavern maid, women who engaged in nonmarital sexual activity could expect a minimum level of support for a child born out of wedlock without facing harsh, punitive sanctions themselves.

During the 1760s and 1770s Philadelphians openly acknowledged casual sexual experiences that led to bastardy. They printed items like "The Half-Joe *Changed*" in their almanacs as they administered child support payments for the children born of these unions. Casual sexual relations in the form of sex commerce, or prostitution, were also important in their sexual culture. The treatment of venereal disease became part of mainstream medical practice, evidence that many Philadelphians acquired diseases through serial sexual encounters. The frequency of bastardy, sex commerce, and sexually transmitted diseases suggests that sexual relations outside courtship and marriage were a regular part of the sexual terrain.

The emergence and recognition of casual sexual relations were part of a broader cultural transformation, part of a new pleasure culture forged in the city after midcentury. During the 1760s the pursuit of personal pleasure and the time and attention given over to leisure activities increased dramatically. New forms of entertainment were created in the city, and the city underwent a kind of cosmopolitanization, embracing European amusements, styles, and fashion. Theaters, dancing studios, horse racing, bullbaiting, cockfighting, lotteries, and bawdy books were among the leisure activities available. Philadelphians took lessons in the latest amusements in vogue in England, from gallant swordplay to the dance steps of "the Masquerarde and *Spanish* Fandogowe." While some city leaders were aghast at these activities, there were worse to be had. Gambling, drunkenness, and sexual intrigues, from seduction to prostitution, were increasingly undertaken as leisure activities.[2]

A committee of ministers, concerned about these developments, described Philadelphians of the 1760s as a people with a "growing fondness for Pleasure, Luxury, Gaming, Dissipation, and their concomitant Vices." In 1764, the Pennsylvania Assembly acknowledged the growing influence of the pleasure culture when it passed An Act for Suppressing Idleness, Drunkenness, and Other Debaucheries, within This Government. By 1775 the city's biannual market fair was abolished because of excessive illicit activity. The fair had been an occasion for the local population to get drunk, gamble, and pursue amorous liaisons. Passage of such acts attests to the fact that some members of the governing elite felt compelled to take a public stance against the vices of the city. But they represent little more than that. There was no organized effort to prosecute or reform those involved in excessive drinking, gambling, pros-

2. *PJ*, June 11, 1761 ("Fandogowe" ad); *PG*, Sept. 9, 1756 (sword instruction). See advertisements for amusements in *PG* and *PJ*. Dance schools: *PG*, Oct. 1, 1767, Dec. 29, 1768, Sept. 9, 1771. Horse racing: *PJ*, Mar. 11, 1762, Oct. 9, 1766, *PG*, Apr. 7, 1763. Lotteries: *PJ*, May 21, July 16, 1761, *PG*, Jan. 7, 1762. Theater: *PG*, June, 21, 1759, *PJ*, July 5, 1759, Nov. 27, 1766. See also Jacob Cox Parsons, ed., *Extracts from the Diary of Jacob Hiltzheimer, of Philadelphia, 1765–1798* (Philadelphia, 1893), 13 (1767), 16 (1769) on theater, 17 (1769) on public dining, 16–17 (1769) on horse racing, 18 (1769) on bullbaiting; J. Thomas Scharf and Thompson Westcott, *History of Philadelphia, 1609–1884* (Philadelphia, 1884), I, II; John F. Watson, *Annals of Philadelphia . . .* (Philadelphia, 1830), 87–91, 96, 120. David S. Shields, *Civil Tongues and Polite Letters in British America* (Chapel Hill, N.C., 1997); Peter Thompson, *Rum Punch and Revolution: Taverngoing and Public Life in Eighteenth-Century Philadelphia* (Philadelphia, 1999).

titution, or the sexual encounters that led to bastardy. Periodic cries against the emerging pleasure culture were voiced by religious authorities but never resulted in a reform campaign in the prewar years. For many Philadelphians *The Universal American Almanack*'s characterization of the modern world in 1769 was apt:

> Cast an eye into the gay world, what see we, for the most part, but a set of querulous, emaciated, fluttering, fantastical beings, worn out in the keen pursuit of pleasure.

In the fifteen years before the Revolution, Philadelphians developed an urban pleasure culture and made sexual indulgence an integral part of it.[3]

Bastardy in the Pre-Revolutionary City

In the fall of 1759 Elizabeth Powell gave birth to a son, born of her sexual intimacies with Philadelphia mariner Edward Butler. Though Elizabeth named her son John Butler after his father, their claim on him was slight. Butler contributed only his seed, his name, and child support payments, secured by his bond and that of shopkeeper Timothy Caroll. Mary Fisher took the same keepsakes from her sexual encounters with the carpenter James Grey in 1766, as did Catherine Brown from the butcher John Everheart three years later. Catherine secured mandatory child support from John while she carried their child, but her child had no place in the home John made with his wife and their children. In the winter of 1770 Elizabeth Montgomery also faced childbed knowing the father, Townsend White, Jr., a Philadelphia merchant, had guaranteed to provide for her coming child. Elizabeth and Townsend had no future together, but the fruit of their union would be provided for. Each of these men and women had sexual intercourse with a partner with whom they would not establish a long-term relationship. But they were not especially noteworthy:

3. "Extracts from the Rule of Life, etc.," in Andrew Aguecheek [pseud.], *The Universal American Almanack . . . for . . . 1769* (Philadelphia: Steuart, 1768); *PG*, Aug. 20, 1761; Samuel Hazard, ed., *Minutes of the Provincial Council of Pennsylvania* (Philadelphia, Harrisburg, 1851–1853), IX, 166. On market fairs: Watson, *Annals of Philadelphia . . .* (Philadelphia, 1823) I, 364; Elaine Forman Crane, ed., *The Diary of Elizabeth Drinker* (Boston, 1991), I, 40. There were organized campaigns against theater and lotteries during the late colonial era. See Thomas Clark Pollock, *The Philadelphia Theater in the Eighteenth Century . . .* (Philadelphia, 1933); Joseph J. Kelley, Jr., *Life and Times in Colonial Philadelphia* (Harrisburg, Pa., 1973), 104; Watson, *Annals of Philadelphia* (1830), 710–712; Scharf and Westcott, *History of Philadelphia*, I, 255.

they were in good company in late colonial Philadelphia, where many men and women made nonmarital sexual pleasure a part of their lives.[4]

We have the opportunity to study the dynamics and meanings of nonmarital sexuality in the pre-Revolutionary period because in 1767 the city's Overseers of the Poor began documenting cases of bastardy that entered their system of child support and poor relief. During the mid-1760s a new group of men, dominated by the city's Quaker merchant elite, wrested control of the poor relief system from the midcentury Overseers, a group comprising primarily men from the middling artisan ranks. The new Overseers built a new almshouse that combined a workhouse for the able-bodied poor and an almshouse-hospital for ailing Philadelphians, hoping to reduce the cost of poor relief by instilling habits of industry in the poor. The year this new group, called the "managers," took control, it began routinely to document cases of bastardy in the Overseers of the Poor records. Quakers' interest in orderly marriage *followed* by sexual intimacy might have influenced their willingness to document bastardy. As artisans, the former Overseers presumably had closer cultural and personal connections to traditions of irregular marriage and family formation among the laboring classes, which probably made bastardy less culturally significant for them. But it appears that the new managers' primary reason for documenting cases of bastardy was fiscal. In order to accurately account for expenses and revenue, recording the sums of money taken in from the fathers of bastard babes and the amounts then given out to the mothers of those children was essential bookkeeping. The new managers also kept careful records of the cases of bastardy where financial support fell to the community because the father was too poor to provide support.[5]

4. OP, Bonds: June 11, 1760, Elizabeth Powell and Edward Butler; Nov. 5, 1766, Mary Fisher and James Grey; May 9, 1769, Catherine Brown and John Everheart; Feb. 1, 1770, Elizabeth Montgomery.

5. The history of the Overseers of the Poor is presented by John K. Alexander, *Render Them Submissive: Responses to Poverty in Philadelphia, 1760–1800* (Amherst, Mass., 1980), 86–94.

This change in record keeping is striking. On Oct. 16, 1767, the day the managers assumed an active role in the day-to-day management of the poor relief system and the first day the new almshouse opened its doors, the minutes record their first case openly identified as bastardy. They wrote: "gave Christiana Fryburger now lying in with a Bastard child by John Wing .7..6." (7s. 6d.). The language used earlier in the year to describe transactions concerning cases of bastardy did not identify them as such. I have identified some of them through cross-references to other, later records.

The minutes for 1767 have survived in both rough daily record form and the re-

During the five years of complete records preceding the Revolution (1767–1769, 1775–1776), the Overseers of the Poor document their administration of child support for 100 children born outside recognizable family units. This figure suggests that the Overseers handled approximately 200 bastardy cases in the decade before the Revolution, representing 400 men and women who produced offspring without subsequently marrying or establishing a conjugal household together. Each year during this period 1 in 380 adult Philadelphians became the parent of a bastard child. Thus over the course of the ten years documented here, 1767–1776, 1 in roughly 38 adults was parent to a bastard child. In the close quarters of the eighteenth-century city, familiarity with bastardy and the nonmarital sexual behavior that it represented extended beyond the parents themselves. For each woman who bore a bastard child, a larger circle of parents, friends, siblings, and acquaintances would become aware of the circumstances of her motherhood. Those close to the fathers would also become familiar with their experiences as they solicited aid to post bonds and made their weekly child support payments. On the eve of the American Revolution, neighbors could expect to encounter a woman nearing childbirth without a mate as an unremarkable event in every neighborhood in the city.[6]

Illegitimate births provide us with an important window into the sexual behavior, social values, and power struggles within Revolutionary and early national Philadelphia. But illegitimate births can be evidence of a wide range of relationships and circumstances, and it is important to define as precisely as the evidence permits what the form of illegitimacy documented in Philadelphia was. Legally, any child born outside a legal marriage in eighteenth-century Philadelphia was illegitimate. But this legal definition had little practical relevance to many of the city's residents. As we have seen, Philadelphians practiced a wide range of marriage rites, and many recognized self-divorce. Children born in common-law marriages were understood to be legitimate. Many of those who practiced serial monogamy also did not consider them-

---

copied final year-end report. Both are labeled "Philadelphia Almshouse—Ledger 1767–1768" and are held at HSP. The use of the term "bastard" has been dropped from the recopied year-end report during this year, but it becomes the standard usage for the Overseers of the Poor minutes from 1768 on.

6. See the Appendix for a full listing of sources and methodology. None of the 200 documented parents enters the record for a second bastardy case during this period. Fragmentary records from 1750 to 1780 document an additional 65 cases to analyze in the late colonial period (60 for 1750–1765, 5 after 1776). The analysis of bastardy in this chapter will use all 165 cases unless otherwise noted.

TABLE I. *Summary of Bastardy*

Span	No. of Bastards	No. of Parents	Adult Population[a]	Annual Ratio of Parents Bearing Bastards to Population
1767–1776	200[b]	400	15,192	1 in 380
1790–1799	711	1,422	27,976	1 in 197
1805–1814	2,193	4,386	44,493	1 in 101
1822–1826	1,226	2,452	72,879	1 in 149

[a]Adults, meaning those over sixteen years old, were approximately half the total population.

[b]Figure extrapolated from the 100 cases from 1767, 1768, 1769, 1775, and 1776.

Sources: Sources and methods are presented in the Appendix; see, esp., "Bastardy Totals." Population estimates draw on Billy G. Smith, *The "Lower Sort": Philadelphia's Laboring People, 1750–1800* (Ithaca, N.Y., 1990), app. B, table B.1, 206; Susan E. Klepp, *Philadelphia in Transition: A Demographic History of the City and Its Occupational Groups, 1720–1830* (New York, 1989), app. C, table 5.2, 336.

selves adulterers or bigamists, nor did they consider their children bastards. The children of these unions had no reason to enter the city's bastardy records, and they did not. They were raised within families comprising parents who acknowledged and supported them. The children of women like Catherine Bryan and men like Thomas Dunbar, who had self-divorced and established new unions, did not come to the attention of the Overseers of the Poor. The form of illegitimacy recorded by the Overseers of the Poor as bastardy, so recognized by Philadelphians at large, identified a particular subset of parents of illegitimate children: parents whose children were conceived in more casual, short-term, or turbulent relationships. These parents never formed marriagelike unions, and the women, finding themselves pregnant, sought official intervention by the Overseers of the Poor to supervise mandatory child support payments from the fathers of their children.

This group of bastard-bearing Philadelphians engaged in sexual behavior divorced from courtship and marriage. These were the individuals the Overseers of the Poor kept track of from the decade before the Revolution until the city revamped its welfare system in 1828, leaving us a record of one important form of nonmarital sexual behavior practiced in the budding new nation. These records reveal a pattern of increasing bastardy from the mid-to-late eighteenth century into the early decades of the nineteenth century (see Table 1). Between

1772 and 1810 the population of Philadelphia almost tripled, but this form of illegitimacy increased tenfold.

Examining bastardy documented in Philadelphia is important because it demonstrates that a particular pattern of sexual behavior, albeit one embraced by a minority of the population, was being forged during the late colonial period and adopted by numerous Philadelphians over the next half-century. Children born outside courtship or marriage show that some men and women were willing to step outside the marital orientation of sexuality. They assumed behavior patterns in which sexual intercourse became a part of relationships in which neither courtship nor marriage was the outcome.

The cases of bastardy recorded by the Overseers of the Poor suggest that the women involved did not perceive their relationships as failed courtships. In the majority of the bastardy cases the women sought community intervention to establish mandatory paternal support soon after they became pregnant and before the birth of the child. They did not wait to see whether a late-pregnancy or postpartum marriage would resolve their situations. The timing of the requests for support demonstrates that in many of these cases the women did not expect to marry their sexual partner.[7]

The mothers' initiation of regulated child support also suggests that the majority of these relationships were probably somewhat casual or short-term, as the mothers had no confidence that the fathers would provide support for their coming child without community intervention. It was rare for these relationships to persist long enough to produce a second child. Only two of the women who bore bastard children in the pre-Revolutionary decade and three of the more than seven hundred in the 1790s had two children with the same

7. In the period 1750–1779, 60 percent of the cases were initiated before the birth of the child (data available in 80 percent of the cases). In the 1790s, 73 percent of the cases were brought forward before the birth; in 1805, 67 percent; and in 1822–1825, 73 percent (data available in 27, 40, and 39 percent of cases, respectively). After the Revolution, almshouse cases were excluded from this analysis, because poverty compelled many of these women to initiate the Guardians' involvement to secure admission to the almshouse. As such, the woman's action does not indicate the nature of her relationship with the father. See Appendix, Table A.1.

In her study of late-eighteenth-century New Hampshire, Laurel Thatcher Ulrich also found evidence of women's engaging in sexual activities in a range of social contexts and not always associated with courtship. Ulrich and Lois Stabler, " 'The Girling of It' in Eighteenth-Century New Hampshire," *Annual Proceedings of the Dublin Seminar for New England Folklife* (Boston, 1985); Ulrich, *A Midwife's Tale: The Life of Martha Ballard, Based on Her Diary, 1785–1812* (New York, 1990).

sexual partner. It was also extremely unusual for these couples to marry after the birth of the child. (Evidence of parents' marriage exists for only one case in the pre-Revolutionary decade and three cases during the 1790s.) Had these parents united and formed a conjugal family, the Overseers would have ended their supervisory role in child support, but they did not. Unlike the rise in premarital pregnancy, which predated it, this form of bastardy demonstrated a fissure in the sexual system that had in the past confined most reproductive sexuality to courtship and family formation.[8]

In the northern and middle colonies premarital pregnancy had been on the rise throughout the eighteenth century. In Philadelphia the premarital pregnancy rate peaked during the late colonial era, with approximately one in three brides pregnant at marriage. Following the Revolution these numbers decreased to one in five, and then dropped to one in six during the early nineteenth century. These couples embraced sexual intimacy as part of courtship. But they did ultimately marry, and most understood their sexual activity as justified by their intent to marry. Unlike premarital pregnancy, bastardy increased throughout this period, becoming more common as premarital preg-

8. OPM, June 12, 1764, case of Mary Taylor and William Murray; and Mary Barry case (discussed below); GPM, 1790–1799. In one of these 1790s cases the impending birth of a second child, when her first child was twenty-two months old, appears to have moved the mother to seek support. The father was a man of some economic resources; he immediately paid a lump sum of £112 to the Guardians of the Poor for the future care of his two children (GPM, Mar. 14, 1795, case of Kitty Dougherty, father's name unrecorded). The other two cases might have been longer nonmarital unions gone sour, as both enter the Guardians' system after the birth of the second child (GPM: June 22, 1797, case of Alamirrta Talbot and Charles Visey; July 8, 1790, case of Charlotte Lawrence and Thomas Proctor [children ages three and four in 1790]).

Eventual marriage: James Carson married Mary McCormick after the Overseers had jailed him to secure his bond for the child Mary was carrying (OPM, July 31, 1775). During the 1790s, in one case the couple married a year after the father had posted bond with the Guardians for the support of the child, and the record includes his request to have the bond canceled. In another case the couple married before the father posted bond. In the third case the father offered to marry his pregnant partner, taking her out of the almshouse without posting bond. See GPM, Dec. 31, 1795, case of Henry Snyder and Elizabeth Huber; PFT, Aug. 29, 1791, case of William Spearing and Ann Lawson; DOD, Apr. 7, 1791, case of Rachel Hazelton and Isaac Leeds.

Marriage of the parties involved was important information for the Overseers to record, because it explained the conclusion of a case, just as the notation of a father's posting bond and obtaining sureties guaranteeing his financial contribution did.

nancy was becoming less common. In the 1760s and 1770s hundreds of Philadelphians found it acceptable to engage in sexual relations and bear children without marrying their partner.[9]

Bastardy was not completely new in pre-Revolutionary Philadelphia, appearing in court records and grand jury presentments throughout the first half of the eighteenth century. The surviving records reveal seven cases of bastardy then, but these were unusual cases: couples had crossed the colonial racial divide, or women were reluctant to name the fathers, and therefore ended up in court. The records of the Overseers of the Poor for 1739 (the one complete year of colonial records) made no distinctions between mothers receiving aid because they were poor and mothers receiving child support payments for illegitimate children. If there were illegitimate children on the Overseers' rolls for 1739, they were given aid in the same ways as poor children. Bastardy certainly occurred in the early eighteenth century, but it is impossible to know how often, what form of illegitimacy the cases represented, or how the larger community viewed the parents. The infrequent reference to bastardy in colonial records before midcentury does suggest that it did not occupy an impor-

9. Robert V. Wells, "Illegitimacy and Bridal Pregnancy in Colonial America," in Peter Laslett, Karla Oosterveen, and Richard Michael Smith, eds., *Bastardy and Its Comparative History: Studies in the History of Illegitimacy and Marital Nonconformism in Britain, France, Germany, Sweden, North America, Jamaica, and Japan* (Cambridge, Mass., 1980), 349–361; Daniel Scott Smith and Michael S. Hindus, "Premarital Pregnancy in America, 1640–1971: An Overview and Interpretation," *Journal of Interdisciplinary History*, V (1974–1975), 537–570; Stephanie Grauman Wolf, *Urban Village: Population, Community, and Family Structure in Germantown, Pennsylvania, 1683–1800* (Princeton, N.J., 1976), esp. 259; Susan Klepp, *Philadelphia in Transition: A Demographic History of City and Its Occupational Groups, 1720–1830* (New York, 1989), 87–88 and table 2.6.

Figures on Philadelphia's premarital pregnancy rate are from Klepp, *Philadelphia in Transition*, 87–88 and table 2.6. Klepp's premarital pregnancy figures are based on extant Philadelphia church records and thus measure premarital pregnancy for that population.

On the courtship context of premarital sex, see Smith and Hindus, "Premarital Pregnancy in America," *Jour. Interdisc. Hist.*, V (1974–1975), 532–570; John D'Emilio and Estelle B. Freedman, *Intimate Matters: A History of Sexuality in America* (New York, 1988), 21–23; Laurel Thatcher Ulrich, *Good Wives: Image and Reality in the Lives of Women in Northern New England, 1650–1750* (New York, 1980), 122; Roger Thompson, *Sex in Middlesex: Popular Mores in a Massachusetts County, 1649–1699* (Amherst, Mass., 1986), 54–70; Michael Grossberg, *Governing the Hearth: Law and the Family in Nineteenth-Century America* (Chapel Hill, N.C., 1985), 45–49.

TABLE 2. *Bastardy Cases, 1750–1779: Father's Class*

Class	No.	Proportion
Poor (rated £0–£1)	16	25%
Lower (rated £1–£2)	22	34
Middle (rated £3–£8)	19	30
Top (rated over £9)	7	11
Total	64	100

Notes: Class could be ascertained for the 64 cases that stated a father's occupation (or 58%) of the 111 cases that listed the father.

Class was determined by finding the fathers on the 1772 and 1756 tax lists for Philadelphia. When the date of the case made this impossible, the father's class was estimated by assigning the most common tax assessment for his occupation. The author wishes to acknowledge the generosity of Billy G. Smith in sharing his data on class and tax lists for Philadelphia. The categories of class used here were adapted from those used by him in *The "Lower Sort": Philadelphia's Laboring People, 1750–1800* (Ithaca, N.Y., 1990); for a discussion of the relationship of occupational category to economic status, see 4–5.

Source: See Appendix, Tables A.2, A.3, and "Establishing Class."

tant place in the community's consciousness and might not have been common. But by the pre-Revolutionary era bastardy was a publicly recognized phenomenon in Philadelphia.[10]

The men and women whose nonmarital sexual behavior was documented by their bastard children were representative of Philadelphia's population at large. The fathers came from all walks of life, distributed across all economic levels and occupations (see Table 2). The city's poor, the indentured servants, apprentices, and men who worked seasonally, like mariner Richard Mason,

10. Colonial court records for Philadelphia can be found in Ancient Records of Philadelphia, Wallace Collection, containing grand jury presentments, 1702–1790; and Philadelphia County Records, which contains miscellaneous grand jury presentments and Mayor's Court calendars, 1730–1786, both held at HSP. The two bastardy cases of couples comprising a slave man and a white woman occurred in 1716 and 1739; the four cases where the woman refused to name the father occurred in 1716, 1720 (two), and 1739, and there was one apparently nonremarkable case in 1737.

The children in the Overseers' record of 1739 were referred to as the child of a named woman, for instance "to Elizabeth Magennies Child 0..5..0." Illegitimate chil-

but earned too little to be counted among the city's taxables, were responsible for 25 percent of the cases. The lower classes, the cordwainers, peddlers, sailors, and journeymen tradesmen who were taxed at the lowest level, comprised 34 percent of the fathers. The middle classes fathered 30 percent. This was a diverse group, including butchers, bakers, carpenters, a carver, a brass founder, a joiner, a hatter, a goldsmith, a blacksmith, a bricklayer, an upholsterer, a weaver, and a schoolmaster. Men of the economic elite, the merchants of Philadelphia, were recorded as fathers in 11 percent of the cases. The fathers of illegitimate children mirrored the city's class structure as a whole. Thus men like Philip Wilson, a merchant rated at forty-five pounds in 1772, appeared alongside men like Thomas Pulford, a cordwainer, or John Studham, a mariner, each rated at two pounds, in the lists of bastardy fathers.[11]

The ethnic composition of the fathers and mothers also mirrored the city's population. British immigrants, the English, Scotch, Irish, and Welsh, dominated the bastardy rolls just as they dominated the ethnic composition of the city (see Table 3). No one ethnic group was substantially overrepresented. Philadelphia's Germans, however, were noticeably underrepresented, comprising only 9 percent of the fathers and 11 percent of the mothers. The incidence of premarital pregnancy among Germans was similar to that of other ethnic groups. Germans engaged in sexual intimacy as part of courtship but moved more easily from premarital sexual intimacy to marriage, and discouraged bastardy. But the sexual behavior producing bastard pregnancies did not take place only within discrete ethnic communities; Philadelphians who bore bastard children often crossed ethnic lines in doing so. In more than

---

dren were referred to as the child of a named father or as a nurse child in the extant records from 1750 to 1767. This suggests that the one child referred to as "a nurse child" in 1739/40 might have been illegitimate; it might also have been orphaned. For examples of midcentury records, see Letters to the Overseers of the Poor from the Mayor, 1751 and 1752, HSP; and OP, Bonds, where there were thirty-three cases of bastardy recorded before the new managers took over in October 1767.

The Poor's Day Book for 1739, cataloged as Philadelphia Almshouse Day Book, in the Simon Gratz Collection, HSP, runs from March 1739 through April 1740.

11. Although the elite were numerically well represented, it must be assumed that men of the top social and economic tier had greater opportunities to circumvent the systems of regulation by handling child support privately. The economic status of the mothers can be established for only a handful of these cases. What little can be documented suggests that the women were also drawn from all segments of Philadelphia society: there were economically independent women, widows, and servants.

TABLE 3. *Bastardy Cases, 1750–1779: Parents' Ethnicity*

Ethnicity[a]	Father		Mother	
	No.	Proportion	No.	Proportion
English	67	61%	82	57 %
Scots[b]	21	19	24	17
German	10	9	16	11
Irish[b]	9	8	11	8
Welsh	2	2	8	5
French	1	1	1	·7
Jewish			1	·7
Spanish			1	·7
Total	110	100%	144	100.1%

[a]Ethnicity was established by surname analysis, so the figures must be taken as approximate. Because names might have been written into the eighteenth-century record in their English form, even if the individual presented a Scots or Irish variation, the figure for the English may be inflated. The possibility of error was less for Germans, whose names might have undergone transformations because of inventive spelling but remained, nevertheless, ethnically distinguishable.

[b]Because my interest is establishing cultural ethnic identity, I have grouped those fathers with Scotch-Irish surnames as Scottish, and those with surnames of Celtic origin as Irish. Some of those listed as Scottish immigrated from Northern Ireland. Ethnicity was determined by surname, using Patrick Hanks and Flavia Hodges, *A Dictionary of Surnames* (Oxford, 1988).

Notes: Deviations from 100.0% in tables are due to rounding.

There were also 2 African-American mothers among the cases and 2 unnamed African-American fathers. One father was listed only as a servant, so no ethnicity could be ascertained.

There are no precise figures for the ethnic composition of Philadelphia in the late colonial period, but the demographic work done by Marianne S. Wokeck, Susan E. Klepp, Jean R. Soderlund, and others suggests that, with the exception of the Germans, these figures are in keeping with the overall ethnic proportions of the city. See, esp., Klepp, ed., *Symposium on the Demographic History of the Philadelphia Region, 1690–1860*, APS, *Proceedings*, CXXXIII, no. 2 (June 1989): Wokeck, "German and Irish Immigration to Colonial Philadelphia," 128–143; Klepp, "Demography in Early Philadelphia, 1690–1860," 85–111; Soderlund, "Black Importation and Migration into Southeastern Pennsylvania, 1682–1810," 144–153.

half the cases of bastardy, the two parents were from different ethnic groups. Bastardy in late colonial Philadelphia was widespread and not the behavior of a particular class or ethnic subculture.[12]

It is not surprising that Philadelphians expanded the contexts within which sexual intimacy was acceptable, since their broader culture lent itself to developing a completely nonmarital form of sexual behavior. The broad range of customary practices in family formation, coupled with the Quaker adherence to freedom of conscience and continuing immigration from abroad, impeded the formation of one uniform moral code. Ethnic traditions that allowed for nonmarital sexual intercourse, such as the rural English and Welsh practices of fertility proving and single parenthood for economically self-supporting women and the Scots acceptance of bastardy, could easily operate in late colonial Philadelphia. The open gender conflict played out in popular print naturalized conflict between men and women in intimate relationships and nurtured an environment where one could consider abandoning a sexual partner despite pregnancy and a coming child. And the urban pleasure culture that embraced personal indulgence in the latest amusements and fashions legiti-

---

12. In Germantown, where German-speakers predominated, premarital pregnancy was about 25 percent during the second half of the eighteenth century (Wolf, *Urban Village*, 259). Wolf uses a figure of 25 percent for births less than nine months after marriage (four-fifths born less than six months after marriage). Because some births were simply premature births conceived after marriage, the premarital pregnancy rate was probably somewhere between 20 and 25 percent. The 20 percent premarital pregnancy figure for births within six months of marriage makes her figures comparable with Smith and Hindus's findings for several New England towns of just over 16 percent.

The low bastardy rates among Germans were also true of Germantown. The Manager of the Poor for Germantown recorded only nine cases in the Minutes from 1809 to 1815. Managers of the Poor of the Township of Germantown, Minutes, 1809–1822, Germantown Historical Society.

Premarital intercourse termed "trying out" was a usual form of fertility testing in several of the German-speaking regions of Europe. Michael Mitterauer and Reinhard Sieder, *The European Family: Patriarchy to Partnership from the Middle Ages to the Present* (Oxford, 1982), 124.

Data to do the cross-ethnic analysis existed for ninety-six cases (or 58 percent of the whole): 45 percent of the couples were of the same ethnicity, and 55 percent of them had different ethnicities. Wolf found the same willingness to cross ethnic and religious lines in romantic pursuit in Germantown (Wolf, *Urban Village*, 131–132).

mated the pursuit of personal enjoyment. Pursuing sexual pleasure for its own sake could be envisioned.[13]

Mid-to-late-eighteenth-century Philadelphians were not unusual in their adoption of nonmarital sexual intercourse. The pattern of bastardy documented through the Overseers of the Poor parallels the trajectory of illegitimacy documented in eighteenth- and nineteenth-century England. In England parish registers reveal a significant increase in illegitimacy during the second half of the eighteenth century, rising to a peak in the 1820s. The ratios of illegitimate to legitimate births in England were higher during the mid-to-late eighteenth century than our first evidence for bastardy in Philadelphia, but then both approached similar levels during the first three decades of the nineteenth century (see Tables 4, 5).[14]

13. For the English and Welsh, see John R. Gillis, *For Better, for Worse: British Marriages, 1600 to the Present* (Oxford, 1985); G. R. Quaife, *Wanton Wenches and Wayward Wives: Peasants and Illicit Sex in Early Seventeenth Century England* (New Brunswick, N.J., 1979). For demographically based work on illegitimacy in England and Wales, see Laslett, Oosterveen, and Smith, eds., *Bastardy and Its Comparative History*, 71–246.

For the Scots, see Leah Leneman and Rosalind Mitchison, "Scottish Illegitimacy Ratios in the Early Modern Period," *Economic History Review*, XL (1987), 41–63, and "Girls in Trouble: The Social and Geographical Setting of Illegitimacy in Early Modern Scotland," *Journal of Social History*, XXI (1987–1988), 483–497; Christopher Smout, "Aspects of Sexual Behavior in Nineteenth-Century Scotland," in Laslett, Oosterveen, and Smith, eds., *Bastardy and Its Comparative History*, 192–216.

14. Laslett, Oosterveen, and Smith, eds., *Bastardy and Its Comparative History;* E. A. Wrigley et al., *English Population History from Family Reconstitution, 1580–1837* (Cambridge, 1997), 219–220; Louise A. Tilly and Joan W. Scott, *Women, Work, and Family* (New York, 1978). English illegitimacy ratios are based on records of births and baptisms in parish registers. Many of these couples subsequently married. Therefore, some of those measured in English parish registers were practicing a form of family formation much like Philadelphia's serially monogamous couples or those self-divorcing and establishing new conjugal households, in that they did eventually establish permanent relationships with their sexual partner. Philadelphia's Overseers of the Poor rarely record this kind of illegitimacy, and thus Philadelphia's bastardy ratios record only a smaller subset for comparison with English sexual patterns.

Analyzing Philadelphia church records, Susan Klepp found that illegitimate births by couples who subsequently married accounted for 2.8 percent of births in church records in the pre-Revolutionary era, 2.0 percent in the Revolutionary, 4.9 percent in the post-Revolutionary, and 3.2 percent in the early nineteenth century (*Philadelphia in*

The significance of bastardy goes far beyond its prominence in the records of sexual behavior. If one looks further than statistics into the broader cultural milieu, one finds that bastardy assumed a new cultural significance during the late colonial and Revolutionary period. As the recorded cases rose, the topic of bastardy emerged in multiple sites within the culture. It became an important theme in popular print, anecdotes, and tall tales and was remarked upon in travelers' accounts and addressed by social commentators. Cultural representations, visitors' writings, and even the systems providing care for illegitimate children evince a general acceptance of nonmarital sexual behavior.

Travelers' accounts represent late colonial Philadelphia as a permissive community, tolerant of variations in sexual behavior and their attendant moral codes. According to Gottlieb Mittelberger, a German schoolteacher who spent three years in Philadelphia in the early 1750s, the town was a place of lax moral discipline, courtship went unregulated, women exercised too much power within marriage, and nonmarital sexuality was rampant. Mittelberger tells three lengthy sexual tales in his short book, *Journey to Pennsylvania*. One is about a happily married bigamous threesome who go unaccosted by the authorities. The other two concern bastardy in the city. He includes these tales to entertain the reader and thus make his book more marketable. Nevertheless, the casual nature of bastardy in Philadelphia made an impression upon him. "If a man gets a woman with child and is willing to marry her, either before or after confinement, then he has atoned for his sin and is not punished by the authorities. But if he is unwilling and she sues him, he must either marry her or give some money. Fornication . . . is not punished."[15]

Transition, 87, table 2.6). These numbers must be used with caution, because the absolute numbers involved were quite small, recording a total of 150 marriages for the pre-Revolutionary era, 150 for the Revolutionary, 143 for the post-Revolutionary, and 31 for the early nineteenth century. If, however, this pattern held for the community at large and was combined with the never-marrying couples bearing bastard children documented by the Overseers of the Poor, the overall illegitimacy rate for Philadelphia would parallel that of mid-to-late-eighteenth-century England and exceed that found in the early nineteenth century.

Illegitimacy rates in the German regions of Europe began to rise in the last third of the eighteenth century, later than in England. Isabel V. Hull, *Sexuality, State, and Civil Society in Germany, 1700–1815* (Ithaca, N.Y., 1996), 35–36, 370, 379; Otto Ulbricht, "The Debate about Foundling Hospitals in Enlightenment Germany: Infanticide, Illegitimacy, and Infant Mortality Rates," *Central European History*, XVIII (1985), 211–256.

15. Gottlieb Mittelberger, *Journey to Pennsylvania*, ed. and trans. Oscar Handlin and John Clive (Cambridge, Mass., 1960), 70–72.

TABLE 4. *Philadelphia and England: Bastardy relative to All Births*

| | Philadelphia | | | |
	1767– 1776	1790– 1799	1805– 1814	1822– 1826
Births	12,535	22,440	33,037	30,299
Illegitimate births	200	711	2,193	1,226
Proportion	1.6%	3.2%	6.6%	4.0%
	England			
	1765– 1774	1790– 1799	1805– 1814	1820– 1829
Proportion				
Raw	4.3%	5.1%	5.2%	5.0%
Adjusted[a]	5.2%	6.1%	6.2%	6.0%

[a]Modern work on English illegitimacy in the seventeenth and early eighteenth century by R. L. Adair has led some scholars to estimate that Laslett's numbers need to be slightly adjusted in light of the larger number of illegitimate births Adair's work has uncovered. The Cambridge Group for the History of Population has suggested a multiplier of 1.2% to render Laslett comparable to Adair and increase the accuracy of these ratios, which multiplier is used here. R. L. Adair, "Regional Variations in Illegitimacy and Courtship Patterns in England, 1538–1754" (Ph.D. diss., University of Cambridge, 1991).

Sources: Philadelphia: births derived from Susan E. Klepp, *Philadelphia in Transition: A Demographic History of the City and Its Occupational Groups, 1720–1830* (New York, 1989), app. C, table 5.2, 336.

England: Illegitimate births, raw, from Peter Laslett, Karla Oosterveen, and Richard M. Smith, eds., *Bastardy and Its Comparative History . . .* (Cambridge, Mass., 1980), 14–15. Illegitimate births, adjusted, from E. A. Wrigley et al., *English Population History from Family Reconstitution, 1580–1837* (Cambridge, 1997), 219–220.

Both bastardy tales are presented in the form of trials in Philadelphia's courthouse. Mittelberger maintains that court hearings were an important source of entertainment in Philadelphia and that the community congregated there to laugh at the entanglements presented. In his Philadelphia bastardy was common and was a source of humor for the community. In the first tale, "an unmarried female, who had gotten herself pregnant, wanted the man who

TABLE 5. *Recorded Bastardy Cases, 1750–1779*

Source	No.
Quaker Minutes	12
Scots Presbyterian Church	1
Second Presbyterian Church	1
Mayor's Court	9
Court of Oyer and Terminer	5
Mayor's Court and Court of Oyer and Terminer	1
Mayor's Court and Overseers of the Poor	6
Mayor's Court, Overseers of the Poor, and Quaker Minutes	2
Overseers of the Poor	128
Total	165

Source: See Appendix, esp. Tables A.2, A.3.

was responsible for a husband." She testified that he had forced her to submit; but, when she admitted that she had not cried out for help, although the house contained those who might aid her, the defense attorney demanded an explanation. She replied, "If she had thought that this time she would become pregnant, then she would certainly have cried for help." Here was a woman who freely indulged her sexual desires but was unwilling to face the consequences alone.[16]

The second case, which followed the much more common path of bastardy adjudication, depicts a young servant maid, pregnant by a manservant of the same household. The ironic twist is that, after she told her master of her predicament, he advised her: "She would be doing herself a great deal of harm were she to charge this dissolute rake with being the father of her child. For . . . he would not be free from service for a long time to come. Furthermore, he did not own a cent. Moreover, . . . he was not a provider." He advised that she should swear the child to a man "having a good name and great wealth." The maid followed his advice. She went before the justice of the peace and swore the child to her master. He was ushered away to prison, there to remain until he either posted bond for the support of the child or married the servant maid.

16. Ibid., 38–39. Mittelberger's account was widely read and accepted as truthful by its eighteenth-century audience (introduction, xvi–xvii).

At this point he decided it was better to have the maid for his own than to support the child without the comfort she could provide. The humor is derived from its play on aristocratic sexual license turned upside down. Mittelberger concludes, "Similar cases frequently happen in this country, especially since the women possess considerable privileges and liberties." Mittelberger was not alone in his assessment. John Adams, writing of tavern life in late colonial Philadelphia, commented, "Here the time, the money, the health, and the modesty, of most that are young and of many old, are wasted; here diseases, vicious habits, bastards, and legislators, are frequently begotten."[17]

It is true that nonmarital sexual behavior was rarely punished and that women enjoyed some protection from shouldering the burdens of sexual intimacy alone. The courts and the system of poverty relief were the only communitywide systems that could have been marshaled to punish nonmarital sexual behavior and enforce a uniform sexual ethic. But the Overseers' role was to regulate child support, not to punish the sexual behavior of their parents, and the courts were rarely used to discipline sexual behavior (see Table 5).

The basic system of regulating bastardy remained largely unchanged from 1705, when it was established, to 1828, when it was substantially revamped. Legally, the first step in obtaining child support was to swear an oath of paternity before one of the city's aldermen or before a judge of the Mayor's Court. Often the Overseers of the Poor were already involved in a case before a woman took that step. She might approach the local guardian responsible for distributing aid to the poor of her neighborhood, or he might approach her as rumor of her coming child came to his attention.[18]

The experiences of Mary Vaughan, who navigated this system in 1766, were typical. In early May, when Mary was five months pregnant, she swore an oath before Samuel Shoemaker, Esq., stating that Edward Leach was the father of the child she was carrying. Following typical procedures, Shoemaker issued a warrant for Leach's arrest, and the Overseers paid to have it executed by the constable. On May 27 Edward agreed to pay weekly child support and presented John Leach to serve as his surety. Both men posted bonds to indemnify

17. Ibid., 39–41; Carl Bridenbaugh, *Cities in Revolt: Urban Life in America 1743–1776* (New York, 1955), 160.

18. James T. Mitchell, Henry Flanders, et al., comps., *The Statutes at Large of Pennsylvania* (Harrisburg, 1896–1915); John W. Purdon, *A Digest of the Laws of Pennsylvania, from the Year 1700 to the Seventh Day of April, 1830* (Philadelphia, 1831); *A Compilation of the Laws of the State of Pennsylvania relative to the Poor, from the Year 1700 to 1795, Inclusive* (Philadelphia, 1796).

the city against the charges arising from the care of Edward's child. The father would be committed to jail until these bonds were posted. Bonds were held by the Overseers until a child reached the age of five (for girls) or seven (for boys), when the law provided that the child could be bound out to service if it should require financial aid. Mary gave birth in September, but by the following March the Overseers had received no support for her child or reimbursement for her lying-in expenses. The Overseers had difficulty collecting support because the one surety had left town and Edward apparently had no assets. Under these circumstances the city assumed financial responsibility for Mary's child and paid her weekly child support from its own coffers.[19]

Men came to one another's aid when they faced legal paternity responsibilities and agreed to serve as the financial backup required by law by acting as the father's surety. The relationships between the fathers and the men who posted bond as their sureties indicate that this was not a disciplinary system. If it had been, one would expect that the sureties would have been men who had authority over the father: his employer, his master, or his relation. Such men could have been seen as enforcing community standards of morality because they helped ensure child support payments. But this was not the situation (see Tables 6, 7). Authoritative relationships, such as relative or master, existed in only 16 percent of the cases.

A shared occupation that might mask a more formal relationship existed in 24 percent of the cases. But in the remaining 52 percent of the cases, the relationship between surety and father had no discernible or structural basis. The fact that these men were neither relatives nor associated through employment or trade indicates a variety of peer or friendly relationships, in which men aided each other by posting the financial bond necessary to keep a father out of jail.

All of this occurred outside the formal court system. Unless the father chose to dispute his paternity, the Mayor's Court, which had jurisdiction over the city of Philadelphia, would never record the case or impose its standard fine of ten pounds for a conviction of "fornication and bastardy." Paternity

19. OPM, May 13, 27, 1776, Mar. 25, 1777, Mary Vaughan and Edward Leach. When the father failed to make his scheduled payments, the Overseers had the power to execute the financial obligation in the bond, garnish wages, and confiscate property. Under these circumstances, and if the father was indigent, the Overseers would make the support payments to the mother. In the majority of the cases the father was required to present two members of the community to serve as his sureties and post their bonds.

TABLE 6. *Father's Relationship to Surety in Bastardy Cases, 1750–1779*

Relationship	No. of Cases	Proportion
Father posted bond (no other surety)	5	8%
Relative or master of father	10	16
Same occupation as father (possible business interest)	15	24
No obvious relationship (friendship, affinity)	33	52
Total	63	100

Note: Surety information included for 57% of the 111 cases that list fathers.

The proportion classified as relatives was based on people who shared the same last name or were identified as such in the records. Relatives on the father's maternal side who might have posted security would not have been discerned and may account for some of the cases where no obvious relationship could be found.

Source: Appendix, esp. Tables A.2, A.3.

disputes rarely occurred. Only twelve of the fathers (or 11 percent) disputed their responsibility and took the cases before the Mayor's Court. These cases were distributed across economic levels and do not indicate that any class of men expected preferential treatment in appealing. Taking the case to court, moreover, did not improve one's chances for a successful outcome. In all cases where the dispositions are given, the fathers were convicted of fornication and bastardy and made to pay a ten-pound fine and the costs of prosecution in addition to the standard support of three shillings weekly child support and lying-in costs.[20]

20. The figure for disputed cases was computed from MCD, QSD, and evidence in OPM. In three cases no disposition was given. Because the Overseers recorded the legal disputes they were involved in, the gaps in the Mayor's Court records have probably only slightly diminished this figure. See, for instance, the cases of Sidney Evans and Archibald Wiseman, OPM, Mar. 23, 1769, Apr. 6, 11, 1770, MCD, October session 1769; Christiana Naglee and Christian Unger, MCD, July session 1763, April session 1765; Catherine Shee and Adam Layer, MCD, April session 1768. Four additional cases (3 percent) were calendared to be heard in the Mayor's Court but were not heard and were presumably settled before trial. The Mayor's Court had jurisdiction for the city of Philadelphia, but the suburbs of Southwark and the Northern Liberties, which the Overseers of Philadelphia were responsible for also, fell into the jurisdiction of the county's Court of Quarter Sessions.

TABLE 7. *Authorities' Involvement and Class of Father in Bastardy Cases, 1750–1779*

Case Brought Forward	Class of Father ($N = 55$)			
	Top	Middle	Lower	Poor
Before birth	11%	25%	43%	21%
After birth	7%	37%	37%	19%

Note: Timing information was available in 131 of 165 cases; 60% (78 cases) were brought forward before birth, and 40% (53 cases) after.

Source: Appendix, Tables A.2, A.3, "Establishing Class."

The lack of punitive measures aimed at changing behavior is especially striking. During this period the Mayor's Court never inflicted physical punishment for the crime of fornication or bastardy, although it did impose public whipping for "intent to ravish" and occasionally pilloried a woman for "keeping a bawdy house." Nor did the Mayor's Court impose the fine for fornication and bastardy upon the women who entered into the records of bastardy cases. In contrast, the county courts, which served the suburbs and the outlying countryside, fined men and women alike. The county court differed as well in processing these cases. In Philadelphia, the Overseers in conjunction with the courts assumed the father's responsibility unless proven otherwise. The county court took a more cautious approach: the pregnant woman herself would come before the Court of Quarter Sessions, be tried, convicted, and fined, and presumably name the father (although his name does not appear in the record of her case). After she had given birth, the father would have his day in court, pay the fine, and be required to establish child support.[21]

The Philadelphia system of private meetings and financial agreements was fairly permissive in comparison to the surrounding county courts and was markedly different from that of New England communities. In 1759 the selectmen of Boston were given the authority to bind out women who bore bastard

21. *PG*, Mar. 21, 1765, June 18, 1772; QSD; Joan M. Jensen, *Loosening the Bonds: Mid-Atlantic Farm Women, 1750–1850* (New Haven, Conn., 1986), 60–61.

In his study of the prosecution of women's crime in Pennsylvania, 1763–1790, G. S. Rowe also found that the counties were much more likely to arrest and prosecute women for fornication and bastardy than was either the city or county of Philadelphia: "Women's Crime and Criminal Administration in Pennsylvania, 1763–1790," *PMHB*, CIX (1985), table 2, p. 348.

children for up to five years to recoup the financial expenses incurred by the city. The Overseers in Philadelphia were keenly aware of the increasing urban poverty during the late colonial era. But, unlike the authorities of Boston, who laid the financial responsibility for indigent illegitimate children on the mothers, the Overseers did not target the bearers of bastard children to curtail the rising costs of public support for the indigent. They also did not use the new almshouse as a punitive deterrent by forcing pregnant women into the almshouse in order to receive aid. Only one of the ten bastardy cases recorded in 1767 after the almshouse opened in October was admitted to receive assistance.[22]

The distinction between Philadelphia's system of adjudicating illegitimacy and New England's becomes clear in an anecdote attributed to Benjamin Franklin. It presents a defense of bastardy and makes the case that sexual behavior should not be a public concern. Franklin tells the story of a Connecticut woman, "Miss Polly," who becomes pregnant under a promise of marriage and bears first one and, then, several illegitimate children. The story argues that the sexual activity that produced bastards was harmless and that bearing a bastard child should not be a crime. When illegitimate children were the product of sincere attachments and were not associated with adultery or licentious seduction, no one was harmed, and society need not intervene. Moreover, mothers of illegitimate children provided a patriotic service by aiding a much-needed increase in population in the North American colonies. Bastardy was not a crime against the community and civil order; if a crime at all, it was against God and should be left to the religious authorities.[23]

When brought before the authorities of New England before whom she had already "several times suffered stripes, fine, and imprisonments," she de-

22. Cornelia Hughes Dayton, *Women before the Bar: Gender, Law, and Society in Connecticut, 1636–1789* (Chapel Hill, N.C., 1995), 198–206; Bridenbaugh, *Cities in Revolt*, 121.

23. The tale of Polly Baker was attributed to Franklin by Bridenbaugh, *Cities in Revolt*, 90. It was written in the late 1740s and reprinted as a factual tale by several colonial newspapers and then made its way into several humorous chapbooks. I have quoted from the version of this story reprinted in the 1807 Philadelphia edition of E[dward] Ward, *Female Policy Detected; or, The Arts of a Designing Woman Laid Open*, 99–104, held by AAS. The text is almost exactly the same as a 1749 London edition printed at the end of Gideon Archer, *Social Bliss Considered . . . with the Speech of Miss Polly Baker* (London, 1749), 99–105. There was also a 1788 Philadelphia edition. Franklin probably modeled this after the London pamphlet *Fornication No Crime*.

livered an impassioned defense of her behavior and an indictment against the system:

> I take the liberty to say, that the act by which I am punished, is both unreasonable, and in my case particularly severe. I have always led an inoffensive life in the neighbourhood where I was born; and defy my enemies (if I have any) to say I ever wronged man, woman, or child. I cannot conceive my offence to be of so unpardonable a nature as the law considers it. I have brought several fine children into the world, at the risque of my life; I have maintained them by my own industry, without burthening the township; indeed I should have done it better but for the heavy charges and fines I have paid. Can it be a crime in the nature of things, to add to the number of his majesty's subjects, in a new country that really wants peopling? I own, I should think it a praiseworthy, rather than a punishable action. I have deprived no woman of her husband, I have not debauched or enticed any apprentice, nor can any parent accuse me of seducing their son. None have any cause of complaint against me, but the minister and justice, who lose their fees in consequence of my having children out of wedlock.
>
> * * *
>
> But you will tell me what I have been often told, that were there not act of assembly in the case, the precepts of religion are violated by my transgression. If mine be religious offence leave it a religious punishment. You have already excluded me from the church communion! You believe I have offended heaven and shall suffer everlastingly! Why then will you increase my misery by additional fines and whippings?

Polly complains she suffered the injustice of a sexual double standard that elevated her seducer to public respectability as magistrate but relegated her to the role of social outcast. Franklin depicts his heroine as a woman of uncommon reason with "grace and captivating softness." Having engaged in a sexually intimate courtship from which her beau departed, she became "the ridicule and contempt of many with less virtue, but more prudence than herself."

Knowing that women in Philadelphia who trod this same path did so within a different social environment gives this anecdote added meaning. Franklin was not simply bemoaning an unjust system; he was using the alternative system of his own Philadelphia to fashion the contours of the sexual system his heroine demanded. Most important, the repeated publication of this story during the latter half of the eighteenth century demonstrates that Franklin's awareness that Philadelphia offered a distinctive sexual culture, to be praised and worth emulating, was shared by others.

The Overseers of the Poor administered a system in which financial considerations were the moving force, discipline was exercised only when the men involved failed to fulfill their financial obligations, and moral or ethical questions about sexual behavior were absent. Discipline and possible punishment of sexual behavior were left to individuals in positions of authority, such as parents, masters, and owners of slaves, and to the city's churches. As Franklin's Miss Polly said: the churches were the place to address sexual sin.

Philadelphia was extraordinarily religiously diverse, with Quaker, Presbyterian, Anglican, Methodist, Lutheran, Baptist, and Catholic congregations, each with its own approach to nonmarital sexual behavior. Quakers and Presbyterians had the largest followings in the late colonial era and had distinct beliefs about what constituted inappropriate sexual behavior and different views on the seriousness with which sexual transgressions should be met.[24]

Religiously diverse! (handwritten margin note)

Philadelphia's Quakers were concerned about the growing importance of sexual intimacy exhibited by their own members both within and outside courtship and marriage. The Women's Meeting for the Philadelphia Monthly Meeting, which had disciplinary jurisdiction over female members, policed behavior ranging from keeping bad company, premarital pregnancy, and unbecoming dress to fornication and bastardy (see Table 8). Between 1760 and 1780 the Philadelphia Women's Meeting cited forty-four women for "committing the sin of unchastity" and brought them before the meeting to answer for premarital intercourse, fornication, and bastardy. The conflicting views among Quaker women about the sinful nature of these acts is evident in the vigilant pursuit by the leadership to root out sexual transgression and the equally spirited response of the perpetrators.[25]

Quakers (handwritten margin note)

24. The extant pre-1780 church disciplinary records for all Presbyterian, Anglican, Methodist, Lutheran, Baptist, and Catholic congregations for the city of Philadelphia as well as the Quaker records for the Philadelphia Women's Monthly Meeting were examined. The discussion here concentrates on Presbyterians and the Quakers, because they kept the most complete disciplinary records. They also had the most members.

The minutes of the Women's Meeting for the Quakers' Philadelphia Monthly Meeting displayed the greatest concern for discipline. The Quaker concern for discipline in general intensified after midcentury. See Jack D. Marietta, *The Reformation of American Quakerism, 1748–1783* (Philadelphia, 1984). Marietta presents the disciplinary action of Pennsylvania Quakers from 1682 to 1776 and explores sexual infractions (10–23).

25. For cases where the meeting went to great lengths to track down sinning members, see cases of Mary Curry, PWMM, Jan. 28, Dec. 27, 1765; Rebecca Calvert, PWMM, Jan. 25, Feb. 22, Mar. 31, 1765.

TABLE 8. *Quaker Women's Sexual Transgressions, 1760–1779*

Offense	No.
Bastardy	14
Fornication	8
Premarital sex	22
Consanguineous marriage	2
Keeping bad company	6
Disorderly house	2
Unbecoming dress	2
Total	56

Note: The most common infraction recorded by the Philadelphia Women's Monthly Meeting was against women who had married outside the Quaker Meeting.
Source: PWMM.

Of the fourteen women whose cases were brought before the meeting for bastardy, eleven can be classified as unrepentant. Mary Cole's response was typical. In August 1769 the meeting reports:

Some Friends inform this Meeting that they have visited Mary Cole (on account of a Scandalous Report concerning her, as being the Mother of an Illegitimate Child) but she not giving them any Satisfaction by endeavoring to clear herself therefrom, and expressed a Desire rather to be testified against.

In November, despite repeated entreaties by her fellow Friends, Mary remained unwilling to condemn her behavior, and the meeting moved to expel her. When guilty women submitted, acknowledged the "evil" of their "sin" within the meeting, and apologized for their breach of discipline, they would be accepted back into the fold. But the majority of Quaker women cited for bastardy refused to comply. Most were like Rebecca Calvert, who would not condemn her own behavior as an "unchaste and sinful act." Despite repeated meetings with fellow Friends initiated "in order to bring her to a sense of her Crime," she would not assume a "suitable disposition to Condemn the same," "she not appearing so convinced." These women likely had many ways of understanding the meanings of their sexual behavior; but, at the moment their bastardy became known to their religious fellowship, they did not adhere to the standard enforced by the meeting's female leadership: that their non-

marital sexual activities constituted "Evil conduct" that required them to publicly condemn their own behavior.[26]

Quaker women were also cited by the meeting for engaging in sex with
their future husbands, betrayed by early births. Some tried to hide their premature intimacy by quickly marrying outside the meeting. These couples
avoided Quaker rules of discipline that required them to come before the
meeting three times before they were married. This "passing the meeting"
ensured that parents consented to the union, that there were no impediments
to the marriage, and that both parties were entering into the marriage freely. It
also required a couple to wait three months before marrying, and pregnant
couples could not afford to postpone their weddings. Hundreds of men and
women circumvented the Quaker system of marriage by being privately and
quickly married by a non-Quaker minister. Certainly, some of these couples
chose to face punishment for the lesser sin of marrying quickly outside the
meeting rather than face the meeting obviously pregnant. For some, having an
illegitimate child by a non-Quaker was deemed less undesirable than marrying the non-Quaker father of the child. This was the judgment made by the
Quaker family of Andrew Craigie's paramour in the midst of the Revolution.
The child's Quaker mother had given her up at birth, under pressure from her
parents to reject Craigie and establish a more suitable marriage with a fellow
member of the Society of Friends: giving birth to an illegitimate child was less
problematic than marrying outside. Despite Quakers' intense concern for
discipline, nonmarital sexual expression was adopted by some of the city's
Quakers, and some refused to interpret their behavior as sinful.[27]

The Presbyterians were much less unified when it came to the discipline of
sexual transgression. The First Presbyterian Church, the church of the city's
prominent and well-to-do, kept no record of sexual misconduct. If the members engaged in unseemly behavior, the discipline of it was not to be public
knowledge. The Second Presbyterian Church was not so secretive, but the

26. Mary Cole, PWMM, Aug. 8, 1769. All eleven of these unrepentant women were
expelled from the Philadelphia Meeting. For cases where women submitted to discipline, see Martha Thomas, PWMM, Feb. 23, 1770, Jan. 25, 1771; Sarah Lloyd, PWMM,
Feb. 22, May 31, 1771; Widow Howel, PWMM, Oct. 28, 1763; Rebecca Calvert, PWMM,
Jan. 25, Feb. 22, Mar. 32, 1765.

27. Marietta found that premaritally pregnant couples married outside the meeting
in 70 percent of the fornication cases disciplined by Quakers in colonial Pennsylvania. Marietta, *The Reformation of American Quakerism*, 13; Frederick Haven Pratt, *The
Craigies: A Footnote to the Medical History of the Revolution* (Cambridge Mass., 1942), 42.
My thanks to Fredrika Teute for bringing this case to my attention.

TABLE 9. *Presbyterian Transgressions, 1750–1779*

Offense	Second Presbyterian, 1750–1779 No.	Scots Presbyterian, 1768–1779 No.
Bastardy	1 (by Negro)	1
Fornication	1 (with mulatto)	2
Adultery	1 (with Negro)	1
Improper conduct		1
Harboring eloped wives		1
Disorderly house	1	1
Domestic dispute	1	
Wife abuse		1
Spousal separation	1	
Drunkenness	1	
Card playing and drinking		2
Slander of "bastard"	1	
Total	8	10

Note: The First Presbyterian Church documented no sexual transgressions in its records for this era.

Sources: Second Presbyterian Church, Session Minutes, 1750–1779, PHS; Scots Presbyterian Church, Session Minutes, 1768–1779, PHS.

congregants inscribed only the sexual infractions of African members in the session's records (see Table 9). All of the cases of explicit sexual misconduct disciplined by the church were committed by African members. By bringing forward "Negro Grigory" for adultery, or "Negro Betty" for bastardy, or "Mrs. Lawrence's Malato wench Jenny" for adultery and fornication, the congregation instructed its African members about proper sexual behavior. It also promoted the belief that racially based distinctions in sexuality existed and that blacks were more likely than whites to commit sexual infractions.[28]

The third active Presbyterian church was the Associated Presbyterian Church of Scotland. Within the Scots Presbyterian Church an ethic of community surveillance prevailed. Congregants watched one another, gossiped

28. Second Presbyterian Church, Session Minutes, Dec. 16, 17, 1754, Nov. 14, 1765, PHS.

about one another's behavior, and informed the church elders when they believed that a sin had been committed. But church members were rarely shocked by such misconduct, and severe discipline was rarely imposed. Despite their watchful eyes, the Scots Presbyterians seemed to tolerate and readily forgive one another for their indiscretions (Table 9).[29]

Evidence of lenient punishment pervades these cases. George Kennedy, who was brought before the session for "attending shooting matches, haunting taverns at untimely hours, playing cards," was dismissed when the elders "agreed that as this was the first offence and finding he had been much drawn aside by bad connexions and his sense of the evil of his ways was so lively they agreed that he be just now rebuked at their bar and solemnly exhorted." When Charles Maise was accused of adultery but maintained his innocence, the session appointed no committee to investigate the charges, but instead "unanimously agreed that nothing be yet done to bring the process to a final issue but this left to a future day, and that he be now recommended to amendment of life and exhorted to serious exercises." Neither Charles, the suspected adulterer, nor the gambling George ever faced the congregation in shame, nor were they expelled for their behavior. Andrew Scot, who admitted that he had "fallen into the sin of fornication with his servant maid who now was with child," was initially required to "make his public appearance in the congregation after sermon and receive a solemn rebuke." When the session next met, a week later, it decided Andrew had been punished enough and that he need not endure another public condemnation before the congregation. Even in this case of fornication and bastardy, the Scots Presbyterian Church of Philadelphia meted out the least severe punishment, departing from the rule of discipline of the Church of Scotland, which, they themselves acknowledged, required a fornicator to come before the congregation on three succeeding Sabbaths "to make profession of their repentance." Even within the churches, nonmarital sexual behavior could be treated with leniency. At best, Philadelphia's churches provided a patchwork system of religious authority, but that authority spoke through many divergent voices.[30]

While Philadelphia's treatment of those whose sexual intimacy led to bastardy was nonpunitive, conceiving a bastard child did affect individuals dif-

29. For an example of the community's entanglements in monitoring one another's behavior, see the case of Margaret Thompson and her husband, Thomas, Scots Presbyterian Church, Sessions Minutes, Oct. 9, Nov. 6, 1775, Feb. 6, 1776, PHS.

30. Ibid., George Kennedy, May 23, 1770; Charles Maise, Jan. 26, Feb. 12, 1776; Andrew Scot, Aug. 26, 30, Sept. 3, 1772.

ferently, depending on their race, labor status, and gender. The legal structure of slavery, which circumvented the issue of legitimacy by denying all slaves the role of legal parent, made bastardy irrelevant to most of the Africans and African-Americans of pre-Revolutionary Philadelphia. Children born of African women in slavery were the property and the responsibility of their white masters. There were only a handful of free Africans then in Philadelphia. In 1767, blacks were 6.7 percent of the city's population, slightly more than fifteen hundred individuals. Only fifty-seven were free, and none of the offspring of free African-American couples came to the attention of the Overseers of the Poor as bastardy cases.[31]

Only when African-American men fathered children with white women would their offspring be born free and the issue of paternal support become relevant. African-American men could, and did, enter the system under these circumstances. During the pre-Revolutionary decade two cases came to the attention of the Overseers of the Poor. In both, the Overseers intervened to seek the identity of the father after the birth of the "mulatto" child. When Catherine Mahoney delivered a child in December 1770, the Overseers appointed a committee to inquire "by whom she was begot with a mulatto child." Such couples sought to avoid public intervention. Not until three months after the birth of her child, when poverty forced Mary Adams to seek shelter in the city's almshouse, did the authorities take notice of her mulatto child.[32]

During the pre-Revolutionary period slavery dominated the structure of social relations between races, and cross-racial sexual relations were a special category of deviance. Sexual relations between blacks and whites had been outlawed in Pennsylvania since 1726. Guarding the sexual boundary between the races was essential to maintaining racially based slavery, and separate, segregated systems policed sexual behavior. Masters were given wide latitude to discipline sexual behavior of slaves, and separate courts enforced the black codes dictating the social and sexual behavior of slaves and free blacks. Except when black men were involved with white women, African-Americans existed only at the edges of the dominant Euro-American sexual culture—with the Overseers of the Poor, before the city courts (which held separate Negro court days), and in the churches, where African-American sexual transgression was used to delineate and maintain racial boundaries (see Table 10). African-Americans were purposefully excluded from the systems that dealt

31. Soderlund, "Black Importation and Immigration," in Klepp, ed., *The Demographic History of the Philadelphia Region,* 148, table 3.

32. OPM, Dec. 12, 1770, Catharine Mahoney; Apr. 11, 1774, Mary Adams.

TABLE 10. *African-American Sexual Transgressions, 1750–1779*

Offense	No.
Mother of bastard child	2
Father of mulatto child	2
Man guilty of fornication with white woman	1
Additional mulatto children (abandoned)	1
Man guilty of adultery	1
Woman guilty of adultery	1
Total adjudicated	8

Source: See Appendix, esp. Tables A.2, A.3.

with nonmarital sexual behavior and were omitted from the cultural representations of such behavior. Denying African-Americans a place in the recognized sexual culture of the city was one way to shore up the racial divide. This exclusion created the illusion of a fundamental difference between blacks and whites, denying that they shared the essential human experiences of sexual intimacy, motherhood, and parenting.

By the mid-1770s it appears that this racial sexual boundary was being challenged. In the decade before the Revolution, African-Americans' resistance to slavery increased, as slaves freed themselves through flight in unprecedented numbers. Some African-Americans rejected racially based sexual segregation. In 1774 the Overseers of the Poor appealed to the legislature to make provision for the support of illegitimate children fathered by slaves, complaining that the "maintenance of children born of white women begotten by Negroes or Mulattoes, who are Slaves" had created "great expenses" "to the public." Under the law, enslaved fathers of illegitimate children could not be held financially responsible for their offspring, because slavery denied them ownership of the fruits of their labor. Just how prevalent bastardy was among African-American men and white women is impossible to say. But the potential this sexual behavior had to disrupt the racial caste system, upon which slavery depended, suggests that the Overseers might have exaggerated its frequency, understanding the danger of cross-racial illegitimacy. This legislative request does suggest that the Overseers perceived a new or growing threat to sexual segregation in the early stages of the Revolution, even before slavery was abolished and a large population of free blacks resided in the city. Their acute attention paid to cross-racial bastardy foreshadowed the important role sexuality would play in the battle for African-Americans' full personhood in the new nation and in the struggles to establish a new social system of white supremacy without racialized slavery.[33]

Unlike the offspring of female slaves, who were a boon to their masters, the children of indentured servants created complicated legal and financial entanglements. Indentured servants in Philadelphia lost control of both their labor and their sexuality during their length of service. When a man entered into a service contract, his labor became the property of his master. Because a servant did not own his own labor, he could not provide the required financial support if he fathered an illegitimate child: the servant's master became responsible for providing support, which he in turn recouped by extending the length of the original indenture, thus extracting the costs from the servant's labor. Servants' status as unfree labor denied them control of their intimate lives. They were to be celibate, or at least nonprocreative, during their terms of service. If they rejected those restrictions, they paid a heavier price for their sexual independence. What cost the free laborer three shillings a week in child support could cost the indentured servant an additional two to four years of service.[34]

Bastardy could also lead to hardships for female servants. When Hugh McCullough petitioned the court to have the term of his servant Margaret Seton extended, he complained that, when Margaret gave birth to "two female mulatto bastards" in January 1777, he "lost the Service of the said Margaret for a long Time and was at great Expense and Charges for her lying-in, Nursing and Attendance, as well as for paying for her Board for some time before her lying-in." McCullough asked for, and was granted, an additional two years of Margaret Seton's time; even more, he gained the future labor of her children by having them bound to serve him until they reached maturity. The extension

33. Almshouse Managers, Minutes, Jan. 6, 1774, CCAP. On the role slave resistance played in the abolition of slavery in Philadelphia, see Gary B. Nash and Jean R. Soderlund, *Freedom by Degrees: Emancipation in Pennsylvania and Its Aftermath* (New York, 1991), 82.

34. Case of Margaret Brooks and a servant of William Todd, OPM, Apr. 28, Oct. 22, 27, 1768, Feb. 23, Mar. 23, 1769; case of Mary Nugent and William Evans, servant of John Landon, Esq., OPM, Jan. 1, Aug. 19, 1776. See also the cases of Wiley Way and Margaret Seton: Mayor's Court, January session 1780 (Wiley Way, servant to Mary McGee, had his term of service extended by four years and six months for having two bastard children, which caused him to take leave of his service for seven months); QSD, September session 1779, case of Margaret Seton, servant maid to Hugh McCullough of Philadelphia. Perhaps the severity of these consequences explains why servants were only a small minority of the parents of illegitimate children.

of Margaret's term of service was unusual. Although the law did make such a provision for female servants, hers is the only case where there is evidence it was carried out. Because the reputed father was required to pay expenses incurred by a woman's bastardy, her master had little just ground to claim financial harm. In Margaret's case it was almost certainly the race of the children and the question of their labor status as free or slave that brought McCullough to court in September 1779. The abolition of slavery was in the air that fall as the state legislature drafted and took its first votes on the Abolition Act that would become law in the spring of 1780. Nearly three years earlier, when the babies were born, McCullough might have imagined that their skin color would allow him to keep them as slaves. He had maintained them within his household during the intervening years without attempting to clarify their status. When it appeared that racially based perpetual slavery was about to be abolished, McCullough brought his case to court and used the provisions against cross-racial sexual relations from the 1726 black codes to bind the children to him. Under the law children of a white woman fathered by a "negro or mulatto" could be bound out until thirty-one years of age. In this instance the master of a white woman used the laws against cross-racial sexual activity to establish slavelike status for her children and extend his ability to use slave labor for another generation. One suspects that McCullough knew he needed to move quickly. The provisions against cross-racial sexual relations and the ability to keep the children of these parents in bondage were repealed in 1780 with the passage of the Abolition Act.[35]

The final group that deserves attention is the mothers themselves. What were the consequences of this regulatory system for these women, and how did bearing a bastard child influence the course of a woman's life? We have already seen that (unlike in New England or the Pennsylvania countryside) the women of Philadelphia who bore illegitimate children were spared public trial

35. QSD, September session 1779, case of Margaret Seton. Philadelphia's treatment of pregnant indentured servants differed from the southern and New England colonies, where such women were regularly penalized for their bastard pregnancies. In pre-Revolutionary Philadelphia the burden of the financial consequences of bastardy fell to the fathers. See Kathleen M. Brown, *Good Wives, Nasty Wenches, and Anxious Patriarchs: Gender, Race, and Power in Colonial Virginia* (Chapel Hill, N.C., 1996), 129–134, 188–206; Dayton, *Women before the Bar*, 157–230; Mary Beth Norton, *Founding Mothers and Fathers: Gendered Power and the Forming of American Society* (New York, 1996), 336–347; Kirsten Fischer, *Suspect Relations: Sex, Race, and Resistence in Colonial North Carolina* (Ithaca, N.Y., 2002), 98–112; Mitchell, Flanders, et al., comps., *Statutes at Large*, IV, 59–64, An Act for the Better Regulation of Negroes in This Province.

and the humiliation of public punishment and were not held financially responsible in lieu of their male partners.

In Philadelphia the adjudication of bastardy through the Overseers of the Poor routinely and consistently provided mothers support for their children. In addition, the costs of lying-in, including the payment of the birth attendant, doctor, midwife, or "granny," and the cost of pre- and postdelivery nursing care were recoupable. If a child died, the father was also responsible for the cost of its burial. The standard weekly support payment during the pre-Revolutionary years was 3 s., or £7 16s. annually. But the cost of feeding alone for the child in the 1760s would run to £6 7s. This left the mother little to cover shelter, fuel, and clothing. While financial support was mandated, the level of that support would certainly not cover the costs of raising the child. Some men took full financial responsibility for their illegitimate offspring and provided a level of support in keeping with their economic resources. Medical doctor Andrew Craigie, who fathered a child by the daughter of an established Quaker family while stationed in Philadelphia during the war, placed his daughter in the home of his New England friends as a child, sent her to the Moravian school outside Philadelphia for education as a youth, and settled a portion of his estate upon her as an adult. Men who were unable, or unwilling, to supplement mandatory minimum child support could leave their partners in a precarious situation. When Mary Nugent gave birth to twins fathered by William Evans, then an indentured servant, she felt compelled to abandon one baby at the doorstep of the home of one of the Overseers. Despite the financial contribution made by Evans's master on his behalf for child support, Mary could not manage the care of two babies on her own.[36]

36. Pratt, *The Craigies* (since Craigie made private arrangements for his illegitimate daughter, his fathering an illegitimate child did not enter the public record); OPM, Jan. 1, Aug. 19, 1776, Mary Nugent. During the 1760s and 1770s the birth and delivery charges ranged from £2 to £6 4s. The cost of feeding a child was calculated using the food budget index for members of the lower classes provided by Billy G. Smith, employing the nutritionist model estimating that a child requires 60 percent of the calories of an adult, and thus calculating the child's annual cost of food at 60 percent of the food cost index for an individual in 1762. Between 1762 and 1770, the adult annual food cost index ranged from a high of £10.12 to a low of £8.9. Smith's figures suggest that shelter, fuel, and clothing costs for one child would also cost approximately £6 each year. Smith estimates that the annual cost for shelter, fuel, and clothing in 1762 for a family of two adults and two children would be £5.60 for fuel, £9.66 for clothing, £14.90 for rent. *The "Lower Sort": Philadelphia's Laboring People, 1750–1800* (Ithaca, N.Y., 1990), table 4, 100–103, 107.

The burdens of bearing a bastard child fell most heavily upon poor mothers whose sexual partners were without financial resources. They ended up in the almshouse as the place of last resort for food, shelter, and medical care during the birth. But fewer than 20 percent of the mothers were in dire enough circumstances to enter the almshouse. Even among them a third were there only temporarily, until the father "was taken," or located by the Overseers of the Poor, and posted bond. The overwhelming majority of women who bore illegitimate children had some resources: 81 percent had enough to navigate through the late stages of pregnancy, birth, and postpartum recovery without using the city's almshouse. Personal and familial resources, and usually the father's financial contributions, provided for their needs.[37]

Although required to provide a minimum level of support for their illegitimate child, fathers were under no legal obligation to the mother. This system did nothing to protect women from the burdens of single motherhood in a society where women typically had half the earning power of men. Thus a system that allowed women some choice to engage in nonmarital sexuality probably also increased male sexual privilege and allowed greater sexual exploitation of women.

To fully evaluate the consequences of bastardy in Philadelphia, one must ask whether bearing an illegitimate child foreclosed a woman's future marriage opportunities. This question will be more conclusively addressed when we return to the subject of bastardy for the 1790s and 1820s, when the life stories of these women are more fully documented. But at this point it is important to understand that, to the extent that bearing a child out of wedlock compromised a woman's opportunity to marry, it jeopardized her economic future. In the preindustrial urban society of Philadelphia, the key moment of class formation for many women was marriage. If bearing an illegitimate child blocked the opportunity to marry, it solidified most single women's temporary lower-class economic status into a permanent condition.

Two women present contrasting examples of the impact bearing a bastard child could have in late colonial Philadelphia. For Elizabeth Lacey it was a detour on the road to prosperity and marital security; for Mary Barry it was the starting block in the race for survival among the underclass of the city.

37. Information to determine the location of the mother during the pregnancy or birth was available in 90 of the 116 cases recorded after the almshouse opened in October 1767. At least a third of those women who entered the almshouse might not have stayed there long enough to give birth. But they did not have the economic resources to provide for themselves until the father's financial support was secured.

Elizabeth Lacey was involved in a nonmarital relationship with Charles Moore, and they had two children together. The first was born in 1769, when Charles posted bond with the Overseers for its support. Five years later, the couple were separated, and Elizabeth met and married Henry Gordon, a fairly well-to-do Philadelphia sea captain. Following their marriage, Elizabeth and Henry sat down together with Charles and a committee of Overseers to settle the financial arrangements for the maintenance of the two children Elizabeth had had with Charles. Elizabeth, it appears, moved smoothly from her life as the mother of two illegitimate children to her status as a financially secure married woman.[38]

Mary Barry's life could not have been more different. For her, bearing an illegitimate child was the beginning of a long string of hardships. In 1765 she was disowned by the Quaker Philadelphia Monthly Meeting for bearing a bastard child. Two years later, in October 1767, she was convicted before the Mayor's Court for keeping a disorderly house, fined five pounds, and ordered to stand committed in jail until her fine was paid. In late September 1768 Mary and two of her children were still in jail because she had been unable to pay her fine. At this point the Overseers of the Poor obtained an order from the mayor to move the children from jail to the almshouse. Mary, probably fearing she would lose control of her children, "found means to send the eldest out of jail and refused to all [to tell] who had her." Pregnant with her next child, Mary was removed to the almshouse in early November 1768 to give birth to her third bastard child, a child conceived in jail.[39]

The sexual culture of Philadelphia allowed these women to establish non-marital sexual lives, and possible poverty more than approbation for sexual misbehavior directed the path each would tread. Establishing nonmarital sexual lives allowed women to enter into and exit from relationships at will. Women who established nonmarital unions were under no legal obligation to submit to the dictates of patriarchal marriage. Their wages were their own,

---

38. OPM, Feb. 23, 1769, Dec. 26, 1774; 1772 Provincial Tax.

39. Case of Mary Barry, PWMM, Jan. 25, Mar. 29, May 31, 1765; MCD, October session 1767; OPM, Sept. 22, Nov. 3, 1768. I suspect that the Overseers became interested in the fate of Mary's children when they became involved in Mary's case because she was expecting another illegitimate child.

"Keeping a disorderly house" was the general term used to describe inappropriate behavior. While it did connote behavior inappropriate to one's gender, it was not usually employed, in the late colonial era, to mean sexual misbehavior such as prostitution, which was termed "keeping a bawdyhouse."

they could move as they chose, and no husband had rights to control their bodies. But these same unions could also place women in extremely precarious positions. When the relationships turned sour or when the man withdrew his commitment, the repercussions were far more serious for the woman.

Some women who saw no better option turned to infanticide as an alternative to single motherhood. In Philadelphia the death of illegitimate infants occupied a small but constant place within the sexual culture. Indictments for murder of a bastard child were scattered throughout this period. Between 1750 and 1780, six, possibly seven cases were prosecuted at least as far as the grand jury inquest. Beyond this, the only evidence of the suspicious death of newborns appears in brief references in the local press and diaries. On February 6, 1766, the *Pennsylvania Gazette* carried the news that "a female infant, just born, was found dead in one of the Cellars of the Barracks," and two years later another dead infant "was taken out of the Brickkiln Pond, in the Northern Liberties of this City, tied up in a Bag." A decade later Elizabeth Drinker noted in her diary, "A new born infant was taken out of the river this Afternoon with a wound in its neck—suppos'd to have been murdered."[40]

40. *PG*, Feb. 6, 1766, May 12, 1768; Crane, ed., *The Diary of Elizabeth Drinker*, I, 373 (Aug. 26, 1780); see also *PG*, Sept. 28, 1769. The *PG* reports only these three instances of the murder of infants in Philadelphia from 1750 to 1780. The paper did also regularly report infanticide and the prosecution of those charged with it in the surrounding countryside as well as in the other British North American colonies.

The criminal infanticide cases were Isabella Larence, September 1757; Margaret Bevan, 1758; Mary Wallace, 1768; Margaret Rauch (late Sebald), 1772; and "mulatto" Elizabeth, *PG*, May 4, 1774 (Court of Oyer and Terminer for the County of Philadelphia, file papers for 1774, PSA). Two other cases surface in OPM: Alice Harper, June 30, 1768, Mar. 16, 1769; Mary Mead and William Clifton, Apr. 11, Sept. 1, 1768, Mar. 23, 1769. It is unclear whether Mead and Clifton were indicted by the grand jury, but the suspicious death of their child did warrant a coroner's inquest. All of these cases except Rauch's occurred in the city of Philadelphia. Rauch's occurred in Frankfort, Philadelphia County. See Appendix, Table A-2.

Historians disagree on the extent of infanticide in Philadelphia. Sharon Ann Burnston argues that infanticide was probably prevalent in late-eighteenth-century Philadelphia because bastardy was socially unacceptable; I have not found a pronounced social sanction against bastardy. Infanticide was probably more common than the disciplinary records reveal, but, because alternatives existed through the Overseers of the Poor, it is unlikely social disapproval of bastardy caused a large number of women to murder their children. See Burnston, "Babies in the Well: An Underground Insight into Deviant Behavior in Eighteenth-Century Philadelphia," *PMHB*, CVI (1982), 151–

Most women who discarded their newborn child were left unmolested by the law. Infanticide did not occupy much of the attention of late colonial Philadelphians. In only one instance was a woman convicted of this felony and executed. She was known only as "mulatto" Elizabeth, and, when she was hanged in Philadelphia on April 30, 1774, the local press made no mention of the nature of her crime, stating only that she along with a man had been executed for murder. Elizabeth was the only woman convicted of infanticide in Philadelphia before capital punishment for the crime was abolished in 1786.[41]

Despite the fact that infanticide convictions were extremely rare, the prospect of prosecution did worry the women who bore bastard children. In provincial Pennsylvania infanticide was defined as concealing the death of a bastard child. To obtain a conviction it was necessary to establish that a child had been born in secret, indicating that its birth had been concealed, that it had subsequently died, and that its body had been secretly disposed of. The state equated concealment of the death of the child with its physical murder, underscoring the vulnerability of women who gave birth to stillborn illegitimate children.[42]

The testimony of Mary Wallace, tried for infanticide in 1768, provides us with an unusually clear view into this world of fear and secrecy. Mary testified

---

186. For nineteenth-century Philadelphia, see Roger Lane, *Violent Death in the City: Suicide, Accident, and Murder in Nineteenth-Century Philadelphia* (Cambridge, Mass., 1979), 96–100.

41. "Mulatto" Elizabeth, *PG*, May 4, 1774 (Court of Oyer and Terminer for the County of Philadelphia, file papers for 1774, PSA); G. S. Rowe, "Infanticide, Its Judicial Resolution, and Criminal Code Revision in Early Pennsylvania," APS, *Proceedings,* CXXXV (1991), 200–232, notes that Philadelphia distinguished itself with the lowest prosecution rate for infanticide of any Pennsylvania county before the early national period (211). Rowe's data do not include some of the cases identified as infanticide only in the Oyer and Terminer file papers. The pattern he identifies, however, holds true, even with these few additional cases. Rowe documents that forty-three women were tried for infanticide in Pennsylvania before 1786, when the law was revised to eliminate capital punishment for the crime. Before 1786 only six cases took place in the county of Philadelphia, and two were outside the city.

42. Pennsylvania's criminal statutes adopted in 1718 followed English law, which defined infanticide in these terms. Provincial Pennsylvania had been forced to bring its legal code into line with English law in 1718. Before that time, infanticide was not specified as a particular kind of murder with the particular presumptions of foul play that English law incorporated. Mitchell, Flanders, et al., comps., *Statutes at Large*, III, 202–203, An Act for the Advancement of Justice, and More Certain Administration Thereof.

that she gave birth to her child, alone in a small room in the house of Joseph Yeates, during the evening hours of September 14. About a quarter of an hour after delivery, "Mr. Yeates's negro woman, Nan," came to the mother's chamber bringing the infant "jacket and forehead cloth" that Mary had made for the child, and Mary told Nan that the child was born dead. About noon the next day, Nan came upstairs to her chamber and "hurried her to go out of the house" one step ahead of the authorities. Mary left the house and headed with the infant's body to Patty Craig's house in the alley behind Walnut Street and asked Patty to go with her to help bury the infant in Potters Field. Patty, aware that such a public burial was dangerous under the circumstances, refused to go with her but "advised her to throw it down the little house," meaning the privy. Together Mary and Patty interred the child's body in the privy behind the house.[43]

Each of the women was keenly aware of the implications of her actions and took steps to evade the authorities. Nan, an African-American enslaved woman, and the alley-dwelling white woman Patty Craig supported another woman of the lower classes through her trials of bearing a bastard child and concealing its death. Mary testified that the only person who knew of her pregnancy was Nan. One can imagine Nan moving about Joseph Yeates's house on the evening of the birth listening for signs of distress from Mary's chamber.

Mary was tried and acquitted of infanticide based on evidence that she had sustained an injury about a month before delivery that had killed the fetus. Mary testified that the baby "used to move before, but did not move afterward." The fact that Mary had made clothes for the infant while pregnant and that they could be found in the possession of her friend Patty Craig added credence to her story.[44]

While Philadelphians were aware of infanticide, they were rarely willing to condemn a woman to death by convicting her of the crime. This reluctance must have been what saved Margaret Rauch, who was investigated but not tried for infanticide in 1772 despite her own incriminating sworn testimony. During her examination before the justice of the peace, Margaret first denied that she was ever pregnant. Next, at the urging of her brother Leonhard she

43. Case of Mary Wallace, Court of Oyer and Terminer, Examination of Mary Wallace, Sept. 17, 1768; inquest, Sept. 19, 1768; PFT, Sept. 26, 1768.

44. Ibid. Proving that the pregnant woman prepared for the coming child by procuring clothing for it was a key aspect of the defense against infanticide allegations. This information was consistently present in the testimony in eighteenth-century infanticide cases.

admitted that she did give birth to a dead fetus, alone in a barn, in the countryside outside the city. After more pressure from Leonhard she added that she had "made tea of Pennyroyal or Pulegium" and drunk it but that "she does not know whether the Child went off by the tea or by a fall or two she had." Margaret swore that she had not murdered the child, that it was born dead, and that it was born only two months after she felt movement.[45]

This is a fascinating story of a bastard-bearing woman's inducing abortion during her second trimester of pregnancy. What makes it more interesting is that, despite its striking resemblance to other known cases of eighteenth-century abortion, it was a fabrication. Margaret with the help of her brothers had created this story, filling it with the minute details that would make it convincing for an eighteenth-century judge and jury. But, as she later testified, it was not what ended her child's life.[46]

Four days after giving her first sworn statement, Margaret Rauch returned to the justice of the peace and requested that he take a second statement. This time Margaret was accompanied by her recent husband, Peter Rauch. With his support Margaret presented another sequence of events. It appears that her second brother, David, had been a party to the concealment of the child's birth and death. It was David who came to Margaret in the barn after she had given

45. Case of Margaret Rauch, Late Sebald, Court of Oyer and Terminer, Examination of Margaret Rauch, Jan. 13, 1772. Pulegi, or pulegium, is an extract of pennyroyal *(Mentha pulogium)*, sometimes used as an abortifacient. J. Worth Estes, "Therapeutic Practice in Colonial New England," in *Medicine in Colonial Massachusetts, 1620–1820* (Boston, 1980).

46. Several aspects of Margaret Rauch's testimony support the assertion made by Cornelia Hughes Dayton in "Taking the Trade" that abortion was widely known and practiced among eighteenth-century young women. In reading infanticide cases I have found that eighteenth-century women did not acknowledge—were not sure—that they were with child until they felt first movement. For these women the first three months of a pregnancy were an uncertain time, when one might or might not be pregnant. This belief was supported by the medical notions that life did not begin until movement was felt by the mother. Margaret Rauch voices this consciousness when she says that "the first day that she felt it that she had a living child within her was the Ninth Day of May last." That Rauch's testimony so closely follows real cases of abortion suggests that precise knowledge of how to terminate an unwanted pregnancy was common among eighteenth-century women. See Dayton, "Taking the Trade: Abortion and Gender Relations in an Eighteenth-Century New England Village," *WMQ*, 3d Ser., XLVIII (1991), 19–49.

birth and took the living child from the straw where it lay beside her. She had not brought on delivery by the use of an abortifacient, but had given birth to a full-term child. Margaret had conspired with her brothers to construct a story of premature labor and suspected abortion to obscure David's involvement. When it looked as if Margaret would be imprisoned to stand trial for infanticide, her husband forced her to break her silence. Now Margaret swore that it was David who took the child, "which was alive then, rapit [wrapped it] up in Hay and went Down with it away from her Killed or Murdered the Child or—whether he Buryed it alive she does not know." This case was not brought to trial. The grand jury failed to bring in the true bill necessary to bring the case before a jury. Margaret Rauch and her brother David were free to go.[47]

That the members of the grand jury in Philadelphia let this case pass by unpunished attests to the community's sexually permissive environment. It appears that the author of the broadside *A Wo and a Warning; or, The Three Cruel Mothers* was right. Philadelphians had turned a blind eye on infanticide.

3. But *Woman* the delight of Man the Paragon of Angels, in the City of *Squares,* hath destroyed the Fruit of her Body with her own Hands.

4. Instead of Nourishing, cherishing and protecting the most helpless of all young, she hath *barbarously murdered* it; and flung it out as dung to fat the Land.

6. Woe to us! the Blood of the Innocent has been spilt in our City; and crieth from the Ground for vengeance.

7. Where are the *Proclamations,* or the Rewards offer'd to discover the Murderers.

8. Ye *Matrons* who have your pretty Babes about your Knees; For whom you would risque your own Lives; will not you give a Reward, *(if there be no other Friend provided,)* for exterminating these Wretches, the Disgrace of your Sex, from the face of the Earth.

12. Ye *Rulers,* what are you doing!

13. Ye *Ministers of the everlasting Gospel,* are Ye Silent.[48]

47. Case of Margaret Rauch, Late Sebald, Court of Oyer and Terminer, examination of Margaret Rauch, Jan. 13, 17, 1772; grand inquest, April term 1772. The events concerning her bastard child had occurred in the spring and summer of 1771, before she married Peter. The reputed father was John George Rothrock.

48. *A Wo and a Warning; or, The Three Cruel Mothers* (Philadelphia: Armbruster, [1765]).

Philadelphians rarely held the mothers of suspiciously dead illegitimate children responsible for their deaths, despite the law. In 1766, the year after this broadside, the newspapers appealed to the city's residents to reveal the identity of "the barbarous Mother" who had murdered a newborn infant. Despite the newspapers' assertion that "it is certainly the Business of every One to be active in discovering the Perpetrator of such a horrid Act of Cruelty," no one disclosed this woman's identity. Despite their fear of prosecution, most of the women who did turn to infanticide were safe in late colonial Philadelphia. Only women at the bottom of the social hierarchy like Elizabeth, a mulatto, needed to fear for their lives.[49]

This sexual culture, which winked at infanticide, was markedly different from the situation in other colonies. Once again, the comparison with New England illustrates this difference. In New England infanticide cases rose throughout the eighteenth century and were well established in the crime pamphlet literature of the day. The publication of "true crime" pamphlets and execution sermons that contained the confessions of convicted felons included cases of infanticide. Before the Revolution, this literary genre was used for spiritual instruction. A combination of criminal autobiography and pious confession, these pamphlets taught the lessons of a moral life on earth and highlighted the importance of spiritual salvation. In Philadelphia, however, the genre did not incorporate tales of murdered illegitimate children within its scope. Even the trial, conviction, and execution of Elizabeth was not seized upon for its sensational literary content. In late colonial Philadelphia, infanticide was not a salient part of the discourse on sex, crime, or salvation.[50]

49. *PG*, Feb. 6, 1766.

50. For a study of infanticide in New England, see Peter C. Hoffer and N. E. H. Hull, *Murdering Mothers: Infanticide in England and New England, 1558–1803* (New York, 1981). For New England infanticide pamphlets, see *A Brief Relation of a Murder Committed by Elizabeth Shaw, Who Was Executed. . . for the Murder of Her Child* (New London, Conn., 1772); *The Declaration and Confession of Ruth Blay, Who Was Tried . . . for Concealing the Birth of Her Infant, Which Was Found Dead* . . . (Portsmouth, N.H., 1768); William Shurtleff, *The Faith and Prayer: A Sermon Preach'd December 27, 1739, on the Occasion of the Execution of Two Criminals, Namely Sarah Simpson and Penelope Kenny* (Boston, 1740) (Simpson and Kenny were executed for concealing the death of a bastard child); *A Sermon Preached on the Occasion of the Execution of Katherine Garret, an Indian-Servant, (Who Was Condemned for the Murder of Her Spurious Child)* (New London, Conn., 1738); *The Declaration, Dying Warning, and Advice of Rebekah Chamblit . . . Concealing the Birth of Her Spurious Male Infant . . .* (Boston, 1733); John Rogers, *Death the Certain Wages of Sin . . . Occasioned by the Imprisonment, Condemnation, and Exe-*

Prostitution in the Pre-Revolutionary City

Prostitution was a vital part of the sexual culture of the city. From all surviving evidence, prostitution occupied a fairly secure position in the pleasure culture of the city in the 1760s and 1770s. Evidence of men and women's engaging in sex commerce slips into the historical record side by side with representations of prostitution in popular culture. Tales of men's debauchery in the taverns relied on women's plying the trade of their bodies. Almanac descriptions of the prostitute's appearance and deportment were specific enough that we can almost see her walk off the pages and onto the Dock Street alleys where she plied her trade: face made up and in "gaudy" dress, she gestured suggestively to men as she called to them to taste her wares. She had an "unseemly Gesture of Body, Lightness of Countenance, Gaudiness in Apparel, [and] Unclean Speech."[51]

The presence of prostitution in the city was strong enough to generate domestic popular print material independent of the almanac. In the mid-1760s, tales of prostitution in Philadelphia were printed as broadsides, in pamphlets, and in plays. As we shall see below, these stories presented prostitution as a real part of the city, and, like the almanac ditties on other forms of nonmarital sexual behavior, they presented prostitution as an acceptable behavior as long as it did not overstep certain boundaries.

Three items produced between 1765 and 1768 present prostitution as it existed then. Given the cost and difficulty of late colonial printing, it is striking that, when Philadelphians took it upon themselves to write and publish popular print materials about sexuality, they wrote about prostitution.

The first was a broadside poem of 1765 called *A New Song about Miss Ketty*, warning young men to turn away from sexual relations with the city's whores in favor of securing wives.

---

cution of a Woman, Who Was Guilty of Murdering Her Infant Begotten in Whoredom (Boston, 1701).

See also Daniel A. Cohen, *Pillars of Salt, Monuments of Grace: New England Crime Literature and the Origins of American Popular Culture, 1674–1860* (Oxford, 1993). Cohen does not study infanticide pamphlets as a particular genre; he does, however, discuss the importance of murder pamphlets and execution sermons as tools for spiritual instruction.

51. Andrew Aguecheek [pseud], *The Universal American Almanack . . . for . . . 1761* (Philadelphia: Steuart, 1760). These descriptions are very similar to the descriptions of actual prostitution in the city, produced immediately after the Revolution (See Chapters 4, 5, below).

About Miss Ketty, leaving the Country to the TUNE
  Derry down, down, down, Derry down.

1. You Lady's of Pleasure, that lives in Delight,
Pray mourn for *Miss Ketty,* who have taking her flight,
Her Silks, and her Sattins, like full spreading Sails,
Her Colours are hist, so adue to your Tails,   *Derry etc.*

2. Rakish young Beaus, that delights in such charms
Sing farewell to *Ketty,* no more in your Arms.
Your gold you may spend, ther's enough of the Game;
That will play at all fours, and tip you the same.   *Derry etc.*

3. They look then so pretty, with their rolling Eyes,
Descending like Angels, that comes from the Skys;
Young men are Intic'd, with so glittering a Show,
Not heeding that they are a fire Below.   *Derry etc.*

4. Come walk in young man, and kiss me my Dear;
If 'tis but a *Negroe,* they do not much Care,
For as long he had money to spend he may Stay:
But when 'tis all spent, you black dog aWay.   *Derry etc.*

5. But when to the Work-House, They are force for to Stear,
For to pick Oakam, they straight must prepaire:
Or else the bear block, they are forc'd for to Pound,
Besied's all the night, they must lie on the Ground.   *Derry etc.*

6. Here's a curse to all Whores, but to honest Wives;
A Blessing may tend them, all the Days of their Lives:
So young men take warning as *Ketty,* is gone,
And dispise all such Whores and hold them to Scorn.   *Derry etc.*

7. So all you fond Bucks, take warning by This,
Ther's no pleasure indeed a Whore for to Kiss
There is honest Women so make them your Wives;
Then you will live happy all the Days of your Lives.   *Derry &c.*[52]

Men were cautioned that a relationship with a prostitute would be fleeting
and insincere, that her inveigling deportment and glittery appearance were

52. *A New Song about Miss Ketty* (Philadelphia, 1765) (numbering regularized).

only illusions that obscured her bankrupt morals and greed for money. To make this point powerfully, the author takes an unusual step for late colonial popular print and openly addresses cross-racial sexual involvement. Miss Ketty's true nature is revealed by her willingness to take any client with money, even African-Americans. This characterization of the prostitute as a white woman who willingly engages in sexual relations with black men speaks to a broader concern that was just beginning to surface in the city before the American Revolution: a fear that female sexuality not tightly bound to courtship and marriage would permit social and sexual mixing across fundamental racial boundaries.

Except for this broadside and a couple of satirical political ones from the 1760s, there was very little printed on African-American sexuality or cross-racial sexual relations. In these few instances, cross-racial sexual intimacy itself was invoked to slander the character of the white partner. While ethnic and class-specific characterizations were crucial to the humor of early Philadelphia print culture, color designation and caricatures of African-American sexuality were largely absent from the print material on sex and gender prior to the Revolution. Neither African-American sexuality nor cross-racial sexual intrigue was an important source of humor in the 1750s and 1760s. While slavery held, white Philadelphians did not use sexual slander of African-Americans to justify their oppression. But neither was cross-racial sexual behavior a joking matter; slavery was too serious and contentious an issue for race to play a key role in sexual humor before the Revolution. As we shall see, all of this changed after the Revolution, when Philadelphians began to dismantle slavery and fashion a system to preserve racial subordination without it.[53]

If the portrait of Miss Ketty allows us a preview of the racial and sexual anxiety to come, it also depicts a real member of the Philadelphia community. In describing the possible outcomes she might face as a result of prostituting herself, the author drew upon references to the city's almshouse and jail. Use of such accurate and specific details as picking oakum (twisting apart tar-

53. *A Conference between the D[evi]l and Doctor D[ov]e: Together with the Doctor's Epitaph on Himself* (Philadelphia: Steuart, 1764), broadside, for political satire using cross-racial sex. Violence, not sex, was the attribute consistently associated with African-Americans in eighteenth-century Philadelphia print culture before the Revolution. References to African-Americans in colonial newspapers were about violence either committed by African-Americans or done to them, setting up the expectation that violence and danger would be associated with them.

impregnated rope) as an almshouse inmate or serving a sentence at hard labor breaking rocks in the city jail made the possible consequences of prostitution real for the broadside reader. In 1765, when *Miss Ketty* was published, Philadelphians were openly grappling with the role of sex commerce in the lives of young men. *Miss Ketty* warned the youth tempted by the willing "ladies of pleasure" that he risked his health—by exposure to venereal disease in the "fire Below"—and lifelong happiness by choosing the whore.

The lessons of *Hilliad Magna: Being the Life and Adventures of Moll Placket-Hole,* also published in 1765, were quite different. This short, seven-page pamphlet about the life of a Philadelphia prostitute gives us our most explicit look at the bawdier side of life in the city. As an artifact of low-life popular culture, it presents the coarser material printed and read in late colonial Philadelphia. As a parody it gives us a glimpse at the practice of prostitution in the city. As we shall see, the description of prostitution in the pamphlet had much in common with the evidence of actual prostitution in the city.[54]

Following in the English tradition of the prostitute exposé, this piece presents the spatial and social geography of vice in the city, depicts several scenes of prostitution, and describes the town's ultimate toleration of the trade. Like many English exposés, this story makes very little attempt to appear to be cautionary. Instead, it is bold, bawdy, and suggestive. Even Moll's name is a play on words. "Moll," which in the eighteenth century often referred to a prostitute, becomes graphically suggestive by adding "Placket-Hole," a reference to the slit pocket of a woman's skirt suggesting easy access to her private parts.[55]

The tale begins by placing Moll in Philadelphia, the bastard child of an aging prostitute:

MOLL PLACKET-HOLE was born in a *Bawdy House* in a Lane in the City of *Brotherly Love.* . . . Her Mother kept a Port of Trade; and as the Duties were all paid down, she had no Clerks in her Custom-House; and therefore could not remember all who *entered,* and *unloaded their freights* there.

The life of prostitution presented through Moll's experiences was not unattractive. She had a loving childhood surrounded by her mother's colleagues and generous clients. When she was old enough, she happily joined the trade. After seven years of prostitution, when her health was ruined by disease, she

54. *Hilliad Magna: Being the Life and Adventures of Moll Placket-Hole, with a Prefatory Dialogue, and Some Moral Reflections, on the Whole* (Philadelphia: Armbruster, 1765).

55. See, for example, *The Night Walker; or, Evening Rambles* (London, 1697). This copy held at the LCP was owned by Benjamin Franklin during the late colonial period.

became the proprietor of her own bawdyhouse. Moll enjoyed the patronage of men and women of all stations of society and became rich from the trade in sexual services.

The Philadelphia of this story tolerated Moll's trade, because men of elite standing enjoyed frequenting her establishment and because Moll wisely kept up the appearance of propriety. Moll brought a man in to live with her "that they might appear to the Publick, as *honest* Housekeepers." When public sentiment was periodically aroused against prostitution, Moll and her friends disappeared until the fervor died down again.

The pamphlet reads like a prescription on the proper uses of prostitution. Frequenting a bawdyhouse and paying for the sexual services of a "hussy" was within the realm of reasonable behavior. When the prostitute was a woman like Moll who was raised to the trade and "shewed all the Eagerness for forbidden Joy," men might enjoy her, and the community indulge them. But, when a man sought a virgin and conspired with a madam to entrap her, prostitution had overstepped its bounds. The pamphlet recounts just such a scenario. Moll, having found a "handsome" country girl in the market, tricked her into staying the night in her home. Unaware that Moll's was a bawdy-house, the country virgin agreed to spend the night:

> In the Evening, a Person (who is esteemed a Gentleman) for whom she was designed, came. He fell in Conversation with her, and thinking he had spent Time enough in *Civility,* began to treat her *rudely.* Which she resented. He was surprized at her Coyness; and let her understand such Nicety was not to be observed, *in the Place where she was.* Upon which, bursting into Tears, she implored his Mercy; told her Story, and who her Parents were. But oh! think of the Confusion of the Man, when he found her the Daughter of his Friend thus inveigled, and on the Brink of Destruction!

In this situation prostitution threatened the community's class and patriarchal relations by infringing on the rights and prerogatives of a gentleman father.

At this point Moll had become too bold and the trade too disruptive to the social order. To show their displeasure at her practice of procuring innocent young maids for her clients, a town mob would set out against her:

> She exulted; and insulted every one who she believed, had complained against her, and their Relatives and Friends also. Till the Town tired out with her Insolence, and her Escape from Justice in a regular Manner, set a Mob (many of whom had been her Beneficiaries) upon her. They pulled down her House, and destroyed her Furniture etc.

But Moll would have the last laugh, for Philadelphia would not be without its house of ill fame. After destroying her house, Philadelphians immediately took up a collection to build her a new one.

> She stormed and raged and swore if her Customers would not build her a better House, she would expose them. A Sense of Shame remains after the greatest Debaucheries. They opened a Subscription, and a hundred Pounds were subscribed in one Day.

Part of the purpose of this pamphlet might have been to advertise the trade to potential customers. The story details how prostitution was carried out, how houses of prostitution operated as boardinghouses run by women, where one could find them (along the waterfront in the alleys by the city's docks), and that one's identity would remain discreetly hidden (because the proprietor "kept no record" and "could not remember" who all her customers were). One learned the cost of specific services and was cautioned to engage only voluntary prostitutes. But the reader also learned of a new world of underground involuntary sexual services, where unprotected young women were tricked and then trapped into prostitution.[56]

The position of the prostitute as a central figure is reinforced by her presence in a comic opera written about life in the city by Thomas Forrest in 1767. Because *The Disappointment* made fun of several well-known figures of the city, it was withdrawn from its scheduled performance at the Southwark theater in April 1767, deemed unfit for the stage. But it was published and sold in Philadelphia that spring as an inexpensive "comic opera" and in New York City later that year.[57] In it we see another version of the city's prostitute, also named

56. I have found documentation of one case of such sexual abduction during this period, where Abigail Hamilton was brought from Ireland for purposes of prostitution. OPM, Apr. 18, 1770.

57. Andrew Barton [pseud. of Thomas Forrest], *The Disappointment; or, The Force of Credulity* (1767), ed. David Mays (Gainesville, Fla., 1976). The play chronicled an elaborate practical joke that was played on men of the city, and it was their objection to public ridicule, not a public objection to the bawdy behavior of the character of the prostitute, that caused the play to be canceled at the last minute. See John F. Watson, *Annals of Philadelphia* . . . (Philadelphia, 1823), I, 73–74. In his introduction Mays presents the production controversy, gives the historical identities of characters, and recaps the events that it was based upon. Moll's historical identity remains unknown.

Advertisement for the theatrical production was run in *PC*, Apr. 13, 1767, announcing the performance on Apr. 20. Advertisements for the published play also ran in the *PC*, Apr. 13, 27, 1767, after the play had been canceled. The play heralded by printer-

Moll Placket, the principal female character. Although peripheral to the main action, she gives us another view of the Philadelphia prostitute of the late 1760s. This Moll made her living as the kept woman of an elderly married man. She explains:

> He thinks I have a prodigious fondness for him—and so I have for his better part, that's his money—He has been deficient in payment for some-time past. . . . But thank fortune, I'm not at a loss for a friend, to make up his deficiency.

Raccoon, her patron, has set her up in a house and maintains her, and she acts the loving paramour for this aging man, despite his sexual inadequacy. But Moll, unbeknownst to Raccoon, entertains other, less permanent "friends" when he is away. Topinlift, a sailor, sings Moll's praises before he beds her:

> No girl with Placket can compare,
> She is so charming, sweet and fair,
> Her rosy cheeks and nut brown hair,
> Theres none like Molly Placket.
> Whene'er from sea I do return,
> For my dear Placket how I burn;
> Good luck, Raccoon, 'tis now my turn;
> Come, come, my lovely Placket.[58]

Had this play been performed as intended, one can imagine that the sailors in the gallery would have joined in the chorus sung to Molly. Like the other characters in the play based on real members of the community, Moll Placket was a familiar face.

Prostitutes surfaced in almanac tales, were characters in plays, and were the subject of songs and broadside poems during the 1760s. But they rarely appeared in court or the newspaper stories of crime in the city. The Mayor's Court and the newspapers record only three women prosecuted for prostitution from 1759 until the Revolution. In March 1765 two women were pilloried for keeping bawdyhouses. They stood an hour in the public pillory at the end of the market on High Street on Saturday, market day, for the town to view. Five years later Susanna Collins was also prosecuted for keeping a bawdy-house. But these women are stark in their solitary example. It seems For-

---

publisher Samuel Taylor as "a new American Comic Opera" was priced at 1s. 6d., making it an inexpensive, affordable text.

58. Barton [pseud. of Forrest], *The Disappointment*, 80.

rest was right: Moll could expect good business and little interference in the port town.[59]

It was only when sex commerce led to other crimes that the community took notice. Two incidents reported in the city's papers make this point clear. In 1769 a house of prostitution was the site of a brawl that led to the death of a city constable. The *Pennsylvania Chronicle* reported:

> On Saturday Night, very late, one Arthur Campbell, a Constable, hearing a Fray near a House of ill Fame, in the Neighbourhood of this City, went with a Companion towards the Place; whereupon they were assaulted in the most furious Manner by a Number of Seamen, armed with Bludgeons, who wounded Campbell in so terrible a Manner that he died Yesterday about one o'Clock. Several other People were knock'd down and very much bruised by the same Gang. Five of them, being the Principals, are taken and committed to Gaol.[60]

What concerned the community was, not the scene of prostitution, but the violence of the rough sailors. The *Pennsylvania Gazette*'s report even omitted the fact that a house of prostitution was the scene. But, while newspaper reports obscured the sexual setting of the crime, it might have been important to the participants. The main perpetrators were members of the lower classes, sailors who refused to give way to the constable's attempt to direct their behavior at the brothel. Quite possibly, Charles Smith and Thomas Furlong stood their ground against Campbell because they perceived this brothel as part of their cultural terrain, where they expected to be able to assert their own notions of appropriate behavior. Pre-Revolutionary Philadelphia's lower classes periodically resorted to mob violence to defend their values and cultural turf when threatened. The surviving evidence of this event is slim, and this analysis can suggest only one likely explanation. We are presented with an instance when members of the lower classes, the sailors at the brothel, violently resisted the attempt by the city's authorities to control their social and sexual behavior.[61]

59. The Mayor's Court Docket exists from 1759 through 1771, with a two-year gap between July session 1764 and July session 1766. *PG*, Mar. 21, 1765; MCD, October session 1770, January session 1771.

60. *PC*, June 5, 1769. In the following weeks two of the sailors were tried for murder, convicted of manslaughter, and "burnt in the Hand" as punishment (*PC*, July 10, 1769).

61. *PG*, June 15, 1769. Charles Smith and Thomas Furlong were tried for the murder

The next mention of prostitution did not appear until three years later, when a member of polite society was murdered in consequence of a fight between a prostitute and her client. This time the *Pennsylvania Gazette* spoke out against the unimpeded trade:

> It is hoped that this unhappy Affair will induce the Constables to exert their Vigilance in apprehending and securing disorderly Persons, which would be a means of suppressing the many Houses of ill Fame which dishonour this City.

The editor of the paper, David Hall, was concerned because the victim in this case was the aged mother of two prominent merchants of the city and because the murder occurred just outside her own home. The murderer, enraged from a quarrel with a "Woman of ill Fame," ran from his house, crossing the street to Mrs. Bartram's, "swearing he would kill the first person he saw," and struck her down as she stood at her front gate.[62]

These two stories, in which prostitution itself was not the stated crime, were the only references to prostitution in the city's papers during the prewar decade. Other crimes, especially crimes against property, like burglary and robbery, were frequently reported, as was a growing concern in the late 1760s that these crimes were on the rise.[63]

The surviving court records, like the newspapers, also give us details about prostitution only when they accompany other, real crimes. A robbery perpetrated by husband-and-wife team Catharine and Peter Dwire upon Andrew Henry in 1768 was such a case. Henry's deposition describing the crime unwittingly records what might have been the common practices in procuring a prostitute. At about seven o'clock in the evening he went to the city market, where he saw Catharine Dwire. She asked him to share his pepper pot, which

---

of Constable Campbell and convicted of manslaughter in July 1769 (*PG*, July 10, 1769). Steven Rosswurm convincingly interprets several mob events in pre-Revolutionary Philadelphia as single-class acts of resistance, where the lower sort united to defend their violated values. *Arms, Country, and Class: The Philadelphia Militia and "Lower Sort" during the American Revolution, 1775–1783* (New Brunswick, N.J., 1987); see chap. 1, "The Lower Sort and the Resistance Movement," 13–48.

62. *PG*, Aug. 5, 1772. Alexander and George Bartram were wealthy merchants and shopkeepers in Philadelphia (Philadelphia Tax List, 1772, HSP; Philadelphia Constable Returns, 1775, HSP). The victim was their mother, Mrs. Eleanor Bartram.

63. Both the *PG* and the *PC* regularly reported crimes against property and warnings about increasing crime during the 1760s.

he did, and "afterwards she asked him to go with her where they might get a nights lodgeing together." He consented, and the two walked out Market Street, stopped to get a drink, but were refused by the proprietor. They walked farther out away from the center of the city. As they turned a corner, they were confronted by Dwire's husband, who demanded to know what Henry was doing with his wife. Henry denied knowing she was his wife and was set upon by the pair, who struck him and robbed him of his pocketbook and comb case. Clearly, Catharine Dwire lured Andrew Henry to where her husband lay in wait. But the tactic she took was familiar enough to Henry to seem plausible: meeting a woman in the market, agreeing to spend the night together, and seeking out an establishment where they might stay without question. Whether Henry had agreed to do more for Catharine than buy her a drink is not known. But it would not be surprising for him to omit such details.[64]

Prostitution, it seems, thrived in the city's emerging pleasure culture of the 1760s. Historians have long believed that prostitution had a place along Philadelphia's waterfront at midcentury.[65] But the picture that emerges for the 1760s displays prostitution in every district of the city. The bawdyhouse of Constable Campbell's raid was on the south side of the city on Society Hill; Mrs. Bartram's assault occurred on Front Street in Southwark; Andrew Henry procured a prostitute on High Street in the city center at the market; and in the Northern Liberties the British Barracks was the site of illicit activity.

The British Barracks, built in 1757, became a gathering place for some of the city's lower sort. Runaway servant women sometimes took refuge there, and rowdy brawls occurred in the surrounding public houses. Prostitution in the bawdyhouses was one of the few options available to runaway servant girls that provided anonymity. Glover Hunt thought his Irish servant girl, Mary McCormick, had made such a career change when he advertised her in the *Pennsylvania Gazette:*

> Since she went off she has been seen in another Dress, and she is supposed to be harboured in some lewd House in this City. Whoever will secure her in any Gaol, or bring her to me, at the Sign of the Key, in Market-street, shall receive four Dollars Reward.

64. Court of Oyer and Terminer, deposition of Andrew Henry, Sept. 12, 1768.
65. Bridenbaugh, *Cities in Revolt,* 317; Kelley, *Life and Times in Colonial Philadelphia,* 182. Kelley asserts that prostitution had "been strongly entrenched since Penn's time" along the waterfront, and Bridenbaugh notes that Philadelphia "had its bawdyhouses." Neither author attempts to explore the subject further.

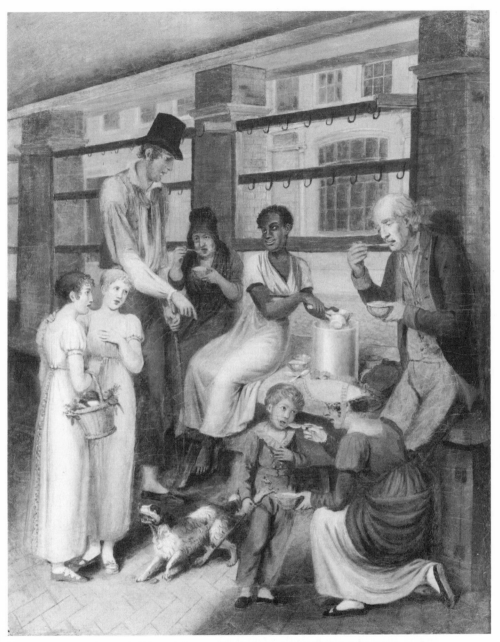

PLATE I. *John Lewis Krimmel,* Pepper Pot: A Scene in the Philadelphia Market. *1811.*
*Selling pepper pot soup in the Philadelphia market, the scene of Catherine Dwire's meeting
with Andrew Henry. Courtesy Philadelphia Museum of Art: Gift of Mr. and Mrs. Edward B.
Leisenring, Jr., in honor of the 125th Anniversary of the Museum, 2001*

The same culture that allowed sexual indulgence of young men could provide young women with a way to make a living.[66]

Participation in prostitution, like bastardy, was an aspect of the pleasure culture that men of all social classes engaged in, not only the sailors by the docks or the soldiers by the barracks. The sons of Philadelphia's well-to-do citizens also participated in such sexual opportunities. In 1770 Samuel Coates described the activities of twelve sons of leading Quaker families in a letter to William Logan, then in England. These young men engaged in drunkenness, gambling, and whoring, and one of them "is said to give a Girl £50 to strip Stark naked before him." The permissive sexual ethic of Philadelphians in the 1760s created an environment in which sex commerce could flourish.[67]

Casual sexual behavior, whether with a woman paid for her sexual services or in the encounters that led to bastardy, created a network of sexual exchanges within the city. One devastating consequence was an increase in the spread of venereal disease. Beginning in the 1760s Philadelphians demonstrate a growing concern about the disease and interest in its medical treatment. Newspaper advertisements for medicines to cure venereal disease and doctors who specialized in its treatment proliferated. The flourishing activity Philadelphians undertook to treat it indicates that many had adopted sexual practices not limited to one lifelong sexual partner. Simply put, venereal disease depends on a series of sexual partners for transmission.

Doctors initiating their medical practice in the city made a special point of declaring their renowned skill in curing venereal disease to attract a clientele. Thomas Wire announced his practice "a few Doors from the Blue Bell" on Society Hill in 1767, informing Philadelphians that "he undertakes particularly to cure, with small Expence and Pain to the Patient, Cancers and Wens, without cutting them, the King's Evil, venereal Disorders, without Sallivation." John Flemor, "SURGEON and Practitioner in PHYSIC" could be found, his 1768 ad proclaimed, "next door to the sign of the Jolly Sailor," also on Society Hill, where clients could take advantage of his supply of medicines "fresh" from "the most eminent hospitals in Europe." Potential customers were reminded of his expertise in treating venereal disease:

> His skill in the cure of that pernicious and destructive disorder, the venereal disease, is well known in this city; he will engage to cure it, from the slightest infection, to the most virulent degree, without sallivation, hin-

66. *PG*, Sept. 18, 1760 (McCormick); *PG*, Jan. 5, 1769 (runaway servant, Jane Greenwood); *PG*, Jan. 26, 1769 (fight by the barracks), also in *PC*, Jan. 23, 1769.

67. Quoted in Bridenbaugh, *Cities in Revolt*, 318.

drance of business, or danger of impairing the most tender constitution, and cures a fresh infection in a few days.

Female medical practitioners, such as Mrs. Steward of Key Alley, and Mrs. Brown in Race Street, also provided treatment for the "King's Evil" for the city's residents. Before the 1760s, doctors' advertisements rarely mentioned venereal disease as a specialty. Only two medical practitioners advertised their skill in treating venereal disease in the *Pennsylvania Gazette* before 1760, and only two shopkeepers advertised medicines specifically designed for its cure.[68]

By the mid-1760s, pills and potions to cure venereal disease became a standard item stocked by shopkeepers and booksellers and were advertised regularly in the city's newspapers. Local doctors and druggists who made their own medicines competed with the latest imported "famous" cures from abroad. By the late 1760s and 1770s, venereal medicines such as "Dr. Sanxay's Imperial Golden drops," "Walker Jesuit Drops," "Maredant drops," and "Keyer's famous pills" were regularly advertised with complete and unambiguous explanations of their use. Advertisements contained personal testimonials of authentic cures and reassurances that they could be used without detection, even by one's sexual partner:

> A full printed plain direction is given with the medicine, that any person, in his own house, or on a journey, or at sea, may cure himself, without the least inconveniencey, or imparting the secret to a bedfellow.[69]

68. *PG*, Jan. 9, 1763, June 11, 1767, Mar. 3, 1768. Mrs. Steward and Mrs. Brown probably serviced clients from the city's laboring classes. They also advertised that they could recommend (meaning connect clients to) wet nurses and dry nurses and could cure children with worms. For other instances of doctors' advertising skill in treatment of venereal disease, see *PJ*, Jan. 22, 1761; *PG*, Sept. 3, 1767, Sept. 15, 1768, July 11, 1772, June 23, 1773.

Pre-1760: *PG*, May 19, 1737, chemist Evan Jones offered "speedy relief" from those who suffered from "the Venereal Disease." *PG*, Jan. 10, 1749, Dr. Vander Kluyt advertised "the arcanum anti venereum; or the secret against the venereal distemper" "without hindrance of business, or fear of discovery; as also, without being sallivated" (meaning without mercury treatment). *PG*, May 31, 1751, Daniel Goodman advertised to cure venereal disease for free. *PG*, Aug. 12, 1756, June 2, 1757, baker, John Atkinson (Hatkinson) offered an oil imported from London that would cure all ailments, including the "kingevil."

69. *PG*, Jan. 31, 1771. See also, for example, *PG*, Apr. 20, 27, Dec. 14, 1769, Jan. 31, Feb. 28, 1771, Feb. 27, Mar. 12, 1772; *PJ*, Nov. 11, 1772, Nov. 3, 1773; *PG*, Nov. 3, 10, 1773, Feb. 28, 1776.

One could undertake a cure from a doctor or buy the latest medicines from a number of Philadelphia shopkeepers. Speakman and Carter, "Chymists and Druggists, at the Bell and Dragon," sold "Very fine Muscadine Raisins, Turkey Figs, and Currants" alongside "Keyser's famous Pills, from the Importer in London, with full Directions for their Use," complete with a certificate guaranteeing their authenticity. John Sparhawk advertised that Walker's Jesuit's drops, "an infallible cure for venereal disease," were available at his "London Book-Store, in Market-street"; William and Thomas Bradford stocked their bookstore with "Dr Keyser's Pills, which infallibly cure a DISEASE, not to be mentioned in a News-Paper"; and Thomas Anderton, bookseller and later self-proclaimed doctor, provided "Doctor *Sanxay's* Imperial Golden DROPS" from his store at the lower end of the Jersey market. Anderton "sealed the bottle with his seal and coat of arms, and signed each bottle in his own hand writing," "to prevent the buyers being imposed on by any counterfeit sort." Anderton thereby hoped to distinguish his cure from less reputable medicines hawked by other entrepreneurs among the city's infected residents.[70]

Venereal disease was not new in late colonial Philadelphia. Periodically, runaway servants had been described in the city's newspapers with the telltale physical signs of the disease since the 1730s. But by the 1760s doctors perceived a demand for venereal cures and advertised accordingly, and men in the import business understood venereal medicine to be a good investment. Enough Philadelphians had adopted expansive sex lives to keep the doctors in business. The general public tolerated these advertisements that acknowledged the sexual practices of those who caught and transmitted the disease and that even catered to the duplicitous practices of those who, as Thomas Anderton's ad stated, sought treatment without "imparting the secret to a bedfellow."

The sexual culture embraced by Philadelphians of the late colonial era was a far cry from the image of sedate Quakers in a restrained society; it was instead a permissive sexual ethic, where members expanded the boundaries of accepted sexual behavior. Serial causal sexual relationships, sometimes resulting in the birth of a bastard child, were common. Philadelphians also created an urban pleasure culture in which a broad spectrum of them devoted their leisure time to recreations and amusements for personal satisfaction. It was within this pleasure culture that Philadelphians developed the discourses on sexuality that would help them make sense of the expanding arenas of sexual expression.

70. *PG*, Apr. 27, 1769, Feb. 28, 1771, Feb. 27, 1772, Nov. 3, 10, 1773.

CHAPTER 3

The Pleasures and Powers of Reading

Eroticization of Popular Print and Discursive Interpretations of Sex

---

The Maids of PHILADELPHIA's Petition

We, the Maids of *Philadelphia* City,
   (The Maids, good lack! the more's the Pity;)
   Do humbly offer this Petition
To represent our sad Condition,
Which once made known, our Hope and Trust is,
That Men of Parts will do us Justice.
Now you must know,—ah! can't you guess
The Subject of a Maid's Distress;
(Plague on the Widows that compel us)
Thus to petition for young Fellows.
But we were saying, you must know,
(Tho' blushing we declare our Woe,)
A Virgin was design'd by Nature,
A weakly and imperfect Creature,
So apt to fall, so apt to stray
Her Wants require a Guide, a Stay.
And then so timorous of Sprites,
She dares not lie alone at Nights;
Say what she will, do what she can,
Her Heart still gravitates to Man;
From whence its evident as Light,
That Marriage is a Maiden's Right;
And therefore 'tis prodigious hard
To be from such a Right debarr'd,
Yet we (poor Souls) can't have the Freedom
To get good Men, howe'er we need 'm.
The Widows, Sirs! the rankest Goats
That e'er polluted Petticoats,
Those Plagues more odious than Small-pox,

Those Jades more subtil than a Fox,
Still cut us out, are still before us,
And leave no Lovers to adore us.[1]

To fully understand the sexual culture of colonial and Revolutionary Philadelphia, one must go beyond the record of sexual behavior and explore what
people thought about sexuality. One avenue is to examine the notions surrounding them in the popular culture and how that culture interpreted the
body, sexual desire, and sexual behavior: to try to grasp the images evoked in
the minds of eighteenth-century men and women when they thought about
sexuality and intimate relationships.

The humorous ditties of popular print are a wonderful entry into this
sexual mentalité. Philadelphia, like other eighteenth-century port cities, maintained cultural links with Britain and western Europe through the importation
and sale of texts, which presented English and European notions of sexuality
throughout the colonial and Revolutionary eras. But the cost of imported print
material limited its circulation to those of the upper economic strata until the
1760s and 1770s, when imported books and cheap domestic reprints came to
enjoy broad circulation. For the majority of Philadelphians the most readily
accessible print material was domestic imprints: the annual almanacs, weekly
newspapers, broadsides, and cheap pamphlets were where they read about
sexuality.

Conflict between husbands and wives dominated representations of gender
in domestic imprints during the first half of the eighteenth century. After midcentury, sexuality emerged as the dominant theme when discussion turned to
gender relations in popular print. Poems, sayings, songs, tall tales, and anecdotes about sexuality, like "The Maids of Philadalphia's Petition" from *Father
Abraham's Almanack,* became very popular in inexpensive print material before the Revolution. Almanacs were exceedingly popular. Printed each year
within a competitive market, they provide a record of changing representations of sexuality and shifts in popular tastes. In almanacs printed between
1750 and 1775, more than three hundred unique items addressed gender and
sexuality. In addition, single-sheet broadsides and short pamphlets were published on prostitution, seduction, and adultery, and even the one play written
in and about late colonial Philadelphia had its sexual themes. Through editing,

1. Abraham Weatherwise [pseud.], *Father Abraham's Almanack . . . for . . . 1762*
(Philadelphia: Dunlap, 1761).

PLATE 2. *John Lewis Krimmel,* Dance in a Country Tavern. *1820.*
Philadelphia artist John Krimmel often placed almanacs in his interiors of
homes and taverns. Bb 61 K89. Permission Historical Society of Pennsylvania

printing, sales, and consumption (reading), Philadelphians shaped and were
in turn shaped by the images of sexuality embodied in these materials.[2]

The representations of sexuality in popular print, like the behavior patterns
already discussed, mark the 1760s as a turning point in the history of sexuality
and gender relations. Midcentury Philadelphians created a newly eroticized
print culture within an expanding market of interested readers, adding erotic

2. A new generation of almanac producers eclipsed earlier ones, beginning in the
late 1750s. Franklin turned production of his almanac over to David Hall in 1758. The
Dunlaps, first William and then John, began producing *Father Abraham's Almanack* in
1759. Many of those Philadelphia almanac producers of the 1730s, 1740s, and 1750s
had left the scene, such as Titan Leeds, Jacob Taylor, Andrew Bradford, John Jerman,
William Burket, Thomas Godfrey, and Matthew Boucher.

Almanacs were still popular in the early nineteenth century, when such artists as
John Lewis Krimmel first portrayed Philadelphia interiors, often depicting almanacs as

content to the popular print material produced from the city's presses, thus expanding the market for bawdy and erotic imports and transforming their popular culture. Analyzing the images produced as new forms of sexual behavior became more prevalent allows us to discern the discursive work these images attempted to do, as sexual desire and sexual behavior were interpreted for eighteenth-century Philadelphians. Here we will first examine the eroticization of popular print culture in the 1760s and 1770s and the creation of a broad multiclass and mixed-gender reading public. We will analyze the representations of sexuality in popular print for the interpretation of gendered sexuality they contain and compare those discursive "truths" to the evidence we have of actual bodily behavior in pre-Revolutionary Philadelphia. Reading these images against the sexual behavior of Philadelphians reveals attempts to interpret sexuality discursively in ways that could shore up the gender system of naturalized male power and female subordination.

Popular print materials can be used as a looking glass into the past: their images mirror the changes in sexual behavior but refract those images through a prism of proper power relations between men and women, casting a fractured and distorted image of sexuality for their readers—an image designed to counter the assertive independence of women in pre-Revolutionary Philadelphia.

Philadelphia Comes of Age: Eroticization of Popular Print Culture

Philadelphia's eighteenth-century almanacs reveal a shift in the tastes of the reading public after midcentury. Beginning in the almanacs for 1759 and 1760, a broader range of sexual topics became printable, and sexual encounters outside courtship and marriage were given greater attention. New tastes as well as tolerance for the bawdy and titillating overcame a propriety that had excluded such items from popular print. Bawdy material formerly confined to English imprints marketed only to the economic elite now entered Philadelphia's popular print culture. By the end of the 1760s, sexual content intensified and became the mainstay of several almanacs. Nonmarital sexual behavior became the dominant theme in almanac material concerned with gender,

---

a standard possession. See *Interior of an American Inn* (1814), *Country Frolic and Dance* (1819), *Country Wedding* (1820), *Departure for a Boarding School* (1820), and *Return from a Boarding School* (1820). Anneliese Harding, *John Lewis Krimmel, Genre Artist of the Early Republic* (Winterthur, Del., 1994); Milo M. Naeve, *John Lewis Krimmel: An Artist in Federal America* (Newark, Del., 1987). Content analysis based on all almanacs printed in eighteenth-century Philadelphia.

scenes of sexual danger for women provided the suspense for many ditties, and sexual encounters offered a voyeuristic sexual experience for the reader. This material depicted and was part of a full-blown urban pleasure culture. As consumers, Philadelphians expanded the market for erotic depictions of sexual behavior and, as readers, participated in the urban pleasure culture.

Father Abraham's Almanack was in the vanguard. William Dunlap, as Abraham Weatherwise, seemed to anticipate the direction of popular tastes, filling his almanac with tales of sexual intrigue and taking the risk of printing the humorous bawdy ditties so popular in contemporary London. In 1762, Weatherwise printed the first explicitly bawdy poem to appear in Philadelphia's almanacs.[3] "The Old Monk and His Young Maid" is typical of eighteenth-century bawdy poems printed in England and France. The poem depicts a monk who peers under his maid's dress and describes his view. The humor of the poem derived from revealing the lustful nature of the supposedly chaste man of God. The scene is set by Peg, the monk's maid, who secretly drank dry the monk's "Ton" (keg) of beer. He discovers the empty keg.

> *Peg* hears th'Alarm, and seeming sore affrighted,
> Hastes to her Master, with a Candle lighted.
> O *Jesu!* what's the Matter, for Heaven's Sake?
> Matter enough!—Our Vessel springs a Leak.
>   With angry Eyes they both peep round about,
> To find, if possible, the Crevice out:
> But all in vain; the Ton proves fast and tight;
> Not one Hoop flown, and all stands safe in Sight.

3. The only almanac produced in Philadelphia that came close to the bawdy content of *Father Abraham's Almanack* before the 1760s was one published in 1726 as an attempt to slander its supposed author. It was printed by Samuel Keimer, who put rival almanac producer Jacob Taylor's name on it. Its bawdy humor was meant, however, to scandalize the public and destroy Taylor's reputation. See Jacob Taylor, *A Compleat Ephemeris for the Year of Christ 1726* (Philadelphia, [1725]); *AWM,* Jan. 25, 1726, for Taylor's reply and denial of authorship. Taylor renounced his authorship, declaring, "Whereas there hath been lately Published and Spread abroad in the Province and elsewhere, a lying Pamphlet called, An Almanack, set out and Printed by Samuel Keimer, to reproach, ridicule, and rob an honest Man of his Reputation, and Strengthening his Adversaries . . ." (*AWM,* Feb. 8, 1726).

For a discussion of eighteenth-century erotica, see Peter Wagner, *Eros Revived: Erotica of the Enlightenment in England and America* (London, 1988), 72–86 (on antireligious erotica), 182–191 (on scatological erotica).

The Maid, commission'd, strait ascends its Head,
And stooping downwards, all behind display'd.
Upwards her [Ho]op, by her Declension, flew,
And every latent Charm expos'd to View.
Transported with the Vision, *Geron* cry'd:
Come, *Peggy;* lay the fruitless Search aside:
Don't take such wond'rous Pains; I plainly spy
The Leak, from whence my Ton is drain'd so dry.[4]

Weatherwise's decision to include the bawdy in his almanac must have met with popular success, for the next year he increased the volume of such material and continued to expand the role of sex in his almanac until the Revolution. Most of the early bawdy jests, like the next one, might have been palatable to Philadelphians of the early 1760s because they were obviously located in a European setting. As such, the sexual humor could be enjoyed without reflecting upon the morality of their own community.

> The Bishop of D——m had a slovenly Custom of keeping one Hand always in his Breeches, and being one Day to bring a Bill into the House of Peers, relating to a Provision for Officers Widows, he come with some Papers in one Hand, and had the other, as usual, in his Breeches; and beginning to speak, I have something in my Hand my Lords, said he, for the Benefit of the Officers Widows—Upon which the Duke of Wh——n immediately interrupting him, ask'd, *In which Hand, my Lord?*[5]

Weatherwise led the way, and Philadelphia's other almanac publishers followed. By 1764 sexual poems had become acceptable enough to Philadelphia's readers that the *Universal American Almanack* used sex as the theme for each of its monthly poems atop each month's calendar. The spring months, not surprisingly, present the most explicit sexual maxims:

> April
> The Stallion and the Bull now rampant grow,
> And Maids to *Silence* turn their modest *No;*
> Which shews the Heart's consenting to the Bliss;
> And serves for Answer just as well as *Yes.*

4. Weatherwise, *Father Abraham's Almanack for 1762.*
5. Ibid., *For . . . 1763* (Philadelphia: Dunlap, 1762). See also anecdote "An Old Parson," *For . . . 1767* (Philadelphia: Dunlap, 1766).

May

Behold the charming, verdant Month of *May*.
All Nature smiles in beautiful Array;
Lovers in Fields now enter into Leagues,
And blooming Hedges hide their close Intreagues.

July

This Month the thirsty Traveller will try,
And southern Maids in Bed half naked lie;
On Hay tricks play the Country-Lass and Clown,
While Lords and Ladies kiss on Beds of Down.[6]

In these poems human sexuality follows the annual cycle of seasons, and sexual desire leads to sexual activity for men and women of all walks of life: 'tis the season for reluctant maidens to be overcome, for lovers to fulfill their desires in rural bliss, and for couples of all classes to take their pleasure.

The poems reflect a permissive attitude toward nonmarital sexuality. The maids and country lasses are sexually active, with no mention of courtship, betrothal, or marriage. Topics rarely raised in the early almanacs, and then only to prohibit them, were by the 1760s sites for humorous sex play. For example, adultery, castigated in the 1750s, was ten years later the vehicle to present a humorous display of libidinous sexuality.

The HAPPY PAIR: *or, Both of one Mind.*

WHO says my Lord and Lady disagree?
    A *Pair* more like in all *Things* cannot be.
    My *Lord* will often *curse* the Marriage Chain;
My *Lady* wishes it unloos'd again,
Ever with Rakes, my *Lord* is *ne'er at Home*:
Ever engag'd, my *Lady* likes his *Room*.
He swears his *Boy* is not his *real Son;*
My *Lady* thinks it is not all his own.
He'll have a *sep'rate Bed;*—'Tis *her* Desire;
Sheets warm'd, Bed made, the *smiling Pair retire;*
The *Cause*, tho' *hidden*, yet the *same* their *Want;*
He sends for *Miss*, and *she* for her *Gallant*.

6. Andrew Aguecheek [pseud.], *The Universal American Almanack . . . for . . . 1764* (Philadelphia: Steuart, 1763).

If *Union* then makes *bless'd* the *Marriage-Life,*
The *same* the *Husband,* and the *same* the *Wife,*
If in *two* Breasts *one* Mind give Joy *sincere,*
What *two* more *happy* than this HAPPY PAIR?[7]

Other sexual behaviors of the new urban pleasure culture also infused popular print material. By the late 1760s and early 1770s the almanacs presented a sexuality that could exist wholly outside established social relationships or the pursuit of marriage. Sexual gratification for its own sake inspired anecdotes about seduction and abandonment, premarital pregnancy, and bastardy. No longer in the shadows, they became the source of lively and light humor.

In the early 1760s the seducer was spoken of as one who "violated virgin innocence, and rewarded the maid . . . with eternal infamy." Ten years later the tricks of seduction earned praise, and the predicament of the abandoned woman was a source of humor.

Says Dolly—"Me, Thomas, you promis'd to wed,
And I, silly Girl, believ'd all that you said."
"That I promis'd to wed you, and love you, 'tis true,
But I've try'd you, my Doll, and I find you won't do."[8]

Premarital sex, too, became a joking matter.

Scarce had five Months expir'd since *Ralph* did wed,
When lo! his fruitful Wife was brought to Bed.
How now, quo[t]h *Ralph*—this is *too soon, my Kate?*
No, *Ralph,* quo[t]h she,—you marry'd me *too late.*[9]

7. Weatherwise, *Father Abraham's Almanack for 1763.* Contrast the letter ten years earlier, supposedly written to the editor, concerning adultery, in William Ball, *The New-Jersey Almanack . . . for . . . 1753* (Philadelphia: Bradford, 1752).

8. 1760s: Andrew Aguecheek [pseud.], *The Universal American Almanack . . . for . . . 1763* (Philadelphia: Steuart, 1762).

1770s: Richard Saunders [pseud.], *Poor Richard Improved . . . for . . . 1774* (Philadelphia: Hall and Sellers, 1773). For others on seduction, see "The Fox and Goose, a Curious Fable," in Abraham Weatherwise [pseud.], *Father Abraham's Almanack . . . for . . . 1772* (Philadelphia: Dunlap, 1771); poem heads September–December in William Andrews, *Poor Will's Almanack . . . for . . . 1774* (Philadelphia: Cruikshank, 1773).

9. "An Epigram," in Richard Saunders [pseud.], *Poor Richard Improved . . . for . . . 1772* (Philadelphia: Hall and Sellers, 1771).

The sexual experiences of these men and women before marriage did not create any real conflict within these marriages. Premarital sexual activity was presented in a casual tone, as was bastardy. In two of the *Poor Richard's* poems for 1774, bastardy was the topic of witty repartee between husband and wife:

When *wedded* Nell was brought to Bed,
    She scream'd and roar'd with Pain;
She'd rather die a Maid, she said,
    Was it to do again.
Pray have a little Patience, Nell,
    And say, why now this Pother?
Before your Marriage you could tell,
    What 'twas to be a Mother.

The woman was the butt of the joke, but in the next poem she had the last laugh. Here the husband declares that he will enlist as a soldier to escape his termagant wife. Not to be outdone she boasts, "Do, Robin, do; I'll raise, the mean while, fresh Recruits," threatening to bear bastard children should he depart.[10]

The city's almanacs from the late 1760s to the mid-1770s present an underworld of sex available to men. In "Written to a Friend after a Debauch," readers view an evening's entertainment among a group of men. While suffering from a morning hangover, the author tells us of his evening drinking with his friends at a tavern. Each man maintained his own ability to drink more than the rest, until he passed out. Our author tells us he preferred the pleasures of a woman to drunkenness and after several drinks left to visit the tavern's prostitute:

I hate the bottle and the glass,
But sigh for ev'ry pretty lass;
My youthful blood don't yet require
A stimulus to warm desire;
With natal heat and vigor bless'd,
The rapt'rous joys of love possess'd,
I leave your dull, phlegmatic souls,
To seek your bliss in flowing bowls;
While I bow down at Venus' shrine,
And they adore the god of wine.

10. "On Nelley," "Epigrams," in Saunders, *Poor Richard Improved for 1774.* For other bastardy jests, see "Jests," in Weatherwise, *Father Abraham's Almanack for 1767;* "All Covet All Lose," in *For 1763;* May poem, in *For 1766.*

The association between heavy drinking and casual sexual encounters was reinforced in several of these poems, and often the tavern was the setting for sexual opportunities.[11]

The rake who makes self-confident use of women and the libertine who moves from one brief and intense sexual encounter to another became frequent characters. Initially, they were recognizably part of European and usually aristocratic society. As such, the rake and the libertine were known but were not necessarily part of Philadelphia's immediate community. But by the mid-1760s the European setting faded away, and the context for their sexual play could just as easily have been Philadelphia as London or Paris. Sometimes they were portrayed as engaging in reasonable and expected behaviors, like the author of "Written to a Friend after a Debauch." At other times the drawbacks of their style of life were expressed.

Of the PLEASURES of LIBERTINES

Let libertines their boist'rous Pleasures boast,
They are but *noisy wretchedness* at most:
The *tott'ring base* of all the *joys* they know
Is *fleeting tumults* or *delusive show.*
They rend the breast, as whirlwinds rend the sky,
And, like the instant lightnings, glare and die.
That *lasting bliss* which bears a *calm review,*
None but the *wise* and *virtuous* ever knew.[12]

Poems like this gave the libertine public recognition and a place in the cultural landscape of the city even as they warned against the quick gratification of passion the libertine pursued. The proliferation of this material validated and supported the sexual lives of such libertines while exposing the limitations of

11. Philo Copernicus [pseud.], *The American Calendar; or, An Almanack for the Year 1771* (Philadelphia: Bradford, 1770).

For other examples of men's activities in the pleasure culture, see "On Love and Acquaintance with the Fair Sex," in Andrew Aguecheek [pseud.], *The Universal American Almanack . . . for . . . 1768* (Philadelphia: Steuart, 1769); "The Parson's Pocket-Companions, or the Cork-Screw, a Merry Tale," in Weatherwise, *Father Abraham's Almanack for 1766;* "Love and Wine: An Epigram," in Philo Copernicus [pseud.], *The American Calendar for 1771;* "An Affecting Anecdote," in Copernicus, *The American Calendar; or, An Almanack for the Year 1773* (Philadelphia: Bradford, 1772).

12. Abraham Weatherwise [pseud.], *Father Abraham's Almanack . . . for . . . 1771* (Philadelphia: Dunlap, 1770).

self-indulgent sexuality. These scenes gave the pleasure culture a life stretching beyond those who engaged in its activities.

The rake and the libertine had their female counterparts in the amorous lady and the coquette. Such characters engaged in succesive sexual intrigues for their personal fulfillment with no intent to marry. In 1770 *Poor Richard* compared the two:

The Amorous Lady and Coquet Contrasted

The Difference between an *amorous* Lady, and a *Coquet*, is, that the first is for being loved, and the other only [f]or passing [f]or handsome and lovely: The one designes [t]o engage us, and the other only to please us: The *intriguing Woman* passes from one Amour to another successively, the *Coquet* has several *Amusements* at once: Passion and Pleasure are predominant in the first, and Vanity and Levity in the other. Gallantry is a Weakness of the Heart, or, purhaps, a Defect of Constitution; but a *coquetish Humour* is an Irregularity, or Debauchery of the Mind. To conclude, an *amorous Woman* makes herself to be feared, and a *Coquet* to be hated.[13]

While the coquet was given the worse evaluation, both types of women were scorned for engaging more than one man. Anecdotes such as this, which provide full-blown definitions and distinctions between different kinds of sexually active women, demonstrate that women too inhabited the cultural landscape of the pleasure culture.

Two years later *Poor Richard* responded to the unbound sexuality of women in the pleasure culture by cautioning them to restrain themselves. In "The Way to Get Him" he derides them for the literal overexposure of their flesh and suggests, metaphorically, that women have failed to conceal and constrain their lusts.

> Girls who intend the Heart to seize,
> Must shew their Beauties by Degrees;
> By full Displays they lose their Aim,
> Tis Expectation feeds the Flame.
>
> And gently fans the amorous Fire
> Which but for that would soon expire.
> The Breast which pants through Cyprus Gauze,
> A Glance of Admiration draws;

13. Richard Saunders [pseud.], *Poor Richard Improved . . . for . . . 1770* (Philadelphia: Hall and Sellers, 1769).

But when we've seen it o'er and o'er,
It strikes us with Surprize no more.
We coolly own its snowy Charms,
But feel no violent Alarms:

We soon grow surfeited with those
Who all their Charms at once disclose,
And from a vain Desire to strike,
Treat all, with what they have, alike;
The female Rattle, Flirt and Rake,
The Point they have in View mistake,
And formal Prudes, and gay Coquettes,
Instead of Cages, deal in Nets.

If Girls, to Admiration prone,
Would only let themselves alone,
And not by studied Arts pretend
The Charms which Nature gives to mend;
Nor ev'n those Charms at once reveal,
But with Discretion half conceal,
Their Prudence would be well repaid,
By every Conquest which they made.[14]

In Franklin's view, Philadelphia's women needed to be warned not to act "the
female Rattle, Flirt and Rake." The temptation to do so was not confined to the
lower levels of female society. While the poorer woman might be imagined as
the harlot in the tavern, the behavior of middle- and upper-class women was
often the specific subject of almanac material.

The images of nonmarital sexuality unfolding in Philadelphia's print culture emphasized the availability of sexual opportunity, the casual nature of
these relationships, and a lack of concern over the hardships created for discarded sexual partners or sexual victims. The pursuit of sexual conquest,
especially for men, had become commonplace and comical. These scenes had
become joking matters, in part, because indulging in sexual intimacies outside marriage had become an option exercised by all classes of Philadelphia
society. Sexuality had been released from its marital moorings in the late
colonial period, and men exercised a heightened level of sexual privilege.

The sexualization of print culture evident in Philadelphia almanacs was
part of a broader eroticization of popular culture in the city after midcentury,

14. Ibid., *For 1772.*

when interest in erotic texts and their availability increased. In part, the greater numbers of bawdy and erotic English imprints encouraged Philadelphia printers to expand the sexual content of their almanacs. Their reading audience increasingly had access to salacious imported reading material independent of the almanac genre. During the early 1760s the book trade expanded and became more competitive and innovative. Prices for books decreased, and rapid importation of the most recent London publications became a key to success. Reading of imported texts spread from well-to-do Philadelphians to the middling and even the laboring classes in the 1760s and 1770s, booksellers turned to auction sales of used books, and they created circulating libraries for the reading public to expand their market. Some printer-booksellers began printing excerpts of fashionable European novels in their weekly newspapers to draw readers to them and into this expanding print culture.[15]

Midcentury Philadelphia was an English city in its love of the bawdy. Philadelphians told coarse jokes and sang bawdy songs in taverns where prints by William Hogarth hung on the walls, providing them with images of London's sexual ribaldry. His popular representations of the vices of the English urban lower classes and caricatures of the moral hypocrisy of the elite were imported and sold. At prices of one shilling to two pounds in London, they were out of reach for most laboring Philadelphians. But the Idle Apprentice's intrigues with his whore and the street scenes of overt sex play in the Times of the Day series, advertised for sale in 1754, were perhaps as popular as in London. Retailers took the unusual step of advertising Hogarth's imported prints by artist and title, believing that advertising them among their imported prints would bring buyers to their shops.[16]

15. My analysis of the eroticization of popular culture is based on newspaper advertisements, catalogs of books for sale, booksellers' inventories, the holdings of Philadelphia's lending libraries, and all eighteenth-century almanacs. See James N. Green, "The Book Trade in the Middle Colonies, 1720–1790," in Hugh Amory and David D. Hall, eds., *A History of the Book in America*, I, *The Colonial Book in the Atlantic World* (New York, 2000), 247–313 (on the development of the book trade). *PJ*, published by William Bradford, made reprinted fiction, often abridged, its signature element during the 1750s. The content of these pieces ranged from sentimental fiction to libertine exposés. They were placed on the newspaper's front page and often serialized. See, for example, the sentimental "Entertainment Story of Leontine and Clora (from a Late Magazine)," *PJ*, Jan. 23, 1754, and the exploration of a rake in "To the Adventurer," *PJ*, May 2, 1754.

16. Hogarth prints were advertised by title in 1754 and 1755: *PG*, July 4, 1754, for sale by Matthew Clarkson; *PG*, May 1, 1755, *PJ*, May 29, Aug. 7, 1755, for sale by Alexander Hamilton. Prices from broadside *Prints Publish'd by W. Hogarth, and Are to Be Had at*

PLATE 3. *William Hogarth,* The Idle 'Prentice Return'd from Sea,
and in a Garret with a Common Prostitute. *1747. Plate 7 of* Industry
and Idleness. *Permission Colonial Williamsburg Foundation*

The cheapest, and therefore the most widely available, bawdy print materials were short pamphlets, broadsides, and songsters that were also imported
and sold in Philadelphia. Unfortunately, they were not advertised by title,
and few have survived. But we can catch a glimpse of their sexual humor in
the songs appended to such books as *The Compleat Academy of Complements,*
which was sold in Philadelphia in the 1740s and 1760s. Such sayings and

---

His House in Leicester Fields, 1754 (London, 1754), reprinted in David Bindman, *Hogarth
and His Times: Serious Comedy* (Berkeley, Calif., 1997), 89. Philadelphia shopkeepers
and booksellers regularly advertised imported English prints at midcentury, at least
twenty-two in *PG* between 1742 and 1767, when the nonimportation agreements interrupted the steady flow of English goods. On tavern life, including bawdy speech and
song, see Peter Thompson, *Rum Punch and Revolution: Taverngoing and Public Life in
Eighteenth-Century Philadelphia* (Philadelphia, 1999), 92, 98.

PLATE 4. *William Hogarth,* Noon. *1738. Plate 2 of* The Four Times of the Day.
Permission Colonial Williamsburg Foundation

jokes provided Philadelphians with another conduit of ribald sexual humor. In one typical song, a soldier, sailor, tinker, and tailor vied for the attention of "Buxome Joan" as she sought a mate.

> The Soldier swore like Thunder,
> He lov'd her more than Plunder,
>
> . . . .
>
> The Taylor thought to please her,
> With offering her his Measure;
> The Tinker too with Mettle,
> Said he could mend her Kettle,
>   and stop up ev'ry Leak,
>   and stop etc.
>
> But while these Three were prating
> The Sailor slily waiting,
> Thought if it came about, Sir,
> That they should all fall out, Sir,
>   he then might play his part,
>   he then etc.
>
> And just e'en as he meant, Sir,
> To Logger-heads they went, Sir,
> And then he let fly at her,
> A Shot 'tween Wind and Water;
>   which won this fair Maid's Heart
>   which won etc.[17]

Although English imprints were the most widely available, by the 1760s Philadelphia booksellers openly advertised French erotica for sale as well. James Rivington imported both the French and English versions of Denis

17. *The Compleat Academy of Complements: . . . Together with a Collection of the Newest Songs That Are Sung at Court and Play-House* (London, 1705) was reprinted in many editions, all with songbooks attached; see also *A New Academy of Compliments; or, The Lover's Secretary* . . . (Worcester, Mass., 1795). *PG*, Feb. 7, 1740, for sale by Franklin; Abraham Weatherwise [pseud.], *Father Abraham's Almanack . . . for . . . 1760* (Philadelphia: Dunlap, 1759), "Books . . . Just Imported," by Dunlap.

Booksellers rarely referred to imported pamphlets for sale by title in their advertisements, preferring instead to make general claims such as "the latest and most entertaining . . . plays . . . pamphlets." See, for example: *PJ*, Oct. 22, 1761; *PP*, Dec. 5, 1778, Oct. 26, 1782.

Diderot's erotic philosophic novel *Les bijoux indiscrets (The Indiscreet Jewels)* in 1762, and *Cloister* in 1764. *The Indiscreet Jewels* was a licentious political commentary on the French monarchy achieved through an erotic oriental tale with Louis XV represented by a sultan. Bored, the sultan summons a genie who gives him a magic ring that, when pointed at a woman's "jewels," or genitals, will make her tell of her sexual escapades. *Cloister* was an English translation of either Jean Barrin's sexually explicit *Venus in the Cloister* or the tamer *Les amours de Sainfroit Jesuite, et d'Eulalie fille dévote*, translated into English as *The Cloister: Containing the Amours of Sainfroid, a Jesuit and Evalalia, a Nun.*[18]

Erotic texts had always been available to the well-to-do men in Philadelphia, either by private solicitation of the city's booksellers or through correspondence with friends and agents in England. Men like Benjamin Franklin owned copies of imported erotic books such as *The Night Walker; or, Evening Rambles in Search after Lewd Women*. Two rare advertisements that included erotic texts from earlier in the century give us some idea of what books were available to elite readers before the expansion of the book trade and popularization of reading in the 1760s. The first, placed by Benjamin Franklin in February 1740, advertised the sexual adventure stories *The English Rogue* and *Edward the Fourth's Amours;* chronicles of wanton women and female sexual lasciviousness in *The Arraignment of Lewd Women* and *Aristole's Last Legacy;* and bawdy poems and songs in *The Compleat Academy of Complements, London Jests,* and *Cambridge Jests*. Franklin did not run another ad with such erotic variety. The Great Awakening made piety, not bawdry, popular in the early 1740s. By the summer of 1740, just months after he had advertised these erotic imports, Franklin himself noted this shift in interest in texts in the *Pennsylvania Gazette*. "No Books are in Request but those of Piety and Devotion; and instead of Songs and Ballads, the People are every where entertaining themselves with Psalms, Hymns and Spiritual Songs." While Franklin almost certainly con-

18. [James Rivington], *A Catalogue of Books, Sold by Rivington and Brown . . .* ([Philadelphia], 1762). Rivington advertised *The Indiscreet Jewels* as *The Indiscreet Toys*. For an analysis of the social and political critique contained therein, see Aram Vartanian, introduction, in Sophie Hawkes, trans., *The Insdiscreet Jewels* (New York, 1993). "Cloister," in *PG*, May 10, 1764, advertised by Rivington and Brown. *Venus in the Cloister* was among the most explicit sexual texts circulating in eighteenth-century France and Britain and is usually classified as pornographic because of its candor. "The Cloister: Containing the Amours of Sainfroid, a Jesuit and Eulalia, a Nun, from the French," was advertised for sale in Robert Bell, *A Catalogue of a Large Collection of New and Old Books . . .* (Philadelphia, 1783).

tinued to import some erotic texts for sale, he had misjudged the moment when open advertisement of erotica would be received enthusiastically.[19]

Tench Francis's advertisement of the books he imported suggests that the full range of erotic texts available in Europe made their way to Philadelphia after midcentury, and probably before. In July 1754 he advertised books from classical Greek and Roman erotica, such as Ovid's *Art of Love;* Restoration satire employing sex and politics, like John Oldham's "Upon the Author of the Play Call'd Sodom"; French erotica, such as Sir Roger L'Estrange's translation of *Lettres portugaises traduites en françois* (as *Portuguese Love Letters*); exposés of the French aristocracy in such works as *The Secret Memoirs of the Duke and Dutchess of Orleans;* Grub Street bawdry by writers such as Tom Brown; and, finally, salacious true crime literature such as *Lives of the Convicts.* Given the range of materials advertised in the city's newspapers, one must imagine that

19. *The Night Walker; or, Evening Rambles in Search after Lewd Women* . . . (London, 1697) consisted of a series of exposés of the lives of London prostitutes.

Franklin's ads: *PG,* Feb. 7, 1740; quotation from *PG,* June 12, 1740. The expansion of Franklin's printing business relied on religious materials generated by Whitefield and other revival preachers in the early 1740s. See Frank Lambert, " 'Pedlar in Divinity': George Whitefield and the Great Awakening, 1737–1745," *Journal of American History,* LXXVII (1990–1991), 812–837.

This shift in popular interest was reflected in early Philadelphia newspapers as well. The *American Weekly Mercury,* which had sporadically reprinted humorous tall tales about London prostitution, English aristocratic bastardy, and Scottish adultery from the London papers during the 1720s and 1730s, shied away from sexual humor after 1740. As circulation of the city's newspapers expanded beyond the elite and as religious revival encouraged piety, humorous and bawdy sexual content receded from its pages.

Periodic use of sexual humor reprinted from London papers in the city's early colonial newspapers (particularly *AWM*) had been used to recruit subscribers. But it did not signal the full-scale adoption of the bawdy into Philadelphia's print culture. Such material was relatively sparse, slipping out of fashion in the 1740s. Early in the eighteenth century the circulation of newspapers was limited to well-to-do readers, the target audience for the humorous reporting of British sex news. These were the same readers that had access to imported print materials. The shift in publication of sexual humor to a broad, multiclass audience did not take place until after midcentury. Unlike Andrew Bradford, the editor of the *American Weekly Mercury,* Benjamin Franklin tended not to reprint humor about sexuality in *PG,* choosing to highlight gender conflict as his humorous theme instead. See *AWM,* 1719–1746; *PG,* 1728–1800. For examples of early sexual humor from British papers, see *AWM,* June 2, 1726 (on Scottish adultery), Jan. 15, 1734 (gentleman's bastardy tale), Oct. 29, 1730 (raid on London houses of prostitution).

the more explicit English and French texts, including *Memoirs of a Woman of Pleasure*, were sold under the counter in midcentury.[20]

The difference, beginning in the 1760s, was that bawdy and erotic print material became available to men and women of all but the lowest classes through its incorporation into locally produced almanacs, an increase in the importation of books, and (by the 1770s) Philadelphia reprints of the most popular European texts. Before midcentury not only the price but also the small volume of imported books confined readership of erotic material to the economic elite. By the 1760s the city's booksellers were widely advertising erotic texts in the city's newspapers and their book catalogs, and their popularity led the printer-booksellers to bring bawdy sexual content into the local print culture. Erotica and bawdy humor were adopted into Philadelphia's popular culture.

By the 1760s Philadelphia's printer-booksellers were competing with one another for the imported erotica market. For instance, William Dunlap advertised *The English Rogue* and *The Irish Rogue*, and William Bradford responded by advertising *The English Rogue* and *The French Rogue*, *The London Bawd*, and

20. *PG*, July 18, 1754, "Just Imported from London, and to be sold by Tench Francis, Jun." This advertisement also listed "school of woman" for sale. This might have been the English translation of Nicolas Chorier's notoriously pornographic novel *L'académie des dames*, known by the English title *School of Women*, or François Génard's newly translated novel *The School of Woman; or, Memoirs of Constantia* (London, 1753). The works of Tom Brown were also advertised by Rivington and Brown for sale: *PG*, Aug. 25, 1763.

Philadelphia's booksellers were more cautious in their advertisement of the century's most infamous English erotic novel, John Cleland's *Memoirs of a Woman of Pleasure: The Life of Fanny Hill*, first published in 1748–1749. Short, oblique references to it appear in the newspapers and catalogs during the 1760s, advertising it as "Memoirs of ——," "Ditto Fanny," or simply "Fanny in 2 vols." Cleland did publish an expurgated version entitled *Memoirs of Fanny Hill* in one volume in 1750. The original was twice as long, in two volumes. The short-title references giving "Fanny" and "2 vols." indicated the longer, explicitly erotic version. See *PG*, June 28, 1764, books for sale by Rivington and Brown; *PJ*, Jan. 8, 1756, books for sale by William Bradford (running weekly from January through May 1756, and again from September 1756 through January 1757); William Bradford's *Catalogue of Books* for 1760; and *Father Abraham's Almanack for 1760*, books for sale by the publisher. *Memoirs of a Woman of Pleasure* was also apparently printed in Philadelphia in 1806 (John Tate to Mathew Carey, July 8, 1806, HSP). Tate complained that Carey's type had been used to print "The Memoirs of a Woman of Pleasure, Other Wise Called Hannah Hill and the Abomible plates are Ingraved in this city."

The London Spy. These were sexual adventure stories following the intrigues of notorious prostitutes and libidinous rogues. Books such as *The English Rogue* allowed readers to vicariously engage in male sexual freedom in a fictional world of never-ending sexual opportunity. Philadelphia readers were introduced to the erotic journeys of characters such as Meriton Latroon, a man happy to attain sexual pleasure through the most calculated chicanery. Latroon's exploits provided readers with the ideal male sexual fantasies of the day.[21] He takes maidenheads aplenty, seduces married women, and enjoys haremlike sexual encounters with groups of women. Avoiding graphic descriptions of sexual mechanics, the narrative creates an erotic charge nonetheless. Recounting one of his earliest sexual intrigues, Latroon writes, "I am sure for our part we slept but little, for it was the first time that I ever enjoyed a woman naked in my arms all night, and I was ravished with delight, never having had so much pleasure." Latroon's earlier sexual encounters all occur in haste and in secret, to avoid the intrusion of protective parents. But this time his companion is a sexual adventurer like himself traveling with two other women, whom he also enjoys en masse before they part:

> And now we all thought of removing to London, but one night more we lay at our old quarters, where we had the greatest frolic I was ever guilty of, for that night I kissed with all three of the women, and pleased them round, by giving each of them a trial of my skill. . . . I thought myself to be as brave a fellow as the great Turk in his Seraglio, he having but his choice of women, which I now enjoyed to my full content.

Later in his life Latroon travels to the Far East, experiencing the sexual paradise it held for early modern imaginations. Here local sexual customs, readers

21. *Father Abraham's Almanack for 1760*, "Books . . . Just Imported from London and to be sold by the Printer"; [William Bradford], *Catalogue of Books* (Philadelphia, [1760]); *PJ*, Nov. 17, 1763, for sale by William Bradford.

The English Rogue was written during the mid-seventeenth century and enjoyed great popularity in Britain for the next century, going through at least twenty-four printings and generating numerous copycat look-alikes. The first section of the *English Rogue* was written by Richard Head in 1665, and the second, third, and fourth sections by Francis Kirkman in 1671. See Roger Thompson, *Unfit for Modest Ears: A Study of Pornographic, Obscene, and Bawdy Works Written or Published in England in the Second Half of the Seventeenth Century* (Totowa, N.J., 1979), 80. *The English Rogue* was advertised in *PG*, Feb. 7, 1740, Franklin; *PG*, Jan. 6, 1742, John Barkley; *Father Abraham's Almanack for 1760*, "Books . . . Just Imported," Dunlap; *PJ*, Nov. 17, 1763, William Bradford.

are to believe, give husbands total authority, allowing them to bring home young women to share their marital chambers without suffering their wives' complaints. Latroon himself, not surprisingly, adopts these customs, taking a "Moorish" wife. "Though my bedfellow was not fair, yet she was young and pleasant, and so far from jealousy that she herself sometimes would procure me a young girl, the fairest in the country, to lie with me, and she also lying by me and taking much pleasure therein." What could be more pleasing to the male sexual imagination than a wife who enjoyed, even facilitated, the wide-ranging sexual experiences of her husband? If, however, this sexual fantasy was not to the reader's liking, *The English Rogue* presented other, equally erotic scenes, with force and trickery at the center of sexual experience. Latroon, for instance, gains entry into a woman's bed (and more) by pretending to be a woman. He succeeds in amours with married women by tricking them into believing that he is their husband. Tricked, these women are nevertheless pleased by Latroon's sexual performance after they have been treated to it. Even when Latroon is held up by a female cross-dressing thief who has assumed a male identity, the encounter is resolved by their sexual union, to her supposed pleasure.[22]

In sexual adventure novels the narrative aim was to excite the reader with anticipation of the sexual encounter. In the encounter with the cross-dressing female robber, the tension of the scene was created by informing the reader of her gender before Latroon begins his groping search for stolen treasure and by employing language reminiscent of a rape. Having pulled the robber from his-her horse and pinned him-her to the ground, Latroon demands, "Yield, or I shall compel you." After "much reluctancy" the robber complied.

With cords I had ready for that purpose, I tied both his hands and feet, and so fell to rifling him. Unbuttoning his doublet to find whether there was no gold quilted therein, I wondered to see a pair of breasts so unexpectedly greater and whiter than any man's; but being intent about my business, that amazement vanished from my thoughts. Then did I come to his breeches (which I laid open) my curious search omitted not any place wherein I might suspect the concealment of moneys. At last proffering to remove his shirt from between his legs, he suddenly cried out (and strove to lay his hand there, but could not) "I beseech you, sir, be civil," said he. I imagining

22. Richard Head and Francis Kirkman, *The English Rogue, Described in the Life of Meriton Latroon, A Witty Extravagant: Being a Complete History of the Most Eminent Cheats of Both Sexes* (London, 1928), 276, 353–354.

that some notable treasure lay there obscured, I pulled up his shirt (alias smock) and found myself not much mistaken.

This teasing erotic scene was common English bawdry of the day, and by 1760 Philadelphia booksellers openly promoted such texts to bring readers into their shops.[23]

New styles of advertising made the salacious content of books a selling point. Transplanted London bookseller James Rivington was pivotal in opening up the book trade to a broad readership by ignoring copyright patents, drawing on the Scottish and Irish reprint trade, and selling books at reduced prices. He also employed sexual allure to attract readers and highlighted British social fashions and vices. Rather than following the customary Philadelphia booksellers' practice of long advertisements stating the short title of each new book from London, Rivington annotated his advertisements and featured particular texts to entice buyers into his shop. Others, like veteran booksellers David Hall and William Bradford, soon followed his lead.[24]

When Rivington advertised the voyeuristic chronicle of famous adultery trials, *Adultery Anatomised,* in the *Pennsylvania Journal* in February 1762, he left the reader with no doubt about the book's erotic content. He highlighted it by devoting a paragraph to it, centered and offset from the rest of the ad:

Adultery Anatomized;
A Collection of Trials for Criminal Conversation, brought down from the infant Age of Cuckoldom in *England,* to its full Growth in the present Time, Containing, amongst others, the following, The Trials of Capt. Gambies, and Admiral K——; of Mr. Sloper, with Mr. Cibber; Lord A——g——s F——z——, with Sir William Morris; Lord B——d, and Mr. Rochford; the Dutchess of Cleveland against her Husband, Lord Fielding, etc. etc. etc.

23. Ibid., 153.

24. Rivington opened his Philadelphia bookstore Dec. 4, 1760, and adopted a descriptive advertising style from the outset (see *PJ,* Dec. 11, 1760, Jan. 22, 29, Apr. 2, Dec. 10, 1761). For the new descriptive advertisement style adopted by Hall and Bradford, see *PG,* Mar. 19, 1761, David Hall; *PJ,* Nov. 10, 1763, William Bradford. For examples of typical colonial short-title book advertisements, see *PJ,* Jan. 21, 1751, June 7, 1759, William Bradford; *PG,* Feb. 22, 1759, David Hall. James N. Green documents Rivington's general role in expanding the book trade of the mid-Atlantic in the early 1760s in "The Book Trade in the Middle Colonies," in Amory and Hall, eds., *A History of the Book in America,* I, 279–283.

The reader understood this book contained not only narratives of extramarital sexual adventures but also an insider's view of the intrigues of English aristocrats.[25]

Booksellers also advertised their wares in book catalogs, both free and posted in their shop windows. Here too sexual exploits solicited buyers. Rivington's first catalog, in 1762, highlighted the sexually titillating aspects of the books. His *Catalogue of Books* began with a lengthy, two-page ad for the *Connoisseur,* which contained "a Collection of elegant Essays and Writings upon the Modern Manners, Customs, Virtues, and Vices of Mankind, written with infinite Vivacity." Readers were promised that they would learn about "Two pretty Letters from a pretty Miss in Breeches, and from a Blood in Pettycoats." They would be introduced to the vices of the English theater by reading "An humerous Survey of the Audience at the Play, the Behaviour of Persons in the Boxes, Pitt, Gallery, of the Ladies of Pleasure, and of the fine Gentlemen on the Stage." Rivington's annotated entry for *The New Atalantis; or, The Secret History of Several Persons of Quality* informed potential readers that this book lay at the edge of decency, as it was "written with vast Freedom, which occasioned the Author to be imprisoned." Readers might buy *The New Atalantis* simply to find out what Mrs. Manley had written about "Persons of Quality" in England that was deemed so unacceptable. Ned Ward's *Nuptial Dialogues and Debates* promised "Fops, Coquets, Bullies, Jilts, fond Fools and Wantons, old Fumblers, Barren Ladies, Misers, Parsimonious Wives, Ninies, Sluts and Termagants, Drunken Husbands, Toping Gossips"; and *The Devil upon Crutches* would provide the reader with "Humerous Satire upon the Vices of our own Mother Country." By the 1770s Rivington was capitalizing on the interest in lowbrow literature by promising that his new weekly newspaper would include reviews and excerpts of books "from the Garrets of GRUBB-STREET."[26]

Each of the books Rivington promoted had been imported, advertised, and sold in Philadelphia for years, but enticing readers to buy these books by flaunting their sexual content was new. His assumption that Philadelphians would welcome greater access to bawdy books about scandals in British high and low culture proved correct. Philadelphians read with interest the illict

25. *PJ*, Feb. 4, 1762.

26. [Rivington], *A Catalogue of Books* (1762); *PC*, Feb. 22, 1773. In 1773 Rivington was no longer operating a bookstore in Philadelphia, but sought Philadelphia readers for his new periodical published in New York.

sexual escapades of the well-to-do, such as Eliza Haywood's *Invisible Spy,* Mrs. Manley's *New Atalantis, Illustrious French Lovers,* and the *Connoisseur.*[27]

The witty periodical the *Connoisseur* was very popular. Originally a weekly from 1754 to 1756, it was soon published as a four-volume set and imported to Philadelphia regularly thereafter, providing readers with humorous commentary on England's fashionable vices of the upper classes and targeting men and women who had adopted a life of licentious pleasure seeking. Readers learned of a new order of women called "demi-reps" that had emerged at the top of English society. Once married, these women discarded modesty and propriety and gave in to the "unbounded licence of their enjoyment," especially sexual intrigues and adulteries. Adopting the ways of high-class "courtesans" and French persons of quality, they were separated from prostitutes only by their wealth and status as married women.[28]

Philadelphia's readers also read commentary on English middle-class debauchees as well as aristocratic rakes in the *Connoisseur.* Such men engaged in fashionable "frolicks," "playing the most wild and extravagant pranks, that wantonness and debauchery can suggest." Mr. Town, the *Connoisseur's* narrator, described English "men of the town" whose usual amusement, known as "beating the rounds," involved touring bawdyhouses, rioting therein, and undertaking "a rape on a modest woman." The *Connoisseur* employed a sarcas-

27. *The Invisible Spy* was published in London in 1755 and was for sale in Philadelphia by May 1755. It was advertised in *PJ,* May 8, 15, 22, Aug. 7, Sept. 4, 11 (and next four weeks), 1755, Jan. 8, 1756, and each week in January, February, March, April, and May, 1756, Bradford; *PG,* July 4, 1765, Hall; [Bradford], *Catalogue of Books* (1760); *Father Abraham's Almanack for 1760,* "Books . . . Just Imported," Dunlap; [Rivington], *A Catalogue of Books* (1762); *Robert Bell's Sale Catalogue . . .* (Philadelphia, 1773).

Mary De La Riviere Manley, *Secret Memoirs and Manners of Several Persons of Quality of Both Sexes, from the New Atalantis. The New Atalantis* was advertised in *PG,* May 25, 1738, Feb. 7, 1740, Franklin; *PJ,* Jan. 21, 29, Feb. 19, 26, Mar. 5, 12, 1751, Bradford; *PG,* Mar. 19, 1761, Hall; *PG,* Nov. 18, 25, Dec. 2, 1762, Dunlap; [Rivington], *A Catalogue of Books* (1762). In *Robert Bell's Sale Catalogue* (1773), the four-volume set was priced at twelve shillings.

Illustrious French Lovers: Being the True Histories of the Amours of Several French Persons of Quality was advertised by Hall in *PG,* Mar. 14, Apr. 5, 16, May 12, Aug. 4, Oct. 12, Dec. 19, 1748, Feb. 5, 1750, May 30, June 13, 20, Dec. 10, 1751, Mar. 19, 1761; by Bradford in *PJ,* Oct. 25, 1750, Jan. 22, Feb. 19, 26, Mar. 5, 1751, July 17, Sept. 11, Nov. 10, 1760, [Bradford], *Catalogue of Books* (1760).

28. *Connoisseur* (Oxford, 1767), I, 46–51.

PLATE 5. *William Hogarth,* The Tavern Scene. *1735. Plate 3 of* A Rake's Progress. *Permission Colonial Williamsburg Foundation*

tic wit that simultaneously ridiculed and embraced the licentious fashions it described.[29]

Philadelphians demonstrated their interest in the *Connoisseur* by making it a consistent seller during the late 1750s and the 1760s. Imported and advertised annually in the city's newspapers by David Hall and James Rivington from its inception in 1757 Tuntil the middle of the 1760s, it was also advertised in the catalogs of William Bradford, William Dunlap, and James Rivington in the early 1760s, and by Robert Bell in 1773. It was held by the city's lending libraries and would be reprinted in a Philadelphia edition in 1803.[30]

29. Ibid., 100–103.

30. The *Connoisseur* was advertised in *PG* by Hall, Rivington, and Bell at least nineteen times between 1757 and 1778 as well as in *PJ* by Bradford; and in [Bradford],

Books that explored the seedy underbelly of English culture, particularly wicked London, also flourished after midcentury. *The Sisters; or, The History of Lucy and Caroline Sanson* presented London as a place where every woman might be "a bawd ready to entrap and betray you" and "every man you behold . . . is a debauched rake," who "already in his heart has committed fornication with you." Here the innocent, unsuspecting young woman who ventured alone to London would be debauched at a masquerade or seduced into prostitution—the fate that befell Lucy. Works such as *The Sisters* incorporated references to well-known Hogarth prints to enhance the visual image of illicit sex for the reader. Lucy's seduction and initiation into prostitution take place in the setting of the third plate from Hogarth's *Rake's Progress*.

> It was not long before the company was compleated, and every lad had his lass; the bowl was pushed briskly around, *Lucy* forgot her former fears, and a sad heart for the mad moment was not found amidst the jocund band.
>
> Deceive not thyself, reader, with the vain expectations, that we shall record in this our history the whole behavior and conversation of this company; their indecencies, of course, became too shocking, and their midnight revels too infamous to be related. The man of pleasure knows them, and knowing them, let him reflect, and must he not detest them? Thou, who, happy for thee, art unexperienced in such iniquity, hast thou never seen that inimitable representation of such a society, in one of the pictures of that moral master, and child of fancy, the excellent *Hogarth,* where the young heir, in happy drunkenness, lolls, with his ladies around him; some of whom, drunk like himself, are venting their fury one at the other, the remainder otherwise laudably employ'd in the several branches of their mystick occupation? Having seen that, thou may'st have some faint rememblance of this wretched company.[31]

The Sisters was first imported to Philadelphia in 1754, the year it was published in England, and was still advertised for sale by each of the city's major

---

Catalogue of Books (1760); Weatherwise, *Father Abraham's Almanack for 1760,* "Books . . . Just Imported," Dunlap; [Rivington], *A Catalogue of Books* (1762); *Robert Bell's Sale Catalogue* (1773). The *Connoisseur* was held by the Library Company of Philadelphia by 1765 and by Bradford's Circulating Library when it opened in late 1769. It was reprinted by Samuel Bradford in Philadelphia in 1803. It was advertised by Bell for three shillings in 1773.

31. [William Dodd], *The Sisters; or, The History of Lucy and Caroline Sanson . . .* (London, 1754), 21–22, 198–199.

PLATE 6. *William Hogarth,* The Quarrel with Her Jew Protector. *1734. Plate 2 of*
A Harlot's Progress. *Charlotte, a woman turned prostitute, acts out the scene from the*
second plate of Harlot's Progress, *in* The Sisters *when she "kicked down, with her angry*
foot, the whole tea-table" and left her lover. Permission Colonial Williamsburg Foundation

booksellers in the 1760s. Booksellers also supplied literate Philadelphians
with an insider's view of the London sexual underworld in books that took the
reader on a guided tour of London's illicit haunts, such as Ned Ward's *London
Spy* and *The Devil upon Crutches; or, Night Scenes in London,* and in criminal
trial reports such as *Select Trials at . . . the Old-Bailey* and *The Lives of the Most
Remarkable Criminals.*[32]

Trial reports, such as *Select Trials at the Old-Bailey,* used the guise of court

32. *The Sisters* was advertised in *PG,* July 18, 1754, Tench Francis; *PJ,* July 17, Sept. 11,
1760, William Bradford; *PG,* Mar. 19, 1761, David Hall; [Bradford], *Catalogue of Books*
(1760); Weatherwise, *Father Abraham's Almanack for 1760,* "Books . . . Just Imported,"
Dunlap; [Rivington], *A Catalogue of Books* (1762).

The London Spy was advertised in *PG,* Jan. 6, 1742, John Barkley; *PJ,* Nov. 17, 1763,

proceedings to assume a more legitimate air than erotic novels but published the prurient details of seduction, rape, and sodomitical intrigue. Because *Select Trials* was published in the form of court transcripts based on actual trials, it succeeded in presenting explicit descriptions of the mechanics of sexual behavior without becoming infamous. Descriptions of rape and sodomy included details of sexual position, penetration, and observers' views of these events. Erotic descriptions of couples watching men in the act of sodomy and testimony of women forced to engage in intercourse were written to take the reader through the behaviors described. The testimony of women such as Elizabeth London, who describes how an acquaintance sneaked into her bed after an evening of drunken merriment and entered her body, was written for the erotic titillation of the reader, not to elicit outrage at the assault done to her. Sexual storytelling, not revelations of criminal violence, was the point of these narratives. *The Lives of the Most Remarkable Criminals,* advertised in Philadelphia as *Lives of the Convicts,* took a more expansive look at the lives and subculture of the criminal element, but this too led to sexual storytelling. Mary Standford appears in *Lives of the Criminals,* the chapter title tells us, as "a Pick-Pocket and Thief." But her story centers on her life as a London prostitute who combines streetwalking with thievery to make her living until her career is cut short by her execution at Tyburn. *Select Trials* and *Lives of the Most Remarkable Criminals* did include appropriate condemnatory introductions, but they were clearly intended to satisfy a voyeuristic gaze into sexual experience.[33]

William Bradford; *PG,* Aug. 25, 1763, Rivington and Brown; *PG,* Nov. 19, 1783, David Hall; [Bradford], *Catalogue of Books* (1760); [Rivington], *A Catalogue of Books* (1762).

The London Spy was typical early-eighteenth-century bawdry. Much of its appeal came from exposing the realistic, if exaggerated, grimy, smelly, and vulgar side of London often inhabited by the lower classes. It used coarse language and vivid description of the sexual underworld of London, from sadomasochistic flogging and sodomy to sex play with prostitutes. The spy genre, or insider's view, of the illicit side of English culture remained popular throughout eighteenth-century England and Philadelphia. But by midcentury the tone had become less vulgar. The Devil upon Crutches; or, Night Scenes in London (1750) was just as much of an exposé but used cleaned-up language.

Philadelphia booksellers imported and advertised the London Spy from the 1740s through the 1780s, whereas the Devil upon Crutches was a hit during the 1760s and 1770s.

33. The Lives of the Most Remarkable Criminals, Who Have Been Condemn'd and Executed; for Murder, Highway, House-Breakers, Street-Robberies, Coining, or Other Offences; From the year 1720, to the Present Time . . . , 3 vols. (London, 1735), I, 283–290.

For examples of this voyeuristic narrative structure, see the testimony of Elizabeth

Philadelphia's readers eagerly took a look. Philadelphia booksellers imported and advertised *Select Trials* from the 1740s through the 1780s. The volumes were owned by the lending libraries, the Library Company of Philadelphia, the Union Library Company, and the Association Library Company by 1765. People did not shy away from acknowledging ownership or readership of the books. The Library Company turned to newspaper ads to solicit the books' return when they had difficulty getting patrons to bring them back, as did individuals who had lent out their copies. *Lives of the Convicts* was also available at the Association Library and was offered for sale during the 1750s and 1760s.[34]

Many of the most popular books imported and sold in pre-Revolutionary Philadelphia invited the reader to take an imaginary erotic journey. Those written as trial proceedings or within the secret spy genre structured voyeurs into the texts, modeling a voyeuristic relationship to sex for the reader. Not

---

London, who describes sexual intercourse for the court, and the descriptions of John Dicks's sodomy with John Meeson, in *Select Trials at the Sessions-House in the Old-Bailey, for Murder, Robberies, Rapes, Sodomy, Coining, Frauds, Bigamy, and Other Offences*, 4 vols. [London, 1742], III, 234–237, I, 158–160, respectively. *Select Trials* also gave the reader vivid descriptions of local customs, such as playful banter or sexual teasing of drunken men and women (III, 237).

34. Book advertisements for *Select Trials at the Old-Bailey* were run in *PG* by David Hall on Oct. 12, Dec. 19, 1749, Dec. 10, 1751; by Dunlap and Company on Dec. 29, 1763; by Mathew Carey on May 14, 1788; by Dunlap in Weatherwise, *Father Abraham's Almanack for 1760*; and in [Rivington], *Catalogue of Books* (1762); it was included in *The Charter, Laws, and Catalogue of Books, of the Library Company of Philaelphia* (Philadelphia, 1764); *A Catalogue of Books, Belonging to the Union Library Company of Philadelphia* (Philadelphia, 1765); and *A Catalogue of Books, Belonging to the Association Library Company of Philadelphia* (Philadelphia, 1765). Advertisements requesting its return were placed on Mar. 7, 1738, by an individual (for the earlier two-volume *Proceedings*); as overdue to the Library Company, *PG*, Oct. 23, 1766, *PP*, Apr. 24, 1784, *PG*, Feb. 7, 1789, and by the Association Library, *PG*, Oct. 23, 1766. It was added to the Library Company's holdings sometime between 1757 and 1765. *Lives of the Most Remarkable Criminals* was advertised as *Lives of the Convicts*, and as *Convicts, an Account of the Most Remarkable That Have Suffered for Murder, Robbery etc. 3 vols*, by the Association Library Company: *PG*, Nov. 1, 1753, Feb. 5, 1754, Jan. 21, 1755, Hall; *PG*, July 18, 1754, Francis; *A Catalogue of Books, Belonging to the Association Library Company* (1765); Inventory Book of William and Thomas Bradford, Nov. 14, 1767, HSP. There was another three-volume criminal biography that these ads might have been referring to, *A Select and Impartial Account of the Lives, Behavior, and Dying-Words, of the Most Remarkable Convicts, from the Year 1700, down to the Present Time . . .* (London, 1745).

only were readers viewing illicit sexual behavior, but the stories were often narrated by characters watching the scenes from within the text, peeking from behind a curtain or keyhole or meandering through brothels and bedrooms. *The Devil upon Crutches; or, Night Scenes in London* exemplified this voyeuristic narrative structure and was a favorite among midcentury Philadelphians.

In *The Devil upon Crutches,* the devil takes a young Oxford college student on a nocturnal tour of London to view, behind a screen of invisibility, the vice that has overtaken the city. The devil narrates the scenes they encounter, explaining the shocking scenarios to the uninitiated youth, and to the reader, as they tour London's famous haunts. They enter the chambers of husbands with their whores, daughters with their footmen, artisans and apprentices with their doxies, and clergymen engaged in amours with their parishioners. They hover unobserved as they tour all the notorious neighborhoods and institutions of the sexual underworld: Newgate prison, Bedlam insane asylum (Bethlehem Royal Hospital), the London Foundling Hospital, theaters of Drury Lane and Covent Garden, and the city's numerous brothels. They peer into the world of prostitution, undertaking a "survey of the City —— Whores" that moves from brothel "strumpets" to the homes of ladies, noblemen, merchants, and lawyers, revealing little difference in the sexual habits of brothel prostitutes and members of the city's respectable classes.

A wide range of literate Philadelphians were interested in these exposés and undertook this literary imaginary journey. *The Devil upon Crutches,* published in London in 1750, was initially advertised for sale in Philadelphia in late 1759, taking on a new popularity with the publication of three new editions in that year. Philadelphia booksellers Dunlap, Rivington, and Hall each advertised the new editions throughout the 1760s, as did John Sparhawk and William Woodhouse in 1770 and 1773. The price of *Devil upon Crutches* put it within reach of Philadelphia's merchants, shopkeepers, and master craftsmen, who could afford to spend five or six shillings on the two volumes. Many of them might also have purchased the lengthier, four-volume *Connoisseur,* for about twelve shillings, to explore the vices of English metropolitan culture.[35]

35. *The Devil upon Crutches; or, Night Scenes in London* advertised: *PG,* Nov. 15, 1759, John Bleakley; *PG,* Mar. 19, 1761, Apr. 28, Sept. 1, 1763, July 4, 1765, David Hall; *PG,* Aug. 3, 1770, Edward Role; *PG,* Apr. 21, 1773, William Woodhouse; *PC,* Dec. 3, 1770, John Sparhawk; Weatherwise, *Father Abraham's Almanack for 1760,* "Books . . . Just Imported," Dunlap; [Rivington], *A Catalogue of Books* (1762); Bell, *A Catalogue of New and Old Books* (1783).

William Bradford paid 5s. 6d. for the two-volume set of *Devil upon Crutches* in 1767,

All but the least expensive imported books were out of reach for most journeymen, apprentices, day laborers, and female domestics, but the desire for popular fiction stretched beyond those who could afford to purchase the latest imports from London. By the late 1760s interest in books like *The Devil upon Crutches* led printer-booksellers to create new methods of making books available to more patrons. Demand for popular print material, coupled with periodic disruptions in the importation of English books due to the non-importation agreements, pushed those in the book trade to produce their own reprints of the most popular books. Domestic reprints reached their colonial-era peak in the five years before the Revolution. *The Devil upon Crutches* was just the sort of book that would appeal to a broad audience, if priced cheaply. As printer William Evitt declared in his 1772 advertisement, his sale price undercut the imports by more than half. "This day published and sold . . . (priced only two shillings, the English edition sold at five shillings) The DEVIL UPON CRUTCHES." Two shillings was the cost of a pair of men's stockings. Accompanying the devil through the night haunts of London was now much more feasible for Philadelphians of the middling to moderate classes. Printers increasingly took the economic and legal risk of producing Philadelphia reprints of English books.[36]

4s. 6d. two years later in 1769. The four volumes of the *Connoisseur* cost him 12s. in 1767, and 9s. in 1769. Robert Bell was selling the *Connoisseur* for 3s. a volume in 1773, *Devil upon Crutches* for $1.00 in 1783. Book prices are based on William and Thomas Bradford's Invoice Book for 1767–1769, and Inventory Book for Nov. 14, 1767; *Robert Bell's Sale Catalogue* (1773); and Bell, *A Catalogue of New and Old Books* (1783).

36. *PJ*, Apr. 9, 1772. During the late 1760s and early 1770s small-format imported books cost booksellers between 4s. 6d. and 5s. for a two-volume set, and 12s. for a four-volume set. Philadelphians could expect to spend between 5s. and 15s. for these texts, depending on the size and quality.

These books were possible luxury purchases for master craftsmen, but difficult for journeymen or apprentices. Billy Smith estimates that a fully employed master cord-wainer (shoemaker) earned £74–£89 a year in 1774 and a master tailor earned £100. The cost of basic necessities during the 1770s was approximately £64, so books could be indulged in. But the journeymen under their charge earned barely enough to make ends meet, with fully employed journeymen cordwainers earning £58 and journeymen tailors £62 annually. Purchases of books must have been difficult for these men. Smith, *The "Lower Sort,"* 117–121, 106 (stocking prices).

On domestic reprints, see Green, "The Book Trade in the Middle Colonies," in Amory and Hall, eds., *A History of the Book in America*, I, 285–295. Sexual exposés of both high and low British culture were good candidates for cheap reprints that would

Seeking to tap into this new readers' market, Philadelphia bookseller Thomas Bradford opened a general circulating library in the fall of 1769. Stocked with his most popular fiction, the library charged the general public six pence for a week of borrowing privileges. Patrons usually returned their books within two to three days, and many borrowed and read several books in a week. The subscription libraries also made their volumes available to non-members for a fee. The Library Company of Philadelphia, the nation's oldest subscription library, charged nonmembers between four and eight pence a week for books from its extensive holdings.[37]

Philadelphia's four lending libraries before the Revolution, a dramatic increase in the importation of books after midcentury, the initiation of a successful reprint trade, and a rising literacy rate gave a broad range of Philadelphians access to popular print material.[38] The patron lending list for Bradford's cir-

---

be good sellers, like *The Devil upon Crutches. The Trial of His R.H. the D[uke] of C.[umberland] for Criminal Conversation with Lady Harriet G[rosveno]r* . . . was reprinted by John Dunlap in late October 1770, and by printer William Evitt in mid-November in an edition that he and bookseller William Woodhouse sold at only nine pence through November and December 1770. Advertisements for Philadelphia reprints of *The Trial* ran in *PG*, Nov. 1, 15, Dec. 27, 1770. Reprints of plays "as performed at the Theatre Royal in Drury Lane" were particularly popular and, as short pieces, could be sold cheaply to a broad audience.

37. Thomas Bradford, Day Book of Bradford's Circulating Library, 1771–1772, HSP. The library initially operated from his house in Second Street but moved at least twice. By 1772 Bradford was calling his library the General Circulating Library to emphasize that it was a public institution available to all patrons. Patrons were allowed one book at a time, but they could exchange it once during the week, or borrow books more frequently for a higher fee, as many apparently did (*PJ*, Oct. 26, 1769, Jan. 13, 1772, supplement). The Library Company also required nonmembers to leave a deposit as security for the book's return. Founded in 1731, the Library Company was the largest and most successful of the four libraries founded before the Revolution (*The Charter, Laws, and Catalogue of Books, of the Library Company of Philadelphia* [Philadelphia, 1764]). The Library Company's holdings included only a few novels before the mid-1760s.

38. Literacy increased over the course of the eighteenth century throughout British North America. Our best estimates suggest that the majority of white women and as many as 75–90 percent of white men could read by the American Revolution (Cathy N. Davidson, *Revolution and the Word: The Rise of the Novel in America* [New York, 1986], 55–61).

James Green establishes that the imported book trade increased dramatically in Philadelphia in the 1750s through the business practices of David Hall (who took over

culating library for 1771–1772 demonstrates that on the eve of the Revolution Philadelphians from many walks of life sought out books and participated in the growing print world around them. Innkeepers, sea captains, carpenters, clerks, shoemakers, shopkeepers, hatters, joiners, tanners, and bricklayers as well as men listed on the tax rolls as occupation "unknown" and rated at zero pounds because of their limited resources all borrowed and read the latest books. More than half the male readers using Bradford's circulating library in 1771 and 1772 did not appear on the 1772 tax list. Many of them were young men not yet financially independent, and others were men of little means, like John Dorsey, whose tax burden was abated because of his poverty. Women too availed themselves of Bradford's lending library. Of his patrons, more than 40 percent were women, many of them young, and most not yet wearing the title "Mrs."[39]

---

operation of Franklin's shop in 1758) and rose again in the early 1760s ("The History of the Book in the Middle Colonies," in Amory and Hall, eds., *A History of the Book in America*, I, 277–279). Stephen Botein, drawing on the work of Giles Barber, notes that the overall volume of books imported from London to the North American colonies increased by two and a half times in the 1750s, became oversaturated in the mid-1760s, and then doubled again in 1771 and 1772, during a lull in the imperial conflict. Botein, "The Anglo-American Book Trade before 1776: Personnel and Strategies," in William L. Joyce, David D. Hall, Richard D. Brown, and John B. Hench, eds., *Printing and Society in Early America* (Worcester, Mass., 1983), 80–81.

39. This analysis of Philadelphia readers is based on a six-week random sample of Bradford's Day Book, which runs from December 1771 through December 1772.

These men not on the tax list also failed to appear in the Philadelphia city directories for 1785, the first year such directories were published for the city. One can only speculate here, but it appears that these nontaxed men of 1772 had not attained high status by 1785. If they were young men in 1772, they were probably of middling or lower economic status. Had they been sons of established families, one would expect them to have grown into their adult professional status more than a decade later. They might also have left Philadelphia. *Macpherson's Directory, for the City and Suburbs of Philadelphia* . . . (Philadelphia, 1785); Francis White, *The Philadelphia Directory* (Philadelphia, 1785).

That more than half the women patrons are named without the title "Mrs." signifies their youth, probable single marital status, or Quaker heritage. Only a few female patrons can be identified: wives of middling or elite men (also library patrons), unmarried daughters of well-established families, and at least one well-off woman of independent means who headed her own household. But the majority are identified simply with a first and last name, and thus their social positions are difficult to establish.

Bradford's library intended to meet the needs of Philadelphians of modest means, and they flocked there. Most patrons paid by the week, few paying for more than two weeks at a time, suggesting that cash was in short supply for many of Bradford's readers. Some were regular borrowers, paying for library services and returning week after week. Others used the library intensively for short periods, seeking to get the most for their money by exchanging their books each day during the week they subscribed. The library did a steady business during 1772, lending 120–160 books a week in the winter and spring, and slightly fewer during the summer. Each week about one hundred Philadelphians borrowed from the library, with new customers coming in and old ones dropping. Bradford had correctly anticipated that interest in reading popular fiction was widespread beyond the well-to-do and middle-class book buyers. Midcentury Philadelphia readers were diverse, but they all shared a thirst for novels, intrigues, tall tales, sexual adventures, and sensational occurrences.[40]

Bradford's library made books available to a class of Philadelphians who had, in the past, been priced out of the imported book trade, and his selection catered to popular tastes. Bradford placed the *Connoisseur* among the circulating library stock, for readers such as innkeeper John Little to entertain themselves with, and bought two copies of *Devil upon Crutches*, believing it would be a frequent choice for readers. As with much eighteenth-century fiction, sexually suggestive titles enticed readers. Thus he stocked *Fair Adulteress, Nunnery for Coquets, Fortunate Footman,* and *Masquerade,* each suggesting the possibility of illicit sex. *Betty Thoughtless* and *Virtuous Orphans* relied on popular understanding of the sexual follies that might befall the unprotected young woman who let down her guard. *The Turkish Spy, Arabian Nights,* and *Persian Tales* promised exotic adventures and erotic oriental tales, and *Fanny; or, The Happy Repentant, Agreeable Magdalens,* and *Magdalen Penitents* suggested tales of female prostitutes, albeit ones who ultimately reformed.

Novels deriving their narrative tension from the sexual pursuit of a young

40. The Day Book does not include payment information for all patrons. In my sample, 84 percent of those patrons whose payment information we have paid either 6d. (for one week) or 1s. (for two weeks). Fewer than 5 percent paid 5s. 6d. or more, the price for quarterly privileges. Some patrons appear to have paid a rate of 1s. per week for unlimited borrowing privileges during that week. The sample indicates that Bradford had a core of perhaps 50–60 percent habitual library users but that as many as 40 percent of his customers were new each week. The volume of patronage remained fairly steady because these periodic users came and went, perhaps as their finances allowed.

woman were abundant and popular. Often closing the scene short of sexual fulfillment, either by the young woman's narrow escape or by drawing the curtain on sexual events, their plots centered on the possibility of male sexual conquest. The classic eighteenth-century novel of sexual pursuit was, of course, Samuel Richardson's *Pamela; or, Virtue Rewarded*, written for fluent readers and a popular choice at Bradford's library. But so were less-refined novels, like *The History of Sally Sable*, written in a plain, direct style that made it accessible to less-skilled readers. *Sally Sable* was the fifth novel Betsy Towers read during the week in March that she subscribed to Bradford's library, after the *Virtuous Orphan* and *The Old Maid*, before *The Husband*, her final selection of the week. Many of the readers of *Sally Sable* were women, who might have been drawn to the fairy-tale quality of the novel, which follows the life of a poor bastard-born girl, abandoned at birth, who becomes loved and admired for her exceptional beauty, innocence, and grace. Sally, of course, becomes irresistible to men of both high and low station as the novel proceeds from one intrigue or trap to another.[41]

Books themselves were understood to play an important role in sex education. Reading particular novels was depicted, within novels themselves, as an essential step in a young woman's sexual development. In *The Cry*, for instance, imported and sold in midcentury Philadelphia and borrowed from Bradford's library, the heroine's cousin instigates his seduction by encouraging her to read to awaken her passions. "Care was now taken by him that *Ovid*'s epistles should never be out of my reach; and there I was to learn that the wit and genius of *Sappho* consisted in the violence of her uncontrouled passions." *The Cry* was fairly tame, but it drew on the convention used by the most explicit English erotica of sexual instruction through reading classical texts and other erotic novels. Reading these fashionable novels of sexual pur-

41. *Pamela*, published in 1740, was a consistent seller in Philadelphia during the second half of the eighteenth century. Those of means purchased it, and many others, often women, borrowed it from Bradford's circulating library. Advertisements in the *Pennsylvania Gazette* appeared fourteen times, placed by eight booksellers, in the thirty years before the Revolution. Bradford stocked at least three copies (Bradford's Day Book); all the readers who checked it out during my sample were women. Six of the seven people who borrowed *Sally Sable* were women, three married and three single. The one man was of middling-low economic standing, rated at two pounds (the lowest tax rate) in 1772. *The History of Miss Sally Sable* was first published in London in 1757 and advertised for sale in Philadelphia in *PJ*, June 7, 1759, July 17, Sept. 11, 1760, Dec. 12, 1772, Bradford; [Bradford], *Catalogue of Books* (1760); Weatherwise, *Father Abraham's Almanack for 1760*, "Books . . . Just Imported," Dunlap.

suit, one Philadelphian opined, could weaken young women's resistance to sexual temptation, even when the heroines successfully avoided sexual downfall. In the *Pennsylvania Packet* in 1773 he reprimanded parents for allowing their daughters "to read indiscriminately the multiplicity of novels which are daily published."

> It is . . . a duty to attend to the books a young lady reads, as to the company she keeps; for if it is allowed, that the frequent hearing of loose conversation naturally prepares the mind for the admittance of vicious ideas, it cannot be denied but books, in which love is the only theme, and intrigues the sole business of the actors, are more dangerous than even bad company; since the recital of lascivious scenes might shock an ear not yet hardened in vice, when the warm representation painted in a novel, and read in the privacy of retirement, cannot fail in exciting desires, and leaving impure traces on the memory.[42]

The widespread consumption of novels and sexual exposés was an important component of the eroticization of popular culture in the fifteen years before the Revolution. Earlier in the century daughters and wives of well-to-do Philadelphians had certainly read widely from their fathers' and husbands' bookshelves. But, after midcentury, women from the moderate to upper classes sought out books of their own choosing, followed what was fashionable, and read extensively in many genres as they increasingly became available. The movement of sexually charged texts into a mixed-gender public sphere of readers from the top to the lower social classes evinces a communitywide transformation of popular culture. Erotic texts that had once safely circu-

42. Sarah Fielding, *The Cry: A New Dramatic Fable* (London, 1754), II, 267; "Character and Effects of Modern Novels," *PP*, Sept. 13, 1773; [Bradford], *Catalogue of Books* (1760). On reading as sexual instruction, see Robert Darnton, *The Forbidden Best-Sellers of Pre-Revolutionary France* (New York, 1995), esp. 295–299; Peter Wagner, *Eros Revived: Erotica of the Enlightenment in England and America* (London, 1988), 264, on visual erotica.

It is clear that some women used books as a source of information on sex, which helped them fashion an identity for themselves. English gentlewoman Anne Lister's secret diary demonstrates that Lister sought out classical texts for their descriptions of Sappho, as a source of information about her own sexuality. She fashioned her own identity through a dialectical process between textual representations of women who loved women and her own understanding of her same-sex desire. Anna Clark, "Anne Lister's Construction of Lesbian Identity," in Kim M. Phillips and Barry Reay, eds., *Sexualities in History: A Reader* (New York, 2002), 247–270.

lated only among the elite were brought into the open. Bawdy jokes and humorous tales, locally produced and imported, were distributed widely to readers through almanacs, plays, cheap fiction, newspapers, magazines, and novels. By the onset of the American Revolution the popular culture of Philadelphia had been transformed as men and women from all walks of life embraced the newly eroticized popular print culture, bringing many of them into the eighteenth-century pleasure culture, if only as readers.

Interpreting Sex: The Discursive Production of Sex

Midcentury Philadelphians also generated sex in popular print culture themselves. A close look at the representations of sex in the city's almanacs illuminates the cultural production Philadelphians themselves created during the quarter-century preceding the American Revolution. Almanac poems, ditties, and anecdotes presented a coherent vision of male and female sexuality and depicted sexual behavior in an expansive range of contexts. But, as we shall see, this discursive production of sex differed in striking ways from the evidence of social behavior of sexuality in self-divorce and bastardy. Although almanacs and other cheap imprints were written to appeal to a broad, mixed-gender reading public, they were produced primarily by men of the middling classes and in many ways reflect those interests in their representations of sex and gender. They obscured some aspects of sexual experience and highlighted others, as they built an intellectual framework through which to interpret the expanded sexual arenas of pre-Revolutionary Philadelphia.

Popular print representations of sex produced at midcentury contained many elements of the long-held beliefs in a one-body understanding of anatomy, with its gender continuum and essential similarities between men and women. But, by the 1760s and 1770s, these representations incorporated newer beliefs based on Enlightenment philosophy and scientific rationalism. What makes the locally produced images in Philadelphia almanacs so valuable is that they capture a worldview and understanding of gender and sexuality in transition between these two conceptual schemes. We can, therefore, see how ideas generated in scientific and medical discourse interacted with more popular conceptualizations of sexuality during this transformation. Most important, we can analyze the discursive work of these representations by comparing them to the social behavior of sexuality of the men and women of the city.

In eighteenth-century England, scientific and medical discourse was in the midst of a radical shift in the understanding of the body and its relationship to gender and sexuality. As Thomas Laqueur demonstrates, the one-body model of human anatomy had dominated from antiquity through the seventeenth century. The body was one fluid corporal economy with fungible fluids, called humors, that could transform from one substance to another. Male and female bodies were each made up of four humors (variously denominated): blood, choler, melancholy, and phlegm; with four aspects: cold, wet, hot, and dry. What made a person male or female and what drove sexual behavior were these humors and their characteristics. Men were men because of greater quantities of dry and hot humors, whereas women had more moist and cold humors. Men and women had a common physiological existence, which required the proper functioning of all four humors for health. Because humors were not fixed but could change from one substance to another, a person's character and even gender could be transformed. Men could slip toward the feminine if the proper humoral balance was not maintained, and women could become mannish; gender was where one stood on a continuum from male to female. Men and women had a common human anatomy, but men were deemed superior because they were thought to be the more fully developed, and more highly perfected, version of humanity. Even the reproductive organs shared an anatomical basis: female genitals were internal versions of male organs. Women, lacking the full heat of the more perfect male, had not developed external, more fully developed reproductive organs.[43]

The impetus to engage in sexual behavior was understood as a vital life force shared by men and women alike, and regular orgasm understood to be necessary for good health in both men and women. Orgasm evacuated humors in order to keep the body in balance. This was true in both men and women, because both produced semen and seed from a transformation of blood into male and female seed. Orgasm functioned like other forms of evacuation (excretion, salivation, perspiration, menstruation, and lactation) to regulate the bodily humors; it was central to the generation of new life, signaling the concoction of seed and its expulsion by both men and women into the female womb. Sexual desire was the result of the accumulation of semen in the body, generating sexual desire and requiring release. Sexual desire also increased the bodily heat necessary to expel male and female seed. In the one-body model, sexual desire and sexual satisfaction were essential to health and reproduction. Here too a gender hierarchy existed within the

43. Thomas Laqueur, *Making Sex: Body and Gender from the Greeks to Freud* (Cambridge, Mass., 1990). Each humor had two characteristics: blood was hot and moist; choler was hot and dry; melancholy was cold and dry; phlegm was cold and moist.

shared anatomy. Men's seed, it was believed, was the more potent and active because men had more active and more fully developed minds. The mind and body functioned as one entity, and thought was connected to physical processes such as the transformation of fluids, the concoction of seed, and the generation of human life.

Gender had no fixed biological base within the one-body model of humanity. As scholars of Renaissance and early modern England have shown, gender was displayed on the body through clothing and the theatrics of deportment, not revealed in biology within the body. Gender, in other words, was not rooted in biological difference. The biological basis of gender difference, that men and women were inherently different in anatomy and biology (what Laqueur terms the invention of radically incommensurable male and female bodies), developed in scientific discourse through the eighteenth century but did not displace the older model until the early nineteenth century. No such oppositional understanding of the body was necessary, before the eighteenth century, to justify and explain women's "natural" subordination to men. In early modern English society women's subordination to men was explained much like other relationships of subordination—ordained by God and necessary for the orderly functioning of society. The cosmos was ordered in the Great Chain of Being from God to the angels, to the monarch, to man, and finally to animals. Human society was also ordered in a fixed hierarchy, wherein people were born into their station and expected to respect and obey those higher in the social order. Women were to obey their husbands and fathers, just as men were to obey their monarch, servants were expected to obey their master, and commoners their aristocratic betters.[44]

44. Laqueur, *Making Sex;* Anthony Fletcher, *Gender, Sex, and Subordination in England, 1500–1800* (New Haven, Conn., 1995); George E. Haggarty, *Men in Love: Masculinity and Sexuality in the Eighteenth Century* (New York, 1999); James A. Schultz, "Bodies That Don't Matter: Heterosexuality before Heterosexuality in Gottfried's Tristan," in Phillips and Reay, *Sexualities in History,* 71–89.
Laqueur demonstrates that the shift from a one-body to a two-body understanding of human anatomy was a product of social and political forces, not scientific discoveries. He finds that the one-body model survived the assaults on its logic in the discovery of anatomical differences, such as the clitoris as distinct from the penis, in the late sixteenth century.
The old one-body model persisted throughout the eighteenth century in many popular medical texts, such as *Conjugal Love Reveal'd: In the Nightly Pleasures of the Marriage Bed* (London, 1770) (based on Nicolas Venette's *De la génération de l'homme, ou*

By the eighteenth century, scientific rationalism and Enlightenment philosophy were undermining the belief in a fixed hierarchy by championing a dynamic model of the cosmos and human society. The scientific revolution of the seventeenth century stressed the human capacity to reason, which could create the new knowledge necessary to perfect humanity and for man to master the natural world. Scientific rationalism developed by Francis Bacon, René Descartes, and Isaac Newton asserted that man could come to understand and control his world through methodical thought, which constituted the essential human quality—the ability to reason. Under the influence of Descartes, the mind and body began to be understood as wholly separate from each other. The search for knowledge with the new tools of systematic, rational thought held the promise of an ever-improving human society and a rationalized comprehensible world. This new worldview recognized human agency as fundamental to the construction of the individual self and human society. Humanity itself could guide human development and shape the organization of society. This radical transformation in the understanding of human nature and the ordering of society undermined the conceptual underpinnings of women's subordination to men.

This rich and dynamic period put a tremendous burden on those reformulating their world to renegotiate the basis of women's subordination to men, or relinquish it as fundamental to the ordering of their world. This was the challenge eighteenth-century Philadelphians faced. During the quarter of a century before the Revolution, they had just begun to reshape their beliefs

---

tableau de l'amour conjugal), Aristotle's Master-Piece, and S. A. Tissot's Advice to People in General, with Respect to Their Health and Onanism; or, A Treatise upon the Disorders Produced by Masturbation, all texts imported to midcentury Philadelphia.

Conjugal Love Reveal'd and The Pleasures of Conjugal-Love Explain'd (London, 1740) were advertised for sale in Philadelphia: Weatherwise, Father Abraham's Almanack for 1760, "Books . . . Just Imported," Dunlap; Bell, A Catalogue of New and Old Books (1783). Franklin advertised Aristotle's Master-Piece in PG, Feb. 7, 1740, as did William Dunlap in Weatherwise, Father Abraham's Almanack for 1760, "Books . . . Just Imported from London and to be sold by the Printer." Robert Bell listed Tissot's Onania and Tissot's Advice concerning Health in Robert Bell's Sale Catalogue (1773). Tissot on Health (translation of his Advice) was advertised in PG, Sept. 22, 1773, Mar. 8, 1775, Robert MacGill; June 23, Sept. 1, 1784, William and David Hall. For another example of marital sexual advice literature available in midcentury Philadelphia, see Daniel Defoe, A Treatise concerning the Use and Abuse of the Marriage Bed (London, 1727), advertised in Robert Bell's Sale Catalogue (1773).

about the body and its relationship to sex, gender, and the necessary order of society.[45]

Representations of female sexuality in Philadelphia's popular print culture at midcentury focused on women's lustiness, presented within the gender hierarchy of the one-body model of humanity. Women openly expressed sexual desire but were depicted as dependent on men's more active sexual nature to ignite their full sexual awareness and experience. Women were often portrayed as longing for sexual involvement and desiring the sexual attention of men, even as they were simultaneously passive in initiating the fulfillment of those desires. "The Longing Maid," part of an inexpensive eight-page songster in Philadelphia in 1767, was typical of late colonial representations of female sexuality. The young woman, complaining of a prolonged maidenhood, longed, moaned, and sighed for sexual fulfillment:

One evening of late
   As I walkt out in state,
I heard a maid making her moan,

   I askt her the matter
   She said, I'll not flatter
I'm wearied with lying alone.

  . . . .

   Let some jolly brisk man,
   Have pity on me,
And make me a wife of his own,
   For I vow and declare
   I'll die in dispair,
If I lye any longer alone.

   A sailor so bold,
   As I have been told,
Hearing this maid making her moan,
   Bade her not lament,
   For if she'd consent
She should not lye longer alone.

45. Anthony Fletcher discusses scientific rationalism in relation to this transformation in the English gender system during the seventeenth and eighteenth centuries in *Gender, Sex, and Subordination*, 285–296. For the impact of Enlightenment philosophy and scientific rationalism on gender, see sources in Chapter 1, n. 1, above.

With kisses so sweet
  He did her intreat,
And made her a wife of his own,
  Now since they are wed,
  Her sorrow has fled,
And she lies no more sighing alone.[46]

This belief in a natural female lust dependent on male initiative for fulfillment was reinforced by depicting women as desiring to engage in sexual relations. In the following anecdote the woman playfully voices the sexual norm that *he* should "have" *her* and that she will willingly comply.

John's Courtship to Betty
"Bett, wilt have me?" quoth John. Quoth Bett, "don't take it ill;
I will not,—But—you may have me, if you will."[47]

Women's innate lustiness was established by repeatedly depicting scenes of women's sexual awakening. The many poems and songs of women's first sexual experiences employed a specific formula. Presented as having secret sexual longings or reluctant to fulfill the entreaties of her suitor, she became the initiator once her sexual nature was awakened by her first taste of intimacy. The poem accompanying the calendar for August 1754 in the *American Country Almanack* tells of Phillis and Colin, who struggle over kisses only to have her reluctance overcome by her lust:

But her Heart grew more soft, as more closely he prest,
The first when he'd stolen, she gave him the rest.[48]

In the 1778 song "The Pipe of Love" the first sexual experience of a maid begins with her sexual longing:

46. *William Crotty: To Which Are Added Five Other New Songs* (Philadelphia: Steuart, 176?). See also "The Maiden's Wish," in Weatherwise, *Father Abraham's Almanack for 1762.*

47. Abraham Weatherwise [pseud.], *Father Abraham's Almanack . . . for . . . 1759* (Philadelphia: Dunlap, 1758) (quotation marks regularized). See also "Anecdote" (on a bastard-bearing woman), in *Father Abraham's Almanack . . . for . . . 1764* (Philadelphia: Dunlap, 1763).

48. Thomas More [pseud.], *The American Country Almanack for . . . 1754* (Philadelphia: Franklin and Hall, 1753).

ONE Primrose Time a Maiden Brown
    Wishing for what we will not say,
By side of Shepherd sat her down,
    And softly ask'd him wou'd he play?
Mild shone the Sun thro' Redstreak Morn,
    And glist'ning Dew-drops pearl'd the grass;
The Rustic, stretch'd beneath the thorn,
    Grinning, reply'd,—*I'll please thee Lass.*

The sexual scene is pastoral, employing the character of the shepherd, with "dew" in the "grass," and later "the green fields turfy bed." Playing the pipes is a metaphor for sexual intercourse; she asks him to play, and he promises to please her. Having consummated their union, the maid asks him to make love to her again:

Blue broke the clouds, the day yet young,
    The flowers fragrant fill'd the breeze;
Wanton the Lass, half wisp'ring, sung,
    Yes, Shepherd—once more if you please.
Awaking from embrac'd delight,
    She heard her Dame, and dar'd not stay;
They kiss, they part, but first—*at Night,*
    She charg'd him, *come again and play.*

The song ends with the "love-cheer'd Lass" singing the praises of the "pipe of Love."[49]

These scenes were presented in a playful and positive way. The pastoral setting evoked a sense of natural love and natural sexual fulfillment, where sexual intimacy was an ideal, a pure and natural desire. Women's lust was understood as inherent to her, and the Enlightenment's veneration of the state of nature bolstered this image of female sexuality.

The other basis of female sexual lust was biblical, based on Eve's role in the Fall, presenting women as vulnerable to sexual temptation. Philadelphians occasionally drew upon the biblical images when they described female sexuality. Biblical and anatomical understandings of female nature complemented

49. George Alexander Stevens, *Songs, Comic, Satyrical, and Sentimental* (Philadelphia: Bell, 1778), 116 (reprint of London, 1772). For the same pattern of sexual awakening, see "Maria," 151; "Dick and Doll," 85; and "Moral Sentences," in Andrew Aguecheek [pseud.], *The Universal American Almanack . . . for . . . 1766* (Philadelphia: Steuart, 1765).

each other, as in "The Maids of Philadelphia's Petition," because both represented women as lesser men:

A Virgin was design'd by Nature,
A weakly and imperfect Creature,
So apt to fall, so apt to stray.

Woman's sexual nature makes her apt to fall because of her less-developed human qualities and her weaker nature, as evident in the Fall. But during the 1750s and early 1760s biblical images were overwhelmed by images of a pure pastoral and positive female sexual nature.[50]

A woman's lustiness developed as her body matured in her middle teen years and persisted throughout her life. An almanac poem for 1754 described the early stages:

At fourteen years young females are
    contriving tricks to tempt ye,
At sixteen years come on and woo,
    and take of kisses plenty,
At eighteen years full grown and ripe,
    they're ready to content ye,
At nineteen sly and mischievous,
    but the D[evi]l at one and twenty.[51]

Virgins, from a young age, were believed to be wanton, because they suffered from unfulfilled sexual desire. Women denied sexual experience could become ill from the resulting imbalance of humors. They were vulnerable to chlorosis, or greensickness, which was caused by a lack of sexual fulfillment, for which coitus, preferably in marriage, was understood as the best cure. The complaint put forth by "The Maids of Philadelphia's Petition" (see above) assumed the need for marriage partners. It is sexual desire that motivates the maids "to petition for young Fellows." The maids have been cut out of the sexual economy by the more sexually assertive widows. Virgin maids might pine for unknown sexual pleasures, but widows avidly sought partners to quench the mature woman's sexual thirst. This conceptualization of widows' sexuality was consistent with the idea that, once a woman's sexuality had

50. "The Maids of Philadelphia's Petition," in Weatherwise, *Father Abraham's Almanack for 1762.*

51. More, *The American Country Almanack for 1754.*

been awakened or engaged, she would become inflamed and seek fulfill-ment. Almost all mention of widows in popular print included references to their taking or seeking to find lovers. "The Maids of Philadelphia's Peti-tion" charges the city's widows with engaging all the young single men, calls widows "jades," and insinuates that these women have the sexual upper hand owing to their sexual experience and willingness.[52]

Almanac poems and anecdotes depict the widows as pining for husbands, quick to remarry, and the ideal partner for adultery. The widow was an ideal target for these humorous gibes: the real trouble with widowhood was, not the immediate grief of losing a husband or economic privation, but sexual need.

The Real Affliction

Dorris, a Widow, past her Prime,
    Her Spouse long dead, Wailings double;
Her real Griefs increase by Time,
    And what abates, improves, her Trouble,
Those Pangs her prudent Hopes surpress'd,
    Impatient now she cannot smother:
How should the helpless Woman rest?
    One's gone;—nor can she get another.[53]

The construction of male sexuality, by contrast, changed over the course of a man's life and enjoyed the tempering influence of reason. Throughout the poems and anecdotes that address male sexuality, reason stands as the anti-dote to passion:

To *Reason's* dictates when I lent an ear,
    Harmonious heavenly Sweetness sooth'd my Breast;

52. "The Maids of Philadelphia's Petition," in Weatherwise, *Father Abraham's Alma-nack for 1762;* Fletcher, *Gender, Sex, and Subordination,* 48–50. Greensickness was known as the virgin's disease and was frequently so diagnosed in seventeenth-century England. Unmarried women between seventeen and twenty-two were the most com-monly diagnosed with the condition.

53. Weatherwise, *Father Abraham's Almanack for 1767,* also printed in Richard Saun-ders [pseud.], *Poor Richard, 1737: An Almanack . . .* (Philadelphia: Franklin, 1736). And see "An Epigram," in Saunders [pseud.], *Poor Richard Improved . . . for . . . 1773* (Phila-delphia: Hall and Sellers, 1772); "A Widow's Complaint," in Weatherwise, *Father Abra-ham's Almanack for 1764;* "Question," in William Ball, *The New-Jersey Almanack . . . for . . . 1753* (Philadelphia: Bradford, 1752).

When *Passion* rul'd, 'twas all tumultuous care,
   A racking Conscience, and distemper'd Rest.[54]

By midcentury, when such almanac material dominated the representations of male sexuality, the one-body model of human anatomy had been adapted to incorporate human agency and the rational mind. The older understanding of male sexuality as demonstrating the greatest active quality accompanied by the most developed mind was compatible with scientific rationalism's emphasis on the mind and the Enlightenment's stress on self-perfection. Building upon the foundation of gendered sexuality within the one-body model of humanity, men were imbued with the capacity to incorporate Enlightenment rationalism. It was men who were granted the agency to struggle with their bodily nature; they could, and should, employ reason to overcome their lust: to be masculine was to rule over one's passions. Poor Richard warned men: Be "no Passion's guilty Friend." "He is a Governor that governs his Passions, and he a Servant that serves them." "Sampson with his strong body had a weak Head, or he would not have laid it in a Harlots lap." "Passion" described a constellation of dangerous behaviors in men.[55]

> Gluttony and Drunkenness stir up Lust, Grief, Anger; and extinguish Memory, Judgment, and Understanding; make the Mind dull and unapt; and undermine Reason itself. PLATO[56]

Passion would lead to excess, and moderation and self-control were attributes of a man of reason. When men were instructed to moderate their passions, they were being told what temperament to embrace in their activities rather than being prohibited from those activities. Thus, a man could be sexually active, but his passion must not lead to lust, which would overwhelm his mind's ability to direct his actions. Even in the scenes of women's sexual initiation, men were portrayed as steadily pursuing sexual activity rather than being swept away by their passions. Natural sexual gratification, not uncontrolled passion, was what should govern men in sexual activity.

54. Thomas Thomas, *The Pennsylvania Almanac . . . for 1760* (Philadelphia: Dunlap, 1759).

55. Richard Saunders [pseud.], *Poor Richard Improved . . . for 1755* (Philadelphia: Franklin and Hall, 1754); *For 1750* (Philadelphia: Franklin and Hall, 1749); *For 1756* (Philadelphia: Franklin and Hall, 1755).

56. Andrew Aguecheek [pseud.], *The Universal American Almanack . . . for . . . 1761* (Philadelphia: Steuart, 1760).

The dangers to men of succumbing to passion were keenly felt. Love itself was often portrayed as dangerous, for it could oppose reason in a battle to control the man. Fear of all-consuming love was expressed in 1764 by the author of "Thoughts upon Love and Marriage":

I never deplore a Man, who by losing his Mistress recovers himself.

A witty Wench used to wish her Lovers all the good Qualities, but a good Understanding; for that (says she) would soon make them out of Love with me.

When Love dethrones Reason, tho' it leaves the Lover alive, it destroys the Man.[57]

Despite men's access to reason, lust could wreak havoc upon their lives, especially young men's. Almanacs depicted "youth's frantic fires":

Temptations press me close, a num'rous band,
Which find me oft too feeble to withstand.[58]

The heat of desire developed during a man's youth and continued until con-quered by the reason of the adult man. Young men were told to expect passion to come upon them as they left childhood and to battle it with reason:

Anon, extravagant desires,
Tumultuous Thoughts, and am'rous Fires,
    Within his Bosom rage;
These Reason long assays to tame,
By dread of pain, and want, and shame,
    And tedious Wars they wage.[59]

57. "Thoughts upon Love and Marriage," in Aguecheek, *The Universal American Almanack for 1764.*

58. "A Christmas Hymn, to Close the Year," in Andrew Aguecheek [pseud.], *The Universal American Almanack . . . for . . . 1762* (Philadelphia: Steuart, 1761). See also "An Elegy on a Tallow-Candle," in *The Universal American Almanack . . . for . . . 1768* (Philadelphia: Steuart, 1767).

59. "On the Vanity and Vicissitude of Human Life," in *Poor Robin's Spare Hours . . . for 1758* (Philadelphia: Bradford, 1757); see also "Life an Ode," in Aguecheek, *The Universal American Almanack for 1766.*

In another poem:

> 'Tis now the Time young Passion to command,
> While yet the plant stem obeys the Hand.[60]

Allowing passions to direct their actions would prevent young men from moving into secure and full adulthood. Yet, even those who had succumbed to sexual extravagance could draw upon the strength of the male mind to restore themselves:

> Tho' youth's gay scenes his vig'rous health destroy'd
> And pompous vice his noon of life employ'd,
> When mild reflection calm'd his heated breast,
> Bright Virtue's lovelier beauties he confest,
> Her awful pow'r with reverence he ador'd;
> And blooming years by temp'rate arts restor'd.[61]

This overwhelming sexual desire of young manhood was a departure from the previous generation's expected pattern of sexual experience. The young men of popular print culture of the 1760s were creating a masculine sexuality that expected a period of youthful sexual experimentation and was distinct from that of their fathers' generation.

At times this emphasis on the sexual intensity of youth was explicit; it was also displayed through the emergence of new male sexual types. New male characters appeared who engaged in sexual behavior purely for their own pleasure without any intention to court or marry their sexual partners. First, the "fop" and the "beau," later, the "debauched," "libertine," and "rake" emerged as sexual players in the cultural terrain of popular print.[62]

Just as the young man was expected to experience a distinct sexually active stage in youth and temper his passions and moderate his lusts as he reached adulthood, the older man should refrain from sexual excess:

60. Richard Saunders [pseud.], *Poor Richard Improved . . . for 1758* (Philadelphia: Franklin and Hall, 1757).

61. *Poor Robin's Spare Hours . . . for . . . 1751* (Philadelphia: Bradford, 1750).

62. See, for example, "Chloe's Choice," in Richard Saunders [pseud.], *Poor Richard Improved . . . for 1760* (Philadelphia: Franklin and Hall, 1759); "Proper Ingredients to Make a Modern Beau," in Weatherwise, *Father Abraham's Almanack for 1759;* "On a Beau," in Andrew Aguecheek [pseud.], *The Universal American Almanack . . . for . . . 1770* (Philadelphia: Steuart, 1769); "The Lady's Form of Prayer for a Husband," in Aguecheek, *The Universal American Almanack for 1767.*

Remarks on Youth and Age

Our passions in youth are very powerful seducers; they hurry us into hasty enjoyments, which have often their ending in very long and very fruitless repentance. Against these imminent evils, which have their foundations in early life, we have no kind of defence, but in the experience of later days, which those are the most happy who soonest acquire and regard.[63]

And

January

THis Month keep near the Fire or else you'll find,
   Your Nose Frost-nipped by the northern Wind;
And i[f] in *Venus-Sports* you must engage;
Consider well your *Strength,*—consult your *Age.*[64]

The association of advanced mental capacity with maturity usually protected older men from the ridicule directed at widows, but age-inappropriate sexual behavior of men occasionally elicited a laugh. In "Cupid and Death" two men are shot with darts. Reversing the normal course, the young man gets the dart of death, and the old man the dart of love.

Tis thus we see old hoary age
   In love's forgotten heats engage,
      And pining with its Smart.[65]

The different representations of male and female sexuality promoted the belief that women were innately lustful and especially vulnerable to sexual temptation, and that men enjoyed a greater distance from the potentially destructive influence of lustful sex and all-consuming love. The representations of male sexuality emphasized the dynamic relationship between the individual man and his sexual longings and behavior. Men wielded sexual agency as they struggled with the physical impulses generated within their bodies. Female sexuality was in comparison persistent, unchanging, and inevitable. Mid-eighteenth-century representations of men grafted Enlightenment

63. Andrew Aguecheek [pseud.], *The Universal American Almanack . . . for . . . 1767* (Philadelphia: Steuart, 1766).
64. Aguecheek, *The Universal American Almanack for 1764.*
65. *Poor Robin's Spare Hours . . . for . . . 1751* (Philadelphia: Bradford, 1750). See also December poem in More, *The American Country Almanack for 1751.*

rationalism's emphasis on agency onto the older beliefs in sexual desire as a vital life force present in all people. This conceptual development enhanced the superior position of men over women already present in the one-body model of humanity and began establishing a new foundation for female subordination to men. These conceptualizations of male and female sexuality justified excluding women from the benefits of the rational mind.

Midcentury women were not granted the agency to transform themselves and were depicted as constitutionally unable to master their own sexuality. Woman's lust was inherent, and she was without the mental capacity to take full control of herself. The distinction between male and female sexuality, initiated in the merger of the one-body understanding of sexuality and scientific rationalism, began the essentializing of female sexuality. What constituted female sexuality would change dramatically over the next fifty years. But its character as innate, static, and inborn had been established in opposition to the dynamic male.

As popular culture was eroticized and female lust accentuated in the 1760s and 1770s, female lust became the primary and double-edged explanation for women's behavior. Lust was the uncontrollable driving force of women's behavior and, simultaneously, the springboard for the creation of the all-powerful duplicitous sexual temptress. Female lust, which women are constitutionally unequipped to influence, thus eclipsed the possibility of their exercising agency and rational choice.

The female character in John Dillon's *Pleasures of a Single Life*, first published in America in 1763 in Philadelphia, exemplifies the dual nature of female lust. In this pamphlet the inevitability of the wife's adultery is set up by her duplicitous, scheming nature and her overpowering desire. She uses her sexual wiles to lure her intended to marriage and then is overcome by her own lust to cuckold him. The young man of reason, enjoying a learned life, is ruined when he succumbs to the apparent beauty and charms of a woman.

> When she by wiles had hightened my desire,
> And fan'd love sparkles to a raging fire;
> Made now for wedlock or for Bedlam fit,
> Thus passion gain'd the upper hand of wit.
> The dame by pity or by interest mov'd,
> Or else by lust, pretended now she lov'd,
> After long suffering her consent I got.

But soon after marriage he found that her pleasing demeanor was only a facade behind which lurked a licentious, adulterous beast. The love-torn man forgives and corrects her, but, despite his "stripes and severe correction," she plunges deeper and deeper into her lustful pursuits. Her unstoppable appetite is credited as the cause of all her actions:

> But all this kindness I dispens'd in vain,
> Where lust, and base ingratitude remain.
> Lust, which if once in female fancy fix'd,
> Burns like salt-petre, with dry touch wood mix'd;
> And tho' cold fear for time may stop its force,
> 'Twill soon like fire confin'd, break out the worse,
> Or like a tide obstructed, reassume its course.
>
> . . . .
>
> Thus brutal lust, her human reason drown'd,
> And her loose tail oblig'd the Country round.

She continues her adulteries until no one of her station will have her, then turns to her husband's servants, and bears bastards sired by the groom in her husband's own bed. In the end her "spurious brood" gives him grounds to divorce her, which he does with speed.[66]

Women's lust was repeatedly invoked as the explanation for women's adultery as anecdotes of cuckoldry and tales of licentious temptresses became regular items in Philadelphia's almanacs during the 1760s and 1770s. The adulterous wife is an enticing siren seducing the innocent youth to her bed in *The Universal American Almanack* in 1762:

> June
> Perfumed it with a lover's care
> With aloes, cinnamon, and myrrs,
> Come, let me fill with love the night,
> And revel till the morning light,
> Come, gentle youth, oh! come, nor fear
> An interrupting husband near.
>
> July
> Thank heav'n he treads a distant way,
> Nor comes till the appointed day.
> Her words, deceitful as her charms,

66. Sir John Dillon, *The Pleasures of a Single Life; or, The Miseries of Matrimony* (Philadelphia: Steuart, 1763) (rpt. of London, 1701, original). All editions printed in America before 1780 were printed in Philadelphia: Steuart, 1763; Dunlap, 1771; and Aitken, 1781.

Seduce the stripling to her arms.
Thus the doom'd on to slaughter goes,
Unconscious of his murd'ring foes.

The motive underlying her loving words was her own sexual gratification, which the pure young man can provide.[67]

The accentuation of the temptress in female sexuality in the 1760s served to make men's sexual involvement with women less their responsibility. For, if women were not only subject to sexual temptation but also sought out sexual fulfillment, men could imagine themselves passive agents. The challenge of extending the use of reason to women was, in part, that it would redirect responsibility for sexual activity back toward a shared responsibility. Instead, through the representations of female lust, men were beginning to be depicted as losing control over their own sexual behavior, if only while developing as young men, and were being excused from the usual social responsibilities associated with sex.

The Enlightenment initiation of self-discovery and the quest to reveal man's character in the state of nature supported the eighteenth-century exploration of man's sexual essence. Midcentury Philadelphians had retained belief in sexual desire as a life force, but it was now cast in a world where individuals could seek self-discovery and self-perfection. For some, pure love in a state of nature unencumbered by social conventions became an ideal, probably impossible to achieve, but worth pursuing. Quests for self-discovery could now legitimate men's participation in nonmarital sexual behaviors of the pleasure culture. In popular print, however, such participation was increasingly depicted as sexual opportunity—for men, without social restraints, and thus without conventional social responsibility. By so depicting sex, almanac ditties promoted the idea that men could engage in sex without incurring the obligations of courtship, marriage, or even long-term commitment.

Female lust corrupted woman's character and made her the conniving trickster in popular print. The most serious consequence of feminine duplicity presented was that a woman, at first appearing pleasing and sincere in her romantic attachment, would become adulterous and make her husband a cuckold. During the 1760s cuckold jokes became common and were, presumably, quite popular. They poked fun at husbands who allowed themselves to be cuckolded, and they simultaneously reinforced the notion that female sexuality could not be trusted and that women were naturally duplicitous.

67. "Precepts from the Book of Wisdom," in Aguecheek, *The Universal American Almanack for 1762.*

PLATE 7. *William Hogarth,* Evening. *Plate 3 of* The Four Times of the Day.
1738. Hogarth's parody on cuckoldry was for sale in pre-Revolutionary Philadelphia.
Permission Colonial Williamsburg Foundation

A certain Gentleman being very angry with one of his Neighbours about some Expressions which had been told him again, cryed out, The Devil take all the *Cuckolds,* I wish they were all in the River. To which his Wife answered, *O, dear Husband, how can you make such a wish, when you know you cannot swim.*

Most cuckold jokes assumed that a woman, given the opportunity, would engage in adultery, because she could not resist her own sexual impulses. In a "Jest" in *Father Abraham's Almanack for 1767,* even a protesting woman, it was assumed, would be thankful for the sexual gift bestowed upon her by her pursuer:

An amorous young Fellow making very warm addresses to a married Woman. Pray, Sir, be quiet, said she, I have a Husband that will not thank you for making him a Cuckold. *No, Madam,* replied he, *but you will I hope.*[68]

Another anxiety expressed in tales of cuckoldry was fear of the social instability created by cross-class marriages. Almanac stories like "A Dialogue between a City Termagant and Her Distrustful Spouse" taught that cross-class marriage, when men married above their class, weakened patriarchal authority and unleashed wives' licentiousness. In this story the wife's money made the husband's rise to comfort possible, but her higher premarriage status has given her grounds to criticize him and has undermined his authority. He is jealous and tries, unsuccessfully, to restrict her freedom. Because of his debt to her, he cannot ultimately keep her from behaving with a moral and sexual laxness unbecoming in a wife. The argument begins:

WIFE

What ails the angry Sot? Poor jealous Fool;
Yes, I'll obey when you have Pow'r to rule.
Marry-come-up, indeed; what's that to you,
Where I have been intriguing, or with who?
What, can't a Wife her Recreation take,
But you must all this noisy Bustle make;
Must I be fearful, on a Summer's Day,
To take a Walk, or see a harmless Play,
Because, forsooth, I've such a jealous Spouse,
To think each Man I speak to, horns his Brows [cuckolds him]?

68. Weatherwise, *Father Abraham's Almanack for 1767.* See also cuckold jokes: "The Danger of a Blind Passion," in *Father Abraham's Almanack . . . for . . . 1773* (Philadelphia: Dunlap, 1772); "Jests," in Saunders, *Poor Richard Improved for 1774.*

HUSBAND

Hussy, I say, you are a wanton Slut,
To steal from Home, when I myself am out:
'Tis to my Shame, you Minx, that you're so free
To gad Abroad with any Man but me.
What, tho' he be your Cousin? 'tis a Crime,
I've heard strange Things of Cousins in my Time.

She then maintains that she will "take what Liberties" she pleases and not obey him, for he misunderstands her social station:

WIFE

High Time indeed, you should be so obey'd;
D'ye take me for your Slave, or Servant Maid . . . ?

· · · · · · · · · · · · ·

Must I, behind your Compter, spend my Life,
That Passengers may view your handsome Wife?
There like a Fool, sit Playing with my Thumbs,
To learn the Price of Sugars, and of Plums?
Not I indeed; I'll not be so subdu'd,
But take my Pleasure, as a Woman shou'd;
Dress, visit, gossip, gad where-e'er I please;
And if you thwart me, study how to teaze.

Because he aspires to the upper classes, he deserves to be burdened with the frivolous activities of an upper-class wife. Having insulted his profession, she now makes the ultimate threat, to "study how to teaze," and cuckold him. He responds in anger:

HUSBAND

Hussy, you are the most provoking Jade,
That surely ever curs'd a Marriage-Bed.
With ev'ry Pound, you've brought a thousand Plagues,
Would I had wedded some poor Wench in Rags,
Rather than one so confidenly bold;
A Jilt, a Slut, damn'd lazy, and a Scold.[69]

Ultimately the husband admits his inability to please or control his wife, no matter how many vain entertainments he indulges her in. This tale makes fun

69. Abraham Weatherwise [pseud.], *Father Abraham's Almanack . . . for . . . 1765* (Philadelphia: Dunlap, 1764).

of both the merchant husband who aspires to the wealth of a gentleman, and the elite wife who will not relinquish her idle pursuits to become the industrious helpmate. Cross-class marriages, which allowed a quick rise in social status, were depicted as dangerous: the husband's authority was usurped, and the wife, freed from his control, would engage in sexual misbehavior. When the woman sought to marry up, the consequences also involved sexual catastrophes. The woman who married only for financial gain becomes frigid when she is saddled with a wealthy old man as her partner; and, when the quest to marry into wealth failed, women turned to prostitution, having compromised their sexual virtue in the pursuit of a rich man.[70]

The problems of cross-class marriages in popular print were resolved by distinguishing between love and lust. By the 1760s almanac ditties began differentiating them and instructed individuals to examine their feelings and discern whether they were embarking upon a relationship based upon the intense but fleeting effects of passion, or upon the enduring effects of affection. In "On Love" Poor Richard divides love into two parts. Passion is produced by sight, built on lust, expects "Fruition, and there usually terminates." It is wild, romantic, and changeable. Affection, by contrast, is produced by the mind, "governed by Reason, instructed by sober Reflection, and confirmed by Honesty." It is built upon "a kind of softness of the Soul," will increase over time, and prove indissoluble. Other authors described this division of emotion as love versus lust.

> It is the Difference betwixt Lust and Love, that this is fix'd, that volatile. Love grows, Lust wastes by Enjoyment: And the Reason is, That one springs from an Union of Souls, and the other from an Union of Sense. They have divers Originals, and so are of different Families: That inward and deep, this superficial: this Transient, and that permanent.[71]

The separation of love and lust helped reconcile some of the conflict over cross-class relationships. Love and lust came to be understood as two distinct forms of sexual desire: love became the appropriate form of desire in a mar-

---

70. See "The Courtship," in Abraham Weatherwise [pseud.], *Father Abraham's Almanack . . . for . . . 1766* (Philadelphia: Dunlap, 1765); "Fortune in a Wife No Ungenerous Demand in a Husband," in Philo Copernicus [pseud.], *The American Calend[a]r . . . for . . . 1772* (Philadelphia: Bradford, 1771); "Marriage a-la-Mode; or, The Penitent Prude," in Weatherwise, *Father Abraham's Almanack for 1764.*

71. Richard Saunders [pseud.], *Poor Richard Improved . . . for 1759* (Philadelphia: Franklin and Hall, 1758); Thomas, *The Pennsylvania Almanack for 1760.*

riage to a suitable partner of one's own class, and lust the form of desire to be exercised with women of the lower classes.

In the articulation of this difference between love and lust a new category was created: the lustful affair, or casual tryst, became a social reality. This is not to say that some casual sexual relationships had not occurred in Philadelphia before the 1760s. But what was new in the 1760s was the creation of a recognized space for this behavior in the cultural milieu as well as an increase in numbers of Philadelphians engaged therein.

The proliferation of cuckold jokes, the concern over cross-class marriages, and the greater attention given to wives' adultery in Philadelphia's popular print coincided with the increase in husbands' claims of wives' adultery in elopement advertisements of the 1760s and 1770s. In print, women's uncontrollable lust drives them to adultery, sometimes assisted by their conniving nature. Lacking a man's mental capabilities, a woman can neither make rational choices to seek a more suitable partner nor use her mind to control her body. The work done in popular print to deny women the possibility of individual agency to control their sexuality is striking when compared to evidence of the actions of Revolutionary-era runaway wives.

In print the initiative of women who left their husbands is contradicted and obscured. It is not their husband's bad temper, lack of support, or emotional inadequacy that drives them to flee or find a new partner, but simply the subterranean lava flow of female lust. In the face of runaway wives who evaluated their marital situation and redirected their lives, cuckold jokes denied that women could engage in rational choice and direct their own actions.

Cuckold jokes served another purpose as well. They poked fun at ineffectual husbands, implying that it was husbands' responsibility to control their wives. If women could not take independent action and female sexuality needed external control, then it was up to husbands, popular print proclaimed, to take charge of their marital situation themselves by subduing their wives to their will. These lessons pervaded the almanac ditties: happy, proper marriages rested upon the twin pillars of husbands' exercising patriarchal power and wives' internalizing the belief that they were the ones responsible for marital harmony. Marital bliss rested upon the wife's ability to fulfill her role as the submissive spouse by silently sublimating her will for her husband's happiness. A husband's pleasure was necessary for a wife's own happiness, and a happy marriage required a husband to rule the roost. Just as early almanacs had laid the blame for marital discord at women's feet, ditties after midcentury asserted that marital sexual fulfillment required wifely submission. And they posited that the antidote to a wife's assertive or independent action was a reassertion of patriarchal power in marriage.

Father Abraham's Almanack for 1759, in "The Medicine: A Tale—for the Ladies," made this explicit when a pair of newlyweds reach an insoluble disagreement over his love of wine and her love of money. The wife is presented as the classic nag, whose tirade sends the husband from his home:

> When she began—for Hat and Sword he'd call,
> Then, after a feint Kiss,—cry, "B'y, dear Moll:
> Supper and Friends expect me at the Rose."
> "And, what, Sir John, you'll get your usual [D]ose
> Go stink of Smoke and guzzle nasty Wine;
> Sure never virtuous Love was us'd like mine!"

When he returns home, at four o'clock in the morning, the couple fight, and he goes off to sleep alone. His wife's quarrelsome character is cited as the cause of this nuptial separation:

> "Some Couch and distant Room must be my Choice[,]
> Where I may sleep uncurs'd with Wife and Noise."
> Long this uncomfortable Life they led,
> With snarling Meals, and each a sep'rate Bed.

The situation continues until her uncle gives her a potion to cure their troubles and reunite them. He tells her:

> "Smile, and look pleas'd, when he shall rage and scold,
> Still in your Mouth the healing Cordial hold,
> One Month this Sympathetick Med'cin try'd,
> He'll grow a Lover, you a happy Bride."

Upon the husband's homecoming, the wife remains mute and immediately becomes sexually alluring to her mate:

> Her busy Thoughts are on the Trial bent,
> And, Female like, impatient for the Event!
> The bonny Knight reels Home exceeding clear,
> Prepar'd for Clamour and Domestic War:
> Ent'ring he cries, "Hey! where's our Thunder fled,
> No Hurricane!—Betty's your Lady dead?"
> Madam, aside, an ample Mouthful takes,
> Court'sies, looks kind, but not a Word she speaks:

Wond'ring, he star'd, scarcely his Eyes believ'd,
But [fou]nd his Ears agreeably deceiv'd.
   "Why, how now, Molly, what's the Crotchet now?"
She smiles, and answers only with a Bow.
Then clasping her about—"Why let me die!
   These Night-cloaths, Moll, become thee mightily,"
With that, he sigh'd, her Hand began to press,
And Betty calls, her Lady to undress,

   "Nay, kiss me, Molly,—for I'm much inclin'd:"
Her Lace she cuts, to take him in the Mind.
Thus the fond Pair to Bed enamour'd went,
   The Lady pleas'd, and the good Knight content.

When the month is up, the wife runs to her uncle asking for more elixir, only to find that she has been drinking water the whole time. The moral of the tale, and the lesson for the young wife, is,

"Such Beauty would the coldest Husband warm,
But your provoking Tongue undoes the Charm,
Be silent and complying.—You'll soon find,
Sir John without a Med'cine, will be Kind."[72]

The representations of marriage of the 1760s and 1770s promoted the idea that troubled marriages, unfaithful husbands, and men's choosing to eschew marriage for the sexual opportunities of the urban pleasure culture were women's fault. Rather than simply characterizing wives as termagant nags, as earlier almanac material did, the stories printed in the bloom of the pleasure culture taught that it was the wives' responsibility to solve marital problems or suffer the consequences of living with unfaithful husbands. The pleasure culture gave a husband extramarital sexual options, but it was the wife's duty to examine her own behavior to ensure that her husband did not choose them.

This theme proved so popular to almanac readers that it became a stock item for *Father Abraham's Almanack* in the late 1760s. Two characters, Lurwell and Loveless, presented stories of marital conflict and infidelity. The column "Female Council; or, The Moot-Point of Matrimony" ran serially from 1766 through 1769. In each of these years a dialogue between these two women appeared in the pages before the calendar, but the message in each installment

72. Weatherwise, *Father Abraham's Almanack for 1759* (quotation marks regularized).

was essentially the same: a woman's happiness depended on marital felicity, and she should do everything in her power to make her marriage harmonious.

Lurwell and Loveless represent two extremes in wives. Lurwell is the happily married matron who, as her name suggests, has successfully lured and kept her husband by carefully guiding her own behavior. Loveless, by contrast, is the angry wife, who demands what she believes she is entitled to in marriage and is therefore at risk of enduring a "loveless" marriage.

Their conversation begins, in 1766, with Loveless seeking advice from Lurwell on improving her marriage. Loveless's husband has failed to meet several of her expectations. He is stingy with his wealth and dresses her worse than "Every Tradesman's Daughter." His drunkenness has made him useless in bed, and he takes his pleasure with whores on the town. When they quarrel, he threatens to beat her but backs down when she shields herself with a chair. He has lost her respect because he does not "act as a Man": he has not forced her to submit to his will, nor has he performed the role of husband in the marriage bed. Loveless claims that, until he does so, she will not treat him as husband and submit to his governance.[73]

In the next year's almanac Lurwell counsels Loveless that, no matter how "unkind or indiscreet" her husband is, her "State is unalterable" because divorce is not legal. With little hope of ending her marriage, she should submit to her husband's will in an attempt to reconcile their differences. Two years later Lurwell tells Loveless, and the reader, stories of marital conflict in which the wife reforms her husband by changing her own behavior rather than chastising him for his. In one the husband takes up with a poor but beautiful woman who lives nearby, often visiting her and neglecting his wife. She visits the other woman under the guise of being the husband's sister and finds the house shabby and poor. She resolves to make her husband comfortable wherever he is and sends all the accoutrements of a comfortable home to her husband's mistress. The husband figures out that his wife was responsible for its improvement and questions her. She replies, "She thought it her Duty, when his Inclination led him to such humble Amusements, to take care that his Reception should be decent at least, tho' not suitable to his Character or fortune." The husband, awakened by her loving care, comes back and remains faithful ever after. In another story the wife invites the other woman to her home to be her friend and thus brings her husband home. In each of the subsequent tales the adulterous husband is reclaimed by his wife's changed behavior, implying that his infidelity was her responsibility

73. Ibid., *For 1766.*

all along, and legitimating the sexual double standard that excused male extra-marital sex.[74]

The stories of "Lurwell and Loveless" and "The Medicine" are prime examples of discursive attempts to shape the sexual culture of pre-Revolutionary Philadelphia to reassert male power and control of women. In the face of sexual behavior suggesting that both men and women had initiated a more open sexual system—one that allowed for exploring sexual behavior in a wide array of relationships and sometimes outside of relationships at all—the authors of popular culture crafted an interpretive understanding of sexual desire and sexual behavior that promoted sexual opportunities for men and sexual responsibility for women: and deflected female agency and self-determination.

By the era of the American Revolution some women were asserting a different interpretation of the meanings of an expanded arena of sexual behavior in the context of the Enlightenment quest for self-discovery. From the 1760s through the 1780s, between one-quarter and one-third of the wives advertised as self-divorcing by elopement had left their marriage for other men or established parallel adulterous relationships. These women were seeking personal happiness by finding a new partner and in doing so rejecting the central tenet of patriarchal marriage—a husband's exclusive rights to the sexual use of his wife's body. Unlike Lurwell and Loveless, these Philadelphia women asserted that personal satisfaction and individual choice in intimate relationships were indeed legitimate goals of the new configurations of gender, sexuality, and the ordering of society. Rather than sublimating one's own will, as Lurwell advised, these women asserted that happiness could be achieved by evaluating the shortcomings of one's spouse and taking action to find a more satisfactory primary relationship.[75]

Some wives expressed this by asserting their desire for deeper emotional satisfaction with their marital partner. Personal happiness became a legitimate expectation, and lack of emotional fulfillment (or, in eighteenth-century terms, sentiment or sensibility) in one's partner now was specified by women as a cause for self-divorce. Sensibility stressed the importance of authentic emotional feeling and expression in primary relationships. Many Philadelphians, like their English counterparts, had come to value the capacity for

74. Abraham Weatherwise [pseud.], *Father Abraham's Almanack . . . for . . . 1767* (Philadelphia: Dunlap, 1766); *For 1769* (Philadelphia: Dunlap, 1768).

75. The proportion of advertisements that asserted sexual misbehavior of the wife was 37 percent in the 1760s, 28 percent in the 1770s, and 26 percent in the 1780s.

sentiment in the individual. Valuing the capacity for sentiment has usually been associated with the educated elite and the emerging middle classes, but the expectation that husbands could be evaluated within the framework of acute sensibility is seen in the language of advertisements by women from the moderate classes practicing self-divorce during the Revolutionary era.

Henry Miller, for instance, found his wife's rejection of their marriage somewhat baffling, writing in 1770 that his wife Mary "will not live with him for want of love, and no other reason." His words revealed a wife who required emotional fulfillment for a satisfactory marriage. In a similar fashion, Leonard Pfouts explained that his wife Rachel "has eloped from me for want of love, and has left my bed and board without a cause." Leonard believed his failure to supply his wife with affection was not fundamental to his marital obligations, but his wife disagreed. Another man had offered Leonard's wife the love he lacked. Rachel, his ad concluded, had "gone off with Samuel Oram, who is the main propagator of her leaving me." The language of sentiment also was used by wives in their responding advertisements. Charity Barr, who complained of her husband's physical abuse, included an accusation of his emotional betrayal when she wrote that she had received "such cruel usage, from a man who ought to have been her best friend." These women had not internalized the lessons from "The Medicine" and "Lurwell and Loveless." They had instead evaluated their husband's behavior and found him wanting. Emotional failings, "want of love," or an absence of a deep emotional connection had become a legitimate grievance for some wives.[76]

In this environment some couples openly advertised their separation by mutual agreement without asserting that either partner was at fault or insinuating that one party had deserted the marriage. Such no-fault self-divorces began appearing in the 1760s and increased over the next two decades. Before the 1760s just two couples had openly declared the termination of their marriage without cause. What was new during the period surrounding the Revolution was the open acknowledgment that a couple who agreed to part could do so by simple notification in the city's newspapers. Hannah and Robert Hill posted such a decree in 1771:

> Hannah Hill, or Hannah Watkinson, having declared, in the presence of several persons, that another man hath a better right to her than I have, and that she is desirous of parting from me, and being *extremely* willing

76. *PG*, Aug. 16, 1770, Mary and Henry Miller; *PP*, July 15, 1784, Rachel and Leonard Pfouts; *PG*, Aug. 10, 1785, Charity and Adam Barr. (Counties: Chester, Cumberland, and Bucks, respectively.)

to gratify her, I took her at her word, and we have mutually agreed to part *forever*."[77]

The Hills had fulfilled one of the customary tenets of self-divorce by declaring before witnesses their intention to separate, and both parties appear to have been satisfied with the termination of their marriage. Daniel Barnes, a Philadelphia bricklayer, declared that he and his wife "by reason of some unhappy differences, not being able to live agreeably any longer with each other, have agreed to a mutual separation." Cordwainer Peter Brown asserted that he and his wife, Mary, "have separated from each other by voluntary act and deed, duly executed before authority." Brown neglected to state what authority witnessed the separation, but it was probably the Mayor's Court or a justice of the peace. By the late 1770s, after the city had returned to patriot control, Philadelphia's Mayor's Court took on the function of ratifying self-divorces. Thus couples like Mary and John M'Kitrick could come before the court to solemnize their marital dissolution.[78]

Women expanded the uses of self-divorce to give themselves greater choice in their personal lives, and by the 1770s some women took direct action to summarily end their marriages by placing their own self-divorce ads in the public presses. The actions of women like Margaret Flack directly refuted the

77. *PC*, Dec. 9, 1771, Hannah and Robert Hill.

78. *PJ*, Apr. 30, 1777, Mary and Daniel Barnes; *PJ*, Aug. 23, 1764, Mary and Peter Brown. See also Philadelphia tailor James Welch, who advertised that he and his wife Rose "by a mutual agreement, have agreed to live sole and separate, and not to cohabit together for the future." *PG*, Sept. 1, 1768.

During the early years of the imperial conflict, divorce in the colony had become a point of disagreement between Pennsylvania colonists and the British government. Having in 1766 allowed the first colonial divorce enacted by legislative decree to stand, the Privy Council moved in 1773 to disallow divorce through colonial legislative action when the second Pennsylvania divorce case reached it. The Privy Council asserted that colonists must follow English law, which prohibited divorce, ruling that the Pennsylvania Assembly had usurped the authority of the crown by granting divorce. Reaction against colonial encroachment on imperial prerogatives was reflected in a brief legal crackdown on separations during the mid-1770s. See, for example, QSD, December session 1773, petition of Mary Johnson (ordered to return to her husband's house); March session 1774, Eva Maria and William Herles (Eva's alimony reduced); *PP*, Jan. 30, 1779, Mary and John M'Kitrick. Thomas R. Meehan, " 'Not Made out of Levity': Evolution of Divorce in Early Pennsylvania" *PMHB*, XCII (1968), 441–464. For Mayor's Court involvement in separations, see MCD, January session 1761, Anna Maria and John Byser; October session 1779, Rachel and Peter Morgan.

advice of Lurwell and Loveless. In 1771, she declared that she was severing her marriage ties: "Margaret Flack, the wife of Robert Flack, declines living with him any longer." Jemimah Wilson expressed a similar sentiment in 1777, that "she never intends to live with him any more, nor have any Concern with him." Other wives advertised their husband's desertion and ended their ties to him. These runaway husband advertisements first appeared in the 1770s. Writing from Berks County in 1774, Mary Seidebander informed the public that her husband Matthias had "eloped from his wife about three years ago without any reason whatsoever." Mary gave Matthias public notice, "Unless he returns in three months after the date hereof, I will disown him as a husband." Two Philadelphia wives gave their husbands no opportunity for reunion, summarily terminating their marital union. Elizabeth M. Jackle declared, "Since my husband Jacob Jackle left me these two years and a half, after misbehaving himself greatly . . . I shall not live with him any more, nor pay anything for him." Barbara Cannaway's husband had also been gone two years when his wife advertised him, saying that she "will have nothing to do with him, and that he shall have no pretensions on me, nor on my goods nor will I have any on him."[79]

The self-divorce advertisements placed by Philadelphia's husbands also exhibited a heightened gender conflict and presented new criteria for justifiably ending a marriage. Husbands asserted that they had a just right to self-divorce from an erring wife without claiming that she had eloped. In many ads in the 1770s and 1780s they claimed that a wife "behaved in such a manner, that I find it impossible to live with her any longer." Such ads simply chastised a wife's behavior and then dismissed her. These husbands asserted their right to separate from a wife whose behavior they found intolerable or unforgivable. Sometimes these ads suggested that the wife's offense was infidelity, as Matthias Pinyard did: "Dorcus Pinyard has behaved herself in [such] a scandalous manner, that I cannot live with her." In other instances husbands cited turbulent, nonsubmissive behavior. Matthias Baxter declared that he and Margaret "have for some time past had several disagreeable quarrels, entirely owing to her misconduct, I am therefor resolved never to have any more connection with her."[80]

79. *PG*, Apr. 4, 1771, Margaret and Robert Flack; Mar. 26, 1777, Jemimah and John Wilson; Nov. 30, 1774, Matthias and Mary Seidebander; Feb. 18, 1784, Jacob and Elizabeth M. Jackle; Oct. 15, 1783, Michael and Barbara Cannaway.

80. *PP*, Oct. 4, 1773, Mary and Patrick Phays; *PJ*, Aug. 9, 1780, Dorcas and Matthias Pinyard; *PP*, Aug. 9, 1780, Matthias and Margaret Baxter. See also *PJ*, July 13, 1769,

While the fictional Lurwell advocated male sexual privilege and the double standard, the words and deeds of actual women in the city's newspapers repudiated it. These wives responded to their husbands' ads by placing their own, publicizing their husbands' extramarital behavior. Louise Leddel was in the vanguard, as the only wife who published accounts of her husband's sexual indiscretions before the 1760s. In 1753 she explained that she left her husband for three reasons: his physical abuse of her, his misuse of money she brought to the marriage, and his long-term parallel relationship with another woman. At the time Dr. William Leddel advertised his wife's departure, he had been involved with another woman for at least two years. As Louise put it, "He kept another woman, by whom he had two children."[81]

During the 1760s, 1770s, and 1780s other women came forward with similar responses. In 1767, rather than following the lessons of Lurwell, Mary Blum accused her husband of adultery, and Elizabeth Perkins lambasted her husband for immorality by keeping "disorderly company" and entertaining "the infamous guests he frequently brought to his house, where, amidst the most notorious scenes of disorder, I often met with treatment what would have shocked a savage of the Ohio." These women had in the 1760s begun to question the necessity of remaining silent about their husbands' sexual exploits. These, the most outspoken wives, were willing to expose their husbands' sexual misbehavior in the public press and reject the sexual double standard. Men had left wives for other women throughout the eighteenth century, and others had established parallel illicit unions, but no wives had dared defame them in the public press with accusations of adultery or bastardy. Rebecca Dunbar, whom we met earlier, demonstrates the more typical response colonial wives made to their husband's infidelity. When Thomas falsely advertised Rebecca as an eloped wife in 1760, she turned to the Overseers of the Poor to secure financial support from her husband. What she did not do was expose him as an adulterer and the father of several illegitimate children.[82]

Elizabeth and John Clark (mariner); *PP*, Oct. 11, 1773, Mary and John Doyle; *PEP*, June 22, 1775, Mary and George Sivewright. All are Philadelphia cases. Husbands from the mid-Atlantic region surrounding Philadelphia did not adapt their advertisements to include general claims that they could not tolerate their wives and thus had parted from them.

81. *PG*, Jan. 23, 1753, Louise and Dr. William Leddel.

82. *PJ*, Nov. 25, 1767, Mary and Peter Blum; *PC*, Aug. 24, 1767, Elizabeth and Joseph Perkins. Thomas Dunbar fathered children with two different women, Elizabeth Koch

Other wives refused to remain silent. In 1782 Philadelphian Mary Sommerset denied that she had left her husband Zachariah "without any provocation" as her husband's ad asserted. Mary's own ad declared that her husband's "whole conduct towards me has been such, that if recapitulated by me, it would shock and offend modesty: nay, the greatest libertine would say 'Sommerset, you are a compleat masterpiece of villainy!' " The following year Barbara Burkhardt gave a full report of her husband's infidelity in response to his advertisement of her. Jacob Burkhardt had alleged her economic misbehavior and left the rest to the reader's imagination by closing, "My grievances shall, if called on by her, be stated at large to a Candid public." Barbara called his bluff and responded with indignation and full disclosure. She refuted his economic grievances against her and declared:

> They have lived happily together till within these six months, when his acquaintance and connections with another woman by whom he has a child, caused this disturbance, and having more affection for this woman than his lawful wife, he is seduced, by her persuasions, to ill treat, abuse and advertise his faithful wife.

Barbara was unwilling to stand by and have her Philadelphia neighbors believe she was the cause of their self-divorce.[83]

These wives had rejected the scripts of popular culture that lay the blame for a husband's infidelity in the wife's lap. They rejected the legitimacy of male sexual privilege and in some instances fought back against their husband's infidelity by asserting their own marital rights. Elizabeth Elliot took to the public presses to derail her husband's plans to marry the woman he had discarded her for. Joseph had informed her that "he intended immediate marriage" with a widow he was living with in Philadelphia County, with whom he "criminally corresponds," and that she could expect nothing from him. Elizabeth refused to relinquish her marital claim on Joseph and closed her ad with a warning to any who might aid in his remarriage: "These may in-

---

and Hannah Houthem, in the two years after he claimed his wife, Rebecca, had eloped. Houthem and Dunbar ultimately established a long-term union, marrying after Rebecca's death in 1765. Evidence of Thomas Dunbar's sexual connections outside his marriage is documented in the vital records of St. Michael's Church and by Susan Klepp in *Philadelphia in Transition: A Demographic History of the City and Its Occupational Groups, 1720–1830* (New York, 1989), 112.

83. *PJ*, Nov. 20, 1782, *PP*, Nov. 30, 1782, Zachariah and Mary Sommerset alias Somers; *PP*, July 26, Aug. 14, 1783, Jacob and Barbara Burkhardt.

form the above named and described parties, that if they marry each other, a prosecution for bigamy will be the result; and all ministers, magistrates, etc. are requested to govern themselves accordingly." Women such as Elizabeth Elliot, Barbara Burkhardt, and Mary Sommerset asserted that husbands' prerogatives did not extend to freewheeling extramarital sexual experiences and turned to the public for judgment of their husband's actions. By their words and deeds these wives created a counterdiscourse to that promoted in the popular press.[84]

While men of the middling class published stories about sex and gender to shape the sexual culture to meet their interests, other Philadelphians were expanding the implications of a more open sexual culture to grant women greater agency to lay claim to individual satisfaction. Many of those practicing self-divorce, and perhaps some of those engaging in casual sexual relations that led to bastardy, had embraced connections between Enlightenment-inspired quests for self-knowledge and human perfectibility, and self-directed choices in personal life and sexual practice.

During the 1760s, 1770s, and 1780s, competing discourses sought to shape the meanings associated with sexual practices undertaken outside courtship and marriage and the new attention given to sexuality in popular print culture. These discourses presented distinct interpretations, each highly gendered. Popular print interpreted nonmarital and extramarital sexual behaviors as both an opportunity for men to engage in sex without the social obligations and, simultaneously, as a dangerous and destabilizing force, if not carefully funneled into specific forms that would not undermine the gender and class hierarchy of their society. Other men and women expressed a broad, more open-ended interpretation of what sexual practice untethered to courtship and marriage might mean for the individual, and they claimed the prerogative to shape the meanings of expanded sexual practices themselves.

84. *PG*, July 30, 1783, Joseph and Elizabeth Elliot. The Elliots had made their home in New Jersey. Elizabeth followed Joseph to Philadelphia County, where he had set up a household with the widow of Peter Hanbest.

PART II

SEX IN THE CITY
IN THE AGE OF
DEMOCRATIC REVOLUTIONS

The last third of the eighteenth century has been characterized as the Era of Democratic Revolutions. Men and women throughout the Atlantic world enacted the natural rights philosophy of the sovereignty of the people, testing through revolution and re-creation the theories of human perfectibility, liberty, and self-governance. Enlightenment political philosophies would shape government in the emerging United States in the 1780s and ignite revolutionary fervor throughout Europe and the Caribbean, sparking revolution in France (1789) and Saint Domingue (1791).

Philadelphia was at the intellectual center of political and social ferment in British North America and soon would be the national capital of the United States. Many of the battles over the nature of the new Republic would take place there. Philadelphia's already strong commercial and intellectual links to Europe would be strengthened by its role as the capital, as European ambassadors resided in the city and Philadelphia personages took on the work of foreign policy abroad. The political debates about the nature of the new government made the city a hotbed of political conflict between Democratic-Republicans and Federalists of the 1790s. Philadelphians were aroused by the French Revolution—its toppling of a powerful European monarchy, the Reign of Terror in 1792–1793, and the revolutionary wake in the French colonial Caribbean that destroyed racial slavery in Saint Domingue and created a Haitian republic that enfranchised freed blacks.[1]

When Americans and their European and Caribbean neighbors sought to

1. Michael Durey, *Transatlantic Radicals and the Early American Republic* (Lawrence, Kans., 1997), 221–250; Susan Branson, *These Fiery Frenchified Dames: Women and Political Culture in Early National Philadelphia* (Philadelphia, 2001), 55–99; David Waldstreicher, *In the Midst of Perpetual Fetes: The Making of American Nationalism, 1776–1820* (Chapel Hill, N.C., 1997), 112–116, 126–140.

put Enlightenment philosophies into action by creating new societies, the theoretical questions concerning individuals' political rights and their relationships to the state came to occupy center stage. Americans were forced to come to terms with the conceptual problems of the position of women in society. The justification for their subordination to men would have to be addressed. The philosophical principles propelling the creation of the first modern republic required it. By the 1790s the more radical French and Haitian revolutions stimulated challenges to American women's limited political role and the patriarchal foundations of marriage. As women in France engaged in direct political action, took up arms, and asserted that they were full citizens, the debates over American women's role in the Republic escalated and became more highly charged.[2]

Questions about the status and power of certain groups of men also took on new Revolutionary importance in Philadelphia. The revolt against the mother country was adapted to critique and delegitimate many other relationships within the social hierarchy. Laboring men participated in the revolt against Britain and claimed equal participation in the governance of the new state and, with middling artisans, organized as a political force to challenge the political and economic interests of their betters. African-Americans articulated their resistance to slavery through the patriot rhetoric of liberty, heightening their demands for freedom and securing the gradual abolition of slavery that forbade the future enslavement of African-Americans in Pennsylvania beginning in 1780. This freedom, however, would not be complete. Many of the first generation of Philadelphia free blacks would live in a semifree state as a special class of indentured laborers in a community where white workers were increasingly wage laborers.[3]

2. Rosemarie Zagarri, "The Rights of Man and Woman in Post-Revolutionary America," *WMQ*, 3d Ser., LV (1998), 203–230; Branson, *These Fiery Frenchified Dames*, 55–59; Carroll Smith-Rosenberg, "Black Gothic: The Shadowy Origins of the American Bourgeoisie," in Robert Blair St. George, ed., *Possible Pasts: Becoming Colonial in Early America* (Ithaca, N.Y., 2000), 243–269.

3. Eric Foner, *Tom Paine and Revolutionary America* (New York, 1976); Steven Rosswurm, *Arms, Country, and Class: The Philadelphia Militia and "Lower Sort" during the American Revolution, 1775–1783* (New Brunswick, N.J., 1987); Ronald Schultz, *The Republic of Labor: Philadelphia Artisans and the Politics of Class, 1720–1830* (New York, 1993); Gary B. Nash, *Forging Freedom: The Formation of Philadelphia's Black Community, 1720–1840* (Cambridge, Mass., 1988); Peter Wood, " 'Liberty Is Sweet': African-American Freedom Struggles in the Years before White Independence," in Alfred F. Young, ed., *Beyond the American Revolution: Explorations in the History of American*

Nor was the politics of governance the only place Philadelphians pursued the Lockean philosophy of equality, liberty, autonomy, and personal freedom. Following the Revolution the nonmarital sexual practices of the urban pleasure culture spread. Philadelphians developed an expansive, permissive, but contentious sexual culture. Sexuality took on added importance in the public political culture, as intimate behavior became a place to express and debate the appropriate power and autonomy to be exercised by specific groups within the new nation. The challenges to authority simultaneously generated great anxiety for some, who worried that the forces of revolution would destroy it, sabotaging the great experiments in human self-governance by excessive freedoms, too much democratic leveling, and licentious indulgence. In the Age of Revolution the Enlightenment would have personal implications, and the personal would become political. For some, sexual behavior was an important manifestation of personal freedom and an assertion of self-expression. Ultimately, too, sexuality would play a central role in framing the conservative anti-Revolutionary response.

Radicalism (DeKalb, Ill., 1993), 149–184. Under the Pennsylvania law those people who were slaves as of February 28, 1780, would remain slaves. The children of these women were required to serve prolonged indentures, held in servitude, until they were twenty-eight years old. Those not manumitted by owners would give birth to "free" children who were required to serve prolonged indentures to their mother's master. Nash, *Forging Freedom*, 62.

CHAPTER 4 To Be "Free and Independent"

Sex among the Revolutionary Rabble

About five o'clock in the morning on New Year's Day, 1802, Joham Thager, a cordwainer, and Frederick Auckenback, a servant, tumbled out of Hay's Tavern, in Fourth Street near Branch, to make their way home after an evening of drinking to celebrate the New Year. They bade each other good night and went their separate ways. But Frederick did not head toward his master's house, where he resided. Instead, he walked to the house where his lover worked at service as a domestic laborer, four blocks away in Arch Street near Third, went up the alley to the kitchen door, and knocked. Justina, his lover, lowered the upstairs window and called to Frederick that the kitchen door was open and he should come up. Frederick went in.[1]

Justina Ristiur was not a single woman living at service, secreting her lover in for a predawn visit. She was a married woman, who kept house with her husband, Jacob, in the Northern Liberties. The New Year's meeting was a secret rendezvous with her outside man, and this was not the first time they had arranged such a meeting. A month earlier, three weeks before Christmas, Frederick and Justina had arranged to meet at a mutual friend's rented room in the Northern Liberties.

On this occasion Thager had accompanied Frederick to visit John Wagner in his rented room. While Thager and Wagner were visiting, Justina and Frederick slipped away downstairs and into the garden, where they were observed making love in the garden behind the house. Thager recalled that he and Wagner looked out the upstairs back window:

> It being a clear Moon light night, when this deponent saw the said Justina lying on the ground with her clothes up and the said Frederick Auckenback on the top of her in the act of copulation; That it was so light that this deponent distinctly saw the bare thighs of the said Justina.[2]

1. The events in the Jacob and Justina Ristiur case are reconstructed from PDP, *Jacob Ristiur vs. Justina Ristiur*, 1802, the events of this case occurring in 1801–1802.

2. Deposition of Joham Thager, Dec. 20, 1802, *Ristiur vs. Ristiur*, PDP.

The lives of the four players in this real-life drama were intricately linked. Thager and Frederick frequently visited Jacob and Justina Ristiur in their home in the year preceding these events. Justina was often seen at her home "in the Evening, at the door, as if waiting for the said Frederick and as soon as she would see the Said Frederick coming she would run to meet him and would after walk off with him." Justina appeared smitten with the man she had taken on as her lover. Ultimately the relationship between Justina and Frederick, which persisted for more than a year of her marriage, led Jacob and Justina to separate. Justina and Frederick then continued their relationship.

The sexual scene that this intimate history depicts was not atypical of Philadelphia in the three decades after the Revolution. Post-Revolutionary Philadelphia had changed from the community it had been at midcentury. Not only had it weathered war, occupation, and the implementation of a new republican form of government; it had also expanded the acceptable arenas of sexual behavior. During the 1760s and 1770s some members of the community had rejected the mandatory marital confines on reproductive sexuality, leaving marriages for new relationships or bearing illegitimate children outside serious or permanent relationships. Others had introduced the pleasure culture to the city, indulging in casual intimacies and sex commerce. Many had indulged in vicarious sexual adventures through reading erotic tales available in the city's pre-Revolutionary print culture.

During the war the city had witnessed the libertine sexual practices of the British military, and some had joined in. For others the social disruptions and physical mobility of the war years led to intimate relationships. Ann, a young domestic servant in Elizabeth Drinker's employ, for instance, made a connection with a British officer when he billeted in the Drinkers' home, and then left with him when he moved on. The war created the opportunity for other women to leave marriages and find new mates. Husbands' military service often separated couples, and new, intriguing men, often soldiers from abroad, proved too tempting for some. When Philadelphian Bernard Corrigan returned to the city after serving with the patriot forces, he found that his wife, Laetitia, had married another man. Betty Bourchier of the Northern Liberties left her husband after striking up a relationship with "a continental soldier, lately discharged," and Mary Miller left her marriage and the city in the company of two soldiers she had met in the barracks across the street from the home she shared with her husband, John. For these women, the husband's absence or the presence of many unattached soldiers in the city facilitated making new matches and ending their marriages. How often women left their marriages because they found them unsatisfactory, or because the war placed them in need of material assistance that a new male partner could provide, cannot be discovered. In either case, the Revolutionary era saw more women leaving their marriages to establish new relationships than had left in the past. These changes helped pave the way for the more expansive sexual culture after the war.[3]

Following the American Revolution, sexual expression in the city blossomed. The numbers of Philadelphians who established intimate lives independent of marriage rose: bastardy increased dramatically, prostitution flourished throughout the city, and adultery became a viable sexual option for many more. The challenge to illegitmate authority embodied in Enlightenment thinking and Revolutionary republican philosophy lent legitimacy to the quest for personal autonomy and fulfillment. These Philadelphians had created a subtle revolution in personal behavior, and individuals like Justina Ristiur and Frederick Auckenback were its foot soldiers.[4]

But the Revolution had fundamentally changed the relationship of the common people to the state. In their turn away from monarchy to a government of the people, Americans embraced a political philosophy that relied on the virtue of its citizens. If the people were to be self-governing, republican leaders professed, they must be virtuous and rational and act for the common good. Uncontrolled sexuality could become dangerous: because the body would come to rule the man, such men would not make good citizens. The implications of the Revolution seemed to lead in two different directions.

Could not have embodied in the new sexuality the new republic + meant the body ruled the man

An Expansive Sexual Culture Takes Root

Post-Revolutionary Philadelphia was full of sexual opportunity. M. L. E. Moreau de Saint-Méry, who lived there from 1794 through 1798, went to great lengths to document the laxity of the post-Revolutionary sexual code. As an aristocratic Frenchman who had resided in both late-eighteenth-century Paris

3. Joseph J. Kelley, Jr., *Life and Times in Colonial Philadelphia* (Harrisburg, Pa., 1973), 179 (on adultery during British occupation and husband's absence), 179–181 (on frolics and mistresses and "whoring" among British military), 177 (on Philadelphia's prostitutes' servicing George Washington's troops at Valley Forge), 183 (on servants' leaving with British soldiers after sexual liasons); Elaine Forman Crane, ed., *The Diary of Elizabeth Drinker* (Boston, 1991), I, 273 (Jan. 4, 1778); *PEP*, Mar. 20, 1780, Bernard and Laetitia Corrigan; *PP*, Mar. 17, 1781, James and Betty Bourchier; *PG*, Aug. 22, 1771, John and Mary Miller. See also *PP*, Aug. 18, 1778, Jan. 8, 1780, for servants' and husbands' flight during the war.

4. See Appendix, Tables A.2–A.5.

and Saint Domingue, he had lived in communities that embraced a permissive sexual ethic. He was struck by what he perceived as the hypocritical nature of the sexual culture. "I repeat that morals in this city, as elsewhere in the United States, are not pure, although they pretend to be virtuous." He supported this assertion with a compendium of the sexual behavior he observed in Philadelphia, including bastardy, prostitution, and adultery. Americans professed virtue but engaged in a wide range of sexual adventures. A retailer of contraceptives in his printing and stationery shop, he wrote, "They [contraceptive syringes] were in great demand among Americans, in spite of the false shame so prevalent among the latter." To a Frenchman accustomed to sexual liberty, Philadelphians' reticence to acknowledge their nonmarital sexual behavior was hypocrisy. The elite and middle-class men of his acquaintance were slightly embarrassed about the extent to which post-Revolutionary Philadelphia had embraced unbridled sexuality.[5]

But it was true. Bastardy was accurately described by Moreau de Saint-Méry as "extremely common in Philadelphia." The number of Philadelphians bearing bastard children outside recognizable family units in the 1790s was three and a half times what it had been in the pre-Revolutionary period of 1767–1776. By the 1790s the population had almost doubled. Thus the rate of bastardy was almost twice what it had been in the pre-Revolutionary decade. The governmental response to bastardy in the new nation remained the same as in the late colonial period, with a system of mandatory child support administered by the Guardians of the Poor aided by the courts when necessary, even though the proportion of Philadelphians bearing bastard children had increased.[6]

5. Kenneth Roberts and Anna M. Roberts, eds. and trans., *Moreau de St. Méry's American Journey (1793–1798)* (Garden City, N.Y., 1947), 176–178, 311, 314; Lynn Hunt, ed., *Eroticism and the Body Politic* (Baltimore, 1991); Robert Darnton, *The Forbidden Best-Sellers of Pre-Revolutionary France* (New York, 1995).

6. Roberts and Roberts, eds. and trans., *Moreau de St. Méry's American Journey*, 293. On bastardy, see Table 1, above. The same kinds of records continued to exist in the 1790s that were available in the pre-Revolutionary eras, and were used to calculate bastardy cases: MCD, QSD (Philadelphia cases only), GPM, and Guardians of the Poor, Bond Book, CCAP. In addition the Guardians maintained admission and birth records for the city's almshouse that indicated bastardy cases. In the 1790s the courts kept an additional record, PFT, which indicates an initial arrest requiring the accused father of an illegitimate child to post bond to appear at court, or settle with the Guardians. Nothing in the procedures or consequences concerning bastardy had changed since before the Revolution; therefore, the increase in cases probably did correspond to the

The data collected here, from court dockets, divorce papers, and the Guardians of the Poor and almshouse records, present the most comprehensive record available of the sexual behavior of Philadelphians during the first three decades after the war. But they are, of course, incomplete. For bastardy they record only those individuals who wanted, or needed, the intervention of the Guardians of the Poor to secure child support for their out-of-wedlock children. They do not include cases that were privately settled, and there were surely many such cases, especially among men of the upper classes.[7]

Benjamin Rush inadvertently recorded several of these in his commonplace book under a section "DEATHS of Persons of Note or Singular Character." Peppered among Rush's personal obituaries for prominent members of Philadelphia society are the expansive sexual histories of several leading men of the community. The Reverend John Hay, whom Rush characterized as "sensible, logical, well acquainted with the Scriptures, and remarkably perspicuous in all his discourse," "seduced" a rich widow from his congregation "and had a child by her." Hay's illegitimate child does not show up in the city's bastardy records, but Hay was not secretive about his relationship or his child. Rush recounted: "While living in a state of concubinage with the woman he had seduced, he rode with her and his child by her through the streets of Philadelphia regardless alike of public opinion and of the public eye." Governor Thomas Mifflin, whom Rush disliked for both his "immoral character" and his politics of catering to "the meanest of people," also fathered illegitimate children while he was married and seeking public office. Rush tells us that Mifflin "had lived in a state of adultery with many women during the life of his wife, and had children by some of them, whom he educated in his own family." Mifflin's bastard children were cared for within his own household and therefore never appeared in the public record. Mifflin was elected governor in

---

increased incidence of bastardy. Nothing indicates any increase in the vigilance of the community in seeking out bastard cases. In fact, there are many indications that the larger community was less interested in pursuit of these cases during this period. The Overseers of the Poor became the Guardians of the Poor in 1788. See John K. Alexander, *Render Them Submissive: Responses to Poverty in Philadelphia, 1760–1800* (Amherst, Mass., 1980), 110–117. The changes in the structure of the city's administration of poor relief did not affect the treatment of illegitimacy. John Purdon, *A Digest of the Laws of Pennsylvania, from the Year 1700, to the Seventh Day of April 1830* (Philadelphia, 1831), 716–759 (on the poor laws), 342–344 (on bastardy laws).

7. The tables on sexual transgression in the Appendix give a full account of the sources consulted.

the autumn following his wife's death, which was said to have been caused by "a broken heart in consequence of his conduct towards her."[8]

Other men of less substantial means also chose to handle the care of their illegitimate children themselves. It is impossible to know how many men there were, like James Mahoney, who felt that it was their responsibility to support their children. Mahoney confided to a friend that his lover, Elizabeth Bender, was with child and "that therefore he considered it his duty to provide for her." This couple ran off together, leaving Elizabeth's husband, recently returned from sea, to seek a divorce.[9]

There were also cases like that of Alexander Fowler, where men made secretive arrangements to care for their illegitimate children. Fowler privately arranged for his child to be cared for in a married couple's household to keep the knowledge of this child from his church. He was unsuccessful. A little more than a year after the child was born, Thomas Jameson, the husband of the couple, testified before the church disciplinary session:

> Alexander Fowler took the child out of its mother's Arms and delivered the child to his wife and desired her to take care of it and he would pay for it.— That Alexander Fowler expressly agreed with Thomas Jameson to give him half a Dollar per week for keeping the child and that he has had the care of the child something better than four months and Alexander Fowler had actually paid him for the nursing of it.[10]

Elizabeth McDougall, the mother of the child, wanted Fowler to continue to contribute to her support after the child had been placed with the Jamesons. She went before "Squire Rush to Swear the child to Alexander Fowler" to accomplish this. "Squire Rush told her there was no necessity of her Swearing the child to him since he has engaged to pay for the nursing of it." Having already set up child support arrangements that mimicked those of the Guardians of the Poor and successfully fulfilled them, Fowler circumvented the normal channels of regulated child support. One must assume that many other men had reason to do just the same.[11]

8. George W. Corner, ed., *The Autobiography of Benjamin Rush: His "Travels through Life," Together with His Commonplace Book for 1789–1813* (Princeton, N.J., 1948), 190 (on Mifflin), 316–317 (on Hay). Mifflin was elected in October 1790; his wife died the preceding summer.

9. PDP, *Daniel Bender vs. Elizabeth Bender*, filed December 1799, events 1799; deposition of John Hallman, Jan. 23, 1800.

10. Scots Presbyterian Church, Session Minutes, Dec. 22, 1788, PHS.

11. Ibid., testimony of Thomas Jameson.

Given this evidence of bastardy outside the public record, especially cases that were common knowledge, the city's official record of bastardy must be understood as only a portion of the actual incidence of bastardy in the 1790s. These numbers, which indicate that 1 in 197 adult Philadelphians parented an illegitimate child each year, or that 1 in every 20 did at some point during the decade, underrepresent the actual incidence. Nevertheless, they indicate a significant increase over the cases in the pre-Revolutionary era. Philadelphia of the 1790s was a city where the popularly elected governor resided in open adultery raising his illegitimate children and where the character of a gentleman, Benjamin Rush complained, included the obligatory begetting of bastards.[12]

While bastardy increased, prostitution had become so pervasive that a Brazilian who visited Philadelphia in 1798 depicted it as commonplace and extremely obvious, even to the foreign eye. "The prostitutes in Philadelphia are so many that they flood the streets at night, in such a way that even looking at them in the streets without men you can recognize them." Moreau de Saint-Méry concurred. "Houses of ill fame" had "multiplied in Philadelphia" and were "frequented at all hours."[13] In 1784 *The Philadelphiad; or, New Pictures of the City* depicted a Philadelphia bagnio, or house of prostitution, as a central and recognized institution of the city, next to its descriptions of Bell's Book-Store and the London Coffee-House:

BAGNIO

Turn we to view the Bagnio's horrid scene,

. . . .

The leg half-naked and the breast quite bare,
With all the studied ornament of hair,
The garments loose to raise the warm desire,

12. During the 1760s recorded cases of bastardy, under this same legal and administrative system, accounted for 1 of every 380 Philadelphians. During the late colonial period there must also have been some undocumented cases of illegitimacy, but there was not the pervasive, openly acknowledged bastardy that there was in 1790s Philadelphia. Corner, ed., *Autobiography of Rush*, 190 (on Mifflin), 225 (on gentlemen and bastards).

13. Roberts and Roberts, eds. and trans., *Moreau de St. Méry's American Journey*, 312; Robe Hipolito da Costa Pereira, *Diario de minha viagem para Filadelfia (1798–1799)* [diary of my trip to Philadelphia] (Rio de Janeiro, 1955), 65. Hipolito da Costa Pereira was a young man when he made this trip. Special thanks to Monica Montero for her translation from the Portuguese.

And touch the passions with a keener fire,
Her syren voice that captivates the ear,
With tempting gestures and inviting leer.[14]

This scene of a scantily clad woman of the trade enticing a young man into her lair was described as a common occurrence that gave the city some of its character. Prostitution probably surpassed bastardy as the most common non-marital sexual behavior of Philadelphians during the late eighteenth century. But little legal action was taken to curb this activity. During the 1790s, when streetwalkers "flooded" the streets and bawdyhouses appeared in every neighborhood, there were fewer than two arrests per month for prostitution.[15]

Members of all classes and both races frequented taverns, bawdyhouses, and "negro" houses for sexual adventure. John York, a free African-American, ran such a house in Philadelphia throughout the 1790s. These establishments were described in the *Pennsylvania Gazette* as places where "all the loose and

14. *The Philadelphiad; or, New Pictures of the City: Interspersed with a Candid Review and Display of Some First-Rate Modern Characters of Both Sexes* . . . (Philadelphia: Kline and Reynolds, 1784), I, 21–22. Advertisements and commentary about the *Philadelphiad* appeared in *PJ*, Sept. 18, 24, 1784, and *PP*, Dec. 14, 1784. *The Philiadelphiad* was inexpensive, volume II selling for a quarter of a dollar. *The Philiadelphiad* is one of the few surviving locally produced descriptions of the social terrain of the city written by one of its residents. It was a humorous look at themselves, and many of the key people and institutions of the city were described. Personages such as Benjamin Rush and Dr. Shippen and key institutions such as the courthouse, the New Jail, Bell's Book-Store, the London Coffee-House, and the Lunatic Asylum were lampooned in its pages.

15. For geographical location of bawdyhouses, see Map 1. For criminal arrests, see Appendix 1, Tables A.2–A.5. From 1790 to 1799 there were 53 arrests for prostitution-related offenses documented in the regular court records (PFT, MCD). In addition there were 142 arrests for vagrancy between 1790 and 1797 (1798–1799 records missing), which indicate a prostitution-related offense. This statute was used to remove the "disorderly" from the streets. James T. Mitchell, Henry Flanders, et al., comps., *The Statutes at Large of Pennsylvania* (Harrisburg, 1896–1915), VII, 84–88, XIII, 251–255; Vagrancy Docket, 1790–1797, CCAP.

Particularly lewd streetwalking women were temporarily removed from the streets in this way. Servants and members of the "unruly" poor were also temporarily incarcerated under this statute for "being taken in a bawdyhouse." Criminal prosecutions for maintaining a bawdyhouse, or being "a lewd woman," in the Mayor's Court required finding witnesses willing to testify before a jury about specific behavior, and few chose to in the 1790s. See Vagrancy Docket, 1790–1797. Prosecuting prostitution is discussed in Chapter 7, below.

PLATE 8. *John Lewis Krimmel,* Worldly Folk and Their Master Questioning
Chimneysweeps before Christ Church (1747), Philadelphia. *1811–1813.*
Permission The Metropolitan Museum of Art, Rogers Fund, 1942. (42.95.15)

idle characters of the city, whether whites, blacks, or mulattoes . . . indulge in riotous mirth and dancing till the dawn." They were also places where couples engaged in illicit sex. Sarah Smith, for example, frequented York's house in 1793 for trysts with her lover. Sarah was a married woman and pregnant with a child reputedly fathered by this man.[16]

These semipublic places of amusement accommodated the multiracial character of the city's sexual culture. During the first decades following the Revolution, open cross-racial intimacy was tolerated in Philadelphia, although by no means accepted as legitimate by many Philadelphians. This toleration must be measured against the pre-Revolutionary legal prohibitions against sexual relations across the color line and the strong disapproval that emerged by the second decade of the nineteenth century. Toleration of mixed racial unions was influenced during the 1790s by French colonial refugees from Saint Domingue who resided in the city with their African and African-French wives and mistresses. These colonials from the Caribbean were more open about their relationships with African women, and such couples exemplified in Philadelphia the possibilities of marriage across the color line. John F. Watson described the scene of his youth in Philadelphia: "Mestizo ladies, with complexions of the palest marble, jet black hair, and eyes of the gazelle, and of the most exquiste symmetry, were to be seen, escorted along the pavement by white French gentlemen, both dressed in West India fashion, and of the richest materials; coal black negresses, in flowing white dresses, and turbans of 'muchoir de Madras,' exhibiting their ivory dominos, in social walk with a white or creole." Street scenes of early national Philadelphia depict the social proximity of this diverse population. Whites mixed with blacks, and the high-born interacted with those of lower origins (see Plate 8).[17]

Despite this relative toleration, cross-racial couples were vulnerable to more vigilant enforcement of the laws against illicit sex. Periodically they were sin-

16. John York appears in court records periodically from 1793 through 1805: PFT, June 19, 1793, Sept. 17, 1796, Mar. 5, 1798, May 3, 1802, July 17, 1805; Vagrancy Docket, June 17, 1797; QSD, Dec. 2, 1805; PG, Aug. 8, 1787. Sarah Smith: PFT, June 19, 1793.

17. John F. Watson, *Annals of Philadelphia* . . . (Philadelphia, 1830), 170. See, for example, on cross-racial relations: PDP, *Robert Irwin vs. Catharine Irwin*, April 1795; PFT, Jan. 14, 1799, case of William McCray and Aley Thomas; PFT, 1802, case of Rachel White. In 1726 Pennsylvania passed An Act for the Better Regulating Negroes in this Province, which prohibited cohabitation or marriage between whites and blacks; it was eliminated with the passage of the Gradual Abolition Act of 1780. Mitchell, Flanders, et al., comps., *Statutes at Large*, IV, 59–64.

gled out for arrest, as when the city watchman plucked William McCray, a white man, and Aley Thomas, a black woman, from the clientele of a local bawdyhouse and deposited them in the city jail, and when Hannah Dougherty was charged with "being taken in a Negro House amongst a number of persons of Ill fame." Nevertheless, during the 1790s cross-racial couples publicly legitimated their unions by marriage and openly participated in the public street culture of the city.[18]

In post-Revolutionary Philadelphia individuals moved in and out of sexual relationships with ease, and the broader society accommodated them. People would watch one another's behavior—it was hard not to in the close quarters of eighteenth-century urban living—but they did not intervene to inhibit non-marital and extramarital sexual liaisons. Rarely was nonmarital sexual behavior criminally prosecuted. The documented increase in bastardy, adultery, and prostitution during the late eighteenth century was not due to an increase in prosecutions. This sexual activity was recorded primarily in public records that noted behavior that was not prosecuted in criminal proceedings. Of the bastardy cases in the 1790s, 80 percent were documented through the Guardians of the Poor adjudication of child support and never appeared in any court records. Thus most cases were resolved by the man's posting bond to secure his intention to pay child support immediately following the woman's appearance before an alderman to swear paternity. Another 17 percent of cases appear only at the initial stage of legal action. In these cases the man was arrested and recorded in the Prisoners for Trial docket with the notation that a particular woman had sworn that he fathered her illegitimate child. Most of these men quickly posted bond, either to appear in court or, more commonly, to guarantee their child support through the Guardians of the Poor, were released, and faced no further legal proceedings.

Bastardy in the 1790s was criminally prosecuted only when the father denied paternity and refused to support the child. Such prosecution occurred in only 2 percent of the cases. These men were tried, found guilty, and fined ten pounds in addition to being compelled to set up child support payments "agreeable to the Guardians of the Poor." Under the law the state could have prosecuted the other 98 percent, or fourteen hundred men and women, and collected the standard ten-dollar fine from each. But it did not: the community

18. PFT: Jan. 14, 1799, William McCray and Aley Thomas; Mar. 21, 1794, Hannah Dougherty. On marriage, see Gloria Dei, Marriages, Jan. 8, 1794, July 2, Sept. 22, 1800, December 1803, Feb. 20, 1817, Feb. 20, 1818. On white-and-black couples in public, see Watson, *Annals of Philadelphia*, 170.

interest in bastardy was financial, and Philadelphians of the 1790s paid attention to it only to secure support for children who were legally "fatherless." They never used the courts as a mechanism to try to curb the growing incidence of illegitimate children and the nonmarital sexual behavior that begot them.[19]

This rise in the incidence of bastardy demonstrates that increasing numbers of men and women were stepping outside the marital orientation of sexuality. While this sexual behavior was embraced by only a minority of the city's population, the increase in bastardy in the early national period demonstrated a protracted rupture in the sexual system that had in the past confined most reproductive sexuality to courtship and marriage. The lax treatment of bastardy by the courts and the regulation of child support through the Guardians of the Poor accommodated those who engaged in nonmarital sexual behavior.

The courts' treatment of other sexual offenses also presents a picture of Philadelphia as allowing a great deal of sexual freedom. Simple fornication, still illegal under the revised penal code, was never the sole cause of arrest or prosecution in the 1790s. For these ten years (1790–1799) the Prisoners for Trial docket and the Mayor's Court docket record only nine cases where fornication was the stated charge, none of which was simple fornication between two consenting single white adults. Two cases were actually adultery where the single partner was arrested and charged; one was a cross-racial couple caught in the act in a bawdyhouse; another was fornication charged by the woman against the man, which was probably a rape; in another the charges were brought against a woman by her landlady, who didn't approve of the fornication's taking place in her house; and two more were couples arrested for public fornication. Women like Hannah Fell, who was charged with "being taken up last night in the street by the Watchman committing fornication with William Band," had crossed the boundary of public decency: it was the location of her sexual activity that brought the criminal justice system into action.[20]

19. In all, only sixteen men (2.25 percent of bastardy cases) were criminally prosecuted for bastardy in the 1790s. As had happened earlier, a man who took his case through the court system usually was also required to pay for the mother's lying-in expenses and the costs of prosecution. Only two men were found not guilty, and two more were found guilty of the fornication but not of the bastardy during the 1790s.

20. Mitchell, Flanders, et al., comps., *Statutes at Large*, II, 180–181, An Act against Adultery and Fornication. For changes to penal code, see XII, 280–290, An Act Amending the Penal Laws of This State; XV, 174–181, An Act for the Better Preventing of Crimes, and for Abolishing the Punishment of Death in Certain Cases. In two of

Criminal charges for fornication were not being brought simply for non-marital sexual intercourse. The instances of fornication that gave rise to bastardy were never causes for arrest until a pregnancy ensued. Modern medical science asserts that it often takes many instances of coitus to achieve a pregnancy. Certainly in a city that had yet to develop the physical infrastructure to provide couples with privacy, some of this sexual activity was observed. But it was not deemed worthy of public intervention. Neither neighbors nor the city watchmen intervened. Given the incidence of bastardy, there must have been a great deal more fornication, which did not result in pregnancy, that went unpoliced.

Like fornication, adultery was usually ignored by the larger society. Of the adultery cases that came to light through divorce proceedings, 70 percent were not criminally prosecuted. Those cases that did enter the criminal records were overwhelmingly initiated by the wronged spouse. In late-eighteenth-century Philadelphia, having one's sexual behavior inscribed in the public record was not the same as being prosecuted for that behavior.[21]

In a very direct way eighteenth-century legal prosecutions reflected public opinion. The legal system relied upon private individuals to initiate and sustain prosecutions. Unlike the modern system of state-sponsored policing, investigation, and prosecution, Philadelphians of the early national period had to take the initiative to bring people to justice themselves. When it came to sexual offenses, they often chose not to. In surrounding rural counties public opinion and the community interest in prosecuting sexual offenses were substantially different. Despite their smaller populations, these counties initiated a larger number of prosecutions for sexual transgressions. In contrast, community interest in Philadelphia did not generate criminal prosecutions against those who indulged in nonmarital sex.[22]

------

these cases there is no indication of what behavior caused the arrest. PFT: July 20, 1791, Mathew Bigger; July 21, 1791, Mathew Wilson; Mar. 19, 1792, Susanna Hammell; May 20, 1793, Moses Forrest; Dec. 31, 1795, Hannah Fell (quote); Mar. 2, 1796, John Hamil; May 4, 1798, Caty Mullin; May 30, 1798, Milford Lee and Flora Butcher; Jan. 14, 1799, William McCray and Aley Thomas.

21. Among the adultery cases recorded in the criminal records (30 percent of the whole), the wronged spouse brought the charges in 85 percent of the cases. The information to establish who brought the charges was available in 81 percent of the criminal adultery cases.

22. During the 1790s the city constables would arrest individuals for public disturbances primarily under the vagrancy laws, and they did not therefore require a criminal trial. The vagrancy laws allowed a justice of the peace or alderman to summarily

Those who did not participate in the burgeoning expansive sexual culture were affected by it nonetheless. Elizabeth Drinker's experience demonstrates the extent to which nonmarital sexual behavior was part of community life. In 1796 her neighbor Dr. George Alberti fathered an illegitimate child. He raised this boy in his own household two doors away from the Drinkers on North Front Street. Drinker records the accidental death of the child in 1807 but never mentions his status in her diary. Nevertheless, his illegitimacy would have been known to her, as Alberti did not marry until 1803. Drinker had also faced a case of bastardy within her own household in 1794 when her servant Sally Brant became pregnant with the child of a black man. Drinker sent her to the country to bear her child, but she would not bring her back into her Philadelphia household. Nor was the city's boisterous trade in sexual service unknown to Drinker. As a pious Quaker of elite polite society she was not shielded from such business but, rather, lived in the midst of it. A bawdyhouse stood a block and a half away from her home. In her diary she departed from her usual restrained and nonjudgmental tone when she complained of the lax policing of prostitution during the 1790s.[23]

The most intimate look into nonmarital sexual relationships in the early Republic is provided by those who observed these couples, recorded in witness depositions for divorce proceedings. In 1785 Pennsylvania passed a divorce law, and some couples used the courts to legally terminate their marriage. Unlike the formal divorce petitions that describe infidelity in formulaic language, witness depositions present detailed accounts of individuals' sex lives.

---

impose a sentence of up to thirty days. When individuals were arrested for crimes adjudicated through the courts, private citizens had to initiate the action and produce the witnesses to convict. If the charges turned out to be maliciously false, the citizen would be charged with the costs of prosecution. For the nineteenth century, see Allen Steinberg, *The Transformation of Criminal Justice: Philadelphia, 1800–1880* (Chapel Hill, N.C., 1989): on private prosecutions, 12–115; on reform of criminal justice and policing after 1830, 119–167.

G. S. Rowe, in "Women's Crime and Criminal Administration in Pennsylvania, 1763–1790," *PMHB*, CIX (1985), table 2, 348, found that, during the 1780s, the less populous counties of Chester and York, for instance, had greater numbers of women charged with sexual crimes (seventy and twenty-six, respectively, from 1783 to 1789), than did either Philadelphia County (sixteen) or the city (fifteen).

23. GPM, June 2, 1796; Crane, ed., *The Diary of Elizabeth Drinker*: on Dr. Alberti: III, 2052 (July 6, 1807); on Sally Brant: I, 581 (Aug. 11, 1794), 584 (Aug. 20, 1794), II, 808 (June 2, 1796); on prostitution: III, 1334 (Aug. 25, 1800). See Map 1, below, for Philadelphia brothels of the 1790s.

Because the new divorce law allowed for divorce when either spouse had deserted the marriage for at least four years, it was often not necessary to prove sexual misbehavior. Under these circumstances the testimony that revealed extramarital sexual activities was probably not manufactured for the courts.[24]

The divorce records reinforce the image of the expansive sexual culture and the community's permissiveness. People made little effort to hide their extra-marital relationships from anyone except their spouse, and the community usually accommodated them. In case after case, friends, neighbors, servants, and relatives described the adultery or bigamy they had witnessed, but they almost never revealed this knowledge to the other spouse. In early national Philadelphia no one was particularly surprised when Benjamin Rush the dis-tiller (not the renowned Dr. Rush) established a relationship with his house-keeper, Elizabeth Moyer, and lived with her in his country house, all the while maintaining his wife, Deborah, in his city residence. Deborah discovered that her husband was maintaining two families only when Rush switched house-hold arrangements and moved his wife to the country and his mistress to the city, and even she was less surprised than angry. The men who worked for

---

24. PDP contains divorces filed from 1785 through 1815. The discussion that follows is based on the 233 Philadelphia divorce cases that were filed then, the majority record-ing behavior during the 1790s. The Pennsylvania divorce act stipulated five grounds for a full divorce: adultery, bigamy, desertion for four or more years, impotence or inca-pacity of reproduction, and remarriage due to to the false but credible belief of the death of one's spouse. In cases of mistaken death, the returning spouse could choose to have the marriage restored or dissolved. In addition, a wife could receive a divorce from bed and board with alimony and inheritance rights if the husband had "by cruel and barbarous treatment endangered her life." Mitchell, Flanders, et al., comps., *Statutes at Large*, XII, 94–99, An Act concerning Divorces and Alimony.

Several factors suggest that the sexual behavior described in divorce depositions was not substantially different from that in the more abbreviated records kept by the courts and Guardians of the Poor. The sexual behavior was the same as in the community at large: bastardy, adultery, and prostitution. If the behavior had been extreme or unusual, one would expect the offended spouse to have reacted quickly, and perhaps in anger, either by bringing criminal charges or by initiating divorce proceedings. The spouses seeking divorce did neither. In only one case did the wronged spouse bring criminal charges against a partner for sexual misconduct (Ann and William Keith, QSD, Mar. 7, 1791; PDP, *William Keith vs. Ann Keith*, 1791). Furthermore, in the vast majority of cases the spouse sought divorce years after the events that served as the cause of action. The couple had often separated and in practice had dissolved the marriage long before divorce papers were filed.

Rush at his country site knew that Benjamin and Elizabeth lived as man and wife and had a child together. A friend and fellow distiller in Philadelphia also noted the details of the relationship, as did flour merchant John Husselback. None of these men told Mrs. Rush of her husband's second family, nor is there any indication that they felt his behavior warranted their friendly intervention to redirect it.[25]

As Henry McMahon told the story: "When Benjamin Rush brought Elizabeth Moyer to Philadelphia, and took his wife home with him when he returned, his wife suspected that he had been connected with Elizabeth Moyer." Once Mrs. Rush began to suspect the nature of her husband's living arrangements, she asked the three men who had lived in the country house and worked with her husband whether "Elizabeth Moyer had been there." McMahon recalled, "We all denied that she had been there and kept it secret for some time from Mrs. Rush." Later, after Mrs. Rush had confronted her husband and he had admitted his relationship with Moyer, McMahon too admitted the truth to Mrs. Rush. Ultimately Benjamin's dual lives collided. After arguments between them, which included his violent abuse of her, she left him and returned to her father's house. But, as McMahon noted, the couple "did sleep together after we told Mrs. Rush that Elizabeth Moyer had been at the house and had slept with Benjamin Rush." Perhaps this comment was meant to suggest that the couple tried to reconcile, or perhaps it simply reflects the expectation that, while a man and wife shared a household, they would indeed sleep together. In either event, this information was produced for the court as a defense for Benjamin. Under the divorce law, admitting "the defendant into conjugal society or embraces" after the fact of the adultery implied a tacit acceptance of the adultery by the wronged spouse and was a good defense.[26]

In another case the husband, Philadelphia merchant John Fousalt, whose

25. PDP, *Deborah Rush vs. Benjamin Rush,* filed 1805, events 1802–1803; depositions of Henry McMahon, Geroge Humes, and John Husselback, Nov. 14, 1805.

26. Ibid. In numerous other cases wives returned to their adulterous husband's bed rather than seek a divorce. Some were quite famous couples, like Alexander Hamilton and his wife Elizabeth. In Philadelphia Alexander Hamilton publicly admitted during the 1790s his adultery to refute the more serious scandal of financial corruption and illegal speculation. See Alexander Hamilton, *Observations on Certain Documents Contained in No. V and VI of "The History of the United States for the Year 1796," in Which the Charge of Speculation against Alexander Hamilton, Late Secretary of the Treasury, Is Fully Refuted* (Philadelphia: Bioren, 1797); Mitchell, Flanders, et al., comps., *Statutes at Large,* XII, 97, An Act concerning Divorces and Alimony.

wife committed adultery in 1796, complained that she conducted her adultery "in so open and public a manner that she received and entertained [her lover] day and night in this libellant's house, while said libellant was absent from the city on his lawful business." When Fousalt filed for divorce several years later, Charles LeRoy described in detail what he had observed at Fousalt's house while Fousalt was away at sea.

> I went there one evening, and found the front door partly open. I went in, and saw John Page and the defendant sitting in at the back room together on a sopha. There was a candle in the room and a glass in the door, thro which I saw them. John Page had one arm around her neck and his hand in her bosom, and his other hand under her clothes, and he was kissing her.

LeRoy did not burst in upon this intimate scene. Instead, he "went back, and made a little noise to let them know somebody was there, and then went into the room." He also testified that he "never told him [Fousalt] of her conduct while he was away." Couples were not overly concerned about being seen together. Ann Fousalt and John Page visited freely and playfully together when Ann entertained in her home, Page fondling her knee under the dinner table while others were present. That adultery was noticed and ignored by those who observed it indicates that it often enjoyed a fairly secure position in the sexual culture of post-Revolutionary Philadelphia.[27]

The community often knew which couples openly lived in adultery, cohabiting as man and wife. In some cases this was general public knowledge, as when men such as the Reverend John Hay openly lived with their mistresses. In other cases, when a couple separated and one partner established a new relationship, openly living with a lover, their circle of family, friends, and neighbors knew of their adultery. When Philadelphia merchant Elias Pinkus charged that his wife "hath lived in the said City in open and avowed adultery with a certain Henry Denkel and yet doth continue to commit adultery with him the said Henry," he was accurately describing the openness of his wife's living arrangements. Anthony Wechter, a family friend of the Pinkuses' for more than a decade, testified that Elizabeth had left her marriage of eleven years to live with Denkel. Wechter continued to visit Elizabeth socially and had "frequently" visited the home she shared with Denkel. Another friend, Henry

27. PDP, *Ann Hermiegiuz Fousalt vs. John William Fousalt,* petition of John Fousalt, filed November 1804, events 1796–1797; deposition of Charles LeRoy. LeRoy also saw Page leave her house in the early dawn on several occasions, noting that the Fousalts had no extra beds for overnight guests.

Bletterman, had dined at the couple's home and testified to the household arrangements. Elizabeth also openly claimed Denkel as the father of her child, swearing his paternity to her friends Sophia Seyfert and Mary Wechter, who attended her in childbirth.[28]

Adulterous couples often readily acknowledged their union. When Maria Stenman set up housekeeping with Peter Lund while her husband was on a voyage to Holland, the couple shared their rented lodgings with Christian and Elizabeth Hekler. Maria openly informed Elizabeth Hekler and her landlord, Mary Donseller, that she was married to John Stenman and that the man who shared her bed was her "sweetheart." These two couples moved their lodgings frequently, renting rooms by the fortnight, as was typical of the laboring lower class. When John Stenman filed for divorce a year and a half after his wife left him for Peter, the Heklers easily supplied the details of his wife's living arrangements with Lund. The couples had taken adjoining rooms in Christian Street, where the Heklers had to pass through Peter and Maria's room to exit. Next they shared a room in Camptown and later a boardinghouse in Penn Street. While Maria and Peter assumed the roles of man and wife, those around them knew that this was an adulterous relationship, and yet they accepted the choices this couple had made.[29]

Numerous other couples set up such illicit relationships and persisted in them for years without community intervention. William Lake left his wife after fourteen years of marriage to cohabit with Salley Shaw. When his wife filed for divorce, he had lived with Shaw for four years and had two children with her. William Kensel had lived with his lover for eight years when his wife filed for divorce in 1801; and, when Jacob Giddeon sued for divorce from his wife of eighteen years, she had been living in adultery with George Smith for more than six years. Sometimes the wronged spouse was quicker to seek a legal divorce, but the level of community awareness of the infidelity was the same. Neighbors had seen the adulterous couples in bed, boardinghouse keepers had rented them rooms knowing them to be married to other individ-

28. PDP, *Elias Pinkus vs. Elizabeth Pinkus,* filed Dec. 13, 1801, events 1800. The Pinkuses and their friends were of middling economic standing. Elias Pinkus was a merchant with a middle-ranking tax assessment in 1798. Anthony Wechter was an innkeeper, and Henry Bletterman a baker. Sophia Seyfert also knew of Elizabeth Pinkus's adultery at the time she moved in with Denkel.

29. PDP, *John Stenman vs. Maria Stenman,* filed December 1798, events July through September 1797. John Stenman was a seaman, and Christian Hekler a laborer living in the district of Southwark.

uals, and friends had heard declarations of their intentions to abandon their marital partners.[30]

Post-Revolutionary Philadelphia easily accommodated nonmarital sexual relationships. Couples could rent rooms for short-term trysts or let houses to set up housekeeping posing as man and wife. And yet the fictitiousness of these marriages was known to many in a town still small enough that friends and relations easily crossed paths during the course of daily activities. This was how Catharine Martin's adultery was discovered when she and Michael Dunstine left Philadelphia aboard a boat. John Dickson, a Philadelphia weaver and friend of Catharine's husband, John Martin, was also aboard and saw the couple take a berth together as they traveled from Philadelphia to New Castle.[31]

Sexual intrigues were not confined to one red-light district or seedy section of town but occurred throughout the city and in almost every conceivable locale. Affairs took place at home while a spouse was away and sometimes even when the spouse was present. Wives had affairs with their boarders, and husbands had sex in their shops. Couples were even known to consummate their love on the ferries that ran along the Delaware River.[32]

Philadelphia had begun to acquire a reputation as a city with a comparatively relaxed sexual code. The Pennsylvania divorce law was the most progressive in the new United States and required only one year of residency to file. Men and women traveled there from other states to legally terminate their marriage, and people who left their marriage in the surrounding countryside often headed to Philadelphia to start new intimate lives. Couples who simply went their separate ways could obtain a divorce in Philadelphia using desertion as the cause of action, allowing them to establish new relationships or

30. PDP: *Mary Lake vs. William Lake*, filed Dec. 31, 1799, events 1796; *Charlotte Kensel vs. William Kensel*, filed 1801, events 1793; *Jacob Giddeon vs. Mary Giddeon*, filed December 1800, events 1796. See also, for example, *Elisha Crosby vs. Ann Crosby*, filed March 1796; *Catharine Britton vs. William Britton*, filed 1797; *Mary Bangs vs. Elijah Bangs*, filed December 1807, events 1805–1807 (on friends' and neighbors' view); *Henry Friday vs. Margaret Friday*, filed January 1790, events 1787; *George Alexander vs. Elizabeth Alexander*, filed March 1800, events June 1799 (on landlord's knowledge); *Matthias Conrade vs. Catharine Conrade*, filed April 1788, events 1785 (on quick filing).

31. PDP, *John Martin vs. Catharine Martin*, filed 1794, events 1792. See also *Margaret Friday vs. Henry Friday*, filed January 1790, events 1787; *Ann Crosby vs. Elisha Crosby*, filed March 1796, events 1792–1794.

32. PDP, *William May vs. Sarah May*, filed 1802, events 1802; *Jane Houston vs. Samuel Houston*, filed September 1805, events 1795; *Joseph Russel vs. Margaret Russel*, filed September 1800, events 1799.

legalize those they had already established. A number of recent Irish immigrants used the law in this way. Ann Mahon, for instance, traveled to Philadelphia from Ireland to obtain a divorce from her husband Charles, who had deserted her in Ireland in 1782. Charles had left Donegal after two years of marriage and sailed to Virginia, where he settled into a long-term relationship with Elizabeth Stone. In 1793, Ann made Philadelphia her destination and filed for divorce exactly one year after her arrival, thereby meeting the minimum requirement of residency. Other American women in the Atlantic world looked to Philadelphia to end their marriage. Jane Carvisier had been married in Charleston, South Carolina, in 1780. Following the Revolutionary war the Carvisiers relocated to Port-au-Prince, Haiti, where Bartholowmew Carvisier founded a plantation and established himself as a transatlantic merchant. In the late 1780s, Bartholowmew initiated a prolonged affair with a woman named Duval while Jane was in France to improve her health. When Jane returned to Port-au-Prince and learned of his mistress, she ended their marriage. Leaving her husband and the Caribbean, she headed to Philadelphia in 1790, where she settled and sued for divorce.[33]

It was during the 1790s that most of those who divorced openly broke with marital traditions by deserting their spouse. Philadelphians filed for divorce throughout the period 1785–1815, having married between 1763 and 1809, but the dates of desertion were concentrated in the 1790s. In 57 percent of these cases the deserter left in the 1790s, 33 percent departed in the 1780s, and only 10 percent left in 1800–1810. The concentration of desertions in the 1790s was not due to a pattern of short marriages during that decade. Many of these couples had lived together for a long time before one partner decided to leave. Of such couples, 28 percent had lived together as husband and wife for more than ten years at the point of departure, and another 20 percent lasted five to ten years. Those data suggest that the social environment of the late eighteenth century made leaving one's marriage partner easier than it would become in the nineteenth century.[34]

33. PDP, *Ann Mahon vs. Charles Mahon*, filed 1794, events 1792–1793. See also *Elizabeth Lowry vs. John Lowry*, n.d.; *Alexander McArther vs. Sarah McArther*, filed 1790, events 1788–1789; *Bela Badger vs. Susannah Badger*, filed March 1806, events 1798 (on coming to Philadelphia for a divorce); *Jane Carvisier vs. Bartholowmew Carvisier*, filed 1795, events 1785–1790.

34. PDP, 1785–1815. Desertion was the grounds for divorce in seventy-six of the Philadelphia divorce cases during this period. Information to establish the date of desertion was available in 80 percent of these cases.

TABLE 11. *Social Class and Sexual Transgressions, 1790s*

	Proportion of Cases by Class	
Transgression	Lower	Middle and Upper
Divorce Cases ($N = 107$)[a]	39%	61%
Adultery ($N = 68$)	40%	60%
Bastardy ($N = 165$)	36%	64%

[a]Data from PDP, filed 1785–1814; the cause of action for the majority of cases took place in the 1790s.

Note: Class was established using the occupational listings in PDP, GPM, or PFT or by finding the individual in the tax lists or city directories.

Source: See Appendix, esp. Table A.2 and "Establishing Class."

Nonmarital and extramarital sexual relationships were established with ease, the community failed to intercede to stem such behavior, and sexual intrigues occurred almost anywhere. But perhaps the strongest indication that expansive sexual experiences were a salient and secure aspect of the broader culture of the 1790s was who engaged in the behavior. Nonmarital sexual activity, in all its forms, was taken up by all classes, both sexes, and both youth and adults. Adultery and desertion in the 1790s, for instance, were not a youthful or generational phenomenon but included a cross-section of the population, with people leaving unhappy marriages throughout their lives.

Philadelphians in the 1790s left their partners both soon after marriage and after long unions. They included all ages and both sexes. Both married men and married women sought extramarital sexual relations. In the adultery and bigamy of the 1790s, 53 percent of the infractions were committed by the husband, and 47 percent by the wife. For 1805–1815 the numbers had balanced out to an even 50:50.[35]

Although elites in Philadelphia often singled out the sexual habits of the lower classes for disapproval as the licentious "rabble," the lower classes were not overrepresented in the practice of nonmarital sexual behavior. Whether one looks at the class of the fathers of illegitimate children or of the couples

35. Information on which spouse committed the infraction was available for 112 of the 123 cases in the 1790s (91 percent of the cases) and 107 of the 147 cases 1805–1814 (73 percent). The gender patterns in adultery and desertion will be explored in detail in Chapter 5.

who committed adultery, roughly 60 percent were from the middle and upper classes, and 40 percent from the lower classes (see Table 11). Although the data here are incomplete, the consistency of the class composition that those figures present, given the variety of sources and range of behavior covered, nevertheless strongly suggests that varied sexual experiences outside marriage were embraced by all classes in the early Republic. Clearly, the lower classes were in good company in their choice of sexual expression.[36]

These assertions do not mean that there could not have been class-based patterns of sexual behavior. The grounds for divorce, however, reveal no distinct pattern of behavior based on class (see Table 12). The percentages of divorces for adultery, desertion, or cruel treatment (physical abuse or failing to provide basic support) were not very different between the lower, middle, and elite classes. But, if we look more carefully at the specific behavior, we see that the character of the sexual behavior varied by class. As we have already seen, many of the cases of extramarital sexual behavior involved serial relationships, where one spouse found a more appealing partner and left the marriage to establish a different long-term relationship. The other pattern of behavior was a spouse's engaging in casual sexual relations while maintaining the marriage. These men and women had lovers on the side or engaged in quick sexual encounters in taverns and brothels with acquaintances they had just met. Often they created intimate lives for themselves with multiple partners. What differentiated these two kinds of extramarital sexual patterns was whether the adulterous partners saw their behavior as inconsistent with their marriage. In the serial relationship the offending partners understood their behavior as incompatible with their marriage and took steps to end the marriage in favor of the new relationship. In the casual relationship the wandering partners saw their behavior as a supplement to their marital sexual lives, as truly extra sexual activity that they could engage in continually throughout their marriage.

36. The class reconstruction in the bastardy cases relied most heavily on city directory listings to establish the class of the fathers. These figures are probably biased toward those who were old enough and settled enough to be listed. The divorce cases could be skewed toward the middle and upper classes by the importance of property. But it is striking that there are as many lower-class petitions, given the expense of legal fees. It might have been important for those lower on the economic scale to establish legal divorces to establish alimony, which the Pennsylvania divorce law provided for. Some might have felt more secure terminating their marriages legally, rather than self-divorcing, once that option was available. Mitchell, Flanders, et al., comps., *Statutes at Large*, XII, 94–99, An Act concerning Divorces and Alimony.

TABLE 12. *Cause of Divorce and Social Class*

			Class	
			Middle	
	Lower	Middle	or Upper	Upper
Cause (N = 107)	(N = 42)	(N = 37)	(N = 8)	(N = 20)
Adultery (N = 68)	64%	59.5%	62.5%	70%
Cruel treatment (abuse)				
(N = 16)	14	19	12.5	10
Desertion (N = 17)	17	13.5	12.5	20
Other (N = 6)	5	8	12.5	0
Total	100	100	100	100

Source: PDP, 1785–1814; and see Appendix, "Establishing Class."

When adulterous behavior is examined in this way, we see that Philadelphia's lower classes were more likely to engage in serial relationships than were their middle- and upper-class counterparts: 44 percent of the cases of adultery of the lower classes were serial relationships while only 22 percent of those of the middle and upper classes were (see Table 13). Given the lower sort's reputation as the more licentious, it is interesting that the divorce petitions demonstrate just the opposite. It was the middle and upper classes who were more likely to be the licentious pleasure seekers. When they committed adultery, they tended to engage in casual, brief, and multiple sexual liaisons and were less likely to see their behavior as incompatible with marriage.

Identifying and understanding the class dimensions of the sexual culture are complicated by the parallel emergence of a lower-class street culture of the "rabble." While Philadelphians sometimes collapsed these two patterns in their descriptions and analyses, it is important to understand these developments as distinct yet related. The late eighteenth century witnessed a new assertion by the lower classes of their own cultural space and the creation of a lower-class street culture. At times the expansive sexual culture and the lower-class street culture were intertwined, such as when women of the lower classes were arrested for lewd behavior in the streets, public fornication, or publicly exposing themselves. Sometimes this behavior was part of the rituals of prostitution. At other times it was simply public intimacy for lack of a better alternative. But these two developments, the extensive nonmarital sexual practices and the lower-class street culture, were not one and the same. The street

TABLE 13. *Adultery Divorce Cases: Serial and Casual Relationships*

	Class	
Relationship (*N* = 68)	Lower	Middle and Upper
Serial	44%	22%
Casual	41	59
Indeterminate	15	19
Total	100	100

Source: PDP, 1785–1814.

culture had dimensions beyond the sexual, and the sexual culture was inhabited by the middle and upper classes as well as by those at the bottom of the social hierarchy.[37]

The class dynamics of sexuality in early national Philadelphia were also complicated by the new importance placed on the morality of lower-class whites and African-Americans that increased the attention on their social-sexual lives. In the minds of Revolutionary elites, republican government had fundamentally changed the position of the lower classes. They could now affect the larger society, and their behavior and character became important to larger societal goals and interests, especially in Pennsylvania, where the state constitution of 1776 radically broadened the franchise to include all tax-paying white men.[38]

The creation of a republic of white male citizens gave men of modest means claims to political and social inclusion. The moral character of African-Americans also gained public interest. In Pennsylvania the increased African-American resistance to slavery by self-liberation through flight, the proliferation of voluntary manumissions in the mid-1770s, and the passage of the Gradual Abolition Act in 1780 meant that African-Americans would no longer

37. On public fornication, see, for example, PFT: May 20, 1783, Peggy Hirot; Dec. 31, 1795, Hannah Fell. On lewd public behavior, see PFT: Aug. 20, 1794, Ann Collins; May 15, 1797, Margaret Thompson; Sept. 22, 1797, Elizabeth Dounell; Oct. 3, 1797, Mary Hopkins, Sarah Bennett, and Hannah Fell, arrested as a group.

38. All men over age twenty-one who paid taxes gained the vote, as did their male children when they reached the age of maturity, whether they paid taxes or not. The poor were still excluded from the franchise, but most artisans and mechanics now had a direct political voice. Michael Meranze, *Laboratories of Virtue: Punishment, Revolution, and Authority in Philadelphia, 1760–1835* (Chapel Hill, N.C., 1996), 56.

be controlled by their outright ownership by white masters. The result was that Philadelphia's African-American population moved from being primarily slaves in 1765 to primarily free by 1783. The release of African-Americans from the controls of slavery made their moral character a public concern. In the new Republic, sexuality was deployed by the lower sort as a form of class-based cultural expression. But it was also used by the community's elites to reassert the social boundaries between races and classes under attack by the democratic revolutions of the late eighteenth century.[39]

Sex and Socializing among the Rabble

The public culture of the lower sorts in Philadelphia was created and displayed along the city's streets and alleyways and among the taverns and private houses that catered specifically to the lower classes. Their lives were often filled with hardship, want, and insecurity. The most prosperous among them were craftsmen who worked at the less prosperous trades: the coopers, cordwainers, and tailors whose families lived with poverty just one crisis away, despite their skilled crafts. Others were manual laborers who worked on daily or weekly jobs they picked up along the docks and mariners whose episodic employment often left them without work for months at a time. Among those dependent on periodic employment were the laundresses and whitewashers (the women who seasonally whitewashed the walls of others' homes). Many

39. Gary Nash and Jean R. Soderlund, *Freedom by Degrees: Emancipation in Pennsylvania and Its Aftermath* (New York, 1991), 74–86; Nash, *Forging Freedom: The Formation of Philadelphia's Black Community, 1720–1840* (Cambridge, Mass., 1988), 44. High mortality among the city's slaves, an import duty of ten pounds established in 1761, and the increase in the use of immigrant German and Scots-Irish laborers all contributed to the demise of slavery in Philadelphia. Nash states that in 1765 Philadelphia's black population was approximately 100 free blacks and 1,400 slaves, and by 1783 about 1,000 free blacks and 400 slaves (*Forging Freedom,* 38). As Nash demonstrates, the transformation of the city's black population from slave to free was accomplished before the Gradual Abolition Act of 1780 was enacted. The law itself freed no slaves immediately except those whose masters did not comply with the required registration.

Exactly how many of Philadelphia's African-Americans lived in this semifree condition in the new nation is impossible to discern. Nash and Soderlund found that half of the black population lived in the households of whites in 1790, as did 56 percent of African-Americans enumerated in the census of 1800. How many of these were indentured free blacks and how many were live-in laborers is impossible to tell. By 1810 only 30 percent of African-Americans were living in white households. Nash and Soderlund, *Freedom by Degrees,* 173.

other women of the lower classes worked in domestic service in the homes of middling and upper-class Philadelphians, an occupation plagued during this period with short-term employment and quick turnover. The less fortunate were the destitute, the crippled, and the mentally ill. They were joined by escaped slaves and runaway servants who hoped to make a new life in a city that had espoused liberty during the Revolution and had enacted laws ending slavery, legalizing divorce, and enfranchising lower-class white men, granting new rights to the underclasses in the wake of the American Revolution.[40]

Although their material lives were grim, the lower classes in Philadelphia found ways to enrich their lives. They embraced a boisterous culture of self-display and rowdy demeanor along the city's streets, asserting their own cultural space while simultaneously assaulting the more staid sense of propriety of the elite and middle classes.

After working a long day with the domestic chores of their masters' and mistresses' households, Philadelphia's servants met one another to revel, cavort, and socialize. Moreau de Saint-Méry reported that servants leave "the house as soon as night has arrived and cannot be persuaded to return until eleven-thirty or midnight." Most often they met one another for an evening's entertainment of music, dancing, and drinking. On Tuesday and Friday evenings, the nights before market days, they might join the evening promenade along the market. But the special night was Saturday, when servants and laborers, Euro-Americans and African-Americans would discard their work clothes, put on their one set of finery, and step out on the town. Moreau de Saint-Méry was struck by this contrast in servants' dress, observing that "they love to dress up for their evening promenade" after shedding the dress they had worn all week. These public strolls, attired in fancy colorful clothes, demonstrated a right of membership in the larger community and simultaneously identified one as part of a distinct group. This public display was meant to be noticed, and noticed it was. Elite Philadelphians often commented that it was accompanied by an assertive, bold attitude.[41]

The leisure dress of African-Americans was particularly noteworthy to elite Philadelphians. Women donned white or pink dresses with white kid gloves

40. For the most complete description of Philadelphia's lower classes, see Billy G. Smith, The "Lower Sort": Philadelphia's Laboring People, 1750–1800 (Ithaca, N.Y., 1990). For a description of the basic economic stratification of early national Philadelphia, see esp. 4–5.

41. Roberts and Roberts, eds. and trans., Moreau de St. Méry's American Journey, 283, 285, 297.

and parasols. To this they might add fashionable chignons of coiled false hair, worn at the back of the neck. Their clothes signaled their new status in society, as Elizabeth Drinker's description in 1799 attests:

> Negro and Negriss [Jacob Turner and Sarah Needham] went to a Wedding this evening Jacob dress in a light cloath coat, white casamer vest and britches, white silk Stockens and New Ha[t,] Sarah, the brides Maid, in white muslin, dizen'd of with white ribbons from head to foot, Yallow Morocco Shoes with white bows, etc. They went in Benjn. Oliver's Coachee, drove by his white Man—'tis now near 11 o'clock and they are not yet returned. They are both honest servants but times is much altred with the black folk.

In their dress these African-Americans expressed the transitory nature of their downtrodden state and asserted their self-respect.[42]

African-Caribbean women brought to Philadelphia by French colonials fleeing the unrest in the Caribbean also dressed in bold attire. Their turbans and colorful clothing of "West India fashion" enhanced their public presence in the city. Caribbean colonial society more easily accepted cross-racial social relations and in so doing opened up places in the social hierarchy for Africans above the lower levels. Moreau de Saint-Méry also comments on "French colored women" who displayed their high economic standing, relative to free African-Americans, through their dress and deportment in public. Philadelphia's African-Americans drew support for their own struggle to assert a new social position from these Africans from the Caribbean, some of whom held middle to elite economic status.[43]

The streets themselves were a central cultural space for the lower classes, an arena for public display and the site for much of their socializing. The streets were also where the lower classes' assertion of their own ways met with the most resistance from their upper-class neighbors. Their bold, boisterous, and often bawdy displays frequently met with the disapproval of the city's

42. Ibid., 301–302; Crane, ed., *The Diary of Elizabeth Drinker*, II, 1127 (Jan. 3, 1799). Nash discusses the street culture of Philadelphia's African-Americans in *Forging Freedom*, 219–222. For the most complete study of African-American culture in an American city during this period, see Shane White, *Somewhat More Independent: The End of Slavery in New York City, 1770–1810* (Athens, Ga., 1991); for description and analysis of dress and public demeanor, see chap. 7, "A Question of Style," 185–206.

43. Watson, *Annals of Philadelphia*, 170. Moreau de Saint-Méry also commented on the obvious grandeur displayed by African-Caribbeans in the city. Roberts and Roberts, eds. and trans., *Moreau de St. Méry's American Journey*, 311.

authorities, and hundreds were arrested each year. The lower classes crossed the boundaries of acceptable public behavior with regularity. Jane Daily, Sarah Evans, and Margaret McLean, for example, were charged in 1796 with "being taken up by Mathew Brown at a late hour in this City strolling and make a noise to disturb the Inhabitants, having with them a Bottle of Rum and Intoxicated." George Miller was charged with "being concerned with a gang of men parading the Streets insulting and abusing the Inhabitants." Timothy Wollington was charged with "being an abandoned Character, who is frequently drunk and raising disturbances in and about the new Market," and Richard Hart was charged "with causing a riot and being stripped naked." One can only imagine the raucous scene of a crowd undressing Hart in the city streets.[44]

This boisterous street culture often led to street fighting, as in 1794 when drunk Charles Reiley tried "to force money from a French mulatto man named Augustine," or when James Cusack was arrested for fighting "two negro women in Dock street." But fighting was an accepted part of this culture, where cursing, bragging, and posturing were part of establishing one's position in a society that could be harsh. During the height of summer, many elite and middle-class Philadelphians retired to their country homes or rented cottages outside the city. Having the means to escape the season of heat and disease, they did so. As the elites took to the countryside, the rabble took to the streets, and their arrests for riotous and disorderly conduct increased.[45]

Unruly women of the lower classes were of particular annoyance to the larger community. They were arrested for strolling the streets at late hours and for being drunk in the streets, disorderly, riotous, and turbulent. They were called outrageous, intolerable, intemperate, and incorrigible. Mary Cheff, for example, was charged with "behaving in a violent, unruly and Turbulent manner in High street and disturbing the Citizens, of which conduct she hath frequently heretofore been guilty." The image that emerges from the records of these arrests is of vocal, assertive women indifferent to the conventions of polite society, exhibiting forcefulness and self-confidence, qualities cultivated

44. PFT, 1790–1799, 1805–1815. Hundreds more were picked up for vagrancy and deposited in the workhouse for thirty days for their behavior in the streets (Vagrancy Docket, 1790–1797). PFT: Sept. 16, 1796, Jane Daily; Jan. 19, 1799, George Miller; Aug. 8, 1797, case of Timothy Wollington; Mar. 6, 1799, case of Richard Hart.

45. PFT: May 6, 1794, Charles Reiley; Sept. 12, 1797, James F. Cusack. Also see, for example, PFT: Apr. 19, 1805, Alexander Gardner, charged with "being intoxicated, rioting and fighting on the drawbridge wharf"; May 12, 1797, Michael Mullen; May 2, 1794, Barney Downey.

to survive in the city. At times these traits were recorded, as when Luesa Sebrant engaged in a loud argument with a Guardian of the Poor and was arrested when she insulted him within the hearing of the constable. Or when Catharine McCoy swore "profane oaths" at Constable McMullin, who intervened in her fight with Mary Fear. Hannah Levey, too, rejected the legitimacy of external controls when she abused and ill-treated her father in an argument. In these instances women explicitly asserted themselves against authority. In hundreds of other cases by their raucous demeanor they did so implicitly.[46]

Servants' behavior also gave the authorities difficulty. The idle could be jailed simply for having no visible means of support, and those refusing indenture could be kept in jail. Masters had the power to charge their indentured servants with lack of obedience and have them jailed, and servants were routinely held for thirty days without trial for forms of insubordination and resistance to their master's control. In 1791 John New petitioned the court to have the indenture of his daughter Elizabeth canceled because of such abuses. He complained that Elizabeth had been frequently and severely beaten without cause by her master and "had been confined in Prison among Convicts for the most trifling Offences." He concluded that it was unsafe for his daughter to remain under the stewardship of her master, Henry Clause.[47]

46. PFT: Sept. 22, 1797, Eliza Dounell; Oct. 5, 1797, Sarah Morton and Catharine Heston; Oct. 4, 1797, Lydia Tennant, Susanna Morgan, and Judith Baker; Aug. 10, 1792, Polly Hamm and Kitty Carltney; May 3, 1794, Mary Blackwell, "a negro"; Aug. 9, 1797, Hannah Bond. For language: Jan. 5, 1795, Mary Clieff; Mar. 27, 1795, Margaret Rogers; July 6, 1795, Mary Johnson. Vocal women: July 3, 1794, Mary Cheff; Feb. 2, 1809, Luesa Sebrant; May 3, 1794, Catharine McCoy; Sept. 10, 1794, Hannah Levey.

47. MCD, Mar. 21, 1791, petition of John New. The Vagrancy Act of 1767, in force in Philadelphia throughout the 1790s, allowed the city watchman to take up and the magistrate to incarcerate any person of obvious poverty for thirty days and was used to remove the "disorderly" from the streets. Thus those who had "no visible means of subsistence," or "were likely to become chargeable to the city" could be sent to the workhouse. Mitchell, Flanders, et al., comps., *Statutes at Large*, VII, 84–88, XIII, 251–255; Vagrancy Docket, 1790–1797.

For instances of incarceration for lack of productive employment, see PFT: May 10, 1791, Silvanus Pratt; July 6, 1793, Ann Taylor; Jan. 29, 1798, Elizabeth Stites. For an example of incarceration for refusing to be bound, see July 28, 1808. In this case a young man charged with "being a Idle vagrant having no visible means for a living" was kept in the city jail because he refused to be bound out to learn a trade, to be confined until he "become willing to be Bound" or posted surety not to become chargeable to the

Masters also had servants jailed for "moral" infractions in attempts to control their social-sexual behavior. Servants' status after the Revolution continued to circumscribe their ability to form legal intimate relationships, and indentured servants increasingly were African-Americans required by the Abolition Act of 1780 to serve prolonged indentures before securing their freedom. The prohibition of marriage denied free blacks one of the fundamental rights associated with freedom—the right to marry and establish a household. Prolonged servitude through indenture could block the ability of African-American men to become patriarchs of their own households, one important benchmark of full manhood status. Marriage without the permission of one's master was still prohibited, and servants' nonmarital sexual relations could be scrutinized by masters and the city's authorities. Masters' policing of their servants' intimate behavior usually occurred privately as part of the masters' stewardship, but they could and did employ the powers of the state to enforce their will. As we have seen, fornication was rarely prosecuted in the post-Revolutionary decades unless it was linked to adultery or bastardy. But fornication among servants could lead to arrest. Such intrusions into the intimate lives of servants occurred when masters had lovers jailed for consensual sexual relations. James Glentworth did so in 1805 when he had Tilghman Fitzgerald jailed after finding him in bed with "his servant Girl" around midnight in his home. William Wimley was also jailed for this offense when he "entered the house of William Huber at [a] late hour of the Night" and committed fornication with his servant.[48]

Arrests for frequenting bawdyhouses also depended on the class and labor status of the offender. Thomas Joice, for instance, was charged on the oath of Jacob Black "with being his apprentice and Disorderly frequenting b[aw]dy houses and deserting his service." As the wording suggests, the dual circumstances of apprenticeship and frequenting bawdyhouses made him vulnerable to arrest. Early national Philadelphia had no criminal sanctions against visiting bawdyhouses, but the sexual circumstances of his disorderly behavior when he absented himself from his service were seen to justify his arrest.[49]

---

town. No discharge date was recorded, so we don't know how long he stayed. Examples of servants held for insubordination are scattered throughout the PFT docket, and the practice was complained about by the Society for Alleviating the Miseries of Public Prisons; see its Minutes of the Acting Committee, Oct. 9, 1806, HSP.

48. PFT: May 25, 1805, Tilghman Fitzgerald; May 5, 1814, William Wimley.

49. PFT, May 2, 1814, Thomas Joice. See also Feb. 27, 1805, Charles Lawden. Even among servants the policing of sexual misconduct was not done often.

The activities within places of amusement that catered to the lower classes also came under greater scrutiny when they undermined a master's control of servants. After seven arrests in a dozen years, John York was convicted in 1805, only after being charged with keeping a disorderly house where he "harbored apprentice boys," thereby interfering with their master's control. When in 1787 another "negro" man was arrested for keeping a disorderly house that was a leisure resort for the lower classes, the city's newspapers warned masters to be wary of the dangers of such places and to "watch the conduct of their servants" in their "nocturnal excursions."[50]

Despite masters' ability to use the city jail to discipline their servants, many servants routinely rejected their masters' control. These young men and women were taken up for not working, getting drunk, and leaving their service without permission. They were servants like Robert English, who in 1795 "absconded from his master John McElerees" and when arrested was "at Present in a state of Intoxication," or Fanny Crail, who was charged with "being the servant of William Richardson Oller and . . . conducting herself in a disorderly idle and illegal manner."[51]

While the lower classes did not organize to protest their treatment by their masters, upper-class neighbors, or city constables, they did individually and in small groups resist the authorities' attempts at control. Often this resistance was spontaneous, as when Thomas Stewart and George Seitz were arrested for "pelting the Constables" who had attempted to subdue the two men "rioting in the streets." Usually anger at a specific assertion of control sparked resistance. When her husband was imprisoned in 1805, Margaret Walker threatened the lives of the prosecutors in a futile attempt to protect him. She was arrested for her bold speech. A few years later Moses Carey was incarcerated for instigating a riot following a public execution. He had initiated a mob action targeting the hangman who had performed the execution of John Joyce and Peter Mathias, two black men executed for the murder of a white woman, Sarah Cross.[52]

50. QSD, Docket, John York, Dec. 2, 1805; PG, Aug. 8, 1787.

51. PFT: Mar. 23, 1795, Robert English; Dec. 1, 1806, Fanny Crail. Masters' charges against their servants were especially high during 1806–1807, and more were turning to the state to enforce their authority. See also, for example, PFT: June 30, 1796, Thomas Fleeson, "a blackman"; July 28, 1807, John Bourrer [Boirrer?].

52. PFT: Mar. 18, 1805, Thomas Stewart and George Seitz; Aug. 21, 1805, Margaret Walker; Mar. 18, 1808, Moses Carey. Walker was charged with "saying that she would have satisfaction for her husbands detention (who was at that time imprisoned) or she would have the life or lives of those concerned (as the deponents believe) in the said

The control of access to marriage itself provoked conflict between the lower classes and the middle and upper classes, as elites sought to contain the lower classes' social-sexual freedom. The marriage records for Philadelphia's oldest church, Gloria Dei, the Swedish Lutheran church in Southwark, reveal the tensions over the control of the lower classes. Marriages performed at Gloria Dei were believed to be especially lucky, so more than three thousand couples were married there between 1789 and 1818, more than in any other Philadelphia church. In addition to recording the marriages performed, the minister of the church, Nicolas Collin, also noted requests for marriages that were denied along with his comments about why he refused to marry the couples. Through the marriage register we can view some of the social practices and marriage customs of the lower classes, witness the clash of cultural values between the classes over marriage practices, and observe the lower classes' rejection of the legitimacy of external controls on their intimate lives.[53]

As already noted, servants were not free to marry without the consent of their master. In practice, at Gloria Dei anyone who looked to be of the age, race, or class of a bound servant or apprentice was turned away unless he or she brought written permission from a master or a certificate establishing the termination of indenture as proof of status as a free laborer. The Reverend Mr.

---

prosecution." The murder and subsequent trial of Joyce and Mathias brought many of the racial tensions in Philadelphia into clear public view (see Chapter 8, below). Carey actively policed his sense of justice. In 1806 he had charged his wife with bigamy when she had married another man while he was away at sea (PFT, Dec. 5, 1806).

This lower-class resistance is consistent with Steven Rosswurm's interpretation of mob actions as a defense of lower-class culture during this era. See *Arms, Country, and Class: The Philadelphia Militia and "Lower Sort" during the American Revolution, 1775–1783* (New Brunswick, N.J., 1987), 13–48. John K. Alexander asserts that the lower classes were instrumental in the post-Revolution protests for food price controls in Philadelphia; see *Render Them Submissive*, 33–37.

53. Collin's remarks are scattered throughout the marriage records during his first years as the church's minister and later, beginning in 1789, are recorded in a special section of the marriage record designated "Register of Remarkable Occurances related to marriage"; see Gloria Dei, Marriages, II–IV, 1789–1825. The Reverend Andrew Goeransson, Collin's predecessor, also made some notes on circumstances of the marriages he presided over, found in Gloria Dei, Baptisms and Marriages, I, 1750–1789. Generalizations are based upon records from 1776 through 1824. On lucky marriages at Gloria Dei, see Susan E. Klepp and Billy Smith, "The Records of Gloria Dei Church: Marriages and 'Remarkable Occurances [sic],' 1794–1806," *Pennsylvania History*, LIII (1986), 126.

Collin was especially concerned that the parties he joined were free to marry, so he also refused to marry those under the age of legal maturity without the presence of a parent or guardian to give consent. He routinely refused to marry all runaways and was especially cautious about marrying African-Americans, believing it likely that they were not free to contract themselves in marriage. He was always leery of the Irish, whom he suspected of being under indenture, but who he believed would lie about their status and claim to be free laborers. Collin also refused to perform marriages across racial lines, fearing, he maintained, public sentiment against such marriages.[54]

Collin regarded the moral character of Philadelphia as degraded. He explained his practice of recording marriage refusals at the beginning of his 1795 log: "The licentious manners which in this part of America, and especially in Philadelphia are evidently striking, and which in matrimonial affairs are so pernicious, render a continuation of these memoirs necessary." He was particularly suspicious of members of the lower classes. After refusing to marry a sailor and a young domestic servant, whose story he would not accept without written proof, he wrote "Refused as no credit can be given to the rabble."[55]

But Collin also recorded many of the marriage practices presented by the lower classes themselves as legitimate, as well as the circumstances surrounding their intention to marry. When couples met Collin's resistance to perform their marriage, they often pleaded their case by explaining why they had to marry immediately—often that night, because the groom was a seaman set to depart the city the next day. One such couple arrived at the church at half past ten at night, and, being refused admission because of the late hour, continued to knock on the door and entreat Collin for fifteen minutes, refusing to leave, because the bridegroom, a sailor, was to set sail the next morning. Another

54. Under the law youths under age twenty-one and indentured servants needed proof of a parent's or master's consent if the parent or master resided within the county. There was, however, an exemption for anyone marrying within "the religious society to which they belong." Clergy were given some leeway to marry acording to the rules of their church, and Collin appears to have been cautious and conservative in his application of the law. See John Purdon, *A Digest of the Laws of Pennsylvania, from the Year 1700 to . . . March 13, 1824* (Philadelphia, 1824), 539–541, Act of 14th February 1729–30. During the 1790s Collin went so far as to keep a record of those servants and slaves advertised as runaways in the city's newspapers so that he could avoid marrying them. Gloria Dei, Marriages, Sept. 22, 1800.

55. Gloria Dei, Marriages, Mar. 21, 1809. The servant worked in a boarding-house. Collin's suspicion was probably due to the use of boardinghouses as fronts for prostitution.

couple who pleaded an impending departure was dismissed "with proper disapprobation, of this absurd but common custom to marry in the hour of departure." Despite Collin's usual refusal of such requests, their frequency suggests that impending departure might spur couples to marriage and that marrying quickly was commonplace.[56]

Couples also insisted on the necessity of prompt marriage due to their need for secrecy from parents or masters. They did not try to beguile Collin but explained their circumstances, expecting that he would share their belief that they had a legitimate claim to make independent decisions concerning their private lives.[57]

Many couples sought marriage when the woman was already pregnant or asked that Collin antedate the marriage. These couples were from the lower classes as well as the more genteel; although Collin refused to marry all of them, he tended to chastise those of the lower sort while counseling and sympathizing with the more elite couples. In 1795 he rejected a poor couple:

> April 20, 1795. Two men urged me to marry a woman pregnant by a man who had taken care of her since the desertion of her husband, who had (as they say) cruelly abused her by stabbing etc. and thereby killing the foetus in her womb. These also remonstrated the impossibility of procuring legal divorce because of her poverty—refused with prolix demonstration. Bad manners, crooked laws! Oh when shall I be cleared from this detestable place.

Of a pregnant couple of middle-class standing he wrote:

> January 1, 1805. Two men and two young women came of genteel appearance. The intended bridegroom 27 years old, told me in private of his premature intimacy with his future bride, and of his firm resolution to conceal the time of wedlock from the parents, to save her reputation; seemed very afflicted and agitated assured me of their perfect acquiescence, et[c]. His friend, a man of mature age and in trade, of decent behavior, affirmed that all was proper. In this case there was considerable weight, the more as the woman was 19, and had also a cousin with her (one of the 2) Yet, I would not consent but offered him gratis any advice.

56. Gloria Dei, Marriages, Feb. 21, 1801, Dec. 9, 1806; also see, for example, Mar. 2, 1795, May 31, Aug. 4, 29, 1807.

Moreau de Saint-Méry also commented on the prevalence of quick marriages in Philadelphia in the 1790s. Roberts and Roberts, eds. and trans., *Moreau de St. Méry's American Journey*, 286.

57. Gloria Dei, Marriages, June 29, 1805, Feb. 5, 1807.

The class standing of this couple and their repentant presentation of their premarital sexual activity mollified Collin.[58]

Unlike premarital pregnancy, some circumstances were presented only by members of the lower classes, such as those who sought to legitimate long-standing live-in relationships and those who sought marriage with a new partner while still legally married to another. Those who sought marriage after bearing an illegitimate child were also from the lower levels of society. What distinguished these couples was not necessarily the nature of their intimate behavior but that they did not see marriage as inconsistent with these circumstances. Marrying one's lover after living together and perhaps having a child together, and establishing a second marriage after one had failed in a previous union were reasonable and respectable patterns for many of Philadelphia's lower sort.[59]

What distinguished the behavior of the lower classes more than their premarital experiences was their demeanor in seeking marriage. The lively, loud, and sometimes drunken behavior displayed in the streets often continued during a marriage ceremony. But this style of rollicking playful marriage embraced by the lower classes clashed with Collin's view that marriage should be a serious and solemn occasion, taken on only after careful consideration. Evidence of this class-based cultural clash runs throughout the marriage register. Collin wrote, for instance, on July 24, 1804:

> An Englishman, sailor, about 22, and a girl about 20 came with a large company; some of whom behaved with rude levity; particularly, her half brother, a young sailor. When I had performed one half of the ceremony, this fellow, who was very groggy, and some others broke into great irregularity; 3 or 4 of the males grasping the bride to get the first kiss. I dismissed

58. Ibid., Apr. 20, 1795, Jan. 1, 1805. See also, for example, October 1800, Jan. 12, 1802, Oct. 19, 1806, Sept. 30, 1807.

59. For marriage by long-term partners, see ibid., Mar. 31, 1805, Oct. 19, 1806. For those entering into a second marriage with a spouse still living, see Jan. 10, 1795, May 11, 1801, Mar. 30, Apr. 20, 1807. With illegitimate children, see July 15, 1795, July 25, 1804. These records cannot be trusted to present an accurate picture of the behavior of middle and upper classes. Their absence in Collin's chronicle of refused marriages does not prove that they didn't engage in bigamous practices or marry after establishing long-term relationships. They might have more carefully disguised their behavior, molding it into a more acceptable presentation for the clergy. But, if they did obscure their behavior, such action suggests that the lower classes and the upper classes held different notions of what behavior could be acknowledged as acceptable.

them with severe reproof, and rejected their entreaties to resume the office. They accordingly went off unmarried.[60]

Collin rejected the notion expressed by many lower-class couples that marriages should be joyous occasions and repeatedly noted the unseemly "levity" expressed. He was particularly uncomfortable with couples attended by large groups. When a Portuguese seaman and a "lusty girl" came with "a large company," Collin rejected them, although he noted that the girl's explanation of the absence of her parents was probably true. He refused them because "the levity of the bride and of some of her attendants also gave suspicion." When couples arrived drunk or late in the night, Collin turned them away with the reprimand that "marriage is no frolic."[61]

The lower-class couples' willingness to openly acknowledge the sexual incentive to marriage also struck Collin as inappropriate. When a couple came to Collin on a Saturday night in May and begged him through the closed door to marry them, the bridegroom argued "that his love was so violent that he might suffer if refrained from bedding with her that night." They were turned away, and Collin remarked that the incident was an example of "impulse without decorum." Another groom arriving late in the evening tried to compel Collin by climbing over the gate and pleading "that they would bed without the nuptial ceremony" if he refused them. These couples, like those seeking marriage the evening before a groom's departure, sought marriage to legitimate their sexual union, but they sought it on their own terms: making the decision and then quickly engaging in the marriage service, making it a raucous occasion by including their friends, and arriving after an evening of drinking and celebration.[62]

For Collin this behavior of the lower classes was similar to the use of marriage to extort money from an unsuspecting mate. Collin noted several cases where he refused the marriage because it appeared that a woman had lured a drunken man to marry her so that she could extort money from him after the ceremony to be free of her. In 1794, for instance, when a drunken man came with "a dirty town drab," Collin refused "and warned the man

60. Ibid., July 24, 1804.
61. Ibid., May 26, 1808, Sept. 20, 1814. The "lusty girl" explained that her father was dead and her mother, a woman of "ill conduct," had not taken care of her: it didn't help the case that the bride's mother was a woman of "ill conduct," probably a prostitute. For examples of intoxication, see Sept. 12, 1794, Jan. 12, 1802, July 25, 1804, Feb. 4, 1807.
62. Ibid., May 1805, May 31, 1805.

of his danger." In 1806 after he had refused marriage to several Swedes who were to marry what he called "heathenish strumpets," Collin exclaimed "that he would sue any person that inveigles a Swedish seaman to marry a strumpet." In another incident, a husband arranged to have his wife wed to someone else to be rid of her debt; the husband stood in as the witness. After the ceremony the first husband, who had posed as the bride's brother, exclaimed that the new husband would now be responsible for the debt his wife had accrued and he would free of her. At this Collin lost his temper: "I tore the certificate, flung the money (the fee) out of doors and pushed the dirty rabble out, threatening them with jail." To Collin these sex scams were an extension of the loose morality he perceived among the lower sorts. To the lower classes themselves there was a distinction between the sexually motivated but spontaneous marriages, and the financially motivated entrapment of the naive.[63]

Collin might have been extreme in the force with which he expressed contempt for the "dirty rabble," but other Philadelphians shared his general assessment of the lower sort's sexual practices. Moreau de Saint-Méry was impressed by the sexual laxity of the community, and he singled out servants for their loose sexual habits. "As a rule they [servants] are immoral, and there is hardly an indentured servant in Philadelphia who can't be had for very little money." His evaluation of the city's African-Americans was much the same.[64]

Elizabeth Drinker, in more restrained language, expressed her disapprobation of her servants' sexual behavior. In 1807 when John, a servant in the Drinkers' employ, informed her of his intentions to marry, she wrote:

Our foolish John inform'd Sister that he was going to be married, to a cleaver woman that has a Son, her Man has left her, some time ago, I rather think that matrimony is not the plan,—be that as it may, I believe he will not long do for us.

John's plans conflicted with Drinker's notions of acceptable personal behavior. She disapproved of John's choosing a woman who had been deserted by her

63. See, for example of luring women, ibid., Sept. 12, 1794, Feb. 23, Mar. 4, November 1806. "Drab" and "strumpets": 1794, March 1806 (as a Swedish clergyman in Philadelphia, Collin felt a special responsibility to protect newly arrived fellow countrymen). Wife sale: June 1796. This one instance of wife sale documented in eighteenth-century Philadelphia is discussed in Chapter 1.

64. Roberts and Roberts, eds. and trans., *Moreau de St. Méry's American Journey*, 297 (quote), 302. The relationship of the lower classes and African-Americans to sex commerce will be explored more fully in Chapter 7.

husband and who had a child. This woman was "clever" because she had secured John as a new partner while she was technically not free to enter into a new union. Drinker suspected that the couple had no intention of marrying legally but would instead set up housekeeping together as an unmarried couple. This kind of an arrangement made John unfit to continue in the Drinkers' service. Drinker displayed the same reticence to accept her servants' right to autonomous sexual choices when she was faced with the prospect of a servant's bearing a bastard child.[65]

Even Benjamin Rush, who believed in the reformability of all Americans, singled out the sexual habits of the lower sort for scrutiny. Rush noted that, following the yellow fever epidemic in 1793, the Philadelphia poor who recovered experienced "a sudden revival of the venereal appetite." He described the behavior of the lower classes in the quarantined hospital tent district: "I wish I could add that the passion of the sexes for each other, among those subjects of public charity, was always gratified in a lawful way. Delicacy forbids a detail of the scenes of debauchery which were practiced near the hospital, in some of the tents which had been appropriated for the reception of convalescents." When one considers that the mortality rate for the poor during the epidemic rose to nearly 50 percent, one can understand this expression of a lust for life.[66]

The general societal interpretation of the lower classes' sexual practices and their danger to the rest of society in the 1790s was reflected in the charges brought against a couple in 1797. They were charged with "being persons of infamous character and Conduct—whose debauched mode of living tends to corrupt the morals of the Citizens."[67] Although many middling and elite Philadelphians associated the lower classes with a permissive, even promiscuous, sexuality, after the Revolution the lower classes rejected this interpretation of their habits, and they resisted external control and asserted their right to independent private lives defined by their own standards. When confronted with the clergy's refusal to marry them based on their class, they often re-

65. Crane, ed., *The Diary of Elizabeth Drinker*, I, 584 (Aug. 20, 1794), II, 808 (June 2, 1796), III, 2008 (Feb. 8, 1807).

66. Rush quoted in Kelley, *Life and Times in Colonial Philadelphia*, 190. While the overall mortality rate for Philadelphia during this epidemic was 5 percent, the lower classes were especially hard hit because they lacked the resources to flee the city. Smith, *The "Lower Sort,"* 25.

67. PFT, Aug. 12, 1797, James Ross and Mary McGilliken. The charges do not specify what acts these two engaged in beyond being drunk, having no legal place of abode, and acting together in their infamous character and conduct.

sponded with harsh words, rejecting the Reverend Mr. Collin's assertion that he had just cause to deny them. In 1794, after repeated entreaties failed to sway Collin, one man swore "he would sooner go to hell than marry" and called Collin's wife a "damned bitch." Another man, when asked for a certificate proving the bride had permission from her family, responded that it was "immaterial," that their witnesses could attest to the legality of their marriage. When Collin refused them and turned to leave, he heard the fellow say, "If he will not marry us let him kiss my back——." Collin, outraged at such an affront, "shook" the man "several times against the wall and pushed him out of the house."[68]

For some, personal independence was asserted simply by seeking to establish a legal marriage. This was true for cross-racial couples in the 1790s and early 1800s. Collin's "Remarkable Occurances" records a small but steady flow of such couples to him. Despite the fact that Collin refused to marry all cross-racial couples, some still came to him seeking to legalize their relationships. Collin's comments generally portray the polite demeanor of these couples, but sometimes they too could be persistent. A black waiter seeking marriage to his white lover in 1803 was described as "very pressing." Although Collin refused these couples, other ministers would marry them. In his most expansive comment on the subject Collin acknowledges this and complains of racial mixing:

> July 2 1800. A negro came with a white woman, said that he had had a child with her, which was dead and was uneasy in this conscience for living in such a state. I referred him to the negro minister, not willing to have blame from the public opinion; having never yet joined black and white. Nevertheless these frequent mixtures will soon force matrimonial sanctions. What a particoloured race will soon make a great portion of the population of Philadelphia.[69]

Many of the couples that Collin rejected during the 1790s and early 1800s expressed their disbelief that he had the right to do so. They manifested surprise that he expected proof of parental consent and outrage that he scrutinized them to establish their status as free laborers. Collin attributed their

68. Gloria Dei, Marriages, Apr. 24, 1794, May 24, 1806. Studies of early national Philadelphia by both Alexander and Meranze found that elites increasingly associated vice with the lower classes during the 1780s and 1790s. See Alexander, *Render Them Submissive*; Meranze, *Laboratories of Virtue*.

69. Gloria Dei, Marriages, Jan. 8, 1794, July 2, Sept. 22, 1800, December 1803, Feb. 20, 1817, Feb. 20, 1818.

responses to the ideas they had embraced since the American Revolution. He believed that their insistence on a right to exercise control over their own private affairs was due to "false ideas of liberty." The assertion of a right to such individual liberties was clearly put by one young shoemaker in 1806 who had finished his indenture and set up shop with another shoemaker. Faced with Collin's insistence that he provide "some good evidence" of the truth of his story, the young shoemaker responded that he "was free and independent" and refused to submit to Collin's paternalistic intervention. The autonomy to be granted to the lower classes within the new nation might have been contested by the society at large, but not by the lower classes themselves. Following the Revolution they took actions to establish their personal independence, and they did indeed contend that they were "free and independent."[70]

Class Conflict and the Political Implications of Sex

Philadelphia's laboring classes, white and black alike, asserted their rights to autonomy in their social-sexual lives as part of their claims to full participation in the new, Revolutionary society. Free choice in marriage and control over their sexual intimacy would be rights they enjoyed in the egalitarian society they envisioned for the Republic. But many elites had grown leery of the social and political leveling within society: fears of excessive democracy and of sexual anarchy were intertwined. By the mid-1780s many political leaders complained that the people, the common citizens of the middling and lower orders, were asserting unacceptable upward social mobility without embracing the virtuous moral character required in a republic. Republican philosophy held that, above all, a virtuous people would be guided by rational thought and concern for the common good. They would be self-restrained and able to control their instinctual urges. Reason must rule over the passions, and the mind control the body. Disruptions in the social hierarchy accompanied by

70. See, for example of disbelief and surprise, ibid., July 15, 1805, Nov. 16, 1807; notions of liberty, May 29, 1797, Nov. 8, 1806, and (no month) 1812. Travelers' accounts for the 1780s and 1790s also noted this assertion of a right to political and social equality by the lower classes. See comments by Johann David Schoepf, *Travels in the Confederation [1783–1784]*, ed. and trans. Alfred J. Morrison (1911; New York, 1968), 99; and in Roberts and Roberts, eds. and trans., *Moreau de St. Méry's American Journey*, 334—both quoted in Smith, *The "Lower Sort,"* 24. Smith found that the lower classes tended not to defer to their betters. Watson describes Philadelphians of the 1790s as caught up in notions of liberty inspired by the French Revolution. *Annals of Philadelphia*, 168–169.

self-indulgent displays of luxury and vice were especially unsettling for elites. Excessive indulgence in such pleasures, characterized as "dull . . . animal enjoyment," left "minds stupified, and bodies enervated, by wallowing for ever in one continual puddle of voluptuousness." Giving in to one's appetites, of any variety from finery and food to liquor and sex, meant that the bodily senses or instincts were winning in the struggle between mind and body. The self-governing republican citizen must develop the self-control to overcome the draw of the body and be led to action through reason. This was especially true for the uneducated lower classes, believed to have less fully developed mental capacities.[71]

During the Revolutionary war both John Adams and Benjamin Rush worried that a military victory that thrust self-government on the people before they had learned to be virtuous, self-sacrificing members of the Republic would lead to its demise. Rush expressed his worries to Adams in 1776 that the war would end too soon:

> I hope the war will last until it introduces among us the same temperance in pleasure, the same modesty in dress, the same justice in business, and the same veneration for the name of the Deity which distinguished our ancestors.

Adams went even further when he confided to his wife Abigail Adams that military defeat and the fall of Philadelphia to General Howe "would cure Americans of their vicious and luxurious and effeminate Appetites, Passions and Habits, a more dangerous Army to American Liberty than Mr. Howes."[72]

Speaking in 1787, Rush called upon Americans to continue the Revolutionary program of moral and social transformation:

> The American war is over; but this is far from being the case with the American Revolution. On the contrary, nothing but the first act of the great drama is closed. . . . The temple of tyranny has two doors. We bolted one of them by proper restraints; but we left the other open, by neglecting to guard against the effects of our own ignorance and licentiousness.

71. Gordon S. Wood, *The Creation of the American Republic, 1776–1787* (Chapel Hill, N.C., 1969), 469–518, and 52, quoting Pinkney's *Virginia Gazette* (Williamsburg), June 15, 1775.

72. Benjamin Rush to John Adams, Aug. 8, 1777, in L. H. Butterfield, ed., *Letters of Benjamin Rush* (Princeton, N.J., 1951), I, 152; John Adams to Abigail Adams, Sept. 8, 1777, in L. H. Butterfield et al., eds., *Adams Family Correspondence* (Cambridge, Mass., 1963–1993), II, 338.

The following year Rush complained that "the present moral character of the citizens of the United States" demonstrated that "the people are as much disposed to vice as their rulers."[73]

Sexual desire was identified as particularly problematic by several Revolutionary leaders. Thomas Jefferson, for one, feared that Americans' inability to control their sexual desire—"the strongest of all the human passions"—would undermine the Republic. Perhaps the most articulate spokesman on the subject was Rush. As a republican thinker, patriot, reformer, and physician, he was uniquely situated to posit the connection between suppressing sexual licentiousness and building the Republic.[74]

Throughout the 1780s and 1790s Rush argued against indulgence in sexual passions and cautioned citizens to avoid "uncleanness," or unlawful sexual intercourse. *The Moral Library*, a collection of essays dedicated to Rush, reiterated this concern:

> Let us next inquire, what solid comfort can arise from sensual pleasure? Infamy and disease never fail to attend them, unless they are constantly kept in subjection to reason. And is it not shameful to place our happiness in such gratifications as put us directly upon a level with brutes?

In his "Address to the Ministers," delivered in 1788, Rush argued that many of the activities of the pleasure culture had "a pernicious influence upon morals, and thereby prepare our country for misery and slavery." Spirituous liquors were dangerous because they would "render the temper peevish and passionate." Fairs created opportunities for "gaming—drunkenness—and uncleanness," and should be eliminated. Horse racing, cockfighting, and Sunday amusements should be "forbidden" because they "beget habits of idleness and a love of pleasure." Taverns and "Clubs of all kinds, where the only business of the company, is feeding (for that is the true name of a gratification that is simply animal) are hurtful to morals": they should be replaced with socializ-

73. Benjamin Rush, *An Address to the People of the United States on the Defects of the Confederation*, January 1787 (*American Museum*, I [1787], 8), and quoted in Ronald Takaki, *Iron Cages: Race and Culture in Nineteenth-Century America* (New York, 1979), 19; Benjamin Rush to David Ramsay, March 1788, in Butterfield, ed., *Letters of Rush*, I, 454.

74. Jefferson quoted in Takaki, *Iron Cages*, 41, from Jefferson to John Banister, Oct. 15, 1785, in Julian P. Boyd et al., eds., *The Papers of Thomas Jefferson* (Princeton, N.J., 1950–), VIII, 636. Takaki suggests that Jefferson's concern about sexuality stemmed from both ideological convictions and his own struggles to overcome sexual desire (40–42).

ing in private families, where "the company of females" can "have an influence upon morals." The "licentious" press, especially "personal scandal," corrupted the moral character of Americans and should be avoided. Hallmarks of
the pleasure culture—drinking, visiting taverns, reading bawdy books, and
nonmarital sexual activity—excited the passions, corrupted the morals, and
had no place in the ideal republican society.[75]

Rush often represented the concerns of the educated Revolutionary elite,
who were acutely aware of the shifting social structure and feared the spread of
social and political corruption from the lower classes. In the *Independent Gaz-
etteer* in 1787, Rush presented the contagious nature of vice from the poor as
an argument for establishing public education for their children. He called on
"the Citizens of Philadelphia" to "awaken at last to check the vice which taints
the atmosphere of our city," lest the vices of the poor infect the rest of society.[76]

Control of the servant class was especially troubling, since the prevalence
of "impertinence and irregular conduct of servants" arose from lax governance by their masters. Poorly controlled unmarried servants, given too

75. David MacBride, "Principles of Virtue and Morality," in *The Moral Library* . . .
(Boston, 1796), 52 (publisher William Spotswood dedicated this publication to Rush);
Rush, "An Address to the Ministers of the Gospel of Every Denomination in the United
States, upon Subjects Interesting to Morals," June 21, 1788, in Rush, *Essays, Literary,
Moral, and Philosophical* (Philadelphia, 1798), 114–124.

76. Benjamin Rush, "To the Citizens of Philadelphia: A Plan for Free Schools," *IG,*
Mar. 28, 1787, reprinted in Butterfield, ed., *Letters of Rush,* I, 413. For a full discussion of
the rising concern about the moral character of the poor in Philadelphia in the 1780s
and 1790s, see Alexander, *Render Them Submissive;* Meranze, *Laboratories of Virtue.* In
Philadelphia during the 1780s, 1790s, and the following decade, Rush was a key figure
in many of the reform movements: prison reform and subsequent penal reform, public health, founding the mental hospital associated with the Pennsylvania Hospital,
the Pennsylvania Abolition Society, women's education, the Young Ladies Academy
of Philadelphia, and the Magdalen Society, which sought to reform the city's fallen
women. He published extensively on reform, and his essays were reprinted in the city's
newspapers.

For Rush's involvement in penal reform, see Meranze, *Laboratories of Virtue;* on the
Lunatic Asylum, see Corner, ed., *Autobiography of Rush;* on his involvement with the
Pennsylvania Abolition Society, see Nash, *Forging Freedom,* 104–105, 124, 182; on his
involvement with vice campaigns and concern over the morality of the poor, see Alex-
ander, *Render Them Submissive;* and for his involvement with the Magdalen Society, see
MSM, 1801, and *Articles of Incorporation* (Philadelphia, 1800).

much freedom, spread vice throughout a household to the other servants and to the children:

> How many young men and women have carried through life the sorrowful marks in their consciences or characters, of their being early initiated into the mysteries of vice, by unprincipled servants of both sexes![77]

Fellow Philadelphians shared Rush's concerns. During the mid-1780s and the 1790s the middling and elite orders expressed a growing disdain for the poor. They portrayed them as "vicious" and "vulgar" and believed their poverty stemmed from moral weakness.

The response to free African-Americans' assertions of personal rights also placed sexuality at the center of the debate. While white Philadelphians like Rush were instrumental in dismantling slavery, the specter of unrestrained racial mixing filled them with anxiety and fear. They believed in both the immorality of slavery and the inferiority of people of color. For many the Revolutionary rhetoric of freedom and liberty had made the presence of slavery a hypocritical embarrassment to the American experiment. A year after the victory at Yorktown, Rush was exhorting General Nathanael Greene to encourage the elimination of the slave trade:

> For God's sake, do not exhibit a new spectacle to the world, of men just emerging from a war in favor of liberty, with their clothes not yet washed from the blood which was shed in copious and willing streams in its defense, fitting out vessels to import their fellow creatures from Africa to reduce them afterwards to slavery.[78]

Yet Rush himself, like many Philadelphians, believed that African-Americans exhibited an inferior moral and intellectual character. The root cause of this inferiority was a subject of debate in the 1780s and 1790s. Some believed that Africans were inherently inferior to Europeans, that their inferior moral and intellectual character was biological and "natural." Others argued that slavery itself created vice among African-Americans and was responsible for their degraded moral condition. Many biological determinists supported colonization of free African-Americans. By removing Africans from the United States, they argued, Americans could become the homogeneous and virtuous people

77. Rush, "An Address to the Ministers," in Rush, *Essays, Literary, Moral, and Philosophical*, 122.

78. Benjamin Rush to Nathanael Greene, Sept. 16, 1782, in Butterfield, ed., *Letters of Rush*, I, 286.

the Republic required. The adherents of environmental causes argued that African-Americans raised outside slavery and educated to virtue could become morally equal members of the community.[79]

To Euro-Americans, African-American sexuality was the fundamental manifestation of their "depraved" character, evidenced by especially strong venereal appetites. Jefferson saw African-Americans as "a libidinal race," and Rush stated that strong sexual desire was "universal among the negroes." Biological determinists and environmentalists agreed that African-Americans were led by their bodies, with instinctual urges taking supremacy over rational thought.[80]

In the formative years of the new nation, white Philadelphians could not think about African-Americans and race relations without thinking about sexuality. The two were inexorably intertwined. Unreformed African-Americans were perceived as oversexed, and sex could transmit this nonrepublican characteristic to the white population. Both camps perceived the presence of a free African-American population as a dangerous influence on society, because blacks were at present unfit to be republicans. Biological determinists feared that African-American sexual immorality would spread through miscegenation: the superior moral character of whites would be diluted through the union with a black race ruled by passion and unable to exercise reason, infecting whites. The presence of a race believed to be ruled by instincts threatened the nation.

Environmentalists also feared racial contagion. Although their main theories suggested the transformability and ultimate equality of African-Americans, environmentalists too saw dangers in sexual relations between whites and blacks. Many believed, as Rush did, that slaves had been "rendered unfit by their habits of vice (the offspring of slavery) for freedom." Now free members

79. Takaki explores the relationship between race and developing republicanism in *Iron Cages,* using the ideas expressed by Thomas Jefferson to represent the biological determinist viewpoint, and by Rush to document those who believed in environmentalism. See part I, "Republicanism," especially chap. 2, "Diseases of the Mind and Skin," 16–35, and chap. 3, 36–66, "Within the Bowels of the Republic."

80. Thomas Jefferson, *Notes on the State of Virginia,* ed. William Peden (Chapel Hill, N.C., 1955), 138–139; Benjamin Rush, "Observations Intended to Favour a Supposition That the Black Color (as It Is Called) of the Negroes Is Derived from the Leprosy," APS, *Transactions,* IV (1799), 292; this text was delivered as a speech to the APS in 1792 (Winthrop D. Jordan, *White over Black: American Attitudes toward the Negro, 1550–1812* [Chapel Hill, N.C., 1968], 518–519). Jordan traces this view of African sexuality back to sixteenth-century English descriptions of Africans (32–40); on Jefferson, see 457–461.

of the Philadelphia community, they could not be expected to assume virtuous character overnight. An outspoken advocate for the rights of Philadelphia's African-Americans, Rush supported setting up separate agricultural communities for African-Americans newly released from slavery and providing for the moral and religious education of their children. In separate communities former slaves could undergo moral and intellectual development without creating a threat to the larger community.[81]

But even Rush continued to perceive cross-racial sexual relations as dangerous. In 1792 he presented his theory explaining the environmental cause of black skin color. Drawing on parallels with sufferers from leprosy, Rush postulated that black skin was due to past exposure to the disease. Thus skin color was changeable, and theoretically the disease could be cured and Africans could be whitened. This argument, explaining away the physical differences between the races, supported the environmentalists' belief in the fundamental unity of humanity.

Despite their assertions of essential equality, most educated elites continued to advocate the sexual separation of the races. Rush argued that, while leprosy in blacks had "in a great degree ceased to be infectious," it could be transmitted through sexual intercourse, giving the racial appearance of a black person to a white one. Although he spoke of a general prohibition against cross-racial sex, Rush's specific examples cautioned against white women's engaging in relationships with black men. He recounted the case of a white woman from North Carolina who "not only acquired a dark color, but several of the features of a negro, by marrying and living with a black husband." A similar case occurred in Bucks County, he wrote. In both cases the white women had borne children. Rush must have been aware of the common practice of white men's engaging in casual sexual unions with African-American women in Philadelphia, but he chose not to enumerate this as a behavior to be avoided. White women were to be the racial gatekeepers. If race was transmutable, the direction of transmission must be controlled. Blacks could be whitened by a medical cure and moral instruction, but whites were not to be blackened by sexual relationships with African-Americans.[82]

Tales of racial transformation were plausible to the eighteenth-century intellectual and the common man. People of the new nation were fascinated by tales of changing skin color. Accounts of such "remarkable" changes appeared in Philadelphia newspapers and magazines of the 1780s and 1790s, and live

81. Butterfield, ed., *Letters of Rush*, I, 286, II, 754–758.
82. Rush, "Observations," APS, *Transactions*, IV (1799), 294.

examples, like Henry Moss, were exhibited in the city's taverns. Such stories gave credence to the possibility of the sexual transfer of race and the sexual transmission of nonrepublican instincts.[83]

Lower sort moral superiority (handwritten margin note)

While middle- and upper-class Philadelphians were writing of the dangers of black and lower-class sexuality, the lower classes sometimes asserted their moral superiority. In the 1790s and the early 1800s, when the public took notice of lower-class sexual expressions, the lower classes were simultaneously privy to middle- and upper-class licentiousness. Just as the rabble could be viewed in the streets, the upper classes could be viewed in their homes, and were. It was their servants who described in divorce proceedings the sexual behavior they had witnessed. Adulterous women, who were more likely to engage their lovers in their own homes, were particularly vulnerable to servants' observation.

The divorce depositions give us a rare view into the relationship between mistress and servant. We can see how the power relations between the two, already complicated by the recent republican assertions of liberty, became more intricate because of assertive domestic help and vulnerable adulterous wives. Within the depositions a subtle controversy surfaced over which class really was the more moral.

Many of the servants' accounts demonstrate that middle-class and elite women expected that their household help would witness their behavior but would, out of deference or fear of reprisal, remain silent about it. Rarely did the mistresses go to great lengths to disguise their behavior, and the servants had clearly recognized their mistresses' sexual encounters as illicit. Priscella Read lived in the family of Lewis and Catharine Vallon for four years as a servant. She testified that Catharine habitually committed adultery in her home

83. Henry Moss was such a source of interest in Philadelphia that he was put on exhibition at Leech's Black Horse Tavern in Market Street in 1796 and advertised by broadsides posted along the city's streets. His story appeared in "Account of a Singular Change of Colour in a Negro," *Weekly Magazine of Original Essays* . . . (Philadelphia), I (1798), 109. It was also printed in a broadside dated July 23, 1796, which advertised his exhibition at Leech's tavern. Moss's case was also recounted in Corner, ed., *Autobiography of Rush*, 307. Corner states that Moss suffered from leukoderma, a disease that changed skin pigmentation. Other examples of racial transformation appeared regularly in Philadelphia's periodicals. See, for example, "Some Account of a Motley Coloured, or Pye Negro Girl and Mulatto Boy, Exhibited before the American Philosophical Society, in the Month of May, 1784 . . . ," *American Museum*, III (1788), 37; James Parsons, M.D., "Account of a White Negro," *American Museum*, V (1789), 234.

during the winter of 1804, while her husband was confined to his chamber with a severe illness,

> during which time a certain young man who before had been in the practice of coming privately and without the said Lewis' knowledge to visit Mrs. Vallon, came, during the said Lewis' said indisposition and eat, drank and slept in the house of the said parties without the said Lewis' knowledge. That Mrs. Vallon during Mr. Vallon's illness slept with him as usual in his chamber up two pair of stairs, and the said young man always slept up one flight of stairs in a small room, wherein the said deponent has repeatedly seen the said Catherine and the said young man in bed together—this deponent has heard the said Catherine embracing and kissing the said young man.[84]

Catharine Vallon had made no attempt to conceal her sexual misconduct from Priscella. Elizabeth Bender took a little more care to keep up appearances, but her servant, Julianna Buck, was not fooled. Julianna testified that she usually slept in the same bed with her mistress while the husband was away at sea. Sometimes, however, Elizabeth "directed" Julianna "to sleep in another room" because she was "restless, but afterwards requested her to come back because she was afraid to sleep alone." It was during these midevening interludes that James Mahoney, a boarder in the house, came to Elizabeth's bed. At other times Julianna witnessed Elizabeth leaving her own bed to go to Mahoney's room. She had "frequently found the said Elizabeth and James locked in the room together, and when the room was opened she frequently found the clothes of the said Elizabeth much tumbled." Julianna concluded that "she does believe from what she saw that the respondent did commit adultery with James Mahoney."[85]

Mistresses' behavior assumed that servants' eyes were not a problem, but several servants' comments suggest that they should have been less assured and should not have assumed "blind" obedience. Margaret Naylor's servant maid, Hannah Kempsey, asserted her own greater morality and rejected her mistress's requests for help in concealing her adultery from her husband. In this case, the servant was the critic of the upper-class mistress's morals, keep-

84. PDP, *Lewis C. Vallon vs. Catharine Vallon*, filed Sept. 1, 1805, events 1804; deposition of Priscella Read, Dec. 9, 1805.

85. PDP, *Daniel Bender vs. Elizabeth Bender*, filed December 1799, events 1797–1798; deposition of Julianna Buck, Jan. 23, 1800. See also, for example, *George Wagner vs. Sarah Wagner*, filed Aug. 4, 1803, events 1802.

ing an eye on her behavior and even intervening to police her sexual conduct. In her testimony Hannah compared and contrasted her own behavior to that of her mistress. When in 1802 James Gillaspie spent the night in their home, Hannah "suspected that something wrong was going on. About two o'clock in the morning she went down stairs to light a candle and get a glass of water." Margaret called to Hannah and "asked whether it was this deponent." Hannah answered: "Who do you suppose it is but me. I have nobody after me in the house at this time of night." Clearly Hannah had noted Gillaspie's presence and was pointing out that she would not behave in a like manner.[86]

Once Mr. Naylor had returned home from his voyage, Margaret became concerned and said to Hannah "that James Gillaspie had told her . . . that her maid was very restless in her sleeping," hinting at the secret knowledge Hannah possessed. Hannah testified that she "upbraided [Margaret] with having connexion with James Gillaspie," but that Margaret "only answered that it was none of her business." The conflict continued. That Sunday, after Mr. Naylor returned, Margaret told Hannah to "look out for James Gillaspie, and if he came to stop him from coming in." Hannah, standing at the door, refused her mistress's order and told Margaret "she might look out for herself." Hannah rejected the role of concealer that her mistress thrust upon her and disapproved of Margaret's sexual behavior. She contrasted this behavior with her own moral-sexual code, suggesting that she understood the hypocrisy of a society that more readily assumed the sexual licentiousness of a woman of the lower class, and the fidelity of the women of the upper classes. Hannah's moral assertiveness did not come without its price. Her mistress threatened and severely beat her for her disobedience.[87]

In another case, domestic servant Sarah O'Neil kept her opinion of her mistress's sexual intrigues to herself until called upon to testify. But she too voiced her disapproval when she described the lover's behavior for the court: "Mr. Gallard was often very familiar and playing with [Elizabeth Dabodie] in the presence of this deponent, and they were chasing each other like children thro the house and yard." Among the Dabodie household help Mrs. Dabodie's sexual behavior was common knowledge. Sarah "had often heard from different servants in the family that a certain Mr. Gallard often slept with the defendant, while her husband was gone to New York." O'Neil's account revealed

86. PDP, *Samuel Naylor vs. Margaret Naylor*, filed March 1803, events 1802; deposition of Hannah Kempsey.

87. Ibid.

servants listening in at their mistress's door, peeking through the keyhole, and gossiping to one another about the behavior occurring behind locked doors when Mr. Dabodie was away. O'Neil made a point of telling about a handsome present given to her by her mistress, suggesting that it might have been a reward for her silence. The servants in this household sensed the advantage they might gain by knowledge of their mistress's adultery.[88]

Other servants openly used their mistresses' adultery to their advantage, recognizing the shift in power relations such knowledge gave them. Rachel Lakine, a bond servant to the Mullowny family, received payment from her mistress for her silence. As the ever-present domestic help, Rachel had seen Mr. McDermott "kiss and toy with Catharine Mullowny" and had seen John Duncan "run into the street with his breaches down" when she had interrupted his intrigue with Catharine. Catharine asked her servant to keep quiet, securing that silence with small payments and passing on some of the money she had received from her lovers.[89]

Clearly, the world of sexual intrigue, nonmarital sex, and adultery in early national Philadelphia was inhabited by both the lower-class rabble and the licentious elite and middle classes. The city's elites associated nonmarital sexual practices with the lower classes, in part because loose sexual morality was seen as consistent with the weaker character attributed to them. When elite Philadelphians engaged in nonmarital sexual behavior, they were seen as behaving in ways inconsistent with their class, deviating from their natural character. They dipped into the sexual underworld of the rabble but were not of it.

This understanding of elite sexual transgression as a minor character flaw is reflected in Benjamin Rush's descriptions of some of his peers. Thus Rush described the life and character of William Wister, an elite merchant:

> [Died] 1801, August. W[illia]m Wister, aged 56, a batchelor who had accumulated a large estate of 300,000 dollars by the sale of British dry goods. He was kind, charitable, generous, friendly, and even just. He had one vice, viz. an unlimited commerce with women. He had four mistresses in keeping when he died.[90]

88. PDP, *John Dabodie vs. Elizabeth Dabodie*, filed March 1803, events 1801–1802; deposition of Sarah O'Neil, Sept. 16, 1803.

89. PDP, *John Mullowny vs. Catharine Mullowny*, filed November 1793, events 1792–1793; deposition of Rachel Lakine.

90. Corner, ed., *Autobiography of Rush*, 310–311.

Tom Paine also had one blemish on his otherwise respectable character:

> He possessed a wonderful talent of writing to the tempers and feelings of the public. His compositions, though full of splendid and original imagery, were always adapted to the common capacities. He was intemperate and otherwise debauched in private life.

Thus Paine's sexual indiscretions were a mere footnote in an otherwise admirable life.[91]

Much of the evidence suggests that the meanings attached to nonmarital sexual behavior differed for the rabble lower classes and the libertine elites. For many of the lower classes, sexual experiences were an extension of the class-based cultural expression fashioned during the upheavals of the Revolutionary era. The practice of adultery as serial relationships, like self-divorce to establish a new union, suggests that Philadelphia's lower classes saw serial relationships as legitimate sexual behavior throughout the eighteenth and early nineteenth centuries. For some of the lower sort, sexual nonconformity was an assertion of the primacy of love or romantic attachment over the propriety of marriage. For many of the middle and elite classes, expansive sexual experience meant casual and multiple sexual affairs, and adultery became a component of their marriages. For them, such behavior was personal indulgence in libertine excess.

But one must be careful not to overstate this class-based tendency. Members of the lower classes also had casual sexual encounters purely for pleasure, and some elites were led into affairs by following their hearts. In many ways, the lower-class rabble and the libertine elite shared a sexual culture, often seeking intimate encounters in the same spaces throughout the city and engaging in a remarkable level of mixing across class and racial lines. In the taverns, before the Guardians of the Poor, and at the brothel, the rabble and the libertine met one another as they broke with tradition and forged a culture that created the space for a diversity of sexual experiences and their multiple meanings, challenging and revising the Revolutionary ideal of a free and virtuous people.

91. Ibid., 323.

CHAPTER 5 Sex and the Politics of Gender in
the Age of Revolution

In 1773 the *Pennsylvania Packet* ran a pair of elopement advertisements.

TO THE PUBLIC

WHEREAS my wife AMERICAN LIBERTY, hath lately behaved in a very licentious manner, and run me considerably in debt; this is to forwarn all persons from trusting her, as I will pay no debts of her contracting from the date hereof.

Nov. 12, 1773   LOYALTY

TO THE PUBLIC

WHEREAS my husband Loyalty hath, in a late advertisement, forwarned all persons from trusting me on his account; this is to inform the public, that he derived all his fortune from me; and that by our marriage articles, he has no right to proscribe me from the use of it.—My reason for leaving him was because he behaved in an arbitrary and cruel manner, and suffered his domestic servants, grooms, foxhunters, etc. to direct and insult me.

November 22, 1773   AMERICAN LIBERTY.

On the eve of the American Revolution, women's subordination to men in marriage could serve as the ideal metaphor to express the strained political relationship between the colonies and Britain. American Liberty is the mistreated wife who takes the understandable and legitimate action of leaving the "arbitrary and cruel" Great Britain. Great Britain is cast as the bristling husband dismayed at his wife's disregard for his authority. American Liberty, just like Revolutionary wives, was justified in her separation from the unappreciative, tyrannical husband Loyalty. But these metaphorical connections between marriage, politics, and women's oppression also foreshadowed the nexus of women's oppression in the new Republic and women's critique of it during the last quarter of the eighteenth century. For women, attaining freedom and liberty would require more than the establishment of a republic. Unless the Revolutionary critique of illegitimate authority could be used to overturn the laws of coverture in marriage, the dual sources of women's subordination

[margin annotation: metaphoric connection b/t the Revolution & Revolutionary wives]

would stand firm in the new Republic. The impediments to women's liberty resided not only in the illegitimate governance of the state but also in the unchecked power granted to her most intimate companion, her husband, in marriage. Women were, to use the sentiment expressed by Abigail Adams, at the mercy of their husband's goodwill. Throughout the last quarter of the eighteenth century the men and women of the new nation debated about woman's place in society, addressing both marriage and politics. They read, discussed, and refined views from both sides of the Revolutionary Atlantic. Commentators from Jean-Jacques Rousseau and John Locke to Judith Sargent Murray and Mary Wollstonecraft understood that woman's particular position as the legal subordinate and dependent of her husband shaped her relationship to the new political state, defined her position in society, and impinged on her individual liberty and political autonomy.[1]

The post-Revolutionary increase in nonmarital sexual behavior, with its assertions of individual choice and personal liberties, took place within this larger debate over the proper place for women in the new Republic. Initially, in the 1780s, the debate centered on questions of women's mental capacity and proper female education. Middle-class men and women also advocated a moderation of husbands' control in marriage by shifting the emotional tenor of the relationship to an affectionate partnership: the ideal became a companionate marriage based on the deepest friendship. But by 1790 the debate had developed into a multilayered analysis of marriage, law, economics, and politics unfolding in the city's public prints. As women in Philadelphia participated in this public critique of their status, they understood that marriage was at the center of their disqualification for equal standing in the Republic.

Women's subordination to men in marriage was a key factor in their exclusion from full citizenship. The Constitution and all states, except New Jersey, denied women the vote based on their gender. The laws assumed that all

1. Abigail Adams to John Adams, Mar. 31, 1776, in Elaine Forman Crane, "Political Dialogue and the Spring of Abigail's Discontent," *WMQ*, 3d Ser., LVI (1999), 770–771, and in L. H. Butterfield et al., eds., *Adams Family Correspondence* (Cambridge, Mass., 1963–1993), I, 369–370; Susan Branson, *These Fiery Frenchified Dames: Women and Political Culture in Early National Philadelphia* (Philadelphia, 2001); Fredrika J. Teute, "The Loves of the Plants; or, the Cross-Fertilization of Science and Desire at the End of the Eighteenth Century," *Huntington Library Quarterly*, LXIII (2000), 319–345; Carroll Smith-Rosenberg, "Black Gothic: The Shadowy Origins of the American Bourgeoisie," in Robert Blair St. George, ed., *Possible Pasts: Becoming Colonial in Early America* (Ithaca, N.Y., 2000), 243–269; Rosemarie Zagarri, "The Rights of Man and Woman in Post-Revolutionary America," *WMQ*, 3d Ser., LV (1998), 203–230.

women, as potential wives, were dependents of men and thus could not take independent political action: could not vote or hold public office. In Philadelphia the creation of a masculine republican polity disfranchised a small group of women. Single, white women propertyowners had participated in the electoral politics of the colonial city but were now disqualified by their gender. They joined the rest of female America as politically disfranchised.[2]

For many patriot leaders the exclusion of women from republican governance reflected their perception of women's inferior mental capacity and their own adherence to republican political philosophies. Gendered notions pervaded eighteenth-century political philosophies. Women were not understood as individuals in the Lockean sense and had no direct relationship to the state. The subordination of women to men through marriage, Locke argued, existed in the state of nature; women were, therefore, excluded from the status of individuals in the state of nature. As individuals formed the social contract upon which republican government rests, women had already been excluded by their position as subordinate wives within male households—and thus excluded from becoming full citizens. Other thinkers, most notably Rousseau, argued that women were naturally inferior to men and lacked the mental capacity to participate in important affairs of the world, particularly governance.[3]

2. Each state defined female citizenship in its own way in the early Republic, granting women different rights. Only New Jersey, however, included a constitutional guarantee of women's right to vote, from 1776 to 1807. See Joan R. Gundersen, "Independence, Citizenship, and the American Revolution," *Signs*, XIII (1987–1988), 59–77.

The Revolutionary thinkers' understanding of dependence and independence was inseparable from the gendering of those qualities. All men, even if currently economically dependent, had the potential of acquiring independence. They could become husbands, heads of households, and acquire dependents. A woman's potential for becoming a wife and thus dependent, on the other hand, disqualified her as a full citizen. Gender had become the main differentiating quality for defining full citizenship. Men were full citizens; women were not. On loss of political rights, see Karin Wulf, *Not All Wives: Women of Colonial Philadelphia* (Ithaca, N.Y., 2000), 181–187.

3. Carole Pateman, *The Sexual Contract* (Stanford, Calif., 1988), 52–53 (on Locke). Pateman analyzes Enlightenment philosophy to show that a sexual contract, by which women were subjected to male authority within the family, preceded the social contract (1–18, 39–60). Jean-Jacques Rousseau expressed these views most stridently in *Émile* (1762), widely available in late-eighteenth-century Philadelphia. The use of human reason, for Rousseau, was "beyond a woman's grasp" (*Émile*, trans. Barbara Foxley [London, 1993], 419). For examples of Philadelphia women discussing Rousseau's ideas, see Branson, *These Fiery Frenchified Dames*, 44–46.

Coverture remained intact in the new Republic, and women lost their individual legal identity when they married. As the legal dependents of husbands, wives could not act independently in economic and political matters. The principles upon which marital coverture rested were exactly those that Revolutionary men rejected as illegitimate in the political realm: arbitrary and unaccountable authority, virtual representation, and subordination based on absolute right. But the political leaders of the early Republic were unwilling to apply republican principles to patriarchal marriage. To do so would have required dismantling the structure of marriage and, by extension, restructuring the family and society. They believed that maintaining the existing marital power structure was necessary to preserve the family upon which the greater society was built. Men in the new Republic were unwilling to relinquish their position as patriarchs, under law, of their wives.[4]

Before the Revolution Philadelphians had begun to identify women's deficient education as the major impediment to their equal intellectual standing with men. While most commentary insisted women possessed inferior reasoning capacity, a few public prints were intimating that female education should be encouraged. They suggested that the primary benefits of cultivating

4. Historians have debated the persistence of patriarchy within families after the Revolution. Most who have explored the position of women and the role of gender in the early Republic have found that relations between husband and wife within the family were the one site where patriarchal relations persisted. The laws of coverture were not altered, nor were married women granted control over their own property until the mid-nineteenth century. See Linda K. Kerber, "The Paradox of Women's Citizenship in the Early Republic: The Case of *Martin vs. Massachusetts*, 1805," *American Historical Review*, XCVII (1992), 349–378; Gundersen, "Independence, Citizenship, and the American Revolution," *Signs*, LVII (1987–1988), 59–77; Michael Grossberg, *Governing the Hearth: Law and the Family in Nineteenth-Century America* (Chapel Hill, N.C., 1985); Kenneth A. Lockridge, *On the Sources of Patriarchal Rage: The Commonplace Books of William Byrd and Thomas Jefferson and the Gendering of Power in the Eighteenth Century* (New York, 1992). On coverture, see Hendrik Hartog, "Marital Exits and Marital Expectations in Nineteenth Century America," *Georgetown Law Journal*, LXXX (1991), 95–129. On married women's property laws, see Carole Shammas, "Early American Women and Control over Capital," in Ronald Hoffman and Peter J. Albert, eds., *Women in the Age of the American Revolution* (Charlottesville, Va., 1989), 134–154. Other historians believe the new sentimentalized relationships within the family, sometimes termed companionate marriage, fundamentally changed the nature of marriage by eroding patriarchal relationships. See, for example, Jan Lewis, *The Pursuit of Happiness: Family and Values in Jefferson's Virginia* (New York, 1983).

female reason were its potential for tempering passion and lust and improving women's abilities to be engaging intellectual partners to their husbands. During the 1760s a few voices championed women's intellectual development. The most explicit almanac piece promoting this position was "On Female Education," printed by David Hall, in *Poor Richard Improved for 1761*.

> Reason's not Reason, if not excercis'd;
> Use, not Possession, real Good affords;
> No miser's rich who dares not touch his Hoards,
> Ca[n], Women, left to weaker Women's Care,
> Misled by Custom, Folly's fruitful Heir,
> Told that their Charms a Monarch may enslave,
> And Beauty, like the Gods, can kill or save,
> And taught the wily and mysterious Arts,
> By ambush'd Dress, to catch unwary Hearts;
> If wealthy born, taught to lisp French and dance,
> Their Morals left, Lucretius-like, to Chance;
> Strangers to Reason and Reflection made,
> Left to their Passions, and by them betray'd;
> Untaught the noble End of glorious Truth,
> Bred to deceive, e'en from their earliest Youth;
> Unus'd to Books, nor Virtue taught to prize,
> Whose Mind, a Savage Waste, all desert lies;
>
> . . . .
>
> Can these, from such a School, with Virtue glow,
> Or tempting Vice treat like a dangerous foe?
> Can these resist, when soothing Pleasure woos,
> Preserve their Virtue when their Fame they [l]ose?
>
> . . . .
>
> Portia, the Glory of the female Race;
> Portia, more lovely in her Mind than Face;
> Early inform'd, by Truth's unerring Beam,
> What to reject, what justly to esteem,
> Taught by Philosophy all moral Good,
> How to repel in Youth th'impetuous Blood,
> How every darling Passion to subdue,
> And Fame thro' Virtue's Avenues pursue.

Women, if encouraged to develop their capacity to reason, could subdue their passion and become virtuous. A few other pre-Revolutionary almanac anecdotes fell short of granting women full reasoning power but did enumerate the cultivation of the mind as an important attribute in a wife.[5]

After the Revolution female education became the springboard for asserting women's intellectual equality and the path to removing the impediments to their full participation in the polity. Education was both the explanation and the antidote to woman's apparent inferiority. Judith Sargent Murray, whose writings were read and discussed in Philadelphia, most cogently developed this line of reasoning to expand woman's rights. Countering claims by men like Rousseau, she argued that lack of equal education, not nature, had made women inferior and dependent on men. Advocates of woman's innate inferiority, she suggested, exalted nature to prevent women from seeking to improve themselves through education. Education, she countered, could "lay the foundation for independence" and undermine the dependent economic status of women in marriage by enabling them to achieve an independent livelihood and give women the intellectual independence necessary for sound political judgment. Mary Wollstonecraft, in *A Vindication of the Rights of Woman*, published in the context of the French Revolution in 1792 and immediately reprinted in Philadelphia, took the next logical steps in this argument. She argued for full economic and personal independence for women. Women should have rights to property in marriage and the right to loving relationships unconstrained by the hierarchical power relations of legal marriage. Her views were widely read and discussed in Philadelphia, initially positively. Charles Brockden Brown reprinted extensive excerpts from *The Rights of Woman* in the *Lady's Magazine*, and positive commentary on it was published in the *Philadelphia Minerva*. Brown also drew upon Wollstonecraft for his essay "The Rights of Women" in the *Weekly Magazine of Original Essays* and his book *Alcuin*.[6]

---

5. Richard Saunders [pseud.], *Poor Richard Improved . . . for 1761* (Philadelphia: Franklin and Hall, 1760) (David Hall had assumed editorial control); Andrew Aguecheek [pseud.], *The Universal American Almanack . . . for . . . 1762* (Philadelphia: Steuart, 1761). When choosing a wife, young men were advised to find a woman who cared for her mind, rather than one interested in cardplaying pleasures, visiting, and dress.

For an example of pre-Revolutionary commentary where a woman argues that woman's education, not her inherent intellectual deficiency, was to blame for women's second-class status, see Annis Boudinot Stockton, "To the Visitant *from a Circle of Ladies, on Reading His Paper*, No. 3 *in the* Pennsylvania Chronicle," *PC*, Mar. 14, 1768 (cited by Branson, *These Fiery Frenchified Dames,* 44).

6. Sharon M. Harris, ed., *Selected Writings of Judith Sargent Murray* (Oxford, 1995), 92. Matthew Carey sold the *Massachusetts Magazine* in Philadelphia in the 1790s, when

The students at Philadelphia's Young Ladies' Academy grappled with the *implications of Wollstonecraft's argument* [handwritten note in margin]. In her commencement oration, Priscilla Mason demonstrated that she had embraced the most radical ideas circulating about woman's rights.

> Our high and mighty Lords (thanks to their arbitrary constitutions) have denied us the means of knowledge, and then reproached us for the want of it. . . . They doom'd the sex to servile or frivolous employments, on purpose to degrade their minds, that they themselves might hold unrivall'd, the power and pre-eminence they had usurped. Happily, a more liberal way of thinking begins to prevail. . . . But supposing now that we possess'd all the talents of the orator, in the highest perfection; where shall we find a theatre for the display of them? The Church, the Bar, and the Senate are shut against us. Who shut them? *Man;* despotic man, first made us incapable of the duty, and then forbid us the exercise. Let us by suitable education, qualify ourselves for those high departments—they will open before us.[7]

Because education could make women men's intellectual equals, it could unleash the most radical implications of scientific rationalism, political republicanism, and the doctrine of the "rights of man" for application to women,

---

Murray's essays appeared in it under the name Constantia. In 1798 Murray's volume of collected essays, *The Gleaner,* was sold in Philadelphia (Branson, *These Fiery Frenchified Dames,* 26–34). Mary Wollstonecraft's *Vindication of the Rights of Woman* was reprinted in Philadelphia by William Gibbon in 1792 and again by Matthew Carey in 1794, priced at one dollar in 1795 (*Catalogue of Books, Pamphlets, Maps, and Prints Published by Matthew Carey . . .* [Philadelphia, 1795]). Branson demonstrates that in the early 1790s many middle-class Philadelphians reacted positively to Wollstonecraft's writings, until political winds shifted against the French Revolution and her nonconventional personal life came to light (*These Fiery Frenchified Dames,* 38–53). Fredrika J. Teute examines the impact that Wollstonecraft's ideas on free love and the discourse on natural sciences had on United States urban intellectuals in the 1790s, in "The Loves of the Plants," *Huntington Library Quarterly,* LXIII (2000), 319–345.

On periodical propagation: *Lady's Magazine, and Repository of Entertaining Knowledge,* I (1792), 189–198 (which Brown devoted to reprinting excerpts of Wollstonecraft's *Vindication of the Rights of Woman* in this, the first year of his *Lady's Magazine*); "The Rights of Woman," *Philadelphia Minerva,* Oct. 17, 1795; "The Rights of Women," *Weekly Magazine of Original Essays, Fugitive Pieces, and Interesting Intelligence,* Mar. 17, 31, Apr. 7, 1798; [Charles Brockden Brown], *Alcuin: A Dialogue* (New York, 1798).

7. *The Rise and Progress of the Young-Ladies' Academy of Philadelphia . . .* (Philadelphia, 1794), 90–95.

threatening to eliminate gender difference and bringing the relationship between men and women fully into the political realm. At the same time, wom-
en's subordination to men in marriage was being threatened from another
vantage point—the expansive nonmarital sexual relationships in the city. In
this environment in Philadelphia, sex itself became a place to renegotiate the
relationship between men and women in the new nation.

The Gender Politics of Sex in the New Nation

When men and women entered into intimate relationships wholly outside
marriage, they stepped into a social terrain where the gender rules were largely
uncharted. They could not rely on the traditional understandings of the patriarchal control of female sexuality within the family. The gendered sexual
rules that granted fathers and husbands guardianship of women's sexuality
were difficult to apply when sexual behavior occurred outside courtship and
marriage. The open and expansive sexual culture required new notions about
where the control of female sexuality resided. But during the early national
period, these were newly emerging and contested issues. Would men wield the
same power to control the sexual behavior of the women they bedded as they
had controlled their wives and daughters? Or would women who exercised
their sexuality outside marriage be the stewards of their own sexuality?

Power plays between men and women over sexuality both heightened male
sexual privilege and expanded female sexual independence. These two contradictory phenomena owed their existence to this moment when the gendered
notions of normal male and female sexuality were in flux, the cultural space
existed for the open expression of nonmarital sexual behavior, and the new
nation grappled with questions about the extent of liberty appropriate for the
Republic.

Male sexual expression outside marriage occupied a more secure position
in the post-Revolutionary decades than in the late colonial period, in part
because of the work of the pre-Revolutionary print culture and the burgeoning
pleasure culture of the city. The creation of the new white male citizen and the
reconstruction of male sexuality as "naturally" venturesome also supported an
expansion of male nonmarital sexual expression. The extension of full manhood status to virtually all white men laid the groundwork for white men of all
classes to claim the sexual prerogatives that in the past had been reserved to
men of elite economic and political status. Nonmarital sexual behavior became one arena where white men of the middling and lower classes asserted
claims to full manhood status on par with the economic and political elite, and

elite men of the new nation acknowledged that shared manhood without conceding their economic, political, or social superiority. The political uses of an expansive white male sexuality help explain why patriot leaders, such as Benjamin Rush, did not attempt to police the behavior of white men in the city. These leaders were willing to share the sexual prerogatives of manhood, even if unwilling to concede political, social, or economic equality to their new fellow citizens. That men like Rush had come to believe that men's sexual nature was inherently lustful and questing reinforced a fundamental similarity and connection among men.

As we have already seen, casual sexual encounters became more common after the Revolution. Married men visited brothels, picked up women in taverns and on the streets, solicited and coerced sex from their servants, and turned to other women when their wives were unavailable. Men, like women, also used the toleration of nonmarital sexual practices within the sexual culture to establish fulfilling relationships outside marriage.

Both men and women established extramarital affairs. Numerically, husbands and wives were equally accused of adultery in divorce cases, but there were some differences. It was not uncommon for either a husband or wife to go off with a new lover after years of marriage; such cases were common in legal divorces and in self-divorce. Both husbands and wives found new lovers, left their spouses, and moved in with their new partners, setting up new households and families within Philadelphia. In these cases the circumstances of the adulterous wives were similar to those of the husbands. These relationships tended to be out in the open when the new couple remained in the city. Mary Gideon left her husband in 1796 after ten years of marriage to live with George Smith. At the time her husband petitioned for a divorce, she had cohabited with Smith for six years and had had a child with him. The situations were similar for Ann Albertus, who left to live with James Davan, and Jane Burnet, who left a nine-year marriage to live with John Hylliard. Mary Bangs had been married for four years before she set up housekeeping with Richard Duffield, and they had lived together for three years before her husband filed for divorce. Like the others, Bangs and Duffield lived openly as man and wife despite her prior marriage. Duffield's servant Reuben Tucker testified that "he has very often seen the said Richard Duffield and the respondent in bed together of which they made no secret." William Brown's adultery and desertion from his wife, for example, followed the same pattern. He left his wife after ten years of marriage and moved in with Hannah Pope, with whom he had a child. In 1800, when his wife petitioned for divorce, he and Hannah had been living together in the Northern Liberties for five years.[8]

But there were also differences. Some men used another, more clandestine approach to creating a second family. They left town with their lovers to create lives elsewhere or left their families to settle elsewhere and then established new families. William Side left his wife of eight years to move to Carolina and set up a new family. When he left, in 1796, the couple had three children, and his wife was expecting their fourth. When he returned to Philadelphia briefly in 1801, he told his wife that he had a second family in Carolina and two young children. William Richard Payne also fled to Carolina, taking his lover with him from Philadelphia and leaving his wife of more than five years. Etienne Nouge stopped first in Charleston and then went on to the West Indies when he left his wife. Fleeing husbands tended to go south, to the Carolinas, Maryland, or Virginia; a few went north to Boston, and others simply went "to sea." Wives usually did not make such moves. When they left husbands, they often remained in the city. If a woman left the city to end a marriage, she was usually in the company of a new mate. Picking up and moving out of the city and establishing a new means of economic survival was simply not viable for most eighteenth-century women. Philadelphia was still one of the most hospitable places for independent women.[9]

8. See Table 16. Women who left for a new partner: PDP: *Jacob Gideon vs. Mary Gideon,* filed December 1800, events 1796; *Lewis Albertus vs. Ann Albertus,* filed 1794; *Samuel Burnet vs. Jane Burnet,* filed 1796; *Elijah Bangs vs. Mary Bangs,* filed December 1807, events 1804–1805; deposition of Reuben Tucker, Feb. 26, 1807. Men who left for a new partner: PDP: *Johanna Brown vs. William Brown,* filed September 1800, events 1795; *Elizabeth Alexander vs. George Alexander,* filed March 1800, events 1799; *Hannah Anderson vs. James Anderson,* filed June 18, 1799, events 1799; *Barbara Burkhart vs. Jacob Burkhart,* filed October 1785, events 1782–1785; *Catharine Conrad vs. Matthias Conrad,* filed April 1788, events 1786; *Susannah Altimus vs. Jacob Altimus,* filed Nov. 18, 1801, events 1797–1801.

9. PDP: *Mary Side vs. William Side,* filed 1801, events 1796; *Alice Payne vs. William Richard Payne,* filed 1802, events 1800; *May Nouge vs. Etienne Nouge,* filed 1802. Two self-divorcing wives left the Philadelphia region, both accompanied by a new male partner: PJ, Aug. 2, 1770, Ann White and John Power; PJ, Nov. 8, 1764, Mary McKinley and William McKinley. There is only one instance in legal divorces when the wife relocated out of the area: Sophia Visimer, who left her husband and moved to Virginia. It is unclear whether she left with her partner in adultery or established her relationship with him once she arrived. PDP, *Nicholas Visimer vs. Sophia Visimer,* filed 1803.

Perhaps the most telling feature of the male sexual histories of the early national period was male boasting about extramarital sexual encounters. We know about the actions of these men because they talked about them with other men. Unlike the adulterous wives, whose behavior was seen by others, the adulterous husbands' actions were usually recounted for the court by their male peers who learned of their sexual exploits through conversation. Philadelphia storekeeper Joseph Garwood often told his friends Joseph Agar and Daniel Murphy of his sexual life. Agar testified that Garwood "told me that he had connexion with other women than his wife, and said that he had connexion with several different women. He told me so at several different times." Garwood also told both men the circumstances of his contracting venereal disease, twice, from "women of ill fame." Lewis Thomas boasted to his friend Nathan Rhodes of having connection with other women, telling such details that Rhodes surmised to the court that "from the kind of woman he kept company with, . . . the disorder which he the said Lewis had as aforesaid was the venereal disease." In the male culture of sexual storytelling, their sexual encounters took on a life beyond the sexual experience itself. They took pleasure in telling of their intrigues and shared their satisfaction in getting away with expanding their sexual lives. By telling one another of their sexual conquests, they asserted their manhood.[10]

This male network of sexual storytelling was quite extensive. Many men believed the quest for extramarital sexual affairs was universally accepted by their fellow men. In two cases the husbands shared their sexual experiences with their brothers-in-law, demonstrating that they believed the male bond superseded the bond between brother and sister. Simon Gore, for example, told his wife's brother of his encounter with a woman he met at the Butchers Arm Tavern, confiding that he had met her a few days before and contracted venereal disease from her. Another husband, Adam Erben, boasted of his bawdyhouse exploits to his wife's brother. When Margaret Erben sued for divorce, her brother, Daniel Bickley, supported his sister's claim, recounting three years of Adam's statements about his sexual behavior. Adam "was almost constantly employed in gaming and frequenting Bawdy houses, of which he would often make mention to this Deponent, naming the lewd women with whom he had been engaged in a criminal and adulterous inter-

10. PDP: *Elizabeth Garwood vs. Joseph Garwood*, filed September 1804, events 1802–1803 (Garwood was a storekeeper); deposition of Joseph Agar, stonecutter, Mar. 21, 1805; deposition of Daniel Murphy, stonecutter, Mar. 21, 1805; *Ester Thomas vs. Lewis Thomas*, filed Sept. 1, 1800, events 1798–1799; deposition of Nathan Rhodes.

course." But there is no indication that Bickley failed to keep Adam's sexual behavior secret from his sister during their marriage.[11]

The basis for this sexual storytelling was the shared belief in the desirability of such sexual practices and a wish to claim successful participation in male sexual prerogatives. For some, sexual storytelling was grounded in their common sexual experiences. Men often went out on the town together seeking sexually available women. The case of David Pemble demonstrates the ways these two aspects of male sexual culture, storytelling and sexual practices, reinforced each other. Pemble not only told the tales of his sexual adventures to his friend and fellow tailor Thomas Lyons, but the two frequently accompanied each other to Philadelphia's bawdyhouses. During the late 1790s Pemble and Lyons habitually visited the brothels in the city and district of Southwark. On one occasion at the house called the China Factory, Lyons described Pemble's taking a woman into the private rooms, and upon returning saying "that by God he had to do with her, meaning as the Deponent understood, he had been connected with and carnally knew the Girl." On another occasion Pemble "declared" "he had to do with her . . . and complained of her not being clean" when he and Lyons were reunited in the parlor after their sexual encounters. For these two men, exchanging descriptions of their sexual encounters was part of the ritual of extramarital sexual practices. Pemble's sexual storytelling also kept Lyons informed of his sexual entanglements when Lyons was not a party to them. "David in conversation told the deponent he had been connected with many Women within seven years then last past [the period of his marriage], and more than he could recollect or name. He named the widow Carragan as one he had often been connected with." At least among themselves, men took pride in their sexual exploits outside marriage.[12]

The wide range of male sexual experiences in the early 1790s is most strikingly represented in an unusual sex diary kept by a Philadelphia man. The author's identity remains a mystery. He was a married man of middling economic standing, literate but unsophisticated in his writing. He had enough disposable income to indulge his sexual appetites in bawdyhouses, taverns, and inns, and he distinguished himself from the lower-class sailors who were

11. PDP: *Sarah Gore vs. Simon Gore,* filed December 1787; deposition of John Camon, tailor, Sept. 5, 1787; *Margaret Erben vs. Adam Erben,* filed January 1790, events 1786–1789.

12. PDP: *Catherine Pemble vs. David Pemble,* filed 1803, events 1798–1799; deposition of Thomas Lyons, tailor, 1803. See also *Deborah Bellot vs. Peter Bellot,* filed Apr. 1, 1797.

the typical clientele of a Dock Street brothel he visited. He employed peri-odic domestic help to aid his wife in her housekeeping but appears in no way well-off.[13]

His diary provides us with an intimate account of a year in one man's sexual life in the 1790s. His experiences were probably more extensive than most men's sexual activities, but they did not differ in kind from those presented in the divorce papers, Guardians of the Poor records, newspaper advertisements, and court records. He might not have been typical, but he was not unique. The patterns of conduct recorded in his log are all documented as widespread in the other sources on male sexuality during this era. What his account adds is a composite view of one man's life and his own representation of his sexuality. We see not only where and with whom he found nonmarital sexual experi-ences but also his thoughts about male and female sexuality and the attitudes he held that supported his sexual license.

On January 1, about 1793, he claimed to have "topped" thirty-six "wenches" in the preceding year. In the new year he would name fifteen women other than his wife with whom he had sexual relations. He also recorded two in-

13. [James Wilson?], Account Book and Diary, MS, APS. The account book was originally owned by James Wilson, renowned Philadelphia lawyer and justice of the United States Supreme Court. The diary was kept in a copy of *Aitken's General American Register . . . for 1773*. The account book appears to have been used at least three times, and perhaps by two or three different authors: there are accounting entries for the early 1780s related to Wilson's sawmills; entries made by Wilson pertaining to his legal practice in 1790–1791; and the entries made by the sex diarist, using a different pen and apparently in a different hand from Wilson's, for one year in the 1790s. Internal references to Dr. Phillip Syng Physick suggest that the year was sometime around 1794, when he practiced medicine in Philadelphia. It was not unusual to reuse alma-nacs and journals at the time. It is somewhat surprising that the journal remained with Wilson's personal papers after his death.

Susan Klepp suggests that the author of the intimate journal might have been a sawyer in Wilson's employ. It is also possible that the journal entries were done as a lampoon of Wilson, as a practical joke, though I think probably not. The similarities are striking between the behavior described and that documented in the divorce papers. The diary also contains details of persons and places that can be documented in the 1790s. For these reasons I have concluded that this was someone's personal diary. If designed as a practical joke, it was written convincingly and was crafted from the sexual scripts available to late-eighteenth-century Philadelphia. In either case, it is a useful source of information about that society's beliefs and expectations. My thanks to Susan Klepp for bringing this source to my attention.

stances when he pursued women who successfully rebuffed his sexual advances. His sexual encounters ran through the full range of sexual possibilities that we have already encountered. He maintained mistresses, visited bawdyhouses, pursued his servants, and picked up women he met about the town and during his countryside excursions. He had ongoing relationships with two women: Martha and a woman identified as "Miller's cook." He described thirteen other single-event sexual encounters; in five he paid the woman for her services. Of the remaining women, five can be identified as laboring women: three servants, a cook, and a washerwoman.

Our anonymous diarist was always on the sexual prowl. His primary interaction with women was sexual. Whether he was meeting them in passing or they were working in his home, he never passed up an opportunity to initiate a sexual encounter. When Nancy Jones came to his house to perform domestic labor, he spent the day pestering her for sexual services.

19 Aug—Nancy Jones came to work at 8—today. Rather old but I found her sympathetic and kind. She is a virgin yet fallen. I sent my wife to Race Street while I tested Ms. Nancy [all?] day.

A month later Nancy complained to his wife, without apparently giving her the details of his behavior.

22 Sept—I found Nancy Jones when I came home. My wife said—The hussy—she says that she [hates?] you—I am glad it is no worse—and so I sent her away.

After expressing relief that she had not directly accused him of sexual misconduct, he went on in the same entry to complain that, if Martha, one of his long-term partners, were more sexually satisfying, he would not stray to other women. His interactions with women in public were also based on sexual pursuit. For instance, on May 17:

To the Falls—A brave coursing—got one mistress Ann King near the wood and in some bushes. All over in ten minutes. a Rare wench thin in flesh but great in motion.

Always on the lookout for sexual opportunity, our diarist almost got himself shot when on March 23 he misunderstood the meaning of a woman's eyeing him from her doorway: "Passing along the Quay a wench eyed me from a house. I entered—a man with a gun requested me to depart—I tarried not— but [——] of the deception in [——]."

Most of our author's encounters were consensual, and he made frequent comments about his partners' sexual enjoyment, but he did not perceive coercion and force as unreasonable behavior in attaining access to a sexual experience. On January 7:

> To night a Ruination at a Soiree. Met a certain young—danced with her and aroused all my passion—She resisted much holding her limbs together, but my flame being up I thrust her vigorously and she opened with a scream—a real joyful fuddle—she screaming much at [Incursion?]
> Weary from last nights Excertions

To the modern reader this is a description of a rape. To our diarist, this behavior was consistent with his understanding of his sexuality as an exercise in pursuit, insistence, and the ultimate submission of his partner. On September 28 he alluded to another occasion when he might have used force. "—ed a Maid last night gave her $5—and told her to forget the incident." Here his payment of cash after the fact was used to compensate her for his overcoming her resistance. Whether these women believed that they had been raped is not clear. If they did, they had little legal recourse. Prosecutions for rape in early national Philadelphia were rare and usually unsuccessful if the perpetrator was a white man.[14]

One could dismiss this man as an aberration if his views about his sexuality and women's sexuality were not so strikingly similar to the ideas emerging within Philadelphia's larger culture. In his descriptions of his sexual encounters he credits women with having greater control over their sexuality than men have. Women have the ability to deploy their sexuality as they wish—to arouse his passion or to restrain themselves. When he committed the "Ruination" at the "Soiree," it was the woman who "aroused all my passion" that led him to act. When he spent the night with a woman on March 14, he credited her with instigating their congress. His entry began: "A great vigorous wench in the Inn did ogle me with lecherous eye. To night I lay too with her."

To our diarist, women are the source of his lack of sexual control; they create his straying sexuality. He opens his first entry, "1 Jan—I promise me in the coming year to avoid lewd women—they are the bane of my life." Later in the year he writes: "12 May. A great coming of Ladies—I must avoid them. I am a poor weak [——] man—with great passion and no self restraint." He, as a

---

14. In only twelve instances in the 1790s was rape or attempted rape the stated offense in arrest records or trial proceedings. The few convictions were for the lesser crime of attempted rape. Successful prosecutions for rape or attempted rape usually involved child victims or men of color as the accused perpetrators.

man, must battle to control his sexuality.[15] But he succumbs to his passion when the opportunity appears. On November 24 he writes of his encounter with Maria, a chamberwoman, "I could not resist her charms," and on July 4 he sums up his basic construction of male and female sexuality:

> 4 July—In evening met Amanda S—Walked with her much discourse of sweet nature. I could not resist and Amanda would not.—god forgive me. but it was good.

Amanda, as a woman, could resist sexual temptation if she wanted to. Our diarist, a man, simply did not have the constitution to turn away from this sexual opportunity. In the thirty years since the idea of male sexual weakness had been introduced to Philadelphians through popular print, some men had come to fully embrace it as the natural state of their gendered sexuality.

One of the consequences of the more open system of sexuality of the 1790s was that it paved the way for men to exercise greater sexual privilege. This was manifested in men's exerting their power over subordinate women to attain sexual access as well as in their disregard for their wives' well-being in their pursuit of it. Our anonymous diarist demonstrated both phenomena. Many of the women he had sexual relations with were of the lower classes, available to him because of their occupations. As washerwomen, domestic servants, and chambermaids, their work took them into his home under his temporary employ or placed him in the establishments where they were charged with attending to guests' needs. Under these circumstances they were particularly vulnerable to his pursuits. In every instance when the diarist mentions a woman working in his home or one he encountered at an inn, he attempts and usually attains sexual access to her.[16]

In divorce petitions, other men behaved in similar ways. John Oldmixon seduced his child's nursemaid Elizabeth Brown in 1799; Samuel Pettit attempted "to ravish" his wife's friend Margaret Skeen when she spent the night in the couple's home in 1791; and Nicholas Gerin regularly brought a "certain Negro woman" to his house to commit adultery while his wife was home and aware of his behavior. In each of these instances men asserted their control over their home dominion—control that included assertions of their sexual

---

15. He writes of his penis as a separate powerful entity with a will of its own and credits it with control of him. For example: "26 Jan—My penis doth annoy me much— He recovering frequently vigorous at onoffentious times—I pray he be not so."

16. For example, Ludorwick's wife, who washes for him in December, is described as "a nice person,—I rolled her over and fuddled her . . . sweet thing."

prerogative. Samuel Pettit seemed very sure of himself when, as Margaret Skeen described it, lying in bed early in the morning, she "was attacked by the Respondent in a most violent and indecent manner, who attempted with all his power to ravish her; but by her crying out for assistance extricated herself from him and took shelter in the room of the libellant." These two women thwarted his designs by locking themselves in a room together. Pettit nonetheless expected to exercise the sexual privilege he enjoyed within his household.[17]

Another symptom of male sexual privilege was husbands' willingness to bring venereal disease home. Venereal disease had become a serious health hazard. Its spread in early national Philadelphia led to the creation of special venereal wards in the Pennsylvania Hospital and special protocol for those admitted with it to the almshouse and the Asylum of the Magdalen Society. The greatest danger to wives was the possibility of contracting venereal disease. While the transmission of venereal disease follows no gender bias, the entrance of venereal disease into marriages from extramarital adventures was almost wholly due to the husband as the agent of transmission. Venereal disease was often what betrayed a husband's infidelity to his wife, in many instances after his prolonged engagment in a parallel extramarital sexual life. In the case of Samuel Tallman, for instance, only when he contracted the disease a second time, in 1802, did his wife learn of it and his infidelity. He had successfully concealed from her his first bout with the disease in 1800.[18]

But what is most striking in these cases was the husbands' disregard for their wives. Many men concealed their illness and adopted a strategy of staying away from their wives while their venereal disease was active. Like our diarist (who noted, "Clapp—much itching in my flopper—must keep away from my

17. PDP: *Mary Oldmixon vs. John Oldmixon*, filed October 1807, events 1799; *Eleanor Pettit vs. Samuel Pettit*, filed 1797, events 1791; deposition of Margaret Skeen, Mar. 27, 1798; *Ann Gerin vs. Nicholas Gerin*, filed March 1798, events 1795–1796.

18. PDP: *Mary Tallman vs. Samuel Tallman*, filed March 1805, events 1800–1802; deposition of David Christie, of the district of Southwark, physician. For other cases where venereal disease revealed a husband's adultery, see PDP: *Hannah Rice vs. Peter Rice*, filed December 1798, events late 1790s (this couple lived in Northampton, and he contracted the disease in Philadelphia); *Elizabeth Smallwood vs. Thomas Smallwood*, filed March 1796; *Catharine Brown vs. Joseph Brown*, filed September 1802, events 1801; *Anne Murphy vs. Timothy Murphy*, filed April 1786, events early 1780s.

Within the divorce petitions, venereal disease was specifically cited as a cause for divorce in fifteen of the adultery cases. In only one is there evidence that the wife might have been responsible.

wife"), these men would refrain from sexual activity with their wives while they suffered symptoms. The doctors who treated them were well aware of their tendency to conceal their condition from their wives. In their depositions for the court these doctors documented their efforts to ascertain whether their patient had a wife at risk of contracting the disease. Dr. Albertus Shilack testified in the Erben divorce case that infected husbands could not be trusted to abstain from sexual activity with their wives:

And this deponent saith, that he enjoined the Defendant not to cohabit with his wife during the continuance of the said disorder, and warned the Libellant of her danger in permitting it, in consequences of which warning this Deponent believes the said Libellant was saved from the infection.[19]

Dr. William Walace of the district of Southwark echoed this sentiment when he stated "that he asked the said Charles [McGee] some serious questions about the manner in which he caught the disease." Dr. Walace's concern was warranted: McGee concealed the fact that he was a married man from the doctor. When McGee solicited the doctor's aid a second time and confessed that he had "caught it from the same woman again," Dr. Walace confronted him with the fact that he had learned that McGee was married. McGee admitted that it was true and said "that if the deponent would cure him again, that she had consented to receive him; and he would go and live with her and would be a new man." Walace's deposition does not reveal whether he believed that McGee was a changed man, but it does demonstrate the role of arbitrator and social conscience that doctors often played in cases of marital venereal disease.[20]

Other men failed to curb their sexual intercourse with their wives despite their venereal disease. Eliza Steinberg suffered from such action. Her husband's case was well advanced when Dr. Isaac Cathcall began treating the couple. Here it was Eliza who initiated the doctor's intervention; early in her pregnancy her symptoms caused her to consult him. Cathcall testified that he found her pregnant and "afflicted with venereal ulcers"; that "in the case of three visits, affirmant [Cathcall] was led to believe from the conversations and confessions of the Respondent [Eliza's husband Jacob] to him, that he had

19. PDP: *Margaret Erben vs. Adam Erben*, filed Feb. 2, 1804; deposition of Albertus Shilack of the Northern Liberties, surgeon, Jan. 6, 1790.

20. PDP: *Elizabeth McGee vs. Charles McGee*, filed Feb. 2, 1804, events 1802; deposition of William Walace, district of Southwark, physician, Sept. 11, 1804.

communicated the venereal disease to his wife." When Cathcall attended Eliza in childbed, she was delivered of a stillborn child, which Cathcall attributed to the mercurial treatment for venereal disease that she had undergone. Cathcall's testimony about the stage of Jacob's disease makes it clear that Jacob knowingly communicated the disease to her.[21]

Jacob Steinberg was not alone. Other men put their sexual interests ahead of their wives' well-being. Thomas Smith maintained a mistress in New York from whom he contracted venereal disease. When his wife visited him there, he slept with her, knowing he had the disease, and swore to a friend that he would sleep with her again when he was in Philadelphia despite the risk to her:

> This deponent [John Brown] asked him [Thomas Smith] whether he had seen his wife when she had been at New York some time before and whether he had slept with her. He answered that he had seen her and slept with her, and that at the time he did so, he had the venereal disorder but could not tell whether he had communicated it to his wife or not.

> The said Thomas then shewed to this deponent that he had the venereal disorder at the time they were conversing together, and this deponent begged him not to go to his family. He answered and swore that he would sleep with his wife that night.

The next day, Thomas confided to John that he had slept with his wife but that "she would not let him touch her." Isabella had indeed contracted venereal disease from him in New York and had just recovered from her treatment for it when he returned to Philadelphia. She would have no more to do with him.[22]

The wives of these men did not always accept their male sexual privilege. While the broad sexual culture of the community allowed more open sexual behavior, women themselves often acted to restrain their husbands. In the criminally prosecuted cases of adultery, wives usually swore out the oaths of complaint, in many cases bringing the charges against her husband's sexual partner, the other woman, and not her husband. These women were laying claim to their exclusive right to their husband's sexuality, and their goal was to bring him home. In 1796, for example, Jemima Brown went in search of her husband, "he having been absent for several nights," and retrieved him from

21. PDP: *Eliza Steinberg vs. Jacob Steinberg*, filed December 1812, events 1811–1812; deposition of Isaac Cathcall of the city of Philadelphia, physick, Dec. 23, 1812.

22. PDP: *Isabella Smith vs. Thomas Smith*, filed 1801, events 1800; deposition of John Brown, mariner, Mar. 17, 1802.

"a house of ill fame." In these instances women took action to restrict their husbands' wide-ranging sexuality, but society in general did not.[23]

Clearly, during the early national era Philadelphians tolerated an increase in male sexual privilege, which in turn increased female vulnerability. But this era also witnessed strong assertions of female independence. When women engaged in relations that resulted in bastardy, established affairs, left their marriages for new men, or participated in sex commerce, they affirmed their sexual independence, that is, created sexual lives independent of marriage. When the women themselves directed their sexual lives, they exercised unprecedented female sexual autonomy, that is, sexual choices unmediated by the interests or directions of others.

Establishing how often those women not just engaged in nonmarital sexual behavior but established sexual lives of their own choosing is difficult. Often the historical evidence fails to give enough information to make such a judgment. For Philadelphia society the nonmarital behavior of women in itself marked unprecedented female independence, and the number of women engaging in sexual behavior outside marriage was remarkable. But for the women themselves, their greater sexual autonomy must have been important and exciting. As we analyze the meanings of women's participation in bastardy, adultery, and prostitution, we will explore first how their behavior signified sexual independence and, second, how it demonstrated female sexual autonomy.[24]

During the 1790s more than seven hundred cases of bastardy were administered through the Guardians of the Poor. Proportionally, twice as many women gave birth to children outside recognizable families as did so in the ten years preceding the Revolution (Table 1). After the Revolution the administration of bastardy cases continued to follow its pre-Revolutionary form, with the Guardians of the Poor promoting gender equity in the responsibility for nonmarital sexual behavior through their adjudication of child support. When the

23. PDP: *Maria Moore vs. John Moore*, filed September 1799, events 1796–1797; deposition of Jemima Brown, Nov. 19, 1799. See also PFT: Apr. 13, 1801, Ann McGuire; Aug. 21, 1803, Mary White.

24. I have purposely used the word "independence" here (meaning sexual behavior independent of marriage) to complicate our understanding of how gendered notions of "dependence" and "independence" operated in early national America. It was this association of men with independence that qualified them for citizenship and became an important aspect of full manhood status—just as women's supposed dependence on men in marriage disqualified them for direct participation in the new political state. But, when women adopted forms of sexual behavior independent of marriage, they demonstrated the fiction of these associations, literally embodying a form of female independence.

fathers of illegitimate children could support them, they were required to; when the fathers were poor and the mothers without resources, the mothers relied on the almshouse for aid during the birth and public support during the child's infant years. Such mothers often bound their children to lengthy indentures to secure a higher standard of living for them in childhood and the prospect of their learning a trade as youths.[25]

At its most basic level, the system of mandatory paternal child support through the Guardians of the Poor routinely and consistently provided support for the children of these unions. On another level, however, this system had a more complicated effect on women and on the sexual system. By protecting the community from bearing the financial burden of illegitimate children, the system of regulating child support through the Guardians of the Poor unwittingly facilitated the separation of sexual intercourse from its marital context. It provided a way for men to be responsible for their children born out of wedlock and thus mitigated the community's insistence upon children's being born within recognizable families. While this system increased male sexual privilege and led to greater sexual exploitation of women, it also allowed women some choice to engage in nonmarital sexuality.

During the 1790s, in the overwhelming majority of the documented instances of bastardy the fathers posted bonds with the Guardians ensuring their financial support of their offspring (68 percent). As they had been in the pre-Revolutionary era, these were men and women who did not intend to marry or establish households together. Again, in most of these cases the woman sought mandatory regulated paternal child support before the birth of her child (73 percent) (see Plate 9). In one-quarter of the bastardy cases in the 1790s the mother used the almshouse to give birth or brought her child there immediately after the birth. In these cases it is difficult to ferret out the relationship between the parents. Those who gave birth in the almshouse were generally poor women whose sexual partner was without financial resources.

25. When the city reestablished poor relief after the Revolutionary war, the Guardians took over practical control and daily operations of poor relief from the Managers, who had run the poor relief system since 1767. Throughout the 1780s the Guardians ran the poor relief and bastardy system, gaining legal authority to do so in 1789 with the passage of An Act for the More Effectual Collection of the Poor Tax (James T. Mitchell, Henry Flanders, et al., comps., *The Statutes at Large of Pennsylvania* [Harrisburg, 1896–1915], XIII, 251–252). See also John K. Alexander, *Render Them Submissive: Responses to Poverty in Philadelphia, 1760–1800* (Amherst, Mass., 1980), 104–116; Priscilla Ferguson Clement, *Welfare and the Poor in the Nineteenth-Century City: Philadelphia, 1800–1854* (Rutherford, N.J., 1985), 40–41.

PLATE 9. *John Lewis Krimmel,* A Woman Swearing Paternity before an Alderman in Philadelphia. *1820. Courtesy, The Winterthur Library: Joseph Downs Collection of Manuscripts and Print Ephemera*

In these circumstances the decision to enter the system of bastardy adjudication administered by the Guardians of the Poor was often based on economic necessity and may not reflect the quality of the relationship or the absence of a long-term partner. In the remaining 6.4 percent of cases the mother used the almshouse on a temporary basis during her pregnancy but found the means necessary to leave the almshouse before the birth of her child (see Table 14).[26]

After the Revolution the Guardians of the Poor chronicled cases of bastardy

26. In the 1790s the information necessary to establish the timing of initiation was available for 27 percent of the cases, of which 73 percent were brought forward before the birth. However, another quarter of the cases appear to have begun in the months surrounding the birth, but the timing cannot be established conclusively. In the period 1790–1795 it was common for the father to post bond before the birth of the child, whereas at the end of the decade the bond was usually not posted until after the birth and thus recorded by the Guardians of the Poor. I suspect that the women in these cases had sworn the child to the father before the birth, but they came into the record only when the bond was posted.

TABLE 14. *Almshouse Bastardy Cases*

Bastardy Cases	1790	1805–1814	1822–1825
	ALL CASES		
Involving almshouse	32%	25%	28%
(Birth in)[a]	(25.6)	(20)	(22)
(Temporary use of)	(6.4)	(5)	(6)
Not involving almshouse	68	75	72
	ALMSHOUSE CASES		
Birth in[a]	79	79	79
Temporary use of	21	21	21

[a] Includes cases where the woman gave birth in the almshouse and cases where a mother or mother and babe came into the almshouse immediately following the birth for aid.

Source: DOD.

in two separate groups, representing two distinct populations: women receiving mandatory child support from the father of their child, administered by the Guardians; and women admitted to the almshouse, not receiving support, pregnant with an illegitimate child. During the last decades of the eighteenth century what placed a woman pregnant with a bastard child in one group or the other was her class, the class of her sexual partner, and her race when she was a woman of color. Recipients of mandatory paternal child support outside the almshouse were generally white women whose sexual partner had been a man with some economic resources, from gentleman to employed laborer. Those entering the almshouse were generally poor women whose sexual partner was also without financial resources, or African-American women. The only women from the out-relief child support system who ever entered the almshouse in the late eighteenth century were those in the few cases where the father fought charges of paternity in court (2 percent). Otherwise, the two groups were documented as distinct populations whose experiences of bearing an illegitimate child differed because of class and race.

During the 1790s the proportion of almshouse cases was somewhat higher than in the pre-Revolutionary era. In the 1790s, 32 percent of the mothers who bore bastard children used the almshouse at some point during their pregnancy or postpartum period, with 26 percent giving birth and recovering there. In the decade preceding the Revolution approximately 20 percent were almshouse cases, with 17 percent giving birth there. Some of this increase in almshouse use was due to the maturity of the system. In the pre-Revolutionary decade the almshouse had just opened its doors, and the Overseers did not use it consistently. By the 1790s the parents without resources were funneled into the almshouse rather than given outside aid. But the increase in almshouse use was primarily due to the difficult financial circumstances of many laboring men and women at the end of the century. During the 1790s the city experienced mercantile expansion and economic growth, but the fruits of the expanding economy did not benefit lower-class laborers. Bearing children in the economy of the 1790s was costly for them. That poverty compelled 25 percent of those known to have parented an illegitimate child to use the almshouse during this era is not surprising. Having a child was a financial hardship. The status of that child as bastard or not made little economic difference to its mother when the father was poor.[27]

Because the public policy on illegitimate children did not penalize their mothers, even women at the bottom of the economic ladder could maneuver though this system of child support without the additional burden of punitive repercussions. While the almshouse admissions clerk viewed poor women and women of color as especially licentious, reflecting his upward class aspirations, the policies of the Guardians toward those women who entered to bear their child were not particularly punitive or unusually disciplinarian. The clerk often attacked the sexual reputations of the women who bore bastard babies within its walls. The admissions log is littered with comments like those about Elizabeth McClenshy (a white woman): "that dirty little hussey Elizabeth McClenshy who lays in here with Bastard, after Bastard, after Bastard with Impunity." His choice of words was crude but reflected the sentiment of upper-class Philadelphians like Benjamin Rush and Elizabeth Drinker. In 1793 when a white

27. During the late 1760s and early 1770s the Overseers and the Managers fought for control over the authority and resources of poor relief. A central dispute was over the use of out-relief, versus compulsory use of the almshouse. Bonded bastardy cases fell outside this dispute because the city often did not extend its own resources in these cases and could recoup money spent in support of bastard-bearing women and their children. But cases of bastardy among the indigent were part of this dispute. During this era the Overseers sought to continue providing aid outside the almshouse, and the Managers worked to force the poor seeking aid into the almshouse. During this dispute some of the indigent bastardy cases were probably handled outside the almshouse, reducing the proportion of bastardy cases cared for in the almshouse before the Revolution. Billy G. Smith, The "Lower Sort": Philadelphia's Laboring People, 1750–1800 (Ithaca, N.Y., 1990), 65–91.

woman brought her newborn mulatto babe to the almshouse for care and left, the clerk asserted that she "goes to get another," and that an African-American woman who also brought in a child she could not care for was "a worthless Hussey of a mother who is runing about the Town and no doubt endeavouring to git another to encrease the burthen of this Institution." Occasionally, the admissions clerk noted a "decent" poor woman who entered the house, but most poor women were assumed to have voracious sexual appetites. Underneath these harsh words the clerk's comments reveal a kernel of truth about poor women's ability to use the poor relief system and the almshouse when facing an illegitimate birth in the 1790s: poor women did come in, bear their child, and then leave the almshouse without punishment or financial penalty.[28]

During the 1790s the Guardians of the Poor did not use the almshouse as a coercive tool to correct or punish mothers of illegitimate children. Women who were pregnant by men with the financial resources to pay child support were not forced into the almshouse, and admission and discharge policies were flexible enough to allow women to use it for a brief period while pregnant but to leave it before the birth. These women were usually taken out by family members who pledged they would care for them during their confinement. In 21 percent of the almshouse cases women made such temporary use of the almshouse. Many of those who did give birth there were discharged after they had secured a place of service, often as wet nurses, and they left to support themselves with their babies in tow.

During the 1790s poor Philadelphians often used the almshouse without adopting the morals advocated by its administrators or adhering to its rules and regulations, including those rules requiring the able poor to work while residing there. The inmates often dictated the atmosphere and behavior in the house and did not submit to their expected subordinate and deferential place. Inmates frequently eloped over the fence (including a few women with pronounced pregnancies!), brought alcohol into the house and got drunk,

28. The incidence of repeated bastard births by women in Philadelphia was quite low. In the out-relief paternal child support cases in the 1790s two cases might have been the same woman, but no evidence connected her to both cases, and her name was too common to make a conclusive link. In the almshouse sample of 3.25 years there were four cases where women used the almshouse for a second case of bastardy. If these figures held true for the decade, the rate of repeated bastardy among the mothers using the almshouse would be 1.7 percent. DOD: case of Elizabeth McClenshy, June 28, 1791; case of Jonathan Trusty and unnamed white woman, May 31, 1793; case of baby Henry Cook, Mar. 12, 1793. Elizabeth Courtney is described in positive, respectable terms; see Mar. 5, 1796.

and refused to work for their keep. Women who made their living through sex commerce often took a hiatus from the trade in the almshouse or retired there for medical treatment for venereal disease. In one instance in 1789, the women of the venereal ward drummed out a fellow inmate who had worked among them as nurse, and probably as a moral reformer, by enacting what they called " 'the Whoars' March." The almshouse clerk reported that a pauper from the Northern Liberties named Jane Bickerdite had

> for some time acted as nurse among the Venereal Women. But her best endeavours, in their filthy Service, not proving satisfactory to them, they quarrelled with and abused her very much. And now when she was going away ["being discharged at her own desire"] they mob'd her severely and raised a bawling Clamrous Noise and clangor with Beating and Rattling, Frying pans, Shovels, Tongs etc. after her all of which Together, they called "the Whoars" March.[29]

The women of the almshouse had apparently rejected Bickerdite's aid and her attempts to turn them away from the sexual behavior that had led to their infection. They turned the tables on her, insinuating that she was the deviant, enacting a customary practice usually used to shame women who had violated a moral code. On their turf, in the almshouse, Bickerdite's reforming ways were the ways of the whore, and their sexual adventures were the accepted shared experiences. Not all the sexually active women who spent time there were so brazen, and some must have perceived themselves sexual victims of cunning and false men. But in the almshouse of the 1790s lower-class women could assert their own interpretation of their sexual behavior.

The experience of entering the almshouse could also be quite grim. Those assigned to the medical wards, including women lying in to give birth, shared the space with those suffering from venereal disease. In 1796, when twenty-nine women gave birth to illegitimate children there, forty-one women and twenty-one men were admitted for medical treatment with telltale physical signs of venereal disease. But the almshouse also provided food, shelter, clothing, and medical care for those in need, and many used the almshouse on their own terms, including women bearing illegitimate babies.[30]

29. DOD, Dec. 22, 1789.

30. DOD. The almshouse operated the only medical facility for indigent patients. Some men of the laboring classes had the financial resources to seek treatment in the Pennsylvania Hospital, which operated a venereal disease ward. But women, with fewer resources, were more likely to seek treatment at the almshouse.

The experiences of Priscilla McPherson and Mary Perkins, who gave birth to illegitimate daughters in the spring of 1796, were typical. Like most such women in the almshouse, they sought admission late in their pregnancy. Priscilla entered during her ninth month and gave birth two and a half weeks later. She and her baby remained there for a recovery period of two months, and, once Priscilla was ready to resume work, they departed, "being now both well and she engaged in a place of nursing they are discharged." Mary Perkins was admitted in May, eight months pregnant. She gave birth on May 24, but her child survived only one day, dying the following evening. Mary left eleven days later, having also "engaged in a place of nursing," probably as a wet nurse to a well-to-do family. Mary was not the only woman to lose an infant to a quick death. One of every six illegitimate infants born in the almshouse died before discharge, usually within days of birth.[31]

Some women who gave birth in the almshouse were frequent residents who used the almshouse seasonally as opportunities for employment slowed or harsh winter weather made living without fuel or adequate housing untenable. Elizabeth Barber was one such poor woman. She entered the almshouse in February 1790, eight months pregnant. She had contracted venereal disease before the birth of her son, who died of the disease a month after birth. When she left the almshouse in April following his death, the clerk predicted that she would "soon be back." He was right. On Christmas Day her admission entry recorded that she was "now returned with the venereal Disease and in a most wretched naked condition, frozen." She was a frequent resident throughout the 1790s, coming in and then "eloping," or leaving without being formally discharged. As the clerk put it in 1796, she "according to her usual custom jumped the fence." Elizabeth Barber lived in poverty for much of this period, but she was able to use the almshouse as a place of periodic refuge and resources. Each time she entered she was treated for her illness and issued a new set of clothes. Often women like Elizabeth recuperated there and then returned to their lives among the working poor in the city streets. Some women, like Sarah Peters, made more direct use of the almshouse's resources. She took several sets of clothing with her when she left after the birth of her daughter in the spring of 1796. The almshouse clerk believed women like

31. Sixty percent were admitted to the almshouse during or after their eighth month of pregnancy, and another 35 percent entered the almshouse in their sixth and seventh months (information available in half the cases). DOD: Priscilla McPherson, Mar. 5, 24, June 23, 1796; Mary Perkins, May 3, June 24, July 6, 1796. Of the illegitimate infants born in the 3.25-year sample from the 1790s, 17 percent died soon after birth.

Sarah sold the clothes they acquired there for support once they left, and he complained that the lax admission and discharge policies of the Guardians allowed the poor to cycle in and out of the almshouse at will, taking a fresh set of clothes with them after each visit. Clothing was a small asset for a poor woman facing raising a child on her own. But such petty pilfering was one of the ways poor women used this system to try to care for themselves and their infants at the end of the century.[32]

During the 1790s the almshouse was used almost exclusively by poor women with few resources. It provided a needed refuge and critical medical services for those in dire need. It would come to play a far different role in the public policy concerning illegitimacy and nonmarital sexuality in the early nineteenth century, when city officials would attempt to lay the responsibility for sexual transgression at women's feet.

If the experience of bearing a bastard child remained in many ways the same for white women in early national Philadelphia as it had been before the Revolution, it changed dramatically for women of color. By 1790 more than 85 percent of Philadelphia's African-American population were free, and the city had become something of a mecca for African-Americans throughout the mid-Atlantic as a place to establish a new life after slavery. Their children would not be the legal property of white masters. During the 1780s African-American women began to participate in the Guardians of the Poor adjudication of bastardy. The experiences of some would be similar to those of white women of the lower classes. If their partners were employed and could post bond and guarantee child support, they could expect the Guardians of the Poor to facilitate paternal responsibility and work to keep them from needing public support. Mary Cary's experience was recorded as rather unremarkable by the Guardians:

> June 9, 1791, Peter Sharp a free black laborer paid to the Guardians of the Poor the sum of 24 pounds, received as compensation in full for the support of his child by Mary Cary, a Black Woman, this being the most that could be got.

32. DOD: Elizabeth Barber, Feb. 2, Mar. 25, Apr. 19, Dec. 25, 1790, May 17, 1793, Feb. 17, 1796; Sarah Peters, Feb. 6, Mar. 16, May 31, 1796. For other examples of habitual almshouse residents who gave birth to bastard babies, see the cases of Catherine Delany, also known as Red-Kate, and Mary Smith, also known as Hannah Sharp. Both women probably supported themselves through sex commerce, and both had contracted venereal disease. DOD, Dec. 2, 3, 1793, Mar. 20, 30, 1798.

Like other members of the laboring classes, the modest economic status of Mary's sexual partner meant that the support Mary would receive for her child was minimal.[33]

During the 1790s, when African-Americans made up 7 percent of the city's population, black couples like Mary Cary and Peter Sharp accounted for only 2.5 percent of the bastardy cases. Many African-Americans probably worked hard to avoid drawing attention to themselves and sought to steer clear of the Guardians of the Poor. In this era, when the abolition law dictated the indenture of children of slaves until age twenty-eight, the Guardians would not hesitate to indenture the children of indigent free blacks. The city's people of color also lived under the daily threat of reenslavement. Slave traders operated within the city, abducting African-Americans by claiming they were the property of men they represented, and children were especially vulnerable to illegal enslavement. Avoiding public notice, including public exposure in the bastardy system, could be an important survival strategy. It is no wonder that women like Sylvia Clow, a newly freed Philadelphian, strove to extricate herself from the Guardians' bastardy system before she gave birth. Sylvia had gained her freedom when a member of the Pennsylvania Abolition Society purchased her in the bankruptcy sale of her owner, Samuel Wharton. In January 1790 she was admitted to the almshouse as a pauper, pregnant with her second illegitimate child. Two months later, before she had given birth, her mother secured her discharge from the almshouse. Sylvia, having assured the Guardians that "her Mother hath now provided a suitable place and accommodations for her lying in," was free to bear her child away from official view. When black women did enter the system of bastardy adjudication, they were

33. GPM, June 9, 1791; Gary B. Nash, *Forging Freedom: The Formation of Philadelphia's Black Community, 1720–1840* (Cambridge, Mass., 1988), table 4, 137. Nash estimates that the black population of Philadelphia in 1790 was 2,078, with 273 enslaved African-Americans and 1,805 free.

African-American women could expect a higher level of support for their children when the father had greater means. See, for example, the case of Elizabeth Long and the white merchant William Cochran, who in 1790 paid more than twice as much (£50 12s. 6d.) to commute his cases (GPM, March 1790).

I use the term "women of color" here to refer to all nonwhite women in late-eighteenth-century Philadelphia, primarily women of African origin or descent. There were few native Americans in Philadelphia, and few Asian-Pacific immigrants. White and black Philadelphians used the term "colored" to identify people of African origin, including those of mixed racial parentage, during the early national period.

much more likely to end up using the resources of the almshouse than to receive out-relief paternal support (see Table 15).[34]

Bastardy cases that involved cross-racial couples came to the attention of the Guardians of the Poor more frequently than cases of black couples. During the 1790s just under 5 percent of cases involved couples who crossed the racial divide to conceive a child. In three-fifths of these cases the mother was a woman of color and the father white, and in two-fifths the mother was white and the father black. The behavior of the white women involved in these cases suggests that bearing a mulatto illegitimate child had harsh social consequences for them. Several abandoned their child soon after birth. In 1793 the almshouse admitted two-week-old Denis Proctor after his mother had run away from her place of service, leaving him behind. Later that same year David Trusty was delivered to the almshouse by his mother, despite the commitment of Jonathan Trusty, the child's father, to provide support. These women desired to be free of their mulatto child, whose presence broadcast their sexual relationships with black men. Even when a white mother did not shun her mulatto offspring, the society around her offered little understanding or support. White women who bore illegitimate children to black fathers were the most likely to require the aid of the almshouse, often having nowhere else to turn for assistance.[35]

A white woman's sexual reputation, even among the mothers of illegitimate children, was harmed by her intimate relationships with African-American men. It was Mary McCulloch's reputation for cavorting with African-Americans in a house of prostitution that encouraged the Guardians to treat her case unfairly. Mary had established a sexual relationship with the almshouse senior apothecary when she was admitted for medical treatment in the summer of 1789. When she became pregnant and swore the child to him, a Dr. Hutchinson gave his bond on behalf of the "young Gentleman." But, when Mary sought aid late in her pregnancy, she was admitted to the almshouse as

34. DOD, Sylvia Clow, Jan. 15, Mar. 22, 1790. This figure of 7 percent for the African-American population of Philadelphia is a midpoint population figure for the decade of the 1790s. In 1790 the African-American population in Philadelphia of 2,078 was within an overall population of 42,520, or 4.9 percent; and in 1800 the African-American population had grown to 9.5 percent, or 6,436 within a population of 67,811. For African-American population figures, see Nash, *Forging Freedom*, table 4, 137; for city of Philadelphia, see Smith, *The "Lower Sort,"* app. B, table B.1, 206.

35. DOD, Jan. 1, May 31, 1793; GPM, Mar. 14, 1793. Jonathan Trusty had posted bond with the Guardians for the support of his son two months before his mother left him at the almshouse.

TABLE 15. *Race and Bastardy Support, 1790s*

Couple	Disposition of Bastardy Cases	
	Almshouse	Out-relief Mandatory Paternal Support
White	31%	69%
Black	60	40
Cross-racial	50	50
(White mother/black father)	(80)	(20)
(Black mother/white father)	(29)	(71)

Note: Individuals identified as mulatto were included in the category "Black."

Source: See Appendix, esp. "Bastardy Totals" and Table A.2.

"a pregnant pauper." Her admission entry explained that she was a woman "of very bad Character having lived among some very ordinary free Blacks at such places of ill fame as made her so *reputed.*" The clerk went on to note that no mention was made of the bond, or that she should have been "a pay Patient," on her order of admission. Mary's reputation as a woman of bad fame who mixed freely with the free blacks in lowlife haunts led the Guardians and almshouse administrators, in this instance, to cover for one of their own and treat her as a pauper.[36]

Cases of bastardy involving white women and black men were also more tightly monitored by the courts. In each of the bonded cases involving black men and white women, the women swore the case in open court, and the cases all appeared in court proceedings. It is unclear whether it was the Guardians that required these women to appear in court rather than make the typical oath before an alderman or justice of the peace, or whether the women themselves thought they could claim some benefit by this open declaration that activated the law against their former partner.[37]

When cross-racial couples were black women and white men, the system of mandatory paternal child support worked surprisingly well in the cases that came before the Guardians. When black women came forward and swore

36. DOD, Feb. 3, 13, 1790.

37. PFT: Mar. 21, 1792, John Douglas and Catharine Able; Aug. 23, 1797, Luft "a negro" and Ruth Bron; Jan. 19, 1798, George Fisher and Elizabeth Brown; Mar. 5, 1798, and MCD, Apr. 1, 1798, Adam James and Sarah Williams.

their child to white men, those men posted bond and provided child support. In only 29 percent of these cross-racial bastardy cases were women left with no choice but the almshouse. In each of these almshouse cases, the reputed white father was away at sea and therefore could not post bond or provide support. Captain Archibald Galt, for example, was off on the aptly named sloop *Willing Lass* when Ann Williams was brought to childbed. Ann had been dismissed from her place of service with Governor Thomas Mifflin when she was six months pregnant and had spent the last three months of her pregnancy in the almshouse. Captain Galt could expect to repay the city for her lodging and medical care when his ship next docked in Philadelphia.[38]

The experiences of Sarah Dempsey, however, exemplified the ways in which African-American women were especially vulnerable to abuses of power by white men. In March 1803 she gave birth to a child fathered by a respectable white Philadelphian. Eschewing the normal system of child support, the father made private arrangements through his friend John Douglass, Esq., city magistrate, to "pay her from time to time for its support, should she not expose him as [the father]." The father kept his agreement and provided support; then, when the child was three months old, he attempted to steal the child from its mother:

> He had paid her, until one day she applying for her stipend when he refusing, attempted to secure the child. But she escaped and sheltered in her friends house.

Next the father went to his friend Magistrate Douglass and procured a warrant for Sarah's arrest. The constable seized Sarah from her friend's house, took the child from her, and committed Sarah to prison. Not only did this man succeed in keeping his behavior as the father of a "mulatto" child out of the public record; he also successfully marshaled the powers of the state to take the child from its mother. But Sarah was not without her own resources. With the aid of the Pennsylvania Abolition Society she appealed to Chief Justice Edward Shippen, who released her from prison, called the father and the magistrate into court, and reprimanded them for their conduct. Sarah's child was returned to her, and the father was required to provide for its support. Had Sarah been white, one can imagine that she would not have been vulnerable to such bold actions by the father and these abuses of the law.[39]

Clearly, women low in the social hierarchy were more vulnerable to coer-

38. DOD, Feb. 3, Apr. 24, May 20, 26, 1796.
39. Pennsylvania Abolition Society, Acting Committee Minutes, June 3, 1803, HSP.

cion and male sexual exploitation. But, given the levels of privilege generally accorded elites in the late eighteenth century, the system of adjudicating bastardy through the Guardians of the Poor was remarkably egalitarian. African-American women successfully secured mandatory child support for their children fathered by white Philadelphians, as did women of the lower classes whose sexual partners were well-to-do merchants. Even Sarah Dempsey, who never entered the official system of bastardy adjudication, ultimately succeeded in securing support for her child.[40]

Some women saw this system as a form of protection and had it in mind when they decided to engage in nonmarital sexual affairs. Recording his casual sexual encounter with an African-American woman in a Philadelphia inn, our anonymous diarist recalled that, following the sexual act, the woman turned to him and asked where she could locate him should she prove with child:

> She caused me much fright on asking me where I dwelleth and that in case increase from contact she would make known to me the fact—I said I lived in the Carolinas—and fled.

Not only did this woman know that he could be held responsible for a child so conceived, but this knowledge seems to have informed her decision to have sex with him.[41]

Evaluating the relationships that produced illegitimate children is difficult. We may never know how many were relationships women welcomed or sought out and how many were the result of coercion. In late-eighteenth-century Philadelphia most women could at any time become the object of sexual pursuit, not only servants and slaves but also women not protected within families by husbands or fathers. They lived in a society where the concept of women's consent as necessary in sexual relations was not well established. Under these circumstances women did not necessarily rebuff sexual advances, but rather sought to make the best of such situations. What is

40. During the 1790s there were fifteen cases of African-American or "mulatto" women's securing child support from white men recorded by the Guardians of the Poor. See, for example, the case of Elizabeth Long and the white merchant, William Cochran, GPM, March 1790. There were also six women admitted to the almshouse expecting babies fathered by white men who were currently at sea and thus could not post bond or provide support at that time.

41. [James Wilson?], Account Book and Diary. See also case of Mary Carn in *Commonwealth vs. John Bissell*, Court of Oyer and Terminer for the County of Philadelphia County, file papers, n.d., HSP.

striking in the 1790s is how many women appear to have chosen to establish sexual lives for themselves independent of marriage.[42]

This initiative is seen most clearly in the women who committed adultery. Their sexual histories suggest that some women of the early national period did exercise heightened sexual autonomy. In three-quarters of the adultery cases, the women had not only been unfaithful but had also deserted their husbands to establish new intimate lives for themselves (see Table 16).[43] Like the Philadelphia women practicing self-divorce in the 1770s and 1780s, these women laid claim to their right to personal happiness and sexual fulfillment by leaving their marriages to establish relationships with new men. This pattern contrasts sharply with New England patterns of female adultery before the nineteenth century, when marital desertion was predominantly a male behavior: it was not only men who abandoned their partners in Revolutionary and early national Philadelphia. Sometimes women left their marriages for love, as Justina Ristiur did, and settled into new, long-term relationships. In other instances, however, they left marriages to establish varied sexual lives for themselves with multiple partners.[44]

42. This attitude toward consent can be seen in the near absence of rape charges in late-eighteenth-century Philadelphia (1790s: twelve cases charged as attempted rape or rape) despite evidence of numerous instances of force used in sexual relations. See, for example, PDP: *Mary Oldmixon vs. John Oldmixon,* filed October 1807, events 1799; *Eleanor Pettit vs. Samuel Pettit,* filed 1797, events 1791.

43. This analysis of adultery used the divorce records (PDP). The petitions for divorce give the details of the adultery necessary to make a distinction between simple adultery and adultery combined with desertion.

Pennsylvania law did not require infidelity to grant a divorce. After 1785 just cause for divorce included simple separation for four years. Because many of the divorce cases that charged adultery also qualified for a divorce under this provision, the evidence of adultery can probably be granted a greater degree of truthfulness than in states where adultery was a requirement for divorce.

44. Nancy F. Cott, for instance, found that female adultery coupled with desertion occurred in only 31 percent of Massachusetts divorce cases between 1692 and 1786 in which the cause of action was adultery. (For these years 101 husbands filed for divorce; the cause of action was adultery in 85 cases, and in 26 cases the wife had committed adultery and deserted her husband.) Cornelia Hughes Dayton's study showed a similar situation in Connecticut. In New Haven, 1711–1789, in only three cases of female adultery had the wife deserted her husband, or 20 percent of the female adultery cases. See Cott, "Divorce and the Changing Status of Women in Eighteenth-Century Massachusetts,"

TABLE 16. *Cause of Action in Divorce Petitions, 1785–1814*

Cause	Husband's Petition (Wife's Fault)		Wife's Petition (Husband's Fault)	
	No.	%	No.	%
Adultery	62	87	68	42
(With desertion)	(37)	(74)	(42)	(62)
(Without desertion)	(13)	(26)	(26)	(38)
Bigamy	2	3	4	2
Desertion	6	8.5	52	32
Cruel treatment	1	1.5	37	23
Impotence	0		1	1
Total	71	100	162	100

Note: A total of 62 husbands filed for divorce listing their wife's adultery as the cause of action. Information whether the adultery also involved desertion was unavailable in 12 cases.

Source: PDP.

Some women who engaged in extramarital affairs did not leave their marriage. These women too exhibited heightened female sexual autonomy, as exemplified by the life of Marianne Montgomery, the wife of a Philadelphia gentleman. Her black indentured servant described her as a woman with a lusty sexual appetite, who enjoyed her lover's company, laughing and talking into the night. She sought out her lovers and engaged in a public social life with her men while her husband was away. Marianne had three lovers during

WMQ, 3d Ser., XXXIII (1976), 586–614; Dayton, *Women before the Bar: Gender, Law, and Society in Connecticut, 1639–1789* (Chapel Hill, N.C., 1995), 135.

For examples of women who established postmarriage sexual lives that included multiple partners, see PDP: *Robert Irwin vs. Catharine Irwin*, filed April 1795; *Reuben Bennett vs. Charlotte Bennett*, filed September 1796; *Thomas Newberry vs. Ann Newberry*, filed June 14, 1800; *John Lovinger vs. Lousia Lovinger*, filed 1800; *Valintine Clemens vs. Catharine Clemens*, filed April 1791; *William Keith vs. Ann Keith*, filed 1791; *Lewis Williams vs. Susanna Williams*, filed September 1789. Several of these women reputedly took up prostitution or moved into houses of ill fame after they left their husbands.

the year chronicled for the court by her servant, Bety Simpson. Bety testified that she listened at the chamber door where Marianne and Peter Baudry spent the night. She heard them "have connection together as man and wife several times, and the bed crack, and they did not seem to sleep at all, but laughed and talked a great deal together." This is a portrait of carefree, indulgent lovers, reveling in each other's company. When Bety and the chambermaid listened in on another occasion "and heard their actions quite plain," they "made a considerable noise," expecting Marianne "to rise and see what it was, as she was accustomed to do when there was any noise, but she took no notice of it." On another occasion Bety witnessed the lovers' sexual relations through a window glass in a door to a downstairs chamber.[45]

These events and Marianne's affair with a second man occurred in her country home outside Philadelphia in Wilmington. But her extramarital relations were not confined to her country residence. When she returned to the couple's Philadelphia home in the fall and winter of 1800, she established another relationship, which she pursued whenever her husband was away on business. In this Philadelphia setting we see Marianne's boldest and most public acts. Every evening while her husband was in Washington, D.C., she entertained a Frenchman named DuRenay. Bety was told to turn away any callers who visited while she and DuRenay were locked away in the parlor. DuRenay came almost every evening, but, when he did not, Marianne "would go for him herself or send a boy for him."[46]

Marianne's meetings with her Frenchman were not confined to her home. Both her manservant, Joseph Spraggs, and her coachman, John Gallagher, testified to their public excursions. Spraggs, age sixteen, testified that the couple often "rode out at night" in the Montgomery carriage. Spraggs rode at the rear and suspected that they used the carriage itself for their sexual encounters, as they "let down the glass and put up the blinds." John Gallagher, the coachman, testified that the couple went very often "together to plays and

45. PDP: *Robert Montgomery vs. Marianne Montgomery*, filed Nov. 5, 1801, events 1800–1801; deposition of Bety Simpson, Jan. 9, 1802. Lawrence Stone found this same female sexual assertiveness in his study of early modern divorce in Britain, in *Broken Lives: Separation and Divorce in England, 1660–1857* (Oxford, 1993). See his case studies of late-eighteenth-century divorces, especially those of Mrs. Beaufort, Mrs. Middleton, and Mrs. Loveden, 117–138, 162–247, 248–269.

46. PDP: *Robert Montgomery vs. Marianne Montgomery*, filed Nov. 5, 1801, events 1800–1801; deposition of Bety Simpson, Jan. 9, 1802.

balls in the carriage" and that "Mrs. Montgomery several times called for the said DuRenay in the carriage to go to Parties."[47]

One might suspect that Marianne Montgomery's intimate life was exceptional, were it not replicated by numerous other Philadelphia women. What makes her case unique is the detail of the descriptions that displayed the positive sexual experiences she created outside her marriage. Among the divorce petitions there was a clear pattern of other women's taking action to find sexually fulfilling relationships. Mary Ann Honnorty, whose class we do not know, established a continuing affair in 1795 with a Mr. Gautier, who shared a rented room with Nicholas Collin. Collin testified that Mary Ann was embarrassed when he first found her there with Gautier but "afterwards witnessed his entrance with great unconcern." Collin stated that he had found Mary Ann with his roommate forty times in the winter of 1795 and that Gautier and Collin "begged her to stay at home and not come so often to their chamber." Mary Ann, however, enjoyed her frequent visits and would not stay away; she "refused his admonitions and continued her visits as frequently as usual." Mary Maffet, the wife of a Philadelphia mariner, also established an intimate life for herself, which provided her regular sexual satisfaction. Over the two years preceding her divorce she engaged in adulterous relationships with four men during her husband's frequent absences. In 1803, she finally left her marriage to marry her fourth lover, William Humphreys.[48]

Another woman of strong forward sexual character was Margaret Naylor. Evidence in her divorce from her second husband, Samuel Naylor, established that she had engaged in sexual familiarities with other men during both of her marriages. Samuel Baldwin, a mariner who had apprenticed with her first husband and stayed on as a boarder after Samuel's death, witnessed Margaret's sexual indiscretions with Captain Logan when her husband was at sea. Later, during her widowhood and perhaps into her second marriage, Baldwin himself became her lover. According to him, Margaret initiated the relationship. He swore

> that he was setting with the Respondent, in the back room of her house, in the winter of 1803; While they were in conversation together, the Respondent came up to this Deponent and threw her arms around his neck and

47. Ibid.; depositions of Joseph Spraggs and John Gallagher, Jan. 9, 1802.

48. PDP: *John Honnorty vs. Mary Ann Honnorty*, filed December 1795, events 1795; deposition of Nicholas Collins, March 1796; *David Maffet vs. Mary Gisbertha Maffet*, filed 1804, events 1802–1803.

offered her person to his embraces. As the family were then moving into another house, a bed lay accidentally in the room to which they retired, where this Deponent had a criminal intercourse with the Respondent.

Margaret and Baldwin continued their affair for some time:

This intercourse after that was kept up between them, and he had very often connection with her, sometimes in her own chamber, and on other occasions in any private place to which they could retire unobserved.

Samuel Baldwin might have downplayed his own culpability in his description of the beginnings of their affair. But it is not hard to imagine the widow Margaret taking the initiative to bring young Baldwin the apprentice, no older than nineteen at the time, to her bed.[49]

Women of the lower classes also exercised increased sexual autonomy after the Revolution. Mary Carn, who gave birth to an illegitimate child in the 1790s, had sexual relations with two men during the spring when her child was conceived. Her interest in sexual relations with these men appears to have been both romantic and financial: with Harmon, the first lover, she felt a romantic attachment; Bissell, the second man she "brought to her bed," offered her a new suit of clothes to encourage her affection. While her motivation for engaging in nonmarital sexual activity was not purely romantic, there is no doubt that Mary Carn made these choices herself.[50]

The women whose sexual choices were recorded in the criminal records also insisted on directing their intimate lives, even when it led them to go

49. PDP: *Samuel Naylor vs. Margaret Naylor,* filed Mar. 14, 1807, events 1803 (probably 1800–1803); deposition of Samuel Baldwin, Mar. 14, 1807. It is unclear from the testimony whether Margaret was married to Samuel Naylor at the time she and Samuel Baldwin were involved. That he described their involvement as "criminal intercourse" suggests that she was indeed married then.

For other examples of cases that demonstrate female sexual assertiveness, see PDP: *Lewis Albertus vs. Ann Albertus,* filed 1794; *Alexander Cochran vs. Phoebe Cochran,* filed December 1796; *James Enefer [Eneser?] vs. Mary Enefer,* filed September 1802; *William May vs. Sarah May,* filed 1802.

50. The details of this case are in the lawyer's papers for the cases of the *Commonwealth vs. John Bissell,* Court of Oyer and Terminer, file papers (n.d., filed in the box for the 1790s at HSP). Bissell fought the state's claim that he was the father, claiming Harmon was the child's father. The record does not reveal how long Carn and Harmon were involved. We know only that she slept with him for a week, three or four weeks before she took up with Bissell. Nor do we know how long the relationship with Bissell lasted.

against social conventions. Women arrested for cohabiting with men not their husbands had left their marriages to establish new, more satisfactory relationships, just as the women whose husbands sought divorce and the wives who "eloped" had. Ann Murry, for example, who had left her husband to live with her lover, John Hamil, resisted both her husband's entreaties and the coercion of the legal system to change her behavior. "Cohabiting" with John Hamil when she was arrested in 1796, she was "with child" and refused to say who the father was. What's more, she and Hamil had also threatened to injure her husband. The behavior of the women, like Ann Murry, arrested for illegal cohabitation, demonstrates that the women in the divorce records and elopement ads were not alone in attempting to direct their intimate lives.[51]

One final factor must be considered when evaluating women's extramarital sexual boldness: the power relations within late-eighteenth-century marriage that these women faced as they carved out expressive sexual choices. No discussion of the gender dynamics of extramarital sexual relations would be complete without acknowledging the role domestic violence played in marriage. During the 1790s the most common cause of arrest in Philadelphia was domestic violence. In the huge majority of these cases the wife, a neighbor, or a relative swore out an oath stating the charges. The husband was then taken up by the constable and held until he posted bond for his future good behavior. Only when a husband repeatedly violated the law were more severe steps taken.[52]

As they had in the colonial era, communities worked through formal systems such as "swearing the peace" and informal channels of gossip and reputation to establish the limits of acceptable and unacceptable patriarchal force. But husbands of the early Republic still wielded the discretionary power to discipline their wives. The divorce papers give us blow-by-blow accounts of domestic violence in this era. Here we see community intervention to stop extreme abuse, but what is perhaps more striking is the extent to which neighbors and friends tolerated the physical abuse of women by their hus-

51. PFT, Mar. 2, 1796, Ann Murry. See also PFT: Dec. 5, 1796, Pompey Carpenter and Eleanor Turner charged; June 17, 1799, John Bush and Catharine Smith charged; July 31, 1797, Ely Holcom charged with cohabiting with Mary Walker, "her being with child"; June 19, 1793, Sarah Smith charged with "being in Bed with a Man not her Husband at the House of John Yorke and being with Child refuses to Indemnify the City."

52. More Philadelphians were arrested for committing domestic violence than for any other criminal offense during the 1790s. PFT, 1790–1799.

bands.[53] Usually only when witnesses feared that a wife was in grave danger did they intervene. Yet witnesses were quite able to detail the patterns of abuse that led up to the specific crisis for the court. Neighbors commented that they had often heard the couple quarrel and fight but that, on a particular occasion, the beatings reached an intolerable level and they intervened. Usually only when a wife's behavior could be presented as exemplary would the larger society reprimand a husband. Women's assertions of their right to individual happiness and sexual choice appear all the more forceful when seen in this context. By taking steps to find personal happiness and establishing sexual alternatives for themselves, these women rejected the legitimacy of control by their husbands implicit in marriage.[54]

Clearly, some women of the new Republic asserted greater sexual autonomy. We see them boldly seeking and attaining sexual pleasure, asserting a right to make their own sexual choices. Some women said as much. In 1797, when her friend and neighbor caught Louisa Lovinger in adultery and asked whether she was not ashamed of what she was doing, Louisa responded "that she [was] not, that her husband was away the whole week at the store and she had not good of him, and that she will not stay with him much longer." Lovinger considered her husband an unsatisfactory lover and planned to leave him. She had found a young man to meet her needs and believed that, under the circumstances, she had a perfect right to consort with him. The reason for Catharine Vallon's adultery was also her quest for personal happiness. In the weeks before she ran off with her lover to New York, she was overheard telling her paramour "that she loved him and that Mr. Vallon was an old Frenchman."[55]

Eliza McDougall made a similar choice. When her husband returned from sea and found her pregnant by her lover, he claimed he would forgive her and

53. See, for example of abuse cases, PDP: *Rosanna McKaraker vs. Daniel McKaraker,* filed Feb. 29, 1792; *Mary Scott vs. Edward Scott,* filed 1795; *Mary Lake vs. William Lake,* filed Dec. 31, 1799; *Margaret McFarland vs. Kennedy McFarland,* filed Feb. 11, 1799. It must be noted that these were the same neighbors who routinely policed one another's disruptive and disorderly behavior. PFT.

54. Here I refer to the overall society. The divorce records also reveal women's working together to create strategies for surviving domestic violence, including outright resistance to husbands' authority. These were acts of resistance by those victimized by this system and did not reflect the overall society's views or treatment of domestic violence. See for example, PDP: *Hannah Harvey vs. Alexander Harvey,* filed March 1799; *Sarah Lloyd vs. Benjamin Lloyd,* filed 1802, events 1801.

55. PDP: *John Lovinger vs. Louisa Lovinger,* filed 1800, events 1797–1800; *Lewis C. Vallon vs. Catharine Vallon,* filed Sept. 1, 1805, events 1804–1805.

take her back. Eliza was not interested. Their conversation was overheard by Thomas Jameson, who recalled that Mr. McDougall said, "Betty I will forgive you all that has happened if you will tell me who was the father of the child." She replied, "It was a better fellow than you." Eliza preferred her new lover to her old husband.[56]

When Eleanor Lightwood left her husband Jacob in 1787, she confided to a friend that "she did not like her husband," "that she saw a number of faces that she liked abundances better," that her husband "was a little ugly fellow, and that she would not end her days with him." Eleanor kept her word. She left Jacob in the country, came to the city, and established a rich sexual life. Supporting herself as a child nurse for the family of John Fulmer, Eleanor lived in the Northern Liberties for the next thirteen years, where she bore an illegitimate child with fellow servant Simon Hetcher and earned a reputation for herself as a woman who "would go after men."[57]

Not all of these women were as cavalier. Julie Guermeteau appeared anguished when she confided to her friend and family doctor

> that she did not love [her husband] and had married him by force; that the child she had had three and a half years before was not her husband's but was her lover's, Barralino's; that she was then pregnant again, and that child also was Barralino's; and she could not consent to live with one man and have children by another.

She too ultimately rejected her loveless, forced marriage and went to live with the father of her children.[58]

There was another group of women who exercised sexual independence within post-Revolutionary Philadelphia—those who engaged in sex commerce. In many ways, their economic and sexual independence was the most obvious

56. Scots Presbyterian Church, Minutes of Session, Dec. 22, 1788, PHS.

57. Eleanor's insistence on her right to make her own sexual choices persisted throughout this period. After the birth of her child, when her employer dismissed her lover, Simon Hetcher, Eleanor responded by claiming that she "would have connection with" Fulmer's black hired man, "if she could not get a white man, she would have him." Fulmer then dismissed his hired man but believed that Eleanor did indeed take on both white and black lovers while she remained in his employ. In *PG*, Aug. 15, 1887, Jacob advertised Eleanor's elopement. PDP, *Jacob Lightwood vs. Eleanor Lightwood,* filed 1805, events 1787–1799; GPM, Aug. 16, 1799, bastardy case of Eleanor Lightwood and Simon Hetcher.

58. PDP, *Joseph Guermeteau vs. Julie Guermeteau,* filed September 1805.

manifestation of female autonomy. Prostitution enjoyed an enhanced position within the community because the world of nonmarital sexual behavior had expanded. Amid the permissive sexual culture of the city, the behavior of those who engaged in sex commerce was less distinct. Women who engaged in sex commerce were more public than in the late colonial era but also more integrated into the broader sexual culture. Evidence from Philadelphia suggests that, during the transition between the sexual system of the late colonial period and that of the nineteenth century, prostitution took on its most fluid and least exploitative form.

Historians have characterized the early national period as a time when prostitution did not have a significant presence in American cities. In Timothy J. Gilfoyle's study of New York City, prostitution appears to have operated on the "fringes of urban society" and had not yet entered the sexual repertoire of middle-class urban men. Before 1820 sex commerce was geographically segregated, solicitation generally occurred out of the public eye, there was little streetwalking, and clients were transients, soldiers, and visitors. Similarly, prostitution in early national Boston has been characterized as confined to bawdyhouses catering to visiting sailors and soliders.[59]

59. Timothy J. Gilfoyle, *City of Eros: New York City, Prostitution, and the Commercialization of Sex, 1790–1920* (New York, 1992), 23–26 (prostitution, 1790–1820). The limited extent of prostitution in early national New York City, as compared to Philadelphia, may be due to the city's slightly later development economically, culturally, and as an international port city. It may also be that the forms and organization of prostitution that become prevalent in New York City, documented through Gilfoyle's careful reconstruction, were different from those of the 1790s. Evidence from Philadelphia suggests that the portrait of prostitution Gilfoyle uncovers in New York City of the 1820s—as a well-organized, specialized commercial venture, run predominantly by women brothelkeepers—was a development of the 1820s. Prostitution of the 1790s has been more difficult for historians to detect precisely because it was not yet institutionalized in the same way. The marginal nature of prostitution that Gilfoyle discerns for the early national period may also be due to the incomplete surviving arrest records for the earlier period (on arrests, see 101–102).

On Boston, see Barbara Meil Hobson, *Uneasy Virtue: The Politics of Prostitution and the American Reform Tradition* (Chicago, 1987). Between the American Revolution and the early 1820s, prostitution was generally confined to bawdyhouses. It was tolerated until the early 1820s, when Boston officials began a campaign to drive prostitution underground. On the late eighteenth century, see 15; on the legal crackdown of the 1820s, see 11–27.

For a comparative perspective, see the summary of the growth of prostitution in

Philadelphia could not have been more different. Sex commerce prospered during the 1790s as part of the expansive, permissive sexual culture and was well integrated into the public and semipublic leisure world of the city. It was neither geographically segregated nor isolated from the urban centers. Bawdyhouses occupied all regions of the city (see Map 1).[60] There were bawdyhouses on the city's main streets and more modest establishments among its alleys. Sex commerce also took place in the backrooms of taverns, in the prison, and in the theater and often spilled out into the streets. Women solicited men in the streets, mixing with the legitimate evening strollers, meeting men, and then retiring to rented rooms or bawdyhouses. Sometimes they even engaged in sexual transactions in the city's alleys and abandoned lots. Much of this activity took place within the public view. Women called to men from their doorways soliciting their business, and others strolled about the street in pairs to meet men. Prostitutes were known on sight when they were seen shopping, socializing about the town, or entering the almshouse. The identities of their clients were also often common knowledge—many men were not concerned about secreting their behavior. Some demonstrated a striking disregard for being seen. One "well known gentleman," Moreau de Saint-Méry tells us, "leaves his horse tied to the post outside one of these houses, so that everyone knows when he is there and exactly how long he stays."[61]

England and Europe in the seventeenth and eighteenth century in Lawrence Stone, *The Family, Sex, and Marriage in England, 1500–1800* (New York, 1977), 615–620.

60. The sixteen locations plotted on Map 1 are of those bawdyhouses for which addresses could be ascertained and represent only a small proportion of bawdyhouse locations during the 1790s. However, even the geographic distribution of this smaller subset of bawdyhouses demonstrates that sex commerce was available throughout the city in the 1790s.

61. Kenneth Roberts and Anna M. Roberts, eds. and trans., *Moreau de St. Méry's American Journey (1793–1798)* (Garden City, N.Y., 1947), 312–313.

Locations of sex commerce: PDP: *Mary Ann Dodd vs. Robert J. Dodd*, filed December 1800, events 1799; PDP, *Sarah Gore vs. Simon Gore*, filed December 1787; Society for Alleviating the Miseries of Public Prisons, Minutes of the Acting Committee, Jan. 12, 1799, HSP; Roberts and Roberts, eds. and trans., *Moreau de St. Méry's American Journey*, 122.

Soliciting: Roberts and Roberts, eds. and trans., *Moreau de St. Méry's American Journey*, 297, 313–314; [James Wilson?], Account Book and Diary, Mar. 14, 23; PFT, 1790–1799, 1805–1815; Vagrancy Docket, 1790–1797, 1805–1814, CCAP. PDP: *Mary Burk vs. William Burk*, filed 1797, events 1797 (William Burk had sex with a "Girl of the Town" "up an alley" and at a "Burying ground in Race street" in 1797); *Robert Irwin vs. Catharine Irwin*, filed April 1795, events 1795 (Catharine had sex for cash in the lot up

Bawdyhouses were not places for secret, anonymous sex, but social places where individuals encountered friends and associates. John Moore, for example, ran into two acquaintances when he spent the night in one. Men often socialized together with the women of the house before they retired to upstairs rooms, and even then they were often still among company: illicit sex regularly took place in rooms shared by more than one couple. Even some wives were familiar with the bawdyhouses used by their husbands and sometimes retrieved them from the premises. Prostitution under these circumstances was a very social event.[62]

Griffith Jones, a Philadelphia storekeeper, recorded one of the fullest descriptions of prostitution in early national Philadelphia in his deposition documenting the adultery of William Burk. Jones was careful not to identify the women involved and to forget the exact location of the house, but his account richly describes his perceptions of the casual, playful, and social nature of sex commerce. On a summer evening in June 1797, he happened upon a group of his friends at the corner of Third and Market. Burk and several "other Gentlemen" asked Jones to join them for their evening's entertainment. When Jones inquired where they were going, Burk replied, "to a whore-House." Jones agreed to join in and "accordingly accompanied the Defendant [Burk], and the rest of the party to a House down Third street into Southwark." When they arrived, Burk "asked for the Girls." "The party was told that the Girls were gone abroad, but would return soon, if the party would stay." While several of the men waited inside, Burk and Jones walked about the neighborhood. When

----

from the Pennsylvania Hospital, at Pine and Ninth Streets); *Elizabeth Garwood vs. Joseph Garwood*, filed September 1804, events 1802–1803; *Anthony Felix Weibert vs. Alfathica Weibert*, filed September 1787, events 1784–1787.

Brothelkeepers and the women who worked in them were identified as such in the almshouse admission log and sometimes in the orders of admission written by the neighborhood Guardians. See DOD, Mar. 13, Apr. 16, Aug. 15, 1790, Jan. 10, 1791, Jan. 13, Mar. 22, 1793, Mar. 15, 1796, Mar. 8, 1798.

62. PDP: *Maria Moore vs. John Moore*, filed September 1799, events 1796–1797; *Catherine Pemble vs. David Pemble*, filed 1803, events 1798–1799; *Mary Burk vs. William Burk*, filed 1798, events 1797; *Mary Ann Dodd vs. Robert J. Dodd*, filed December 1800; *Sarah Lloyd vs. Benjamin Lloyd*, filed 1802, events 1801.

In the case of *Maria Moore vs. John Moore*, one acquaintance was a woman neighbor who was reputedly in the house in search of her husband; the other was a male acquaintance whom he shared the room with in the company of two women of the town.

they came back, the girls had returned. Jones recalled that he initially refrained from going in but that "one of them [the girls] knocked at the window, insisting that the defendant should bring this deponent in." In the parlor he saw

four girls who appeared to him to be common Prostitutes; that the defendant took the girls one after another upon his knees, kissed, and hugged with them; that they seemed to be perfectly acquainted and familiar with each other, and much love passed between them; that after a while this Deponent observed to the rest of the party, that there did not seem to be more girls than would be wanted without him, and that he would therefore go away, which he accordingly did leaving the defendant in company with the said Girls behind him.[63]

Whether we can trust Jones's account of himself as a reluctant participant is doubtful. He carefully named no other members of the group that we, or the court, could consult for corroboration. Nevertheless, the beckoning behavior of the women just returned from a walk about town and the social context of prostitution, for both the men and the women, rings true.

Sex commerce of the early national period was part of a continuum of illicit sex, and it was not always easy to distinguish which encounters crossed its fluid boundaries. Prostitution operated in many of the same social spaces as other forms of nonmarital sex, integrated into these worlds of socializing and public amusement. Women brought men to the same disorderly houses for prostitution that couples frequented for illicit sex. Taverns and "negro" houses accommodated those who sought socializing, drinking, gambling, and "lewd company." Bawdyhouses themselves were not always highly organized. Women residents would come and go as their needs required. Some rented rooms by the night or the week, and others worked as operatives in houses run by other women. As such, prostitution was mixed up with the social and sexual activities of those engaging in noncommercial sexual ventures.[64]

People of all walks of life had sexual encounters that were not markedly different from those of prostitutes and their clients. The woman who supplemented her income by periodically strolling the streets to meet a man who would pay for a sexual encounter had much in common with the woman who frequented taverns accepting food and drink from a gentleman with whom

63. PDP: *Mary Burk vs. William Burk*, filed 1798, events 1797; deposition of Griffith Jones, city of Philadelphia, storekeeper (date illegible).

64. Men alone and in couples with women also operated bawdyhouses in Philadelphia. PFT, 1790–1799, 1805–1814.

S. TWELFTH STREET
S. ELEVENTH STREET
S. TENTH STREET
S. NINTH STREET
S. EIGHTH STREET
S. SEVENTH STREET
S. SIXTH STREET
S. FIFTH STREET
S. FOURTH STREET
S. THIRD STREET
S. SECOND STREET
S. FRONT STREET
S. WATER ST.

SOUTH OR CEDAR STREET
PINE STREET
SPRUCE STREET
WALNUT STREET
UNION STREET
LAUREL STREET

FEDERAL STREET
PINE STREET
CARPENTER STREET
CHRISTIAN STREET
QUEEN STREET
CATHERINE STREET
GERMAN STREET
PLUMB STREET
SHIPPEN STREET
SWANSON STREET

DELAWARE

MAP I. *Philadelphia Bawdyhouses, 1790–1799. By Claudia Lyons*

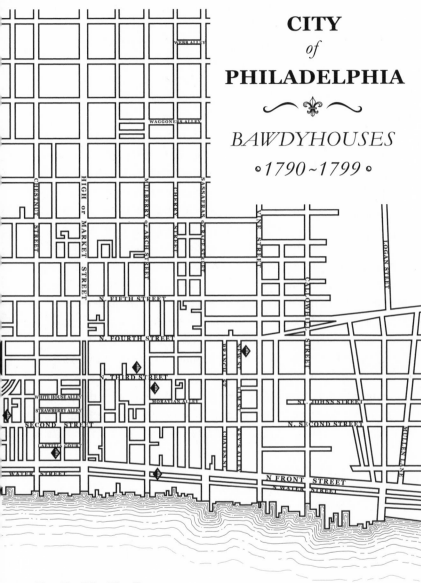

CITY

of

PHILADELPHIA

~❦~

BAWDYHOUSES

∘*1790~1799*∘

RIVER

A Scale of 2000 Feet

100   500   1000   1500   2000

she later had sexual relations. Gifts of goods, food, or drink were part of the sexual exchange in many relationships. Prostitutes who worked the theater expected the gentlemen in the boxes to treat them to the wines and liquors served during the performances. This custom was not that different from the gift giving that accompanied adulterous liaisons, where lovers presented gifts and sometimes cash to their partners. Like the women of the town, women who engaged in adultery were treated to gifts by their lovers.[65]

Prostitution of the 1790s was neither fully commercialized nor fully professionalized; many women moved in and out of it. Some engaged in prostitution as a casual supplement to their meager wages from other labor, others participated for longer periods without permanently foreclosing their opportunities to reenter more polite society, and still others made a career of it.

Prostitution in this environment, often controlled by the women themselves, could support women who sought independence and nonmarital lives. One reason prostitution could serve as an avenue for independent womanhood, during the early new nation, was that it was not completely incompatible with marriage. Some women who had been prostitutes married quite reputably. In 1806 Lucy Ridgeway, for example, married a respectable religious man after living the life of a woman of ill fame. Three years later the marriage of William Penn, great-grandson of the colony's founder, to "a common Prostitute of this city" caused a bit of a sensation. But it did not keep the couple from living among the community of their peers in Philadelphia for the next three years. The belief that former prostitutes could have reputable futures was shared by the sexual avant-garde and social reformers alike.[66]

65. Roberts and Roberts, eds. and trans., *Moreau de St. Méry's American Journey*, 122 (on prostitutes in the theater). On giving gifts in adultery, see PDP, *John Mullowny vs. Catharine Mullowny*, filed November 1793; Alexander Hamilton, *Observations on Certain Documents Contained in No. V and VI of "The History of the United States for the Year 1796," in Which the Charge of Speculation against Alexander Hamilton, Late Secretary of the Treasury, Is Fully Refuted* (Philadelphia: Bioren, 1797). Hamilton admitted giving such gifts to his mistress.

66. Lucy Ridgeway was one of the first women whose readmission into polite society was supported by the Magdalen Society (MSM, May 29, 1806). The careers of these women will be examined in Chapter 7.

On Penn: George W. Corner, ed., *The Autobiography of Benjamin Rush: His "Travels through Life," Together with His Commonplace Book for 1789–1813* (Princeton, N.J., 1948), 285. Penn was thirty-three years old and was described by Rush as "an accomplished Scholar, but wanted understanding upon all the affairs of life." The couple married the day after Penn's father sailed for England, suggesting that the couple understood but

For many of the women involved in prostitution, sex commerce was both an economic venture and a sexual lifestyle. They were part of the subculture that embraced sexual independence for women. Mary Bangs, whom we last saw living in "open adultery" with Richard Duffield, turned periodically to prostitution. She confided to a friend that "she was obliged to see a gentleman, and have intercourse with him, in order to get money to support herself and the said Duffield." Mary's choice to leave her husband to live with Duffield required expanding her sexual life to include commercial transactions. She appears to have engaged in prostitution with Duffield's blessing, and perhaps at his urging.[67]

Other women engaged in sex commerce over the objections of their husbands. Catharine Clemens slipped into prostitution by taking in lodgers to her home in Black Horse Alley. While her husband worked as a cordwainer away from home, Catharine held dances that reputedly devolved into illicit scenes of debauchery with the lodgers. When Valintine Clemens confronted her with the unacceptability of her behavior and threatened to evict the lodgers, Catharine responded "that if he turned the lodgers out of the house, she would go into [J.?] town, and become a common Whore." This drove her husband out of

_____

disregarded the scandal their marriage would raise. James Abercrombie, *Documents relative to the Celebration of a Late Marriage* (Philadelphia, 1809). The Magdalen Society of Philadelphia was founded in 1800 upon the premise that fallen women could be reformed and reenter polite society. The experiences of those women who used the society in its early years bore this out. MSM, 1800–1814.

67. PDP, *Elijah Bangs vs. Mary Bangs*, filed December 1807, events 1805–1807. For an exploration of the complicated position these women inhabited in the 1830s, see Patricia Cline Cohen, *The Murder of Helen Jewett: The Life and Death of a Prostitute in Nineteenth-Century New York* (New York, 1998).

It is unclear how often husbands encouraged their wives' prostitution. Some cases, however, suggest that the financial rewards of commercial sex were attractive to husbands as well as to their wives. Some couples ran brothels, but again it is unclear whether the women only helped run these establishments or were engaged in prostitution themselves. The language of the divorce law of 1785 suggested that society at large believed husbands sometimes prostituted their wives: it excluded sexual intercourse undertaken by a wife at the instruction of her husband as adultery. The law read: "that the said plaintiff (if the husband) allowed of the wife's prostitutions, and received hire for them, or exposed his wife to lewd company whereby she became ensnared to the crime aforesaid; it shall be a good defense and a perpetual bar against the same [a divorce on grounds of adultery]." Mitchell, Flanders, et al., comps., *Statutes at Large*, XII, 94–99, esp. 97, An Act concerning Divorces and Alimony.

the house. When Valintine finally filed for a divorce five years later, Catharine was reputedly making her living by keeping a bawdyhouse in the city.[68]

Some wives moved into houses of ill fame when they left their husbands, some of them clearly maintaining themselves there through prostitution. But other women were simply using the network of independent women who resided in the bawdyhouses of the city when they left their homes to establish new lives. Ann Keith took up prostitution while her husband, a mariner, was away at sea, when she moved in with Mrs. Curtis, who ran a brothel in Southwark. But Susanna Williams was probably only a boarder in the house of ill fame she removed to when she left her husband in 1797.[69]

Whether living in a house of ill fame to accommodate one's adultery or turning to sex commerce as a means of support, bawdyhouses provided women who left their marriages with spaces for independence. Those who turned to prostitution created an alternative to marital sexuality and a source of income greater than the usual female wages. While the consequences of long-term prostitution could be grim, during this era it could serve as a transitional vehicle for women seeking new lives and provide one strategy for establishing economic and personal independence.

What are we to make of these women who created expansive sexual lives for themselves in the new nation? Some of them set out to create fulfilling sexual lives for themselves outside marriage. They built upon the earlier traditions of self-divorce that allowed a degree of female self-determination and took advantage of the slippage in social control afforded by the social and political revolu-

68. PDP, *Valintine Clemens vs. Catharine Clemens*, filed April 1791, events 1785; deposition of George Filker, city of Philadelphia, cordwainer, sworn July 14, 1791. See also PDP, *Anthony Felix Weibert vs. Alfathica Weibert*, filed September 1787, events 1784–1787.

69. PDP: *William Keith vs. Ann Keith*, filed 1791, events 1790; *Lewis Williams vs. Susanna Williams*, filed September 1798, events 1797. For examples of other women's utilizing brothels as an alternative to their marriages, see PDP: *Robert Irwin vs. Catharine Irwin*, filed April 1795; *Catharine Britton vs. William Britton*, filed 1797, events 1795–1796; *Thomas Newberry vs. Ann Newberry*, filed June 14, 1800, events 1799. Ann Newberry visited disorderly houses to engage in prostitution while living with her husband, and then left him and moved into a house of prostitution. Evidence of wives' living in bawdyhouses was also recorded in the court dockets and almshouse admissions records. See, for example, PFT, Oct. 24, 1806, case of Hester French; PFT, Apr. 17, 1805, case of Mary Reylee; DOD, Dec. 28, 1811, Sarah Thompson; DOD, May 26, 1812, Lydia Ross.

tions of the late eighteenth century to assert their own version of freedom and liberty. The intentions of others are less clear. Nevertheless, they too participated in the expansive sexual culture of the city, and their behavior in and of itself was a marked departure from the past.

We are left with the task of trying to imagine how these women understood their actions. In many ways their behavior was not in sharp conflict with the colonial model of the woman vulnerable to sexual temptation. Perhaps some women understood their nonmarital behavior as a logical extension of their natural sexual weakness. Given the predatory nature of male sexual pursuit in the late eighteenth century, this is certainly plausible. Other women, however, expanded the colonial model of the sexual woman to include sexual fulfillment outside marriage. They exercised greater sexual autonomy and asserted their right to seek fulfilling sexual and personal lives with the partner of their choosing. Their behavior indicates that they viewed their own sexuality as integral to their happiness and pursued their rights to claim that happiness in early national Philadelphia.

Perhaps some of them had imbibed the political critique of marriage implicit in the political philosophies of the day and put forth explicitly by Judith Sargent Murray and Mary Wollstonecraft. These ideas were circulating in Philadelphia magazines, the theater, and political commentary and through the lips of citizens in taverns and salons. Did women such as Marianne Montgomery consciously embrace the political notions they encountered in print, or were their decisions to adopt expansive sexual lives more visceral? When Marianne went to the Philadelphia theater with her lover, did she see Susanna Rowson's *Slaves of Algiers,* which critiqued women's slavelike status in marriage, or Elizabeth Inchbald's *Everyone Has His Fault,* which promoted companionate marriage?[70] Was her choice to take on a series of lovers guided by a political critique of her own, or was she simply seeking personal pleasure in a world that made such pursuit possible? Were women like Justina Ristiur and Lousia Lovinger inspired by the stories of the women in the French Revolution they heard in the city's streets? If French women could take to the streets and become *citoyennes* and their fellow Philadelphians could address one another as "citizen" and "citizeness," displaying enthusiasm for a revolutionary reordering of their world, could they stage their own rebellions, choosing love or equality as the basis of their intimate unions rather than marriage? Perhaps when Julie

70. For the gender politics of these plays and their reception in Philadelphia, see Branson, *These Fiery Frenchified Dames,* 110–123. Susanna Rowson's *Slaves of Algiers* was performed at least once each season in Philadelphia in the 1790s (181 n. 38).

Guermeteau finally put an end to her clandestine double life by divorcing her husband to be with the father of her children, the whisperings of Mary Wollstonecraft's indictment of marriage and pleas for free love tickled her ear.

In post-Revolutionary Philadelphia some women, from all classes, exercised new levels of sexual independence, acting to achieve self-fulfillment and undermining patriarchal authority. The intimate details of their lives suggest that more gender trouble was brewing in Revolutionary America than we have previously acknowledged. When women adopted forms of sexual behavior independent of marriage, they undermined the tidy binary gender association of women as dependent and men as independent, thus denaturalizing women's perceived inherent dependence and their exclusion from the polity. If, as scholars of eighteenth-century England and feminist theorists have posited, gender is performative, then the performance of these women destablized the gender system in early national Philadelphia. Their behavior, in the streets, in the places of leisured entertainment, and in their private relations, denaturalized and assaulted the legitimacy of women's subordination to men in marriage and the basis of their exclusion from full participation in the Republic.

Gender is performative

Reformulating Sexuality to Secure the Republic

The behavior of the most sexually assertive women in late-eighteenth-century Philadelphia was consistent with the radical philosophies of the 1790s. For some Philadelphians, especially those who most vociferously objected to female independence, the expansive sexual lives those women exhibited were a disturbing development, signifying women's rebellion against their subordination to men in marriage and threatening to disrupt the social organization of America. Sexual freedom also symbolized women's claims to individual independence and their assertions of Lockean rights of self-determination at precisely the moment when political conservatives declared that the republican experiment was out of control. The political, intellectual, and sexual actions of Philadelphia's women in the early Republic demonstrated the slippery ground gender distinctions occupied and the need to anchor women's subordination to a more secure foundation.[71]

71. This sexual behavior was an expression of individual action consistent with Lockean rights. As Rosemarie Zagarri demonstrates, it was this Lockean definition of rights as liberties that the political parties of Philadelphia resisted applying to women. In 1790s Philadelphia, the Democratic-Republicans promoted the idea of citizens' rights as liberties in an attempt to draw a broad constituency of workingmen to their party. They

The reconceptualization of female sexuality provided one promising avenue for bolstering the gender hierarchy. During the early national period the core attributes of female sexuality promoted in the public sphere underwent a remarkable redefinition. Whereas women in the colonial period had been understood as more vulnerable to sexual temptation than men, after the Revolution a new understanding of female sexuality emerged in popular print in which women had metamorphosed into the lesser sexual beings. During the last decades of the eighteenth century both constructions of female sexuality competed for cultural supremacy. But by the opening of the nineteenth century the new, sexually inert woman had been embraced by the middle class as both the inherent female nature and a symbol of the distinct and superior status of those who embodied it.[72]

For many of the most vocal architects of the new nation, such as Benjamin Rush and Thomas Jefferson, active female sexuality expressed outside marriage threatened the Republic. Late colonial notions of woman as more vulnerable to sexual temptation and the pre-Revolutionary tendency to depict her as the sexual temptress marked her as an especially dangerous member of the Republic. Moreover, as the target of men's lustful ways, women's sexual demeanor could have enormous consequences for the morality of the citizenry. Winthrop Jordan's summation of Jefferson's view of female sexuality represented the larger community of elite men: "If unrestrained sex seemed a dangerous trap to Jefferson, he was deeply certain which sex had set it." For these men, containing female sexuality would be a key to establishing a moral community and a virtuous citizenry.[73]

The advocates of female chastity drew on models within Enlightenment philosophy to demonstrate the importance of the moral and specifically sexual

---

also tended to provide far fewer opportunities for female participation in the public political culture of their party. The Federalists, by contrast, embraced the notion of rights as duties, an idea consistent with female participation in party politics. It was the Federalists, working within the rubric of Scottish Enlightenment ideas of rights as duties, that allowed women greater participation in the public political culture of the city. Zagarri, "The Rights of Man and Woman," *WMQ*, 3d Ser., LV (1998), 203–230.

72. Nancy F. Cott, "Passionlessness: An Interpretation of Victorian Sexual Ideology, 1790–1850," *Signs*, IV (1978–1979), 219–236; Thomas Laqueur, "Orgasm, Generation, and the Politics of Reproductive Biology," *Representations*, no. 14 (Spring 1986), 1–41.

73. Winthrop D. Jordan, *White over Black: American Attitudes toward the Negro, 1550–1812* (Chapel Hill, N.C., 1968), 463.

character of a republican nation. The Scottish Enlightenment four-stage theory of history specifically addressed the character that male-female relationships should take in a republic, explaining the evolution of sexual relations in human society from uncivilized (their term) hunting and gathering through pastoral, agricultural, and finally mercantile societies. In this system, human sexuality had begun with open sexual relations between men and women motivated by "animal love" (according to Lord Kames). When society reached its most advanced stage, "women [would be] valued for their accomplishments rather than viewed as mere sex objects." In this evolved society sexual attraction between men and women would be diminished, and men would choose partners for their charm, conversation, and accomplishments. Early national periodicals were peppered with stories evaluating the republican qualities of past civilizations, using the condition of women and the nature of sexual relations as one standard. In these models women's positions as domestic mothers and their characters, especially their chastity, were central to republican interests. Passion and, certainly, animal sexual attraction were not the social foundations upon which the American republican experiment would be built.[74]

Female sexual restraint would also be necessary if women were to safeguard the nation's virtue. As republican wives and mothers, women were granted the custodianship of the nation's civic virtue. As participants in the political culture of the new nation, Philadelphia's women claimed the virtue necessary for political judgment. By the 1790s the changing understanding of the male republican citizen and economic individual gave women's sexual transformation added importance. As the republican citizen evolved from one acting from a disinterested concern for the common good to one motived by

74. Rosemarie Zagarri, "Morals, Manners, and the Republican Mother," *American Quarterly*, XLIV (1992), 199 (quote), and 198, quoting Henry Home, Lord Ka[me]s, *Six Sketches on the History of Man* (Philadelphia, 1776).

See, for example of past republican qualities, "Short Account of the Women of Egypt," *American Museum*, VII (1790), 56; Gilbert Stuart, "State of the Female Sex, among the Ancient Germans," *American Museum*, XI (1792), 38–40, 97–99. For an example of an American's incorporating these ideas into his own writings (a reader response), see Benjamin Rush's comments on how a republic holds women in the correct position, and his comparing that to France and Turkey: "A Thought on Monarchy and Aristocracy," in Corner, ed., *Autobiography of Rush*, 197–198.

The four-stage theory of history was put forth by the jurisprudential school of the Scottish Enlightenment. See Zagarri, "Morals, Manners, and the Republican Mother," *American Quarterly*, XLIV (1992), 192–215.

personal interest, his capability for civic virtue eroded. With the implementation of the Constitution and the rise of political parties, it became more important for woman's sexual virtue to be congruent with her personification of
republican virtue. As men engaged more openly in individual interests, the
virtue of the state became more closely associated with women's virtue secured and safeguarded in the home. The feminization of religion, as women
were increasingly associated with piety and dominated church membership
over the eighteenth century, also gave credence to women's positive moral
character.[75]

This new construction of the sexually restrained republican woman was
advanced in the public print culture of early national Philadelphia, particularly
through almanacs, newspapers, and magazines. After the Revolution Philadelphia's public print culture assumed new significance for the republican
patriot leaders, who believed that the nation's character was fashioned through
and reflected in its published discourse. The upper- and middle-class men
controlling publishing confronted the question of what was appropriate for
the republican public sphere. The arguments by men such as Benjamin Rush
to excise morally questionable, erotic, and scandalous material from the public
presses were accepted by the city's printer-publishers. Rush contended that

75. During the 1790s, women in Philadelphia established a place in the public
political culture by participation in public displays of partisan politics, engaging in the
political debates as the authors and readers of political commentary, and establishing
the political salon; see Branson, *These Fiery Frenchified Dames*. The definitive work on
republican motherhood is Linda K. Kerber, *Women of the Republic: Intellect and Ideology
in Revolutionary America* (Chapel Hill, N.C., 1980). See also Mary Beth Norton, *Liberty's
Daughters: The Revolutionary Experience of American Women, 1750–1800* (New York,
1980); Zagarri, "Morals, Manners, and the Republican Mother," *American Quarterly*,
XLIV (1992), 192–215; Jan Lewis "The Republican Wife: Virtue and Seduction in the
Early Republic," *WMQ*, 3d Ser., XLIV (1987), 689–721. On the gendering of virtue, see
Ruth H. Bloch, "The Gendered Meanings of Virtue in Revolutionary America," *Signs*,
XIII (1987–1988), 37–58. See also Gordon S. Wood on the constitutional era: *The
Creation of the American Republic, 1776–1787* (Chapel Hill, N.C., 1969), 469–562. On
womanhood and the feminization of religion, see Nancy F. Cott, *The Bonds of Womanhood: "Woman's Sphere" in New England, 1780–1835* (New Haven, Conn., 1977), 126–
146. Women, it was believed, were more susceptible to religion because of their softer,
delicate disposition and the more open nature of the female soul. On the gendering of
religion in the eighteenth century, see Susan Juster, *Disorderly Women: Sexual Politics
and Evangelicalism in Revolutionary New England* (Ithaca, N.Y., 1994); Elizabeth Reis,
Damned Women: Sinners and Witches in Puritan New England (Ithaca, N.Y., 1997).

American newspapers should shun the "anecdotes of British vices and fol-lies." "What have the citizens of the United States to do with the duels, the murders, the suicides and the thefts, the forgeries, the boxing matches, the wagers for eating, drinking and walking etc etc, of the people of Great Brit-ain?" Philadelphia papers should refrain from reprinting the sordid details of intrigue: "What have the citizens of Philadelphia to do with the criminal amours of Mr. M— of Boston?" Rush encouraged newspaper editors, "Never publish an article in your paper that you would not wish your wife or your daughter (if you have any) should read or understand." Erotica and overtly sexually active women no longer belonged in popular print material. Phila-delphia's printer-booksellers would reserve such matter for elite and middle-class men by developing a parallel but private print market.[76]

The matter deemed worthy of a mixed-gender public sphere was reshaped to exclude the most explicit sexual material and to promote a reserved female sexuality. Newspapers, almanacs, and magazines now devoted little space to the sordid details of intrigue and discouraged voyeuristic sexual adventures. These were the genres that still reached the widest reading audience and were the most likely to influence the city's lower classes. Not only could print influence the new, expanded male citizenry to temper its personal indulgence and cultivate republican virtue, but it could also instruct women about the appropriate sexual attributes of the republican woman.

The public print discourse of the late 1780s and 1790s played a central role in promoting women's proper sexuality. Women's natural sexual character, as represented in popular print, was modest, chaste, and virtuous. Female con-stancy within marriage became both the ideal for women to strive for and simultaneously described their natural condition. Under this new configura-tion of gendered sexuality, premarital chastity and marital constancy were the work of a good republican woman. But this work came almost effortlessly to women, because they were seen as naturally disposed to it. Like the earlier, mid-eighteenth-century construction, woman's sexual character was consid-ered innate. This new construction of female sexuality was evident in represen-tations of women in Philadelphia's almanacs, whose ditties by the 1790s high-lighted women's modesty and chastity and excluded her sexual desire. The bawdy or sexually venturesome women of the pre-Revolutionary almanacs had

76. Benjamin Rush to Andrew Brown, Oct. 1, 1788, "Directions for Conducting a Newspaper in Such a Manner as to Make It Innocent, Useful, and Entertaining," in L. H. Butterfield, ed., Letters of Benjamin Rush (Princeton, N.J., 1951), I, 487–488.

been dropped from the pages and replaced by modest and chaste women, who were vitally concerned with maintaining their spotless reputations.[77]

The primary reorientation in the construction of sexuality was the gendering of sexual control. Under the new version, men did not have absolute control over their own sexuality. The virile male depicted in popular print had a dual character: when men were at their best, their sexuality was virile and they controlled it, but desire could easily take control of them. The portrayals of men as losing control of their sexuality evident in popular print of the 1760s and 1770s had become accepted as reality by the 1790s. Now control had become the universal attribute of the female. Women who had embraced the new female morality had their sexuality under control, albeit through their acceptance of their inherent female nature, not through the use of reasoned self-control; and those women who were boldly sexual put their sexuality to specific uses—they purposely deployed it. Passion no longer took control of women as it did in the colonial era: it was men who were at the mercy of uncontrollable passion. Lust was such a natural and vital part of masculinity that Benjamin Rush believed it was impossible for a single man to remain chaste. He therefore prescribed marriage as the cure for men's natural tendency to lust after women. While Rush would have condemned the behavior of the anonymous sex diarist, they both shared the belief that men, by their very nature, could not deny the sexual urge. Women's lesser ardor, Rush believed, would allow them to remain chaste outside matrimony. Rush's characterization of moderate desire as women's natural state, requiring no action to control, essentialized this new female sexuality.[78]

Redefining the nature of female sexuality to highlight woman's innate reserve and downplaying her desire meant that the woman who engaged in sexual behavior outside marriage not only contravened social convention but also went against her very nature. What had been sexual excess consistent with her weak nature now became abnormal and unwomanly.

77. Compare, for example, the poems and ditties in *Father Abraham's Almanack* for 1770 and 1795, for bawdy versus chaste women (Abraham Weatherwise [pseud.], *Father Abraham's Almanack for . . . 1770* [Philadelphia: Dunlap, 1769]; *Father Abraham's Almanack for . . . 1795* [Philadelphia: Stewart and Cochran, 1794]).

78. Rush registered his astonishment at the celibacy of an acquaintance, a Mr. John Steward, who abstained from sexual relations for fourteen months (Corner, ed., *Autobiography of Rush*, 209). See his letter to his sister, Mary Stockton, where he explains marriage as the only sinless form of sexuality (ibid., 483–486). See Chapter 7, below, for Rush's medicalization of overactive sexual desire in the early nineteenth century.

According to this construction of sexuality the proper location for female sexual behavior in the early Republic was marriage, and marriage only, and popular print worked hard to redirect women's erotic interest back to it. Not only did magazines of the 1790s, the voice of the intellectual republican middle class, explicitly extol the virtues of marital bliss, but the almanacs also reworked their material to conform to this new republican marital ethic. An example of this is the rewriting of "Corydon and Phyllis," a popular broadside ballad written by John Cunningham at midcentury. This was a pastoral love poem chronicling a scene of premarital sex: a shepherd meets a woman in the woods, is instantly overcome by his love for her, makes love to her, and marries her the next day. Another version was even more explicit, and there was no reference to marriage. This version was simply a playful voyeuristic account full of sexual allusion and double entendres.[79] A third version, "Phillida's Riddle," published in Pennsylvania in 1795, was not about illicit or premarital sex, but had been reworked to depict the couple's marrying before they have sex. The tension in this version derives from the reader's knowledge of the original story. Throughout, Phillida's mother and the reader are led to believe that Phillida, like Phyllis, has been seduced by Corydon and is now pregnant.

> Transported with joy, with a heart light as air,
> Lovely Phillida tript to her cot from the fair:
> Her Mother would fain know the cause of her bliss;
> Which arose, she insisted, from Corydon's kiss.
> "From Corydon's kiss!" said the lass, with a smile;
> "He gave me much more, ere we journi'd a mile!"
>
> . . . .
>
> "Come, hussy, disclose! I'm determin'd to know,
> What the Shepherd has done, thus to tickle you so!"

79. Authorship of *Corydon and Phillis* is attributed to John Cunningham (1729–1773) in Thomas L. Philbrick, "British Authorship of Ballads in the Isaiah Thomas Collection," *Studies in Bibliography: Papers of the Bibliographical Society of the University of Virginia*, IX (1957), 255–258. I used the copy held by the American Antiquarian Society in the Isaiah Thomas Broadside Collection, printed by Nathaniel Coverly (Boston, between 1810 and 1814).

This other version is also part of the Isaiah Thomas Broadside Collection at the American Antiquarian Society. These broadsides were purchased in Boston and presented to the society in 1814, printing date assumed between 1810 and 1814, printer unknown, date originally written unknown.

"Dear Mother, 'tis only what pass'd, in your youth,
'Tween my Father and you; as I live, 'tis a truth!
So press me no farther; for Time will reveal,
What now, with such rapture, I wish to conceal."

"Yes, yes; I know well, what will happen in Time;
And I know, what misfortunes await on that crime!"
"A crime!" said the fair one. "Believe me, dear Mother,
Each virgin, around, would embrace such another.
He gave me, this morn, the delight of my life;
He gave me, himself: for he made me his wife."

Even the generational reference suggests that what was done in the past (pre-marital and nonmarital sex) was not to be done now.[80]

This promarriage message was addressed to young men as well. The bachelor life, presented variously in the 1770s as an exciting life stage for sexual adventure and a path with hazards for reckless youth, had in the 1790s become unacceptable in public print culture in the city's newspapers, magazines, and almanacs. In the "Court of Apollo," a column in the *Philadelphia Minerva* devoted to poems and sayings on matters of love, "The Bachelor" appeared in 1795. The subject was described as "the dry, dull drowsy" young man who is "stupidly free from Nature's tenderest ties." Bachelorhood led to all the evil consequences of nonmarital sexuality, but the married man, by contrast, endured no hardships:

No husband wrong'd, no virgin's honor spoil'd,
No tender parent weeps his ruin'd child.
No bad disease, nor false embrace is here,
The joys are safe, the raptures are sincere.[81]

There was no sexual middle ground between the destructive bachelor and the joyous husband. Sexuality expressed within marriage brought contentment, and outside marriage it brought only ruin.

Under this new construction of male and female sexuality the politics of sexual transgression shifted greater responsibility for sexual misconduct to women. Because women were presented as naturally better able to control

80. *The Balloon Almanac . . . for 1795* (Lancaster, Pa.: Bailey and Dickson, 1794) (quotation marks have been regularized).

81. "The Bachelor," *Philadelphia Minerva*, Nov. 28, 1795.

their sexuality, policing the limits of sexual intimacy became their responsibility. In addition, women were expected to exercise their influence over
men. At midcentury it had been men, through their use of reason, who were
the cultural targets for sexual responsibility. Now it was women.

Often this dictum went so far as to place the responsibility for men's sexual
misconduct on women. For example, in an article addressed to the "Ladies" in
the *Philadelphia Minerva,* women of polite society were chastised for socializing with men who were known to engage in the sexual intrigues of the pleasure culture.

> You ladies, who ought to be patrons of every thing that is modest, lovely, ami-
> able and virtuous, will smile with approbation on a known debauchee. . . .
> Why do you not frown upon those sordid mean wretches, who associate with
> the abandoned of your sex, and yet wish to keep a fair show in the world, and
> to insinuate themselves into your graces, when you are acquainted with their
> characters.
>
> What little encouragement do you give to virtue and chastity, when a
> libertine can with as great ease, or perhaps greater, gain your affections,
> and consequently consent to marriage, than a man whose character is
> unblemished in the world.[82]

To this male author, it was women's responsibility to transform the loose
sexual habits of the men within their community. He suggested that they
initiate a boycott against such men.

> Ladies, much depends on you, towards a reformation in the morals of our
> sex; if you were to join as a band of sisterhood, and resolve to spurn from
> your company, and treat with contempt, every profligate libertine, and to
> give encouragement to men of common sense and morality, what an alter-
> ation would not shortly take place.

In the response the following week, Dorothy Glibtongue, supposedly a female,
concurs with Adolescens that women can and should reform men's sexual
habits: it is because women can reform such men through marriage that they

82. Adolescens, "Ladies," *Philadelphia Minerva,* Dec. 5, 1795. Much of the material
reprinted in Philadelphia periodicals of the 1790s was influenced by the evangelical
revival flourishing in late-eighteenth-century Britain. The emphasis on women's ability
to transform men's behavior was part of these religious reformers' efforts to effect the
spiritual transformation of moral transgressors. In Philadelphia, religious enthusiasm
led to moral reform campaigns in the early nineteenth century (discussed in Chapter 7).

must be free to receive them in courtship. In short, men in the 1790s were told that they were not fully responsible for their sexual conduct.[83]

There was no cultural space in the new construction of sexuality for the woman who was sexual simply for her own satisfaction. Gone from the pages of the almanacs were the positive images of women overcome by passion who succumb to the caresses of the shepherd. Fear of the socially and politically disruptive consequences of overactive female sexuality eliminated the lusty, overtly sexual woman from the public print culture geared for general consumption. The sexually active woman of the 1790s became the sexual victim, and the seduced woman came to harm.[84]

In early national public print culture, nonmarital sexual activity of women meant sexual danger for them, as witnessed in the proliferating seduction tales, prostitute histories, and courtship follies that dominate the 1790s. Sexual danger was also employed in the symbolism of the Revolutionary generation describing political relationships. As several historians have astutely pointed out, the language of the American Revolution was deeply gendered. Seduction, rape, and marriage were the primary metaphors used to describe the political relationships of the times. Americans were warned to guard against the rape of liberty and to beware of the seduction of British corruption. They were told that the ties that bound citizens together in a republic were like those of a good marriage, based on mutual affection, not tyrannical rule or force. The metaphors describing the evil forces battling against liberty as well as the positive models representing republicanism were forms of male-female relationships, used because they were so universally understood. Men, in particular, could read them and know how to respond to the political situation at hand. People got their meaning from the sexual referent. In this way these sexual metaphors were a lingua franca to explain politics.[85] But they simultaneously conveyed the

83. Adolescens, "Ladies," *Philadelphia Minerva*, Dec. 5, 1795, and Dorothy Glibtongue, "To Mr. Adolescens," Dec. 12, 1795.

84. The literature on seduction and prostitution is discussed in detail in Chapter 6. Cott first made the connection between a passionless construction of female sexuality and sexual danger in "Passionlessness: An Interpretation of Victorian Sexual Ideology," *Signs*, IV (1978–1979), 219–236.

85. On the gendered language of the Revolution, see, for example, Bloch, "The Gendered Meanings of Virtue," *Signs*, XIII (1987–1988), 37–58; Lewis, "The Republican Wife," *WMQ*, 3d Ser., XLIV (1987), 689–721; James Jasinski, "The Feminization of Liberty, Domesticated Virtue, and the Reconstitution of Power and Authority in Early American Political Discourse," *Quarterly Journal of Speech*, LXXIX (1993), 146–164. Lewis suggests that sexual seduction stories were read metaphorically as the battle

changing dynamics of the politics of sex in the new nation. All of the sexual metaphors employed, whether depicting the dangerous forces of corrupt Britain as seduction and rape or celebrating the forces of American republicanism as companionate marriage, depended on and depicted the subordination of women. The widespread use of these metaphors gave the depiction of female sexual vulnerability and women's subordination to men in marriage, albeit under the new gloss of companionate marriage, a huge new cultural arena of play. With the reconstruction of sexuality under way, these symbols of female subordination not only would have been read metaphorically but also would have reinforced the association of women's sexuality with sexual danger.

One has to wonder what happened to the construct of the lusty woman. Dangerous to the Republic, the sexually assertive woman was no longer appropriate in popular print for a general audience. But she remained an erotic interest for men of means, who—despite claims to republican virtue—sought her out in the flesh and in fiction. The sexually lusty woman survived in a parallel print market created for an exclusively male readership. Printer-booksellers of the new Republic continued to import expensive print erotica from Europe, and a few ventured to print erotic texts of their own—but they were no longer publicized in the city's newspapers. It was no longer politically responsible or fashionable to advertise them. Becoming more overtly sexual, domestically produced books for the first time illustrated amorous encounters. An 1807 Philadelphia edition of *Female Policy Detected,* for instance, included a somewhat crude illustration of a naked couple opposite the title page, and a later New York edition of it printed a series of images of scantily clad women to illustrate women's efforts to use their sexual charms to entrap men (see Plates 10, 11). *Female Policy Detected* was an exposé of women's conniving ways. It remained popular in the new Republic, with at least nine American printings between 1785 and 1810. The very word "policy" in its title meant a calculated plan of action, here applied to women's use of sexuality to entrap men. Men were cautioned not to trust or highly regard sexually active women, even as they were excused for engaging in licentious nonmarital sex with them.[86]

---

between virtuous republican society and corrupt society. Seduction tales, she asserts, functioned as a metanarrative to describe the challenges facing the new political organization of American republicanism.

86. E[dward] Ward, *Female Policy Detected; or, The Arts of a Designing Woman Laid Open* (Philadelphia, 1807); Ward, *Female Policy Detected* (New York, 1830). *Female Policy*

PLATE 10. *Frontispiece to E[dward] Ward*, Female Policy Detected; or, The Arts of a Designing Woman Laid Open *(Philadelphia, 1807)*. *Permission The American Antiquarian Society*

Other domestic imprints of English books inserted erotic illustrations to increase their sexual charge. A 1795 edition of Laurence Sterne's *Sentimental Journey through France and Italy*, for instance, was enhanced by explicit illustrations of sexual intercourse. Women, as the frontispiece caption suggested,

---

Detected was originally published in London in 1695 and reprinted numerous times in England throughout the eighteenth century.

See, for example of guidance to helpless males, the opening maxim in chapter 1, "Of the Allurements of Women": "Of all vices, unlawful freedom with the female sex is the most predominant, and of all sins has the most powerful temptations; and many allurements to betray and draw men into this folly. The inducements of the fair sex are so prevalent, a propensity in nature so forcible, it is hard to stand unmoved, when tempted by the charms of a subtle woman, and drove by the foul desires of unbounded lust." He soon follows: "Be not tempted to pick up any woman in the street; but if you should, be sure that you have one eye before and another behind, for wherever lust leads, danger follows." Ward, *Female Policy Detected* (Philadelphia, 1807), 3, 4.

PLATE II. *Frontispiece to E[dward] Ward,* Female Policy Detected; or, The Arts of a Designing Woman Laid Open *(New York, 1830).*
Permission The American Antiquarian Society

presented constant sexual temptations that men often succumbed to (see Plates 12, 13). Men from Philadelphia's well-to-do and middle classes continued to have access to erotic prints and such English fashionable magazines as the *Bon Ton Magazine* of the mid-1790s, illustrated with graceful erotic pictures and Thomas Rowlandson's sexually explicit engravings. But public recognition of this sexually explicit material and the sexually indulgent world fashioned within its pages was shut out of the public sphere of the new nation.[87]

Some humorous material similar to that printed before the Revolution was reprinted in jest books, but the sexual content was toned down. In *The New Entertaining Philadelphia Jest-Book, and Chearful Witty Companion* of 1790, for instance, the most ribald pieces made jokes on the old themes of premarital pregnancy and bastardy. But they were much less sexually explicit pieces than those published before the war. A piece on bastardy read:

> A young gentleman having got his neighbour's maid with child, the master, a grave man, came to expostulate with him about it. Lord, Sir, said he, I wonder how you could do so; prithee where is the wonder? said the other, if she had got me with child you might have wondered indeed.[88]

Almost thirty years later the same modest tone persisted in published jest books. Writing about prostitution, a Philadelphia collection of humorous stories and anecdotes in 1817 contained a witty play on words, but with no erotic implications:

> An old bawd being carried before the late Justice Bond for keeping a disorderly house, strongly denied all that was charged against her — "Housewife! Housewife! (said the justice) how have you the assurance to deny

87. *Memoirs of a Woman of Pleasure* was apparently printed in Philadelphia for sale in 1806. See John Tate to Mathew Carey, July 8, 1806, HSP. Tate wrote to complain that Carey's type had been used to print "The Memoirs of a Woman of Pleasure, Other Wise Called Hannah Hill and the Abomible plates are Ingraved in this city." For an example of the material produced exclusively for this separate male market, see *The Origin of Evil and Elegy* (n.p., 1793), HSP, an eight-page pamphlet erotic poem of the first encounter of Adam and Eve, published domestically in 1793. Surviving editions of domestically produced erotic early national books are rare, and it is impossible to know how often they were produced. Nineteenth- and early-twentieth-century archives did not actively collect such materials, and some purged their collections of them.

Copies of Rowlandson prints owned by members of the Rush family in the early nineteenth century are in LCP.

88. *The New Entertaining Philadelphia Jest-Book, and Chearful Witty Companion* . . . (Philadelphia, 1790), 68.

PLATE 12. *"Such Were My Temptations." From [Laurence Sterne],*
A Sentimental Journey through France and Italy *(New York, 1795).*
Permission The American Antiquarian Society

PLATE 13. *"He Shut the Door. . . ."* *From [Laurence Sterne],* A Sentimental Journey
through France and Italy *(New York, 1795). Courtesy The Lilly Library,*
Indiana University, Bloomington, IN

it? You do keep a bawdy house, and I will maintain it." "Will you (replied the old lady;) the Lord bless you; I always took you to be a kind hearted gentleman."[89]

In early national print culture, sexual humor (collected in volumes such as jest books) tended to focus on ethnic humor or depict active female sexuality as a lower-class attribute. The anecdotes themselves were often reprinted or reworked from earlier eighteenth-century material. But what made them acceptable for inclusion was their association of female lust with particular ethnic groups and women of the lower classes. It was the peasant maid who displayed sexual longing and sexual availability to upper-class men in a lengthy anecdote explaining the acquittal of a lord for the rape of his tenant's daughter, in both the *American Jest Book* (1798) and *The Witty Exploits of George Buchannan* (1813). It was the Scottish woman who was depicted as sexually voracious. When asked by her clergyman how many commandments there were: " 'Eleven,' she answered. — 'Eleven!' said he, 'what is the eleventh?' 'Increase and multiply' answered the woman." And it was the Irish wife who ran away from a man she wasn't really married to:

From a late Clonmel Journal.
Ran away last night, my wife, Bridget Coole; she is a tight neat body, and has lost one leg; she was seen riding behind the priest of the parish through Feemoy, and as we were never married, I will pay no debts she does not contract; She lisps with one tooth, and is always talking about fairies, and is of no use but to the owner.
  Phelim Coole.

Even the print erotica available to men often presented women of the lower classes as sexually available, in contrast to the restrained, respectable woman of the upper classes. In the *Bon Ton Magazine,* a man of means tussles with a domestic maid, her bare breasts exposed by his roaming hands, while a respectable middle-class woman (his wife?!) stands off behind them, refined in dress, composed and unperturbed by his sexual escapades. Elite and middle-class men could cross over into this world while their wives, quite literally, stood sentinel for public propriety and the nation's virtue (see Plate 14).[90]

89. *A Mess of Salmagundi, for Modern Laughing Philosophers: Consisting of the Most Admired Anecdotes, Bon Mots, and Modern Approved Songs* (Philadelphia, 1817), 47–48.

90. *The American Jest Book; or, Merry Fellows Companion* (Philadelphia: John M'Culloch, 1798), 65–66, 76 (quotation marks regularized); *The Witty Exploits of George Buchannan . . . to Which Is Added Paddy from Cork . . . and Humorous Jests* (Philadelphia,

The older model of the lustful woman remained in a parallel print world created exclusively for men to inhabit. When female lust was depicted in print material that circulated broadly in the city, it was associated with women of the lower classes or ethnic women. The lustful woman remained a cultural type to be applied to women who failed to live up to the new construction of middle-class womanhood as pious, pure, and chaste. As we shall see, this older, now pejorative model of the lustful woman was resurrected by men to justify their sexual encounters with women deemed to fall outside the realm of virtuous republicanism.

This was the model of gendered sexuality promoted by the public print culture of the new nation. The depiction of male sexuality was consistent with the behavior of men in Philadelphia during the late eighteenth century, but its presentation of women was in direct conflict with the sexual lives of women participating in the expansive sexual culture of the city. With women like Marianne Montgomery openly entertaining their lovers in public and men like Benjamin Rush writing about the dangers of licentiousness, all within the same small city, something had to give. And it did. By the 1790s the reconstruction of gendered sexuality was under way within the upper and middle classes. The cultural work undertaken to transform the notions of natural and normal female sexuality from carnal to restrained took place with women like Justina Rustiur and Marianne Montgomery in mind. For women, passionlessness held the promise of eradicating their lustful nature, thus qualifying them to participate in building a new nation. But it also delegitimated the sexual independence and greater self-determination in personal life that other women had initiated in the era of the American Revolution.

The new construction of female sexuality represented a compromise of the political initiatives advanced by women in the new Republic. This compromise acquiesced to women's comparable, albeit different, mental faculties, legitimating women's involvement in the public political culture of the city. But it solidified her essential difference from man by creating a female sexuality that was the polar opposite of men's and lodged it securely in the female body. Judith Sargent Murray was right when she wrote in 1782 that women

1813). This story was added at the end of the "Witty Exploits" in the "Humourous Jests" section. The same tale was printed in both books.

Clonmel Journal: *A Mess of Salamagundi*, 14–15. Many of the humorous ditties in this volume made fun of the Irish as bumbling idiots.

PLATE 14. *"Royal Indignation; or, The Pot-Girl in a Pickle,"* Bon Ton Magazine
(1792). Courtesy The Newberry Library, Chicago

could establish the foundation for female independence by the cultivation of the rational mind. Revolutionary-era women had fought a battle against the imputed lack of reason as woman's primary disability. But by the early nineteenth century the battleground of women's subordination had shifted. It had migrated from the brain to the womb, where nineteenth-century science could substantiate that woman differed from man. Female sexual restraint, which arose without effort from the female body, was the evidence in daily life of this difference. Gender difference would now depend upon sexuality.

PART III

NORMALIZING SEX IN THE NINETEENTH CENTURY: THE ASSAULT ON NONMARITAL SEXUALITY

In the new nation, sex had become an important battleground for contesting social and political hierarchies. Intimate behavior was now a place ripe for claims to full and equal status in the Republic, a place to debate the power to be granted to groups that elites understood as lesser citizens. Control over the sexual self was an expression of equal standing for many among the city's lower classes and African-Americans—both those demanding rights to traditional forms of sexual practice, such as legal/patriarchal marriage, and those adopting expansive, nonmarital sexual lives.

Sex had also become the linchpin in the logic of a new gender system under construction by the emerging urban middle class. Gender difference, this new conceptual framework asserted, was based in the anatomical differences between men and women and in distinct male and female forms of sexual desire and deportment. This new gender system countered both the assault on patriarchal prerogatives that the sexual independence of Philadelphia women represented and the political assertions of equality by women of the emerging middle class. It also held the promise of establishing one normative form of sexuality and created the mechanism to pronounce the deviancy of those whose independence threatened the gender, racial, and class hierarchies of the new Republic.

The expansive sexual culture fashioned in the wake of the American Revolution did not go unchallenged. The period 1800–1830 saw increasing conflict and resistance as elite and middle-class Philadelphians responded to the threats they perceived in expansive sexual practices and the permissiveness of the city's sexual culture. They assaulted sexual nonconformity in three successive waves: a cultural attack, benevolent reforms, and ultimately harsh legal reforms. The first attempt at reform of sexual behavior was via cultural subversion. Beginning in the 1790s sexual nonconformity was attacked through the

[handwritten margin note: Three attempts at reforming sexual behavior]

representations of sexuality, when new models of male and female sexuality were adopted in the public print culture of Philadelphia. Then, in the first decade of the nineteenth century, private benevolent societies led by the city's religious leaders set out to reform the lives of sexual transgressors, often employing religious instruction and conversion. These campaigns failed to transform their fellow Philadelphians. When the reform efforts of elites met resistance from those embracing expansive sexual lives, the elites turned to more punitive measures. The third and final wave, during the 1810s and 1820s, established legal reforms mandating compliance. The regulation of sexuality intensified and moved from private to public control. Beginning about 1810, the flexible possibilities of the immediate post-Revolution years gave way to rigid morality and punitive sexual discipline. Philadelphians supported new laws regulating bastardy and enforced laws against illicit sex in ways that targeted the lower classes and shielded elite men from prosecution.

Delegitimating expansive sexual behavior and its meanings hinged on separating these forms of sexuality from the emerging normative construct of romantic marital monogamy and segregating them in another realm entirely. Splitting the sexual culture into two opposing constructions was at the heart of all three waves of reform. None of the reform campaigns successfully transformed the behavior of those engaged in nonmarital sexuality. But they did change the social and cultural context within which sexual nonconformity took place. By the mid-1820s reforms had removed expansive nonmarital sexual behavior from the middle-class culture that dominated the public sphere.

Philadelphia thereby created a two-tiered system of sexuality, which reinforced both class and racial divisions. Between 1790 and 1830 the understanding of sexuality split, creating two sexualities: the dominant and public version of virtuous women and virile men, and a lustful, uncontrollable sexuality of the rabble. This reconstruction was used by the elite and middle-class Philadelphians to reinforce the boundaries delineating the social hierarchy and legitimate their economic and political dominance. By 1830 the middle-class gender system had established the appearance of hegemony through the bifurcation of sexuality, attributing licentiousness to the rabble and forcing such behavior out of the public eye and underground.

Recasting the gendered meanings of sexuality and the subsequent move, in the early nineteenth century, to construct one normal sexuality in contrast to deviant ones was a way of resolving the long-standing instability of the eighteenth-century gender system. Battered by the political developments in the Age of Revolution, this new gender system based on a strictly bounded notion of inert female sexual desire could reestablish an acceptable basis of difference between men and women. But it also served the class and racial interests of the emerging middle classes and was part of the strategy they used to secure the subordinate status of African-Americans and the lower classes in antebellum society.

[handwritten margin note:] New gender system — reestablished differences b/t men & women and secured subordinate status of African-Americans & lower sort

CHAPTER 6

Through Our Bodies

Prostitution and the Cultural Reconstruction of Nonmarital Sexuality

---

> *Behold the house of incontinence: the mark of infamy is indelibly stamped on the*
> *threshold, and on the posts of the door.*
>   *At the window sitteth misfortune forcing a smile; and within are remorse, and*
> *disease, and irretrievable misery.*
> —*Whole Duty of Woman.* By a Lady (Philadelphia, 1798)

The hundreds of women who bore bastard children, engaged in adultery, or practiced prostitution during the early national period did so in an environment in which their behavior was being reinterpreted by the larger society around them. Culturally their behavior came under attack, as the stories used to tell of their lives narrowed into one dominant narrative that eliminated the sexually independent woman from the cultural landscape.

In the sexual tales produced in magazines, newspapers, almanacs, and true crime pamphlets of Philadelphia, the variety of sexual practices and range of sexual meanings in the popular culture of the late colonial era were reduced to a single theme—prostitution. The joking gibes about forward women engaging in adultery and bastardy, so popular in the almanacs of the 1770s, had been replaced with sentimentalized tragic stories of fallen women, who all became prostitutes and usually died. In this transformation of the cultural images of female sexual behavior, female sexuality outside marriage became associated with economic necessity, poverty, and ultimately the lower classes.

These cultural associations took several steps. First, all nonmarital sex became prostitution, because prostitution became the inevitable outcome, for all women, of premarital or extramarital sexual behavior. Adultery, once the source of ribaldry, was no longer represented as funny or tragic, because of the injustice to the other spouse. Adultery was now the first step in a debauched life that could only lead a woman to prostitution. In a tale in the *Philadelphia Repository, and Weekly Register* in 1802, for example, a wife moves from infidelity to prostitution in a house of ill fame:

(From a London Paper)

A young sailor was on Friday tried at the Clerkwell Sessions for an assault upon his wife. Jack did not deny the fact; but according to his mode of telling the story, he had also cause to complain. He could never get her to keep in the same birth with him, and caught her out cruizing under false colours! notwithstanding this provocation, he confessed he was still fond of his spouse; but having found her one day in a house of bad fame, he owned that his passion overcame him, and he beat her with a cat-o'-nine tails. The Jury, whose risible faculties were provoked, acquitted him.

The reader is to understand that the wife's actions were universally condemned by society: the jury acquitted her husband.[1]

Premarital sexual behavior of women also led to prostitution. Gone are the lusty maids of "The Pipe of Love" and the young couples fulfilling their desire in rural bliss.[2] Premarital sex was now represented as the seduction of women by duplicitous, insincere men in countless poems and stories. In "An Inscription for the Tomb of an Unfortunate Prostitute," a young woman is portrayed as the seduced, dying prostitute, giving her life's story as a cautionary example to those tempted to engage in "unlawful love."

> A WRETCHED victim of a quick decay,
> Reliev'd from life, on humble bed of clay,
> The last and only refuge of my woes,
> A lost!—love ruined female! I repose.
> From th' sad hour I listened to his charms,
> And fell, half forc'd, into perfidious arms,
> To that whose awful veil hides every fault,
> Shelt'ring my sufferings in this welcome vault.

Seduced, she turns to prostitution, which tortures her soul while it ravages her body:

> When pamper'd, starv'd, abandon'd, or in drink,
> My thoughts were rack'd in striving not to think;
> I durst not look on what I was before;
> My soul shrunk back, and wish'd to be no more:

1. *Philadelphia Repository, and Weekly Register,* Oct. 9, 1802.
2. These motifs are analyzed in Chapter 3, above. "The Pipe of Love" appeared in George Alexander Stevens, *Songs, Comic, Satyrical, and Sentimental* (Philadelphia: Bell, 1778), 116.

Nor could rejected conscience claim the pow'r,
T' impose the impulse of one secret hour;
Cover'd with guilt, infection, debt, and want,—
My home a brothel—and the street my haunt.
Full sev'n long years of infamy I've pin'd,
And fondled, loath'd, and prey'd upon mankind;
'Till the full course of sin and vice gone through,
My shatter'd fabric failed at twenty-two.

Stricken by venereal disease, she dies:

Then death with every horror in his train,
Here clos'd the scene of riot, guilt, and pain.
Ye fair associates of my opening bloom,
Oh! come and weep, and profit at my tomb;
Let *my* short youth, and blighted beauty prove
Your antidote against unlawful love.
Oh! think how quick my foul career I ran,
The dupe of passion, vanity, and man:
Then shun the paths where gay delusions shine,
Be *your's* the lesson!—sad experience *mine,*
And let me leave one hint, ye giddy swains,
For you, who to deceive us take such pains;
Think how you'll shudder at the bar of God,
When justice smites with his vindictive rod.[3]

Seduction, which within this language meant premarital sex achieved
through the entreaties of a lover, had only two possible outcomes: death or
prostitution. Writing on "seduction" in 1799, Pheonine concluded that "the
unhappy victim" will either "sink in the cold arms of death, for relief from
miseries of which thou [the seducer] art the cause," or "plunge (by thee led
to the brink) into the gulph of woe and infamy." Our "WRETCHED victim,"
like many seduced women of popular print culture, suffered both outcomes.
Within this emerging discourse there was no provision for premarital sexual
intercourse with a happy outcome: virginity must be preserved.[4]

Not surprisingly, the images of bastardy had to change.

3. *Philadelphia Repository,* Feb. 7, 1801.
4. Pheonine, "Seduction," *Weekly Magazine* (Philadelphia), Mar. 16, 1799; "Seduction," *Philadelphia Minerva,* Oct. 22, 1796.

A Girl complaining to a Justice of Peace of one who had got her with child upon a promise of marriage—the more fool you, says the Justice, to trust him, as if any man would do that for you upon his repentance, which he would not upon his temptation.[5]

All sexual encounters that led to illegitimacy became seduction, and bastardy was incorporated into the sequence that transformed seduction to prostitution. The details of the road to ruin varied in every tale, but they all followed a basic pattern: a woman was seduced by her lover, who abandoned her after his conquest. She was then expelled from polite society and thrust into the sexual underworld.

The story of Maria recounted in the *Philadelphia Minerva* was a classic seduction tale of the period. Published as "a fragment" in 1797, it was one of a series of seduction stories in the *Minerva* during the late 1790s. Maria's story began like many others, with her courtship, wooed by an insincere young man. Their wedding set, the couple found themselves alone in her house the week before the nuptials. Frederick, her betrothed, swore to her that without her he "would cease to exist." To Maria, "he appeared sincere, and I viewed him as singled out by fate for my companion thro' life." He pressed her, "Still manifest for me your love."

He continued protestations of his love—the minutes were swift—and ere the evening had elapsed he triumphed over my innocence and credulity— in time he left me miserable.

When her parents returned that evening, Maria was overcome with regret, became deathly ill, and was bedridden for two weeks. Frederick, meanwhile, left for France, abandoning the defiled Maria.[6]

Maria's life quickly moved to the brink of prostitution. She fled from her parents' house to conceal her shame and took a job as a kitchen servant, where she remained until the birth of her bastard son forced her to move on.

I lived in this manner until I was taken ill, when I gave birth to this child—I called him after his father.

My recovery was slow; and when I could not walk I was unable to work as before; consequently I was forced to give up my place.

5. *The Columbian Almanack . . . for . . . 1790* (Philadelphia: Stewart, 1789).
6. "Maria; or, The Seduction," *Philadelphia Minerva*, Mar. 4, 11, 1797. See also "Caroline; or, The Seduced American," *Philadelphia Minerva*, Jan. 21, 1797, and "The Honourable Seducer; or, History of Olivia," Dec. 19, 26, 1795.

Now living only on the charity of strangers, Maria wandered the streets in search of better prospects.

One morning she encountered Frederick, who at first did not recognize her. She asked him for money for their child. "I told him I was in poor state of health, and requested only a small boon." But she was rebuffed. Maria, shocked at such treatment by the man who so passionately had professed his love for her, and facing no reputable prospects for making a living, swooned in the street. But she, unlike most seduced characters, was rescued by a passerby who caught her in his arms and took her home. Maria was saved from the life of a streetwalking prostitute only by the benevolent intervention of a good Samaritan. Caroline, the main character in "The Seduced American," was not as lucky. She ended her days alone, dying of venereal disease, a more typical ending for the women of popular print.[7]

During the early national era, these tales of seduction leading inevitably to prostitution were the staple fare of inexpensive popular print. They were produced as poems in newspapers, written as short stories in installments in weekly magazines, and printed in individual pamphlets as leisure reading. In virtually every one the women have lost all sexual agency, duped or tricked into sexual intimacy. They often experienced an immediate regret after their fall, even before the dreadful consequences of their sexual misconduct arose. This expressed their natural remorse at nonmarital sexual intimacy. Sometimes they lost their wits or became physically ill as a result of sexual intercourse.[8]

The meanings attached to the stock male characters were more ambiguous. The majority of these stories portrayed the sexual partners of fallen women as male sexual villains, describing them as "night wolves which hunt for prey," "a fiend and a monster," one "who lays a snare."[9] Read within the sexual context of the city and the broader, changing constructions of female and male sexuality, these characters could have been interpreted in at least two quite different ways. The repetitive use of these images probably desensitized readers to the manipulative, self-centered pursuit embodied in this male sexual behavior. The uniform deployment of this character familiarized the reading public with the sex-driven man and reinforced the construction of male sexuality as beyond his control. In this way, through familiarization and repeti-

7. "Maria," *Philadelphia Minerva*, Mar. 4, 11, 1797, and "Caroline," Jan. 21, 1797.

8. "Maria," *Philadelphia Minerva*, Mar. 4, 11, 1797; "Crazy Jane," *Philadelphia Repository*, Nov. 22, 1800.

9. Charles Crawford, Esq., *The Dying Prostitute: A Poem* (Philadelphia, 1797); Pheonine, "Seduction," *Weekly Magazine*, Mar. 16, 1799.

tion in the absence of other models, the characterization of men as sexual predators legitimated male license and sexual privilege. Rather than challenging male sexual dominance, these stories supported the idea that such behavior was natural for men.

These images could also have been read as a condemnation of predatory male sexual behavior. Cathy Davidson argues that early national readers understood these narratives less as cautionary tales for women than as critiques of male sexual license. I imagine that these stories were read both ways in the Philadelphia community. But both interpretive readings adopt the new models of male and female sexuality. This is obviously true of a reading of seduction tales that validates a predatory male sexuality through the popularization of such images. But it is also true of a reading of seduction literature as an indictment of male sexual license. The reader must accept the representation of the woman as the sexual victim in order to interpret the male sexual predator as villain. These characters were interdependent, and both readings understood female sexuality as naturally restrained. In neither reading does the woman maintain sexual agency. She does not and, in fact, cannot assert her own sexual will successfully.[10]

The proposition that seduction tales were read as subversive resistance to male domination, as a "cry for female equality" (as Davidson argues), is less satisfactory for readers outside the circle of middle-class women to whom sentimental novels were marketed. Seduction stories also had a strong presence in other forms of cheap popular culture, in magazines and newspapers, broadsides and songsters. While some stories, particularly in literary magazines, were written for an affluent female audience, most were for broad public consumption. Readers, particularly the men wielding power based on their gender and the women of the lower classes especially vulnerable to that power, might have read these tales in different ways. One must imagine that men gained validation of male sexual privilege from this genre, which depicted their sexual power as invincible. The lesson to all women was to protect themselves by restraining their own sexuality. For the women of the lower classes the power granted to men must have been all too familiar. In poems and anecdotes, just as in life, men succeeded in their designs and were left unchastised. For those women, so much more vulnerable to male sexual privilege, these seduction tales were an attack on an active female sexuality, a cultural assault on their sexual autonomy.

10. Cathy N. Davidson, *Revolution and the Word: The Rise of the Novel in America* (New York, 1986), 105, 135.

The conversion of nonmarital sexual experience to seduction and prostitution, along with the cultural representation of female sexuality that emphasized a natural female restraint and sexual vulnerability, greatly increased the real sexual danger to women of the lower classes. Through these cultural transformations, nonmarital sexual practices and female sexual independence became marginalized.

The next narrative step in reducing all nonmarital sexual experience to prostitution was moving from seduction to financial desperation. The cultural tales about prostitution narrowed the possible inducements the trade could offer to only one: the remedy for dire financial need. Only through economic necessity could, or would, a woman prostitute herself. Not only did a woman of the town have no sexual desire, but she also could not exercise any agency to choose, or choose not, to engage in prostitution. Once fallen, she was swept down an inevitable stream to poverty and prostitution. This formula, which focused on economic necessity as the vehicle by which the seduced or fallen woman became the prostitute, facilitated the association of nonmarital sexuality with women of the lower classes.[11]

"The Prostitute," a poem printed in 1795 in the *Philadelphia Minerva*, typified the era's prostitute narrative. Seduced by her lover, turned out of doors by her father, Maria turns to prostitution:

> At first, Oh! horrible to name!
> She's infamous *for bread;*
> Till lost to every sense of shame!
> She meets it without dread.

Prostitution corrupts Maria's moral sense, and she plunges into the sexual underworld.[12]

Most prostitution narratives represented the sexual underworld in one-

11. While this scenario was certainly accurate for some women, it seriously underplayed the variety of experiences of "seduced" women in early national Philadelphia. Some women managed to conceal their sexual behavior. For those who became pregnant, the Guardians of the Poor system of child support provided an economic alternative to inevitable prostitution. Other women put their children out to nurse, which allowed them to work or to keep up an appearance of propriety, as their class required. Still others sought legal redress through civil suits for a failed promise of marriage. In that world, seduction did not automatically lead to outcast status and economic ruin.

12. "The Prostitute," *Philadelphia Minerva*, July 18, 1795. See also, for example, "The Prostitute—A Fragment," *American Museum*, I (1787), 44–45.

dimensional terms as a place fraught with poverty, disease, and death. If a narrative occasionally recognized the existence of a heterogeneous dynamic sexual culture surrounding prostitution, it was only to portray it as enervating. For Maria this sexual underworld proves fleeting and only adds to her descent:

A while in folly's giddy maze,
    Thoughtless her time she spends;
While pleasure seems to wait her days,
    And joy each step attends.

But vice soon robs her lovely face
    Of all its wonted bloom;
While black remorse, and pale disease,
    Her tender frame consume.

The bloom she now supplies by art
    And cheerfulness she feigns;
But still her poor dejected heart
    Feels agonizing pains.

Plung'd in distress none would relieve,
    Maria walks the streets;
By casual prostitution lives,
    Expos'd to colds and heats!

Other portrayals emphasized the long-term economic inviability of prostitution. The subject in "The Dying Prostitute," for example, suffers "want and woe; disease and endless shame," until her life of prostitution devolves to where she can no longer successfully solicit clients:

Who now beholds, but lothes my faded face,
    So wan and sallow, chang'd with sin and care?
Or who can any former beauty trace
    In eyes so sunk with famine and despair?
.   .   .   .
Expell'd by all, enforc'd by pining want,
    I've wept and wander'd many a midnight hour,
Implor'd a pittance Lust would seldom grant,
    Or sought a shelter from the driving shower,

Of't as I rov'd, while beat the wintry storm,
    Unknowing what to seek, or where to stray,

To gain relief, entic'd each hideous form;—
Each hideous form contemptuous turn'd away.[13]

Sometimes these narratives began with lower-class women facing poor economic choices. Mary was a typical character who struggled with poverty, her father dead and her mother with too many mouths to feed. Unable to support the family on wages from washing and nursing, Mary turned to prostitution at the age of fifteen, with her mother's aid and support. Such stories, in which poverty led to a woman's initial fall, accounted for lower-class women's prostitution. But even the elite or middle-class woman's fall led to prostitution. When the road to ruin began with the seduction of the economically advantaged woman, society's rejection of her left her with the economic necessity to prostitute herself. Nonmarital sexuality, in popular print, transformed the woman of secure economic means into a woman of the lower sort.[14]

These images of the woman forced into prostitution through economic want not only undermined the legitimacy of female sexual independence but also obscured and denied the economic independence of the prostitute. In the early national city, prostitutes were the most obvious manifestation of economically independent women. They commanded fees that were believed to be higher than for any other female employment, they generally worked for themselves and controlled their income themselves, and they walked the city's streets to market their trade. During an era when most women's economic well-being was tied either to their husband's income or to poor wages as domestics, the prostitute stood out as a symbol of independent womanhood. Popular print representations of prostitution that denied this reality were attacks on the gender deviancy of such women.[15]

13. T. Holcroft, "The Dying Prostitute: An Elegy," *Literary Miscellany*, I, no. 2 (1795), 26–27.

14. *The Penitent Prostitute* (London, 1800). This was available to Philadelphians through the Library Company of Philadelphia's collections.

See, for example of the better-off woman, "Caroline," *Philadelphia Minerva*, Jan. 21, 1797.

15. Marcia Roberta Carlisle discusses the economic independence of the prostitute in "Prostitutes and Their Reformers in Nineteenth Century Philadelphia" (Ph.D. diss., Rutgers University, 1982). She analyzes the city's prostitutes as working women and suggests that the prostitutes of early-nineteenth-century Philadelphia had much in common with the new mill girls.

Historians and feminist theorists have debated whether prostitution should be

Female sexual and economic independence and the expansive sexual culture were all under attack in popular print in early national Philadelphia. Beyond this, cultural representations of seduction and prostitution were sometimes used more explicitly as tools of reform. Prostitution born of economic necessity was incorporated in the popular print that advocated reform in the period 1790–1810. One of the first pieces of prostitution reform literature produced in Philadelphia was a prefatory essay to the pamphlet *The Dying Prostitute* in 1797. It addressed the lack of honest employment available to women, a sentiment reiterated into midcentury by reformers like Mathew Carey, who decried the low wages and poor conditions of working women. "The prostitution of women," the essay begins,

> which prevails to a high degree in all large cities, might be considerably lessened by giving them encouragement to enter into various occupations which are suitable to them.

Women should be encouraged to be staymakers and milliners, and men should leave such work to them. They could also take over part of the work of male tailors, sewing together the pieces of suits "once they were cut out by the tailor." Farm work could keep women from the trade as well, "by preventing their living in the cities (which are very mischievous to a country) where, through the want of bread, they might be tempted to prostitution."[16]

The essay went on to emphasize, however, that chastity could be assured only through adoption of Christianity:

---

understood primarily as work or as sexual practice. In the early national period in American cities prostitution transgressed the prescribed gender attributes of proper middle-class womanhood in both ways: the prostitute was both a sexual and an economic deviant. It was her independence in both realms that made the secure and independent prostitute such a potent threat to the nineteenth-century middle-class gender system. For a cogent discussion of this question, which synthesizes the main arguments within this debate, see Barbara Meil Hobson, *Uneasy Virtue: The Politics of Prostitution and the American Reform Tradition* (1987; rpt. Chicago, 1990), preface to rpt. edition, vii–xiv, introduction, 3–8.

Jeanne Boydston discusses the ways in which labor, work, and cash-earning power became gendered male during the first three decades of the nineteenth century in *Home and Work: Housework, Wages, and the Ideology of Labor in the Early Republic* (New York, 1990).

16. Crawford, *The Dying Prostitute*, preface, iii–vi.

The best preservative, however, from the prostitution of women, especially of the lower class, may consist in the instruction of First-day or Sunday schools.

To this end, the essayist called upon the citizens of Philadelphia to found a Magdalen Hospital modeled after the one in London, to transform fallen women through industry and religion.

When prostitution narratives turned to reform, they usually focused on transforming the fallen women into repentant Christians. Citizens were encouraged, not to turn away from the fallen woman, but to embrace her, take her in, and lead her to God. Such action not only saved souls but also provided a wonderfully rich subject and plot for the conversion narratives of the evangelical revival.

Only rarely did the call to action against prostitution address the culpability of men as seducers and clients perpetuating the trade. One such piece in 1796 suggested that, if libertines were met with reproofs of their behavior, there would be far fewer fallen women. The analysis of the fictitious love of sex commerce is surprisingly candid. The prostitute, speaking to a "gentleman," challenges him to look past the illusions of prostitution:

> Sir, what pleasure you ever tasted, or can possibly expect, in the arms of a prostitute? You are indisputably aware that I am so unhappy as to be of this wretched description: why, therfore, are you anxious to make me still farther miserable? Can you reasonably imagine that I covet your false smiles, and empty applause?

But critiques like this were rare. Much more common were the deathbed scenes of religious conversion facilitated by benevolent reformers. As turn-of-the-century popular culture focused on these new sexual scripts, reformers would turn their attention to the prostitutes who worked the city streets.[17]

17. "Female Prostitution," *Philadelphia Minerva*, Apr. 2, 1796. See, for example of conversion, "The Prostitute," *American Museum*, I (1787), 44; *The Penitent Prostitute*.

CHAPTER 7 **Through Our Souls**

The Benevolent Reform of Sexual Transgressors

Interest in prostitutes and prostitution narratives was growing in Philadelphia around the turn of the century. Women like Elizabeth Drinker read the stories of prostitution in pamphlets such as *The Histories of Some of the Penitents in the Magdalen-House* and *Modern Seduction; or, Innocence Betrayed*. While Drinker read about penitent prostitutes, other women of Philadelphia continued in the trade. They were women like Eleanor Robinson, who engaged in prostitution and kept a bawdyhouse in Welch's Alley, and Elizabeth Johnson, who visited brothels in the evening while she lived at service in the city. Unlike Robinson, Johnson never made prostitution a full-time occupation, but she did frequent the city's bawdyhouses from age seventeen until twenty-two.[1]

Drinker was not alone in her interest in the reform of prostitutes; a small movement was growing among prominent men of Philadelphia to reclaim them. Led by the Reverend William White, bishop of the Episcopal Church, these men formed the first organization in the United States dedicated to reforming prostitutes. The founding members included physician Benjamin Rush and bankers Robert Rolson and Joseph Morris as well as prominent Philadelphia merchants and doctors. Incorporated in 1800, membership in the Magdalen Society was restricted to white men. It undertook the reform of the city's fallen women with a combination of utopian reform sentiment, born of the Enlightenment, and Protestant evangelical revivalism.[2]

---

1. Elizabeth Drinker read these pamphlets in 1801 and 1802, respectively. Both were published in London and imported for sale to Philadelphia: *The Histories of Some of the Penitents in the Magdalen-House* . . . (London, 1760); *Modern Seduction; or, Innocence Betrayed: Consisting of Several Histories of the Principal Magdalens Received into the Charity* (London, 1780) (Elaine Forman Crane, ed., *The Diary of Elizabeth Drinker* [Boston, 1991], II, 1371 [Oct. 7, 1800], III, 1609 [July 14, 1802]). Examples: PFT, Feb. 9, 1792, Eleanor Robinson; MSM, Feb. 7, 1809, Elizabeth Johnson (Johnson engaged in casual prostitution from 1804 to 1809).

2. MSM, June 3, 1800. Biographical information on the society's founders from

The Magdalen Society's actions were motivated, in part, by a concern shared by many elite Philadelphians over growing social disorder. During the 1790s and the next decade, elite Philadelphians undertook numerous reform campaigns against a perceived increase in vice and immorality, hoping to reconstitute authority among the city's upper classes. Citizens, led by prominent Philadelphia men, created organizations to improve conditions in the prisons, to reform the penal code, and to severely limit capital punishment. They developed an asylum to treat the mentally ill and hired Benjamin Rush to run it. They established schools to educate the children of the poor. Reformers believed that prisoners, children, and the insane could all be reformed through proper treatment. So too, it appeared, could the city's prostitutes. In the face of an apparent epidemic of social corruption, elite Philadelphians set out to transform their fellow, if lesser, citizens.[3]

The efforts to reform prostitutes were part of this movement. During the

---

Marcia Roberta Carlisle, "Prostitutes and Their Reformers in Nineteenth Century Philadelphia" (Ph.D. diss., Rutgers University, 1982), 156.

In 1804 the board opened up membership of the society to "all male persons of mature age (people of color excepted) and of good moral character" (MSM, Feb. 1, 1804). In February 1819 the society agreed to "associate" with "a number of pious discreet females." These women served in an auxiliary fashion, visiting the Magdalens in the Asylum to facilitate their moral instruction (MSM, Feb. 16, 1819, June 6, 1820).

The board of managers appears to have responded to a group of women who sought involvement in the society when they took this action. The exclusion of pious women in the organization for its first twenty years suggests that the board initially understood the redemption of fallen women to require male instruction and guidance. In Philadelphia of 1800–1820, numerous female charitable and reform societies were founded.

3. For an example of citizens' concern voiced through a petition to the Assembly, see PP, Dec. 30, 1785, "To the House of the Assembly." This petition linked prostitution to property crime, the corruption of youth, and declining morals. This concern over social disorder and its relationship to the reform movements of early national Philadelphia are fully examined in several works. See John K. Alexander, *Render Them Submissive: Responses to Poverty in Philadelphia, 1760–1800* (Amherst, Mass., 1980); Priscilla Ferguson Clement, *Welfare and the Poor in the Nineteenth-Century City: Philadelphia, 1800–1854* (Rutherford, N.J., 1985); Michael Meranze, *Laboratories of Virtue: Punishment, Revolution, and Authority in Philadelphia, 1760–1835* (Chapel Hill, N.C., 1996), esp. chaps. 2, 3. There was a double-edged nature to these reforms, as Michel Foucault has pointed out. Reforms undertaken in the name of humanitarian interests, such as penal reform and the creation of the mental asylum, created deviant individuals in the process of reforming their transgressions. Foucault, *Discipline and Punish: The Birth of the Prison*, trans. Alan Sheridan (New York, 1979).

1790s, before the Magdalen Society was founded, several antivice citizens' groups were formed. The first, The Association of the District of Southwark, for the Suppression of Vice and Immorality, was organized in 1790. By the late 1790s the citizens of Philadelphia proper had created a similar organization. These citizens' groups were concerned with the growth of gambling houses, brothels, dance halls, and tippling houses, which seemed to operate unimpeded. Exactly what these groups did and how long they existed remain somewhat of a mystery. We know that they believed a crackdown on the haunts of the pleasure culture was needed and that they took it upon themselves to police Sabbath breaking. They did not, however, generate the community support necessary to challenge the public policy of lax law enforcement against illicit sex.[4]

The Magdalen Society was different. The members saw their purpose as "relieving and reclaiming unhappy females who have Swerv'd from the paths of virtue." They sought to replace the habits of vice with those of industry and chastity through a program of regimented living and religious instruction secluded within a city retreat. To this end the society opened a Magdalen Asylum at the edge of town in 1807. The board of managers hoped that women who had awakened to their sins would use the Asylum to transform their lives. Here the city's prostitutes could escape the trade, take shelter, and emerge months later as reputable members of society.[5]

4. Alexander dates the Philadelphia organization from 1797 or 1798 (*Render Them Submissive*, 82). Calls by citizens for the formation of such organizations had begun by 1785; see *PP*, Dec. 30, 1785, "To the House of the Assembly." There is no evidence, however, that this petition resulted in the incorporation of such an organization.

It appears that the Southwark organization of 1790 had ceased to exist by 1795, when a new Southwark Association was founded (Alexander, *Render Them Submissive*, 81–82). The latter was still operating in 1797 when the Guardians of the Poor noted that they had received a sum of money from the Southwark Association for the Suppression of Vice and Immorality collected for breach of the Sabbath violations (GPM, May 4, 1797). Beyond this, the only record of these groups comes from a few brief newspaper notices. By 1814 some of the surrounding communities had also formed such organizations. Blockley Township formed a Society for the Suppression of Vice and Immorality in December 1813. *Poulson's American Daily Advertiser* (Philadelphia), Jan. 1, 1814.

5. MSM, Feb. 10, 1801 (quote). The first Magdalen was admitted in July 1807 (MSM, Aug. 8, 1807). The Asylum was located at Schuylkill, Second and Race (Carlisle, "Prostitutes and Their Reformers," 163). The nine-member board of managers was the governing body of the Magdalen Society.

From 1807 to 1820, 138 women entered the Asylum. Many were like Mary and Sarah Wood. Mary Wood entered in March 1808 after a life of "debauchery" for six years in the city. At age twenty-two, after taking shelter in the almshouse medical ward, she turned to the Magdalen managers for aid, who admitted her to the Asylum, where she remained for four months. By the following summer Mary Wood had achieved the transformation of character and soul necessary to allow her departure. The managers arranged for her removal to the country, where she would reside in service for "a respectable religious family." Here, it was hoped, she would continue in her religious reformation and maintain her chastity. Sarah Wood, who probably was Mary's older sister, also came to the Asylum in March 1808, and remained for nine months. Twenty-four years old, she had spent several years frequenting disorderly houses before her change of heart. She too took a place at service in the country in a religious family when she departed.[6]

The women who entered the Asylum during its first years, 1807–1814, were mostly from Philadelphia or nearby states. The largest group (38 percent) were born or raised in Philadelphia and had engaged in illicit sexual activity there. Many others (30 percent) came to Philadelphia as young women from New York, New Jersey, Delaware, and Maryland. Women born and raised across the Atlantic also sought refuge in the Asylum. Of the inmates, 17 percent were born in Europe, with more than half from Ireland. But only 6.5 percent of the

6. MSM, 1800–1819. During this period the society admitted an average of 12.5 women annually. In the early 1820s this number rose to 25 (1820–1824) (MSM, 1820–1824). Figures presented in the discussion are based on my own computations from MSM, 1800–1824. Carlisle used the same materials in "Prostitutes and Their Reformers," where she did some statistical work. My own statistical analysis allows me to address specific questions about the earliest stages of prostitution reform in Philadelphia, and, unless otherwise stated, the figures are my own. While Carlisle discusses prostitution from 1800 to 1890, much of her focus is from the 1830s on, and her research for the earlier era relies upon the Magdalen Society records entirely. I have, therefore, drawn my own conclusions on the nature of prostitution and on its policing, based on my use of court records and popular cultural material, in addition to the Magdalen Society records. Carlisle's work provides a rich description of the world of sex commerce and the conflicts over its regulation from the 1830s on, when accounts begin to appear in Philadelphia newspapers.

Woods: MSM, Mar. 7, July 5, 1808, Mary Wood; MSM, Mar. 7, Nov. 11, 1808, Sarah Wood. Sarah was also admitted from the almshouse, although poverty appears to be what brought her there. She was in the regular, nonmedical ward when she met the visiting committee members of the Magdalen Society.

inmates came from the surrounding Pennsylvania countryside. Statistically, at least for those admitted to the Magdalen Society, the road to ruin was less likely to lead from the country to the city than popular lore professed.[7]

More than half these women entered the Asylum directly from the city's almshouse, having entered the almshouse medical ward for treatment. Most of the Magdalens were admitted for gynecological disorders identified as venereal diseases. Upon their "cure" they could, if they appeared repentant, enter the Magdalen Asylum. Members of the society visited the almshouse and, in the early years, the city's prison, to talk with fallen women about their sinful condition and the possibility of converting to respectability. Only when they professed a sincere and convincing desire to transform their lives were they granted admission.[8]

Admission and departure both required permission from the board of managers or the visiting committee members. The program of transforma-

7. These numbers are based on an analysis of the first seventy-six women who entered the Asylum, from its founding in summer 1807 through 1814, and paralleling the data from the sexual transgressions database developed from court records and the Guardians of the Poor. This parallel chronological sample allows for a comparison between the two groups. The place of origin was unknown for 8 percent of those seventy-six Magdalens.

8. Information on where the managers found the Magdalens was recorded for only the first thirty-seven cases, those admitted from 1807 through August 1811. For these years 54 percent were admitted from the almshouse, all except Sarah Wood coming from the medical ward. The others came from the prison (11 percent), were referred by the Guardians of the Poor for their poverty (11 percent), applied directly to the managers (14 percent), or were referred by reputable friends when ill (5 percent); another 5 percent are unknown.

The rules of the Asylum forbade the admission of pregnant women and women with venereal disease. However, the medical understanding of venereal disease interpreted the asymptomatic stages and remission of syphilis as a cure. When symptoms reemerged, people believed they had been reinfected. Therefore, women treated in the venereal wards of the almshouse could enter the Magdalen Asylum despite the prohibition against "diseased" women. This prohibition did mean, however, that, when a woman's syphilis developed to its final stages, where the disease was manifest through physical disfigurement, she would not be an acceptable candidate for the Asylum. Just how many of the women admitted from the almshouse suffered from venereal disease and how many simply suffered from common gynecological infections is unclear. The board of managers' minutes generally concluded that the "disease" that brought women to them was venereal and noted by contrast cases when the woman suffered from an illness that was "not the usual disease" suffered by prostitutes.

tion required the elimination of outside stimulation and an adherence to discipline. The inmates theoretically had the right to request their own discharge, but they could not leave the house at will. The doors were kept locked, and a fence surrounded the grounds. Only a few of the women who wanted to leave because of a change of heart made the official request and awaited permission. Most of those who left before the managers believed they were ready did so by climbing over the fence. The majority stayed, for a rather prolonged period. Those who were discharged with the blessings of the managers as reformed women had resided in the Asylum an average of eight months. Some had stayed a few months, others up to a year. Sarah Proctor, the first woman admitted, lived there for eleven months before she was ready to reenter society. Even those who eloped or were expelled stayed, on average, two and a half months. They used the Asylum as a temporary shelter where they could regain their health and enjoy a decent diet and comfortable surroundings. For those who ultimately rejected the character transformation and required habits of living, the Asylum was, for a short time, a better alternative than the almshouse.[9]

Perhaps the most remarkable thing about the Magdalen Society in its early years was the extent to which the women it served were truly redeemable. Its premise was that fallen women could reenter society: these men believed that the fallen women of turn-of-the-century Philadelphia were not inevitably destined to be social outcasts. The Magdalens' experiences bore this out. When they left the Asylum, most entered respectable households as paid domestic servants. Some took on the care of children, and others married respectable men (see Table 17).

Elizabeth Ogden, the first woman the society took under its wings, opened a school for children with the aid of the board of managers. Elizabeth came to their attention in December 1804, before the Asylum was established. In January 1805, she was placed as a boarder in the home of a respectable

9. From 1807 through 1814, only five of the seventy-six women admitted left by gaining such permission. They were described as "discharged at her own request." Of the inmates, 34 percent left before they were "reformed" (24 percent eloped, 4 percent were expelled for improper behavior, and 6 percent were discharged at their own request). Information on their departure was available on all seventy-six women. A steady stream of women "eloped" over the walls throughout the Asylum's history, roughly a third of the inmates during its first thirty years. MSM, Aug. 8, 1807, June 3, 1808, Sarah Proctor. Information to establish the length of stay was available for seventy-two of the seventy-six women.

TABLE 17. *Magdalens, 1804–1814: Departure from Asylum*

Disposition	No.	Proportion
Eloped	18	24%
Dismissed	3	4
Discharged with permission	5	6
Placed at service in a family	34	45
Returned to relatives	7	9
Discharged to almshouse for medical aid	5	6
Married	2	3
Teaching and care of children	2	3
Total	76	100

Note: The 3 women who were aided by the Magdalen Society before it opened the Asylum are included in this group. Information was unavailable for 3 of the inmates.

Source: MSM.

religious family. There Elizabeth had the use of a private room, which the society paid for, and spent her time reading religious works and taking in sewing. Elizabeth lived with this family for a year, members of the society visited her to converse on religion and salvation, and she regularly attended religious services. At the end of the year Elizabeth became a member of the Second Presbyterian Church of Philadelphia. In May 1806 she removed to her own residence and opened a school. The managers described her "prospects" as "flattering," and they believed "she was likely to do well." Within two months she had eighteen students, and within four she had thirty.[10]

Elizabeth Ogden, a fallen woman, became a school teacher in the city and successfully attracted pupils. Anne Hudner took a position in a household to care for young children. Lucy Ridgeway married a respectable man, and Eleanor Rose was reunited with her estranged family after "about four years in habits of prostitution." These women effectively used the Magdalen Society to

10. Elizabeth Ogden was one of the three women the society assisted before the Asylum opened. While under the society's care, she was supported in the home of a religious family and was admitted as a member to the Second Presbyterian Church in February 1806. Second Presbyterian Church of Philadelphia, Session Minutes, Feb. 6, 1806, PHS; MSM, Jan. 14, Feb. 11, 1805, May 29, June 23, Aug. 11, 1806, Oct. 10, 1807, Elizabeth Ogden. From October 1806 to April 1807, she required no assistance from the managers.

redirect their lives, and during the first decade of the nineteenth century they could do it.[11]

From 1807 on, the women who engaged in sex commerce within the city had at least one avenue out of the trade. They could turn to the Magdalen Society and attempt to enter the Asylum. The huge majority resisted or ignored reformers' efforts to redeem them. From 1790 through 1799, 195 people had been arrested for illicit sexual activities that constituted prostitution; from 1805 through 1814 another 312 were arrested, only 13 of whom ever became inmates of the Magdalen Society, and 2 of these were arrested after their stay in the Asylum. This represents a near-unanimous rejection of the life of the penitent prostitute by those Philadelphians who were the targets of law enforcement's efforts against illicit sex.[12]

For the women who did enter the Asylum after a run-in with the law, the stay in prison rarely motivated their decision to turn away from the trade. Five of these women had been arrested two years or more before they became Magdalens. Mary Charleton was typical. Mary was born in Delaware and bound as a servant to a widow who took her along with her when she moved to Philadelphia. After serving out her time, Mary continued to live in Philadelphia and work at domestic service. Here she was "enticed to Houses of Ill fame" and practiced prostitution for seven years, until illness forced her into the almshouse. Mary's years of sex commerce had not gone unnoticed by the city's authorities. In May 1806, three years before she became a Magdalen, Mary was arrested and convicted of "keeping a disorderly Bawdy House." She served three months at hard labor in the city prison, but her prison stay was not what brought her to the Magdalen Society. Only at retirement, after a long career in the trade, did Mary seek the aid of reformers. Ultimately, she became one of the society's success stories. She stayed in the Asylum for eleven

11. Ogden's school prospered for a year. By the following summer she was having difficulty collecting tuition from her clients, a fate common among all small-business people then. During the summer of 1807 she turned to sewing full-time and was reported as doing well in February 1808, three years after she had come under the care of the Magdalen Society. MSM: Feb. 9, Apr. 9, June 11, 1807, Feb. 2, 1808, Elizabeth Ogden; May 3, 1808, Anne Hudner; May 29, 1806, Lucy Ridgeway; Aug. 12, 1808, Eleanor Rose.

12. The Court Dockets and the Vagrancy Dockets were checked against the list of women who became Magdalens through 1820. The methodology provided a way to detect women who might have turned to the Asylum years after an arrest for prostitution: as, for example, if a woman was arrested in 1814 but continued in the trade for another five years and then became a Magdalen.

months, underwent a suitable transformation of character, and was placed at service with a respectable family.[13]

Most of the women who engaged in sex commerce did not see themselves as seduced victims in need of rescue, nor were they overcome with regret, guilt, or shame that popular culture attributed to them. The moral and spiritual transformation offered by the Magdalen Society required accepting and ultimately internalizing that vision. As Mary Ann Stevenson wrote in a remarkable letter to discourage her brother from rescuing her from prostitution:

Philadelphia August 12th 1827
Henry Stevenson,

As my only desire is to remain in my present situation unmolested and free to act as i think proper, I must insist that you give up all further exertions to discover and molest me as I assure you I shall use my best endeavours to avoid your impertinent interference. And I also assure you, that however disagreeable my present life may be to those who once had authority over me that it is perfectly agreeable to me, and that the authority once exercised over me having expired I claim my privilege in acting according to my own inclinations. All further exertions to discover me would prove fruitless and unavailing. . . . In the mean time I'll endeavour to call your attention or in other words transfer from me to a female relation now residing in the family, who having got tired of the life, which vexes you so much in me, has returned home to carry on her amours privately. For my part when I get tired I'll act in partnership with her and we will divide or at least give you a part of our gains to keep a blind eye and silent tongue.—

I will condescend to inform you that I am perfectly happy and contented, have nothing to wish for, or desire and that there is no likelihood I shall, but if I ever should, I have too much spirit to return, and partake of the comforts I once enjoyed at home, (not meaning that I do not enjoy any comforts now.) No! Sooner would I beg my bread in the street than stoop to such a humiliating condition.— . . . [I] conclude, with, begging you my dear brother to accept of the love

Your affectionate and dutiful Sister
Mary Ann Stevenson

13. MSM, July 7, 1809, June 5, 1810; PFT, May 22, 1806; QSD, June 2, 1806. The exact times elapsed between arrests and admittance to the Asylum were 2 months, 6 months, 2 years (two), 3 years, 4 years (two); four women were admitted directly from prison, and two were arrested for prostitution after their stay in the Asylum.

The cultural assault waged through popular print had not been successful in converting these women to a new interpretation of their lives. If it had been, more would have turned to the Magdalen Asylum and would have fashioned their life stories and future hopes to correspond to the expectations of the society. But they did not.[14]

The narrative of prostitution had, however, influenced how the reformers saw these fallen women. They often wrote of their stories in ways that mimicked the representations of seduced women in popular print. Thus of Mary Anderson in their minutes in 1808 they wrote:

> Magdalen No. 7—Nineteen years of Age, this young Woman a few months past lived in the Country where (as she informs) she was Seduced by a Young Man, who left her and came to this City, to which place she also followed in pursuit of him, but not being able to find him, and ashamed after the loss she had sustained to return to her Friends, she went into a disorderly House, remained there some time and in consequence of disease was compelled to go to the Almshouse.[15]

We cannot know whether Mary felt the shame these reformers attributed to her, but it is clear that the member of the Magdalen visiting committee who wrote down her story believed it. The details included and omitted followed precisely the seduction-to-prostitution narrative so dominant in the print culture of the era. Mary, like the fictional characters in print, moved directly from seduction to prostitution with no acknowledgment of all the other possibilities within the early national world of Philadelphia.

The impact of the new popular cultural representations of female sexuality was also evident in the ways the Magdalen members interpreted resistance to reform in their inmates. Magdalen No. 6, Elizabeth Brooks, entered the Asylum on December 18, 1807, and eloped three weeks later. Her entry in the minutes describes both her admission and her departure because of the short duration of her stay. Written after her departure, it thus became an explanation for her rejection of reform. Elizabeth's illicit life was the result of her own character faults:

> Magdalen No. 6—Twenty years of Age—This poor unhappy young woman by her depraved propensities, and wicked life of debauchery and Ideleness, was lately reduced to such a State of misery and distress, as well as weakness of body, as to afford but little hopes of her recovery.

14. Mary Ann Stevenson to Henry Stevenson, Aug. 12, 1827, LCP.
15. MSM, Feb. 2, 1808.

Despite these faults, she appeared to feel the remorse necessary to effect a transformation:

> She seemed much to lament the wicked life she had lived, and expressed an earnest desire to come under the care of the Society.[16]

When Elizabeth recovered sufficiently from near-deathly illness to scale the wall, she eloped. Her choice to return to her "former associates" was interpreted by the managers as the work of the devil and was attributed to Elizabeth's losing her mind:

> But her heart being deceitful and desperately wicked, and urged on by the grand tempter to pursue her evil propensities; and convictions of the impropriety of her former conduct, conflicting in her mind it is conjectured by, the Committee and Matron that a partial derangement of intellect was the cause of her Elopement on the 8th instant.[17]

As devoted Protestants involved in the evangelical revival of the early nineteenth century, the Magdalen board of managers drew upon and promoted images of sin and salvation, temptation and redemption. These Christian symbols were woven into the prostitution narrative, complementing the powerlessness and lack of agency attributed to women in the Magdalen model. In 1801, for instance, the managers solicited two publishers to reprint excerpts from the tracts published by the London Magdalen Hospital. Samuel Bradford, editor of the *Free Daily Advertiser,* and Zachariah Poulson, editor of the *American Daily Advertiser,* agreed to publish the Magdalen stories interpreted through this evanglical Christian lens.[18]

Law enforcement in the city was also affected by the cultural reinterpretation of female sexuality. The administration of criminal justice during the early national period reinforced the association of licentiousness and criminality with the lower classes. As we have already seen, Philadelphia never mounted a sustained attack on prostitution through mass arrests and criminal prosecutions (see Table 18). Arrests for prostitution, averaging one and a half per month during the 1790s, increased to only two and a half per month from 1805 through 1814, not even keeping up with the population increase. Arrests

16. MSM, Jan. 11, 1808.
17. Ibid.
18. MSM, Jan. 11, Feb. 10, 1801.

TABLE 18. *Prostitution Arrests, 1790–1814*

	Criminal	Vagrancy	Overall
	1790–1799		
1790	0	20	20
1791	3	17	20
1792	3	13	16
1793	2	10	12
1794	4	24	28
1795	7	33	40
1796	1	4	5
1797	9	21	30
1798	5	—	5
1799	19	—	19
Total	53	142	195
	1805–1814		
1805	14	4	18
1806	19	7	26
1807	17	5	22
1808	23	6	29
1809	9	7	16
1810	45	17	62
1811	35	28	63
1812	15	5	20
1813	27	13	40
1814	16	0	16
Total	220	92	312

Source: See Appendix, Table A.2.

were few and sporadic, those arrested usually being released as soon as they posted bond for their future good behavior.[19]

But an examination of the administration of criminal justice can be instructive, revealing one way in which early national Philadelphia began to focus concern about illicit sexuality on women and the lower classes. The separation and polarization of the licentious woman from the virtuous woman, evident in

19. The sexual behavior prohibited by law remained the same throughout this era. When Pennsylvanians rewrote their criminal statutes following the Revolution and

the cultural refashioning of female sexuality in popular print, was put into practice in the policing of prostitution. Through this process the cultural assumptions about greater licentiousness of lower-class women were made to appear real.

The policing of all categories of misbehavior was done in ways that highlighted the criminality of the poorer classes and obscured that of the more affluent. The standard procedure upon an arrest was to post bond immediately to secure a release from the city jail, sometimes just posting a bond to guarantee future good behavior sufficing. Other times a bond guaranteed an appearance in court. If the defendant failed to appear, this bond was forfeited to the court. People routinely failed to appear, and bonds functioned unofficially as fines.

When one did not have the money to post a bond, one remained in jail, so access to money meant one could often avoid a trial altogether. Members of the lower classes often spent weeks if not months in jail awaiting trial for petty crimes. When they did appear in court, they wore the marks of prison in their gaunt appearance and tattered clothing. Insufficient funds to post bond for one's future good behavior also kept many in jail. It is small wonder that many Philadelphians thought the lower classes were more criminal. The poor not only had greater need to relieve hunger and want through thievery, but their movement through the criminal justice system was more protracted and obvious. During the last decades of the eighteenth century their presence became even more prominent, when Philadelphia experimented with public penal labor as a means to reform its male criminals, assigning work gangs throughout the city. The presence of prisoners in public, performing penal labor, reinforced well-do-to Philadelphians' fear of increasing criminality. It probably also increased their sense that it was the lower classes who were criminals.[20]

---

revised the penal code in the 1790s, they continued the colonial prohibitions against fornication, bastardy, adultery, sodomy, and maintaining a bawdyhouse. There was no statutory prohibition against prostitution. When criminally prosecuted, it was under the laws against fornication or, more commonly, under the laws against disorderly behavior. Women were charged with "lewd" behavior. Prostitution was policed also through the vagrancy statute. The term "prostitution" was employed to describe behavior in vagrancy arrests, but the legal charge was vagrancy.

20. See PFT, 1805–1814. Poor Philadelphians continued to be vulnerable to incarceration under the vagrancy statues throughout the 1810s. A grand jury inquest in 1817 found that many people were being held in jail "as vagrants without trial and who not

Arrests and prosecutions for prostitution were especially chaotic. Weeks would go by without any arrests, and then a particular constable would bring in several groups of women in one night. Some women were arrested through the criminal system, and others were picked up only as vagrants and imprisoned for thirty days. Most proprietors of bawdyhouses were never arrested, but a few were. Philadelphia had neither the mechanisms nor the inclination to police prostitution systematically.[21]

Prostitutes who were arrested were rarely brought to trial. Of those arrested for maintaining bawdyhouses in the 1790s, only 25 percent were prosecuted. The proportion of prosecutions was higher in the next decade, 42 percent from 1805 through 1814, but still erratic. A person was just as likely to be released as to stand trial (see Table 19). For the small minority who were tried and convicted, sentencing was equally haphazard. One might be sentenced to one month in prison or one year, with an additional fine of one cent to one hundred dollars. For those charged with keeping a bawdyhouse but convicted only of keeping a disorderly house (treated as a separate charge), the sentence was similar to that for keeping a bawdyhouse. Sentencing did not correspond to the severity of the offense: if keeping a disorderly house was a lesser charge,

---

being charged with any specific offence do not come under the Cognizance of any Court of Justice." Grand Jury Inquest, Court of Oyer and Terminer, Eastern District, Philadelphia County, Jan. 10, 1817, HSP.

From 1786 to 1794 Philadelphia put its prisoners to work throughout the city. This was the first stage in the penal reform Philadelphia undertook following the Revolution. Dressed in prison garb and in chains, male convicts moved among the citizens performing the labor that penal reform theorists believed would effect their reformation. Female convicts were also put to work but were enclosed within the almshouse walls sewing and making textiles (Meranze, *Laboratories of Virtue*, chaps. 2, 3). Meranze demonstrates that public penal punishment reinforced the associations between the lower classes and criminality. He interprets penal reformers' turn away from public punishments in the mid-1790s as a manifestation of their fear of the contagious nature of criminality and social decay.

21. This distinction between those cases charged through the criminal statutes against sexual misconduct and those charged through the vagrancy statute is important, because each required a different level of community involvement to support the prosecution. The vagrancy statute allowed a city magistrate to incarcerate, without any form of due process, any person without visible means of support arrested by a city watchman. Those arrested under the vagrancy statute had no trial, no jury, and no courtroom witnesses. Prosecutions for statutory sex offenses required the support of more members of the community.

TABLE 19. *Arrests for Keeping a Bawdyhouse, 1805–1814*

Outcome	No.	Proportion
Brought to trial	62	42%
(Defendant appears)	(57)	(39)
(Defendant fails to appear)	(5)	(3)
Settled before trial	66	45
(Defendant posts bond for future good behavior)	(21)	(14)
(Case dropped)[a]	(38)	(26)
(State declines prosecution/nolle prosequi)	(7)	(5)
State determines charges false/ignoramus	7	5
Miscellaneous (defendant died, moved)	4	3
No information	8	5
Total	147	100

[a]Most of these cases were calendared for trial but never went to trial. It is unclear whether defendants' posting bond for good behavior was not noted or whether the cases were dropped after the persons posted bond. Most of these defendants were released from jail within a day or two after arrest. They did not, however, show up in the trial docket, nor was there a notation that they had failed to appear and therefore forfeited their bonds.

Source: See Appendix, esp. Table A.2.

it did not carry a less severe sentence (see Table 20). Even those convicted were likely to be pardoned before they served out their sentences, unless they were persons of color.[22]

Clearly, few firm rules governed the adjudication of prostitution. This absence of clear and specific jurisprudence allowed Philadelphians to follow their informal notions of what was appropriate or right when enforcing the laws. They could, and did, apply the laws in ways that reflected and reinforced their biases. For those engaged in sex commerce, that meant that women working in the streets and women obviously of the lower classes were more readily arrested for prostitution. The patterns of arrests for prostitution in the

22. For example, Elizabeth Brown served only one week of her six-month sentence for keeping a disorderly house in 1805, and Mary Row was out after serving ten days of her sentence for the same offense in 1808. James Grant, a black man, and Sarah Roach, described as a "yellow" woman, each served their full six-month terms in 1808 for the same offenses. Convicts' Sentencing Docket, II, June 1804–August 1810, CCAP.

TABLE 20. *Bawdyhouse Arrests, 1805–1814: Sentences and Fines*

	Bawdyhouse Conviction	Disorderly House Conviction
	JAIL TIME	
none	7	4
1 month	1	6
2 months	2	0
3 months	7	3
4 months	2	0
6 months	3	3
1 year	1	0
7 years	1	0
No information	2	5
	FINE	
None	1	0
$ .01	2	0
.06	2	2
.25	2	0
.50	0	2
1.00	4	7
2.00	1	0
5.00	1	0
10.00	2	1
15.00	1	0
20.00	2	2
50.00	2	2
100.00	1	0
No information	2	5

Note: Most sentences included both a fine and a jail sentence, the low fines usually combined with jail time: for instance, 6 months and $1.00 (bawdyhouse), but not always, as in 6 months and $50.00 (for disorderly house). There was no recognizable pattern to the severity of the sentences.

Source: Appendix, esp. Table A.2.

TABLE 21. *Prostitution Arrests, 1790–1814*

Offense	Criminal Arrests	Vagrancy Arrests	Total
	1790–1799		
Keeping bawdyhouse	34 (27 houses)	15 (3 houses)	49
Fornication in bawdyhouse	9	10	19
Street prostitution	10	117	127
Total	53	142	195
	1805–1814		
Keeping bawdyhouse	147 (118 houses)	0	147
Fornication in bawdyhouse	8	0	8
Street prostitution	65	92	157
Total	220	92	312

Note: In addition to arrests where the term "bawdyhouse" was the stated charge, some arrests for disorderly houses probably involved sexual misbehavior. During the 1790s an additional 116 disorderly house raids probably involved sexual misbehavior, and during 1805–1814 there were an additional 165 such disorderly house raids. Such disorderly houses were determined as those disorderly houses recorded in the dockets that did not specify gambling, tippling, or fighting as cause.

Sources: See Appendix, esp. Table A.2.

1790s demonstrate two trends: first, violations that occurred on the streets were more likely to result in arrest; and, second, women who could be construed as vagrants were the most likely to be arrested (see Table 21). During the 1790s, 152 of the 195 people arrested for prostitution fell into these two categories: 78 percent of those arrested were arrested either as vagrants or for street solicitation, or both.

The huge majority of those arrested for prostitution were taken in as vagrants. The city watchmen and the magistrates interpreted the statute that allowed them to incarcerate anyone with no visible means of support to mean anyone with no legal employment. They often recorded the infraction as "having no visible means of making an honest living." Women arrested under the vagrancy statute were also simply charged with being "abandoned" or "notorious prostitutes."[23]

Solicitation in the streets was what landed most women of the trade in jail. But the low number of arrests suggests that most women who engaged in

23. Vagrancy Docket, Dec. 4, 1811, CCAP.

streetwalking were left undisturbed by the authorities. Those arrested probably distinguished themselves by particularly bold behavior, perhaps like Elizabeth Holton, who was charged through the regular court system with "being a disorderly Strumpet, so entirely devoid of Decency or Modesty that she is unfit to be at Large." They might also simply have been less adept at maneuvering through a system of informal rules, corruption, and bribes.[24]

The focus on street behavior was evident in some of the bawdyhouse arrests as well. Joseph and Mary Hines, for instance, were arrested twice in 1795 for maintaining a bawdyhouse. In both instances the charges emphasized their establishment's connection to public solicitation. In May they were charged with "keeping a house for admitting street walking women," and the following November with "keeping a disorderly house for the reception of common prostitutes in the night time."[25]

By 1810 Philadelphia had begun to shift more prostitution prosecutions from vagrancy arrests into the regular criminal court system, increasing also the proportion of prostitution arrests of those who ran houses for prostitution, thereby recognizing prostitution as a specific form of criminal sex. But this shift did not mark a significant increase in policing. Overall arrests for prostitution still averaged only two and a half a month from 1805 through 1814, and convictions were still hard to come by. Of the 42 percent of bawdyhouse arrests brought to trial, 5 percent were dismissed as false charges, and the rest were settled and dismissed (Table 20). Obtaining a conviction for maintaining a bawdyhouse was difficult. Witnesses were needed to establish that sexual behavior had taken place, and few participants in sex commerce would have been willing to testify. Bawdyhouse charges were often dropped and prosecuted only as disorderly houses, but often the general disorder of an establishment was proved without establishing that illicit sexual activity took place (see Table 22).

There were a few signs that some members of the Philadelphia community

24. PFT, July 28, 1798. Elizabeth was held in jail for two weeks and then released without further action. During the 1780s and early 1790s Philadelphians complained of corrupt magistrates and abuses of the law. Some believed arrests were made simply as a means of raising funds for the personnel who worked in law enforcement. See Meranze, *Laboratories of Virtue*, 117–120, on "trading justices." It is unclear how much corruption occurred, but, in a system where the city watchmen, the sheriff, and those who served warrants were paid a percentage of the fines imposed, one must assume a certain number of women who engaged in prostitution paid informal fines to stay out of jail.

25. PFT, May 21, Nov. 26, 1795.

TABLE 22. *Bawdyhouse Trials, 1790–1814: Dispositions*

Outcome	1790–1799		1805–1814	
	No.	%	No.	%
Guilty of keeping a bawdyhouse	5	38	26	45
Guilty of keeping a disorderly house (not guilty on bawdyhouse charge, or bawdyhouse charge dropped)	7	54	21	37
Not guilty	1	8	9	16
Case forwarded to Supreme Court, no disposition given			1	2
Total	13[a]	100	57	100

[a]Only 13 of the 53 people arrested for keeping a bawdyhouse were brought to trial in the 1790s, or only 25% of the cases.

Sources: See Appendix, esp. Table A.2.

were growing impatient with the flourishing trade in sex commerce early in the new century. In 1800 a group of Philadelphians took it upon themselves to close down a notorious brothel in Southwark commonly known as the China Factory. Their action was precipitated by a violent altercation between two men in the brothel, which resulted in one man's death. The survivor of the fight and the men's female partners in the house of ill fame were indicted for manslaughter, rather than murder, prompting a crowd to descend on the establishment and tear it down brick by brick. This mob action went unimpeded by the authorities during the two days it took to accomplish the destruction. The newspaper account suggested that the action was welcomed by "well-disposed Citizens of Southwark." That Philadelphia had few such riots makes the words ring hollow and indicates that prostitution was fairly secure. Elizabeth Drinker's comments on the subject were likely more accurate.

> I was pleased to hear that such Creatures were routed—I am not pleas'd to hear of riots and could wish that a more justifiable power had taken them in hand long ago 'tis a shame to our police that any such houses is suffered.[26]

26. *Claypoole's American Daily Advertiser* (Philadelphia), Aug. 23, 1800; Crane, ed., *The Diary of Elizabeth Drinker*, II, 1334 (Aug. 25, 1800).

This brothel riot followed the same pattern of extralegal action that occurred in other cities during this era, where the precipitating event was not about prostitution

The Pennsylvania Assembly did take one action to curb the growth of sex commerce when it made "masquerades and masqued balls" illegal in 1808. In Philadelphia, dances were a common meeting place for those interested in sex commerce, and masked balls created anonymity for the participants. In eighteenth-century London and Paris, masked balls were places of erotic amusement, where sexual abandon reigned. People met anonymously, and some made illicit connections. In London and mid-nineteenth-century New York, prostitutes attended masked balls to meet clients, and men attended to meet them. In Philadelphia the move to outlaw masquerades was spurred by the introduction of large commercial public masked balls in January 1808. The advertisements for them in the city's newspapers suggested the sexual danger possible, even as they promised that care would be taken to avoid it. Messrs. Hipolite and Epervil assured potential patrons "that every care shall be taken not to admit any improper persons," and Mr. Auriol stated that he "assures the ladies, that they may depend upon his care, as to improper persons being admitted."[27]

---

itself. Historians of antebellum prostitution have found that "brothel riots" usually had more to do with gender or class conflicts than with any sentiment directed against prostitution. Timothy J. Gilfoyle suggests that it was not until the 1820s that brothel riots were instigated as a manifestation of men's resentment over the independence of women of the trade, particularly women brothel owners. Gilfoyle, *City of Eros: New York City, Prostitution, and the Commercialization of Sex, 1790–1820* (New York, 1992), 76–91; Barbara Meil Hobson, *Uneasy Virtue: The Politics of Prostitution and the American Reform Tradition* (1987; rpt. Chicago, 1990), 23–24; Pauline Maier, *From Resistance to Revolution: Colonial Radicals and the Development of American Opposition to Britain, 1765–1776* (New York, 1972), 4–5, 14.

27. An Act to Declare Masquerades and Masqued Balls to Be Common Nuisances, and to Punish Those Who Promote or Encourage Them (1808), in James T. Mitchell, Henry Flanders, et al., comps., *The Statutes at Large of Pennsylvania* (Harrisburg, 1896–1915), XVIII, 751. The law suggested that masked balls were held in private homes in the city, making it illegal for any "housekeeper" to permit a masquerade to be held in "his or her house" and for any person to attend such a ball "in mask or otherwise." Conviction required imprisonment up to three months and a fine between fifty and one thousand dollars. I found no evidence of any arrests or convictions under this statute from 1808 through 1814 or 1820 through 1824. On dances and sex commerce: Court of Oyer and Terminer, File Papers, case of William Gross, Nov. 21, 1822, testimony of Caroline Smith, Mary Newcomb, and Mary Allen. These three women worked the city's dances for clients as prostitutes during the early 1820s. Terry Castle, "The Culture of Travesty: Sexuality and Masquerade in Eighteenth-Century England," in G. S. Rous-

Only two masquerade balls were held in the winter of 1808. Before Epervil could carry out his plan to hold a series of three, the Philadelphia representative to the House of Representatives rushed the antimasquerade law through the legislature. The opponents of masquerades clearly saw them as designed to induce vice. The *United States Gazette* praised Representative Sergeant for his action "to put a stop to a species of amusement which . . . if successful could not be otherwise than very injurious to the public morals." Quoting from the *Journal of the House,* the newspaper indicted masquerades as "obviously demoralizing and injurious." When the Pennsylvania legislators outlawed all masked dances, they were acting on their belief that masquerades facilitated illicit, even anonymous, sexual liaisons, and were attempting to close one avenue of the trade in sex commerce.[28]

Philadelphia experienced a slight surge in arrests for prostitution in 1810 and 1811, when arrests rose to just more than sixty a year, from an average of twenty-two a year in the preceding five years. But, after 1811, the rate of arrests dropped back down to about thirty a year (Table 21). In the winter and spring of 1811–1812 the constables from Southwark tried a new tactic to discourage the trade. With the Guardians of the Poor, they attempted to force prostitutes who sought medical treatment in the almshouse to turn against their bawdyhouse madams, and solve their problem of a lack of witnesses to prosecute the madams. They would coerce prostitutes suffering with venereal disease into identifying their bawdyhouse keepers and testifying against them in court as a condition of admission into the almshouse. Establishing one's place of residence was part of all almshouse admission interviews. So from December 1811 through the following fall the women who came to the almshouse from bawdyhouses were required to promise to testify that they had contracted their venereal disease in the said establishment. By this means the constables and guardians hoped to establish evidence of illicit sex commerce without bringing unwilling male customers into court.

Eleanor Fury was the first woman to be given this ultimatum when she

---

seau and Roy Porter, eds., *Sexual Underworlds of the Enlightenment* (Manchester, 1987), 156–180; Gilfoyle, *City of Eros,* 232–235; *Aurora General Advertiser* (Philadelphia), Feb. 2, 1808 (see also Jan. 22, 28, 30, Feb. 4, 1808).

28. *United States Gazette* (Philadelphia), Jan. 30, 1808; *Poulson's American Daily Advertiser,* Jan. 30, 1808; *Journal of the Eighteenth House of Representatives of the Commonwealth of Pennsylvania* (Lancaster, [1807–1808]), Jan. 28, 1808, 319. The bill passed the House on February 3, and the last publicly advertised masquerade ball was held on February 4. The governor approved the law on February 15.

returned to the almshouse for treatment of her chronic venereal disease in December 1811. Eleanor readily admitted she lived at Mrs. Doyle's "house of ill fame" on Fifth Street between Shippen and South Streets. But, when she refused to become an informer, she was discharged the next day. As the alms-house log read, "Discharged, Elenor Fury (or Terry) in consequence of her refusing to give evidence against a person with whom she lived, for keeping a house of ill fame." News of her experiences must have traveled quickly to the women involved in sex commerce in Southwark, because no other women took the same stance. Instead, each of the women admitted from bawdy-houses during the next year agreed, before admission, to stand as witness against her former bawdyhouse keeper. When, for instance, Elizabeth Saunders was admitted on January 7, 1812, her admission entry stated, "She is willing to be qualified that she got it at the house of Ann Williams a place of ill fame, that she lived in said house about 2 months, and desirous to have her indicted for keeping a bawdyhouse." Two days later Harriot McCoombs's admission entry also asserted, "She is willing to qualify that she got the dis-order at Eliza Aldbergers in Shippen street between Forth and Fifth, who keeps a Bawdy House."[29]

This campaign was short lived and not very effective. The constables and guardians did succeed in extracting promises from eighteen women to turn informant, but the prosecutions never materialized. Only one of the madams named was ever arrested, and she was released from prison before her trial, on the day that her informant left the almshouse for the Magdalen Asy-lum, thereby freeing the state's witness from the almshouse. Three days after Mary Ann Mann swore that she had contracted venereal disease in Hannah Hughes's bawdyhouse, Hughes was arrested on a charge of keeping a disor-derly bawdyhouse. But on the same day that Mary Ann was discharged from the almshouse into the custody of the Magdalen Society, Hughes was released from jail, with the charges dropped. Hughes's one-month stay in jail was the closest thing to success this attempt at policing bawdyhouses ever had, and Hughes had probably been an easy target. One year after her arrest she entered the almshouse herself, an aging casualty of the trade in sex commerce, so "deranged" from the advanced stages of venereal disease that she could not articulate her life story to the admissions clerk. Business at Harriot Gambles's, Mrs. Doyle's, Mary Carr's, Eliza Aldberger's, Ann Williams's, Sarah Cooper's, Mary Ann Curley's, and Mrs. Duffy's houses went on as usual. Julian Nixon operated her brothel for at least six years without interference in the same

29. DOD, Dec. 3, 4, 1811, Jan. 7, 9, 1812.

house at 88 German Street and continued to do so after Ann Murphy so informed the Southwark Guardians of the Poor.[30]

The men of Philadelphia were of divided opinions on the place of prostitution in the city and the appropriate responses to it. The evangelical reformers of the Magdalen Society probably objected to forcing diseased prostitutes to turn witness against their former colleagues as a condition of receiving medical treatment. That they facilitated Mary Ann Mann's transfer from the almshouse to the Magdalen Asylum at the expense of the prosecution of Hannah Hughes suggests this was so. The failure of the prosecutions for the other seventeen bawdyhouse keepers must have been due in part to a reluctance by members of the judiciary to carry out the coercive plan of the Southwark officials. Whether this was due to some sense of fairness and justice or to their own interest in ignoring the trade is not clear. Some of the almshouse prostitutes almost certainly reneged on their pledges when their course of treatment was complete. By 1811 some middle-class public servants, constables, and guardians were willing to single out and punish the women who operated at the lower levels of the trade. But their actions and sentiments were not widely shared by others. Prostitution, in the sexual system of the early nineteenth century, had become an important symbol of male virility and male sexual prerogatives, and many men of middle and elite economic standing had a personal interest in it. Despite these sporadic attempts at policing prostitution, most of those engaged in sex commerce were not seriously restrained by the law during the early nineteenth century. Bawdyhouses remained a presence in most Philadelphia neighborhoods during the first decades of the century (see Map 2).[31]

The uses of the law during this period, however, did visibly mark the sexual behavior of the women of the streets, usually of the lower classes, as criminal. Of all the men and women who participated in the expansive sexual culture of

30. On Mann and Hughes: DOD, Mar. 23, Apr. 27, 1812; PFT, Mar. 26, 1812; MSM, May 5, Sept. 1, 1812. On brothels: DOD, Oct. 11, Dec. 3, 14, 1811, Jan. 7, Feb. 13, May 28, June 29, Oct. 23, 1812. Court moves to not prosecute: PFT, June 3, 1806; MCD, June 2, 1806. Julian Nixon: DOD, Apr. 4, Sept. 23, 1812.

31. During the 1820s bawdyhouse arrests almost doubled, though the numbers remained small: from an annual rate of 15 in 1805–1814 to 28.5 in 1821–1824. The population increased by 38 percent, from roughly 105,000 in 1815 to 145,000 in 1825. Not until the mid-1830s and into the 1840s did prostitution come under serious attack. For the 1830s and 1840s, see Carlisle, "Prostitutes and Their Reformers," chaps. 3, 5. The forty-two bawdyhouses plotted on Map 2 are only those whose exact location could be established. Each was a unique establishment run by a different woman.

DELAWARE

MAP 2. *Philadelphia Bawdyhouses, 1805–1814. By Claudia Lyons*

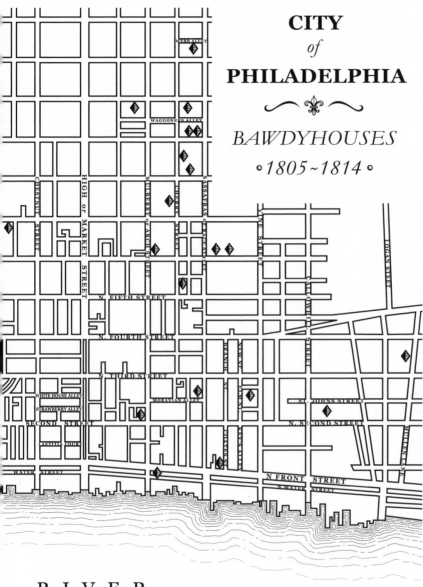

CITY
of
PHILADELPHIA
BAWDYHOUSES
∘*1805~1814*∘

WEBB ALLEY

WAGGONER'S ALLEY

CHESTNUT STREET

HIGH OR MARKET STREET

MULBERRY OR ARCH STREET

CHERRY STREET

SASSAFRAS OR RACE STREET

N. SIXTH STREET

CALLOWHILL STREET

LOGAN STREET

N. FIFTH STREET

N. FOURTH STREET

N. THIRD STREET

WHITE HOUSE ALLEY

STRAWBERRY ALLEY

SECOND STREET

MORAVIAN ALLEY

ST. JOHNS STREET

N. SECOND STREET

MULBERRY STREET

LAETITIA COURT

WATER STREET

N FRONT STREET

N. WATER STREET

RIVER

A Scale of 2000 Feet

100   500   1000   1500   2000

the city, it was these women who were seen being carted off to jail by the watchmen. This use of the law was one way middle-class public officials constructed an oppositional sexuality of the "other" and enhanced the association of nonmarital sexuality, or licentious sexuality, with the rabble.

By 1810 the environment in which women of the trade operated had changed. The images of prostitution that surrounded them undermined their independence and agency. The amorphous legal system left the enforcement of the laws up to the discretion of the night watchmen and city magistrates. When these men policed prostitution, they focused on the women of the lower classes, reinforcing the cultural associations of class and sexuality. Thus cultural assumptions became social reality.

Even the reformers began to lose their conviction that all women were redeemable. Beginning in 1810 the Magdalen Society turned away from the experienced prostitute as the object of its reform efforts. The women admitted to the Asylum after July 1810 were younger and less experienced than those the society had worked with in the past. The median age of the Asylum inmates admitted before August 1810 was twenty-one and one-half years; after that date it dropped to nineteen; the inmate population grew younger and younger (see Figure 1). More important, the sexual experiences of those admitted changed dramatically. After July 1810 only four women were admitted who had engaged in prostitution for longer than a year. The majority of Magdalens were recently fallen women, who came to the Asylum within a few months of their initial sexual experience. Before August 1810, 37.5 percent of the inmates were recently fallen, but after that date 73.5 percent were recent initiates to sexual experience (see Figure 2).[32]

The Asylum no longer took women like Mary Charleton, who was seven years in the trade. After 1809 the Magdalen Society never admitted another woman from the city prison. Now it brought in women such as Catharine Croneman and Ann McKinzey. Catharine entered the Asylum in October 1810 when she was nineteen. Born and raised in Philadelphia, she was bound out as an adolescent to a family in Bucks County. When she returned to Philadelphia, she was "Seduced by a young man (whom she says was the only one she ever had Criminal connnexion with) she thereby became diseased and was sent to the Almshouse." Ann McKinzey had more sexual experience than Catharine, but she too made only a short trip into the world of illicit sex. Ann had lived in Philadelphia for four years, making her living at service, when she was

32. Information was available for 58 (or 76 percent) of the inmates. Before August 1810, 9 of 24 were recently fallen, and, after that date, 25 of 34 were.

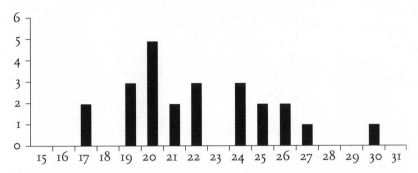

1807–July 1810

(25 Women: Median Age 21.5)

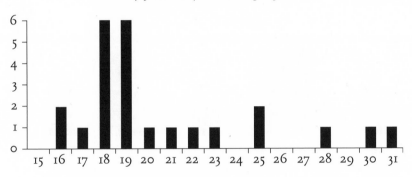

August 1810–December 1812

(25 Women) Median Age 19

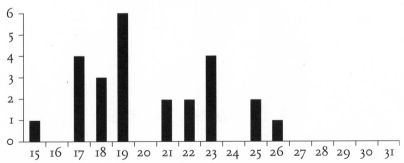

January 1813–December 1814

(26 Women) Median Age 19

FIGURE I. *Age of Magdalen Society Inmates Entering the Asylum.*
Note: *Information was unavailable for 3 of the inmates, 1 from each time period.*
Source: *MSM.*

1807–July 1810

(25 Women)

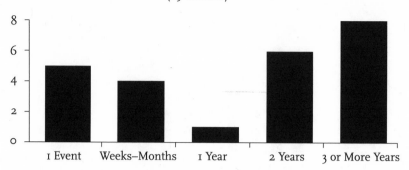

August 1810–December 1812

(25 Women)

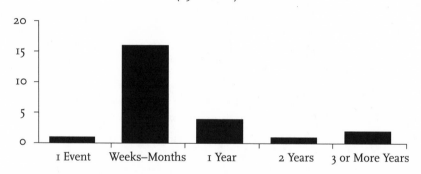

January 1813–December 1814

(26 Women)

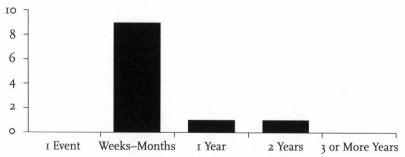

FIGURE 2. *Sexual Histories of Magdalen Society Inmates before Entering the Asylum.*
Note: *Information unavailable: 1807–1810, 1 inmate; August 1810–December 1812,*
1 inmate; January 1813–December 1814, 15 inmates.

"seduced." Ten weeks after her initial experience she "entered into a House of Ill fame, where she stayed about two weeks." While there she wrote to Bishop William White, the president of the society. She expressed "the danger she found herself in" and her fear of a future of "ruin" and was admitted to the Asylum in July 1812.[33]

The shift in the targets of reform was accompanied by an intensified emphasis on moral and sexual weakness as the cause of a woman's turn toward prostitution. While the reformers' explanations of the causes of prostitution had always highlighted moral character, that now became the sole cause. The economic reasons behind prostitution all but disappeared from the discourse on prostitution and reform. The grim economic realities of poor wages and poverty were articulated only by the rare advocate of the female working class, like Mathew Carey. This narrowing of the discourse on prostitution further obscured the realities of working women's lives, including prostitutes', and removed their experiences from the purview of the public constructions of gender and sexuality.[34]

Many of the Asylum inmates in these later years would hardly qualify as prostitutes by an eighteenth-century or modern definition. They had established sexual relations outside marriage, usually with their first sexual partner. The path back to respectability was certainly shorter under such circumstances. But the shift in the Magdalen Society's targets of reform was of greater significance than that. It was a shift away from redemption and toward prevention. By admitting women who had only just stepped off the path of virtue, the society hoped to prevent their fall into serious prostitution: the Magdalen Society had thus abandoned the career prostitute. Within the circles of elite reformers, the prostitute now became an unredeemable member of the underclass—a member whose very existence now seemed in doubt as reformers co-opted the language of seduction and prostitution to describe heart-

33. The last woman admitted from the prison was Magdalen No. 18, Susan Robeson, in May 1809 (MSM, Oct. 6, 1810). Catharine Croneman remained in the Asylum for ten months and then was placed out to service with a respectable family (MSM, Oct. 6, 1810, Aug. 12, 1811). Ann McKinzey stayed two months in the Asylum and was placed at service in a respectable family in the city (MSM, July 7, Sept. 1, 1812).

34. [Mathew Carey], *Essays on The Public Charities of Philadelphia, Intended to Vindicate the Benevolent Societies of This City from the Charge of Encouraging Idleness, and to Place in Strong Relief, before an Enlightened Public, the Sufferings and Oppression under Which the Greater Part of the Females Labour, Who Depend on Their Industry for a Support for Themselves and Their Children* (1828), 4th ed. (Philadelphia, 1829); Carey, "Report on Female Wages," Mar. 25, 1829, in Carey, *Miscellaneous Essays* (Philadelphia, 1830).

broken, despoiled virgins. The board of managers were not the only important Philadelphians to adopt the language of prostitution to describe all forms of nonmarital sexuality. During the early 1820s court records also used the term "prostitution" to describe adultery and nonmarital cohabitation.[35]

The move to catagorize all forms of nonmarital sexuality as deviant by employing the language of prostitution corresponded to an increase in policing of nonmarital sexuality in medical discourse. Benjamin Rush in his nineteenth-century works on illness and madness reflects this same move, from variety within a range of possibilities to one simplified deviant understanding of overt sexuality. In his earlier works, in the 1780s and 1790s, Rush had described nonmarital sex as one of an interconnected constellation of vices that signified overindulgence in luxury and a failure to secure bodily restraint through the use of reason. But by 1812, when he published *Medical Inquiries and Observations, upon the Diseases of the Mind,* excessive sexual appetite had become a disease. In opening his chapter "Of the Morbid State of the Sexual Appetite," Rush wrote that the sexual appetite, "when excessive, becomes a disease both of the body and mind." Excessive sexual activity, such as "promiscuous intercourse with the female sex" or "onanism" (masturbation), would cause everything from seminal weakness and impotence to pulmonary consumption, dyspepsia, dimness of sight, vertigo, loss of memory, and death. To Rush and his peers, the sexual appetite that was not constrained had become a disease. Pathologizing overactive sexual desire contributed to the construction of male sexuality as out of control and to the move away from male responsibility for sexual activity. Overactive sexual desire was presented

35. The move away from the more-experienced prostitute was not precipitated by greater difficulty reforming these women. Those who eloped were evenly distributed between novices and experienced prostitutes. (From 1807 through July 1810, four novices and five experienced prostitutes eloped.) After the admission policies shifted toward novices, elopements continued apace. From August 1810 through December 1812, 32 percent of inmates eloped, and, from January 1813 through December 1814, 29 percent eloped. Carlisle found that elopements continued at about 30 percent from 1821 through 1836 ("Prostitutes and Their Reformers," 175).

On use of the language of prostitution, see, for example, PFT, Sept. 14, 1821, case of John Moore, where the adultery was described as "living in a state of Prostitution"; PFT, Mar. 10, 1823, and MCD, Mar. 25, 1823, case of Reason Powell, "being guilty of fornication he being in a state of prostitution with a certain Rachel Cassidy he being a single man and she a married woman"; PFT, Apr. 11, 1823, case of Benjamin Morris, whose wife charged him with adultery and bastardy with the words "keeping a prostitute by whom he has had a child."

as a male disease, and its cure required more than moral guidance. It required outside help—medical treatment—to overcome, as such control of sexual desire moved away from individual responsibility.[36]

Rush also stressed that overactive sexuality could lead to inappropriate cross-class sexual liaisons. When men did not marry, sexual desire would lead them to forget social divisions and consort with women of the lower classes:

[handwritten margin note: Need to maintain class divisions]

> While men live by themselves (says La Bruere) they do not view washer-women or oyster-wenches as washerwomen or oyster wenches, but simply as women.[37]

Morbid sexual appetite was also responsible for men's marrying below their class and creating unseemly, unequal matches. Maintaining class divisions was a concern for men like Rush.

Once reformers, law enforcement, and the courts adopted the language of prostitution to describe courtship intimacy and lovers' cohabitation, the behavior and lives of women who engaged in sex commerce as a career became unintelligible and inexcusable. Their lives were now shut out of the dominant discourse on sexuality and excluded from the agenda of reform. They belonged to the underclass of unredeemables who practiced a sexuality of the "other." The bifurcation of sexuality into two opposing sexualities had been accepted by the benevolent reformers; the city's prostitutes would now belong unequivocally to the rabble.

36. Benjamin Rush, "An Address to the Ministers of the Gospel of Every Denomination in the United States, upon Subjects Interesting to Morals, June 12, 1788," in Rush, *Essays, Literary, Moral, and Philsophical* (Philadelphia, 1798), 114–124; Benjamin Rush, *Medical Inquiries and Observations, upon the Diseases of the Mind* (Philadelphia, 1812), 347.

37. Rush, *Medical Inquiries*, 351–352.

CHAPTER 8

Through Our Children

Bastardy Comes under Attack

By 1810, Philadelphia's middling classes had begun to believe that women alone were responsible for sexual transgression and that lower-class and African-American women were especially licentious. The policies and practices of the Guardians of the Poor demonstrate that they supported such attitudes and had come to believe that lower-class women bore primary responsibility for their situations. Like the upper-class benevolent reformers who reshaped attitudes toward prostitution and prostitutes, the Guardians' policies toward the least-advantaged women of Philadelphia shifted the burden of bearing a bastard child to its mother. Also by 1810, the Guardians were using the almshouse as a coercive tool against poor women pregnant with illegitimate offspring. Singling out African-American women for special ill-treatment, they soon expanded the reach of punitive measures. This move was significant for several reasons. First, it created greater hardship for women already in a difficult situation. Second, it initiated the schema whereby the Guardians of the Poor used the power of the state to drive a wedge between women who engaged in nonmarital sexual behavior and women who confined their sexual experiences to courtship and marriage. Finally, these new policies reveal that a growing segment of middle-class Philadelphians embraced the cultural reconstruction of female sexuality and concern about illicit sexual habits among the lower classes and free African-Americans.

The Guardians of the Poor who implemented new policies were drawn primarily from the emerging urban middle classes. Between 1800 and 1828, when the welfare system was fundamentally restructured, two-thirds of the Guardians were well-established artisans or proprietors of small businesses. For most, community service as Guardians was the only public service they would take on during their lives. The remaining third were men of more substantial means, drawn from the city's economic elite, who played leading roles in the philanthropic and political life of the city. The majority of the Guardians in the early nineteenth century continued to favor giving each neighborhood Guardian the flexibility to respond to the needs of the poor under his care, such as giving poor relief in the form of a regular financial supplement, material aid in food or fuel, or permission to enter the alms-house. During the early nineteenth century the majority faction among the Guardians fought off attempts to centralize control of poor relief and elimi-nate out-relief. But the Board of Guardians' policies on bastardy demonstrate that, despite their commitment to the needs of the poor, they had begun to see bastardy, in some instances, as a special case.[1]

The growing animosity of many middle-class and lower-class whites to-ward the city's free blacks had set the stage for the punitive policies the Guard-ians would develop during the early nineteenth century. By the early 1800s white Philadelphians were expressing their rejection of racial equality. In 1805 a group of white citizens chased the assembled people of color from the Fourth of July celebration in front of Independence Hall, excluding the city's blacks from the annual celebrations and ending the biracial celebration of Independence. That was also the year Philadelphians first entertained legisla-tive proposals to close the state to the immigration of free blacks. Fears that free blacks represented a potential enemy within the community were accen-tuated by the success of former slaves in Saint Domingue in establishing the republic of Haiti in 1804 and, later, by the concerns raised by the War of 1812. Exclusionary legislation was proposed again in 1806 and 1807, and renewed attempts were pressed in 1813–1814. In 1813 a bill—a "black code"—was intro-duced to require registration of all people of color and to provide for the sale of any black convicted of a crime. Philadelphia's representatives in the senate had supported closing the borders, and the city's mayor and aldermen supported the 1813 bill. Although none of these bills was successful, they did express the increased racial tensions in the city.[2]

Morality and sexual behavior were often at the forefront of the attacks on the city's African-Americans and in the responses by African-American lead-

1. Priscilla Clement found that Guardians from the middle classes had occupations such as "sea captains, editors, owners of small manufacturing and business enter-prises, and craftsmen" (*Welfare and the Poor in the Nineteenth-Century City: Philadelphia, 1800–1854* [Rutherford, N.J., 1985], 42–43). Clement analyzes the politics of poor relief and correctly presents the majority faction's interest in humanitarian aid to the poor during the first two decades of the nineteenth century. During this period the Guard-ians consistently were able to increase aid to the poor because of the increasing tax base available due to Philadelphia's growth. She does not examine their policies regarding the care of illegitimate children. See chap. 2, "Evolution of the Public-Welfare System," 38–66.

2. Gary B. Nash, *Forging Freedom: The Formation of Philadelphia's Black Community, 1720–1840* (Cambridge, Mass., 1988), 176–183.

ers. Cross-racial sexual relations took on heated political importance, as fear of aggressive sexual behavior of African-American men was used to advocate racial segregation. In 1805 Thomas Branagan promoted racialized notions of sexuality to advance his plan to remove all blacks to the Louisiana Territory. An abolitionist and a segregationist, Branagan made his case by depicting the special horror of cross-racial sexual relations. In his 1805 pamphlet against the slave trade, *Serious Remonstrances,* Branagan asserted that free black men in Philadelphia frequently debauched white women. He claimed that free blacks released from slavery sought sex with white women and used every means, from rape of servant girls to "inveigl[ing] white women in to the bonds of matrimony," to attain it. He called upon the white men of the lower classes to imagine their daughters "who have been deluded, and are now married to negroes, living in little smoking huts, despised and scorned by both blacks, and whites," and to take preventive action by ending slavery and establishing a separate black state in the West.[3]

While men like Branagan publicized all cross-racial unions as illicit, other Philadelphians began to police cross-racial sex more aggressively. By the early 1800s arrest records display heightened indignation at sex between whites and blacks. In 1802 Rachel White's transgression was described as "keeping a bawdy house by letting black men and white women go to bed together," and Elizabeth Flanagan's as "frequently going to Bed with different black men." White women were arrested for failing to be the racial gatekeepers of sexual segregation. When Margaret Fisher was arrested in 1803, her crime was "being found in bed with a negro man and with a white man at another [time]." Like White and Flanagan, she had permitted the mixing of races. Rosanna Grovis, an African-American, was also arrested for racial mixing, but her "crime" was "keeping Girls of Different Colours" in her bawdyhouse. The use of racialized sexual slander also suggests that cross-racial sexual behavior had become particularly notorious for the city's whites. Vitriolic diatribe insulting a woman's sexual virtue was the standard slander made by the city's women. But, when these verbal assaults moved from general claims of "whore" or "strumpet" to specific assertions of sexual behavior across the color line, they were particularly insulting. Thus, Diana Smith's declaration that Harriet Mourey "was kept by a negro, thereby meaning," according to the court records, that "Harriet lived in habits of fornication with a negro," warranted Harriet's suit for damages. Susannah Rees meant to suggest Susannah Karaher's utter moral

3. Thomas Branagan, *Serious Remonstrances, Addressed to the Citizens of the Northern States . . .* (Philadelphia, 1805), 101–104.

and sexual bankruptcy when she called the latter "a negro whore, you had three negro bastards and I can prove it," and it was the base nature of Margaret Taylor's whoring that William Esher implied when he called her "an infernal ordinary whore, a whore to every one that runs the Street both black and white."[4]

The leaders within the African-American community sought to counteract such interpretations of racialized sexuality by encouraging adherence to marital monogamous sexuality. Men such as the Reverend Richard Allen and Absalom Jones understood that sexual behavior and deportment would be central to their struggle for racial justice. From the first years of freedom, religious leaders worked to cultivate rigorous moral standards. They supported the efforts of the Pennsylvania Abolition Society to counsel and instruct free blacks in behavior proper for freedmen and women. Religious practice, education, economic industriousness, and frugality were always encouraged, but so too were cultivating a respectful public demeanor, establishing legal marriages, and avoiding creating disturbances. Broadsides distributed by the society instructed the city's blacks to "avoid frolicking and amusements," because "they beget habits of dissipation and vice, and thus expose you to deserved reproach amongst your white neighbors."[5]

4. See, for example, Barbara Clifford's arrest for "being caught in Bed with a Black man" and her partner Samuel Chaney's arrest for "being caught in Bed with Barbara Clifford (a white women)," PFT, Mar. 28, 1801; PFT, May 31, 1802, Rachel White; PFT, May 31, 1802, Elizabeth Flanagan; PFT, Mar. 27, 1803, Margaret Fisher; PFT, Sept. 10, 1804, Rosanna Grovis; Narratives in Slander, Philadelphia District Court, *William and Diana Smith vs. Harriet Mourey*, Sept. 12, 1814; *George and Susannah Rees vs. Samuel and Susannah Karaher*, September 1814; *William Esher vs. John and Margaret Taylor*, June 1816. Records for slander do not exist for Philadelphia before the 1810s, so a comparison with the eighteenth century is not possible.

5. See the rules of governance established by the Pennsylvania Abolition Society, Committee for Improving the Condition of Free Blacks: Minutes, Committee for Improving the Condition of Free Blacks, PAS, Apr. 8, 1790, HSP; Nash, *Forging Freedom*, 176–177; Pennsylvania Abolition Society, *To the Free Africans and Other Free People of Color* (Philadelphia, 1796), broadside, LCP. The attacks on frolics in crime pamphlets aimed at the city's African-Americans were begun in 1797 with the publication of the pamphlet "confession" of Abraham Johnstone, a black man, executed for murder in New Jersey. Frolics and other public amusements led to "every species of licentiousness, debouchery and excess." The only crime Johnstone confessed, as he faced the hangman, was "a too great lust after strange women." *The Address of Abraham Johnstone, a Black Man . . . to the People of Colour* (Philadelphia, 1797), 28–29, 40, 43–45.

In 1808 Allen elaborated on these sentiments, drawing on the murder trial and execution of John Joyce and Peter Matthias to attack public licentiousness. As racial tensions increased and cross-racial sexual practices were cited by some whites to confirm their beliefs in the moral depravity of the city's African-Americans, Allen hoped to use the public focus on Joyce and Matthias to repudiate loose sexual habits associated with public amusements. The motive for this murder was theft, and neither Joyce nor Matthias had lived a particularly notorious life, but for Allen the sexual morality of the men (and of Philadelphia's community of free blacks) was linked to their downfall. John Joyce's life story revealed fairly common but, to Allen, objectionable personal circumstances: fathering two illegitimate children by different women, losing his wife to another man while he was at sea, and soliciting sex from women "of loose character." Peter Matthias seems to have been guilty only of running in bad company and frequenting dances where he sought his livelihood as a fiddle player. In Allen's prefatory "Address to the Public and People of Colour," he implored "People of Colour" to see the chain of sin that led to dishonor and damnation:

> See the tendency of dishonesty and lust, of drunkenness and stealing, in the murder, an account of which is subjoined. See the tendency of midnight dances and frolics. While the lustful dance is delighting thee, forget not, that "for all these things God will bring thee into judgment."

Allen instructed his fellow black Philadelphians to "fly for thy life from the chambers of the harlot" and break off their "guilty assignation[s]." "God," he declared, "would rather see me in rags, in the house of God than in the gayest attire in a riotous tavern, or in the chambers of pollution." Sexual morality and reform of public licentiousness were fundamental concerns for the city's African-American leaders.[6]

Many of Philadelphia's free African-Americans did join churches, marry, remain constant to their spouses, and live sober, industrious lives. They built African-American churches, schools, self-help benevolent organizations, and businesses. The commitment of these Philadelphians to moral rectitude is reflected in strict adherence to sexual propriety in the disciplinary records of the African Methodist Episcopal Church of Philadelphia. But the continued existence of slave status for some, semifree status of prolonged indentures for others, and fragile economic conditions of many made it difficult to at-

6. [Richard Allen], *Confession of John Joyce ... with an Address to the Public, and People of Colour ...* (Philadelphia, 1808), 4–6.

tain the standards of the romantic, monogamous, patriarchal, marital family. Many were women like Lenah, a free woman of color who worked as a domestic cook and, when she became ill, became a public charge, because her husband was a slave in the same household. The normal rhythms of family life could look deviant and licentious when women married to slaves, such as Patience Amos, had to seek shelter in the almshouse to give birth to their legitimate children. Free women of color were often compelled to become as economically self-sufficient as possible, because husbands had to follow their work, often to sea. Sannet Legrane, a mulatto woman born in Cape Francis who had come to Philadelphia as the domestic slave of a French colonial fleeing Saint Domingue, supported herself for nine years after her husband had left for Haiti upon learning of the new republic. Sannet assumed he was dead when he failed to return or send for her. But, for these Philadelphians, establishing personal lives that whites would view as moral, chaste, and virtuous was an uphill battle. Others rejected the primacy of such a task and the sexual constraints advocated by leaders such as the Reverend Richard Allen. For all Philadelphians the connections between race and sexual morality were of growing importance as struggles to negotiate the place of African-Americans intensified.[7]

In the nineteenth century the Board of Guardians' administration of bastardy became an important place to work out the community interest in the politics of nonmarital sexual behavior. During the first two decades a minority faction among the Guardians sought, unsuccessfully, to restrict the Guardians' role in adjudication and administration of bastardy, periodically proposing changes that would undermine the aid given to women pregnant outside permanent relationships. Thus, by 1805 some Guardians were objecting to their role in facilitating the support of illegitimate children. In August 1805, for instance, two members proposed terminating the Guardians' role in procuring paid nurses to take in illegitimate infants given up by their mothers but paid for by their fathers: "Whereas it appears improper for the Guardians of the Poor to pay for the nursing of bastard children in bonded cases, Therefore resolved . . . that no Guardian shall provid for the maintenance of any such child or children, except when the father or mother or bail refuse or neglect to provide for

7. A.M.E. Church members vigilantly protected and policed the sexual reputations of their brethren. See Minutes and Trial Book, Mother Bethel African Methodist Episcopal Church, 1822–1835, HSP microfilm; DOD: Lenah, Dec. 20, 1793; Patience Amos, May 3, 1805; Sannet Legrane, Oct. 12, 1813. See also DOD: Kesia Robertson, Oct. 7, 1813; Elizabeth Anderson, May 22, 1805; Dianna Young, Dec. 21, 1813.

such child or children." The proposal went on to say that in cases of total lack of support the Guardians could set up nursing arrangements just as they did in commuted cases. This proposal was voted down.[8]

The majority in 1805 still sympathized with the woman bearing a child without a marital partner and sought to ease her financial burden. And in 1808, for example, the board directed a committee to meet with the attorney general to persuade him to stop his recent practice of producing indictments for criminal fornication and bastardy against the mothers of bastard children. One week later the board met with the attorney general and "received his assurance that he would enter nolle pros. [not prosecute] in the indictment for fornication agreeable to the wishes of the Board." Here the Guardians intervened to keep women pregnant with illegitimate children from being prosecuted and fined for bastardy in court. Avoiding court action helped everyone involved: the mother stayed out of court and was not saddled with a fine she could often not afford to pay; the fathers, too, avoided being named in open court and being fined; and the Guardians avoided one more financial charge that they would have to extract from the reputed father.[9]

For most women, mandatory paternal child support through the Guardians' administration of bastardy continued to facilitate paternal responsibility. In the ten years 1805–1814, three-quarters of the more than two thousand bastardy cases processed through the Guardians were supervised cases where the fathers had the means to provide support and did so. In the remaining one-quarter the mother turned to the almshouse. Most of these women used the almshouse to give birth, just as they had in the 1790s. In four-fifths of the almshouse cases in both decades the mothers entered the almshouse pregnant and stayed there until they had recovered and were ready to resume their working lives (Table 14). The same proportions of women, one-fifth, used the almshouse only temporarily in both eras. But the nature of their use had changed dramatically. Whereas most women who used the almshouse temporarily in the 1790s entered of their own free will and left by choice before the birth of their child, those in 1805–1814 were coerced into it.

This coercive use of the almshouse only increased over time. In the 1790s, 13 percent of the mothers who entered it left before giving birth by establishing

8. GPM, Aug. 6, 1805. In commuted cases the father had discharged his financial obligation by providing the whole sum necessary for the five to seven years of support mandated by law.

9. GPM, May 17, 23, 1808.

better options for themselves. Their families or friends came to their aid, or they simply chose to make do on their own, and they eloped over the fence. In the period 1805–1814, only 3 percent of the almshouse cases had such outcomes, and by the early 1820s none of them did. Instead, the Guardians' new policies created other situations that brought women into the almshouse on a temporary basis. In 1812 and 1813 most (89 percent) of the women who used the almshouse temporarily during their illegitimate pregnancy were placed there to coerce them into cooperating with Guardians' administration of their cases. Half of these women were admitted after they had sworn an oath of paternity naming a father but before his bond had been secured, and they were released once the father's bond had been taken. In the past poor pregnant women would have typically been advanced a small financial stipend to tide them over until the father's support was secured and the funds could be recouped by the Guardians. By the early 1810s some of these women were forced into the almshouse by lack of financial aid from the Guardians. Poor women pregnant with children fathered by men of means were beginning to be treated less equitably. The other new use of the almshouse was as a holding facility for women who were not legal residents of the city, pregnant with bastard babes. The Guardians were working more assiduously to ferret out nonresidents from their bastardy child support system. The almshouse of the 1790s had sometimes been used by "New Jersey Girls," who crossed the river to give birth. In the early nineteenth century, women who had not established legal residency by residing one year in the city before their lying-in could expect to be forced into the almshouse and then relocated to their place of legal settlement, even when the father of the child was a Philadelphian and could have been called upon to provide mandatory support. Through these policies poor women, once able to rely on the financial good standing of their non-marital sexual partner to support them in their confinement, were increasingly lumped together with the almshouse poor population. These new policies indicate a new public policy that would over time coalesce the two populations of women bearing bastard babies into one.

The Guardians of the Poor also began to target African-American women for special treatment, striving to keep this group out of the almshouse when they were pregnant with an illegitimate child. In 1810 the board passed a resolution prohibiting the admission of

> any Manumitted or Indented female servant that is pregnant, unless the
> Master or Mistress of such servant agrees to pay the lying in expenses and

also engages that the said servant shall bring with her out of the said house when she leaves it, such child or Children of which she may be delivered of, if living.

If the case was bonded by the father of the child, the rule would not apply. In the early nineteenth century the majority of indentured servants were free blacks who were required by law to undergo prolonged indentured service as a condition of manumission. Reworded later to obscure its race-based criteria, the Guardians' intended targets had been stated clearly in their original proposal:

> Resolved that no Guardian of the Poor shall give an Order for admittance into the Almshouse (unless by special Order of this Board) of any Coloured servant that is pregnant unless the Master of such servant agrees to pay the lying in expenses and also engages that the said servant will bring with her out of the house when discharged such Child or Children of which she may have been delivered of, if living.

By this time the Guardians were careful to avoid overtly pejorative language when undertaking formal business. But they were more likely than in the past to enact policies that discriminated against women of color and poor women.[10]

The Guardians' greater concern with providing almshouse aid only to city residents and their interest in establishing a legally responsible solvent party to pay for that care led them to carefully document the life histories of the women admitted to the almshouse. We can learn something about the most-disadvantaged women who bore bastard children in the early nineteenth century in these almshouse records. In many ways their lives did not resemble the cultural images promoted in popular print of nonmarital sexual experiences in the early nineteenth century. Unlike the fictitious seduced young women of popular print, the women admitted to the almshouse ranged in age from fourteen to fifty when they gave birth. Most were not engaged in the youthful folly of despoiled innocence but were fairly evenly distributed throughout all stages of reproductive life (see Table 23). Nor were they primarily recent arrivals to Philadelphia (less than one year's residence) falling into the clutches of the life of infamy in the corrupt city; only about one-quarter (24 percent) of them could fit this description of the friendless young woman new to the city. Many of these women might have come to Philadelphia already pregnant and in search of work and anonymity. Another one-quarter (28 percent) who entered the almshouse were longtime city residents who had either been born

10. GPM, Aug. 28, Sept. 4, 1810.

TABLE 23. *Almshouse Mothers: Age at Birth of Illegitimate Child, 1805–1814*

Age	All Women	White Women	Women of Color
14–19	22%	15%	40%
20–24	37	40	31
25–29	22	24	18
30–34	11	12	9
35–50	7	9	2

Note: Information on the mother's age was available in 76% of the cases.

Source: DOD; Guardians of the Poor, Almshouse Hospital Registry of Births.

there or lived there for at least a decade. They would have been part of commu-nity networks of family, friends, and working colleagues. Their poverty, not their friendlessness, sent them to the almshouse to bear their bastard chil-dren. One-third (34 percent) had resided in the city between one and nine years, and the remaining one-seventh (14 percent) were legal residents whose length of residency is unknown. As one would expect in this seaport urban center, the majority of the women were born outside the city. Thus, almost half (45 percent) were born in the region surrounding Philadelphia, in Delaware, New Jersey, and Pennsylvania; one-quarter (23 percent) had been born in Philadelphia; and the rest were evenly split between those born abroad and those born in the more distant eastern United States. The poor women who became mothers of illegitimate children were much like their mobile neigh-bors: they were part of the constant influx of people that made up the popula-tion of this rapidly expanding city.[11]

Most of the women who entered the almshouse pregnant with a bastard child between 1805 and 1814 were white (76 percent); 24 percent were of color, most of them pregnant with children fathered by black men. Like the black community at large, many of the women of color in the almshouse had been residents of the city for a shorter period than the white women. Many, 40 per-cent, had been legal residents for less than ten years, and only 21 percent (against 31 percent for whites) were long-term residents, either born in Phila-delphia or resident for at least ten years. Fewer black or mulatto women who were not legal residents entered (16 percent, versus 27 percent for whites). This was almost certainly due to the Guardians' insistence on establishing a

11. Information on residency was available in 65 percent of the cases; information on mother's place of birth was recorded in 56 percent of the cases.

legally responsible party for as many women of color as possible, and to the women's interest in steering clear of the almshouse until they had established legal residence and thus the legal right to it. One can see the Guardians' greater vigilance in establishing financial responsibility among black women in the greater frequency with which women of color had named a reputed father upon admission to the almshouse. In 1805–1814, 42 percent of the white women had given the name of the father, but among African-American and mulatto women 64 percent had, which was recorded in their admission entry. They were women like Nancy Petterson, who gave clear details identifying the father. She was twenty-nine years old when she entered the almshouse in 1810 to give birth to a son. Born in Maryland, she had served her term of indenture in Philadelphia to a Mr. Rowan who lived in Chestnut Street, between Second and Third. She stated that Peter Stall, a black man, was the father of her child. Stall, she informed the Guardian, "sails in the Brig Good Friend, [of] captain Davis." At her confinement he was at sea, but the Guardians had obtained the Philadelphia address of the captain's wife, who could be prevailed upon to advance the Guardians a portion of Stall's wages to reimburse the city for Nancy's lying-in expenses. Nancy, however, did not wait in the almshouse to see whether her expenses would be reimbursed and she would be discharged. One month after she had given birth she eloped from the almshouse with little Isaiah clutched to her bosom. Even when the fathers were away from Philadelphia and unavailable to post bond, women of color were more likely to have established a financially responsible party to pay for their use of the almshouse. When Harriet Burnie, a twenty-year-old legal resident of the city, was admitted, it was her "Godmother" Madam John Jack who gave security that Harriet's expenses would be paid. Harriet had sworn her child to Bowman Trijon, who was then in the West Indies. Harriet's godmother could not accommodate her at her own residence, because she lived in a white man's household. But she could use her own financial resources to ensure that Harriet had medical care during childbirth and was free to leave the almshouse with her child after her recovery.[12]

The composite sketch of women of color who bore illegitimate children in the almshouse reveals they were more likely to be young than were white

12. In addition, 11 percent of whites and 24 percent of women of color were legal residents, but the exact period of residency is unknown. Only 3 percent of almshouse bastardy cases were cross-racial couples in the period 1805–1814. Information on residency was available in 72 percent of the cases of women of color. DOD: Nancy Petterson, Aug. 27, Sept. 18, Oct. 15, 1810; Harriet Burnie, Feb. 26, 1812.

women. Of the black and mulatto women, 40 percent were under twenty when they gave birth, compared with only 15 percent of the white mothers. In the antebellum South a similar fertility pattern existed of one early birth among slave women, which was culturally accepted by African-American slave communities. Philadelphia's women of color might have been operating in a similar cultural context, bearing a first child out of wedlock without social disapprobation. But, because the age at childbirth for most women of color bearing a bastard child was under twenty-five and, unlike with white women, fertility declined rapidly after age thirty, poverty and poor nutrition were also factors responsible for the compressed and younger age structure (Table 23).[13]

African-American women distinguished themselves in another way. By the 1820s they were much more likely to give their illegitimate child their own surname than were white women. Most women, white and black, named their child after the father. In 1805–1814, 68 percent did so, and, in 1822–1825, 65 percent did. These women asserted the child's claim on its father by giving it his name. But, interestingly, by the 1820s, those mothers who chose to give their child their own name were overwhelmingly women of color, at 74 percent. They probably had a strategic purpose. In a slave society children derived their status from their mother. By the 1820s most women of African descent in Philadelphia were free, and many had served out their compulsory indenture. By giving their child their own name they established beyond a doubt the child's lineage and its status as a free person.[14]

As the Guardians worked to more closely monitor the use of the almshouse and sought ways to recoup the expenses paid by the city for illegitimate births, the almshouse became less hospitable for the poor of the city. As we have seen, women were more vigorously interviewed to establish financial responsibility, and nonresidents were removed to their former homes. Admission of indentured servants, especially women of color, was tightly monitored. By 1810 more women were keeping themselves out of the almshouse until late in their pregnancy. In the 1790s, 41 percent of the expectant mothers entered sometime during the first seven months of their pregnancy. In 1805–1814, this

13. Herbert Gutman, *The Black Family in Slavery and Freedom, 1750–1925* (New York, 1976), 61–83. Of the women of color, 71 percent were under age twenty-five, compared to 55 percent of the white women; and only 11 percent were over thirty, compared to 21 percent of white women.

14. Information for this analysis of naming patterns was available in 61 percent of the cases in 1805–1814 and 65 percent of the cases in 1822–1825.

TABLE 24. *Bastardy Cases: Father's Class, 1822–1825*

Class	No.	Proportion
Poor	15	5%
Lower	129	43
Middle	104	35
Upper	49	16.5
Total	297	99.5

Notes: Class was established for 297 of the 957 cases.

These figures underestimate the number of men at both the lowest and highest end of the economic scale. When men commuted their cases by paying a onetime lump sum in the 1820s, their identities were rarely recorded. It is impossible to tell how many of the 217 nonalmshouse cases that omitted the father's name were commuted cases. Only men of the middle and elite classes had the financial resources to make such a payment.

Class was established by internal evidence of wealth and occupation in the Guardians of the Poor records and by establishing occupations through the city directories. Because the very poor rarely listed themselves there, identifying them relied on the Guardians' comments. While the guardians were acutely interested in their financial resources, one must assume that not all poor men were identified as such in the records.

Source: See Appendix, esp. "Bastardy Totals," Table A.2, and "Establishing Class."

number had dropped to 27 percent, and in the early 1820s it was only 22 percent. The almshouse was no longer a refuge where a poor pregnant woman could retreat from the hardships of poverty and recoup her strength. Despite the economic dislocation created by the War of 1812, women bearing bastard children spent less time in the almshouse than they had in the past.[15]

Despite the cultural assault on the meanings attached to nonmarital sexuality, the reform efforts initiated by upper-class moral reformers, law enforcement's focus on the sexual transgressions of the lower classes, and the middle-class Guardians' more stringent administration of bastardy among poor women, nonmarital sexuality continued to flourish in Philadelphia. By the decade 1805–1814, the number of bastardy cases documented through the

15. Information to establish the stage of pregnancy at admission to the almshouse existed in 49 percent of the 1790s cases, 32 percent of the cases in 1805–1814, and 46 percent of the cases in 1822–1825.

Guardians was three times what it had been in the 1790s, although the city's population had increased only by half. Thus the bastardy rate had doubled since the 1790s. Documented cases of bastardy reached their peak in this period when 6.6 percent of births were instances of bastardy adjudicated through the Guardians. During the early 1820s the incidence of bastardy remained higher than in the 1790s, although it had declined somewhat since the 1805–1814 era (Table 1).[16] Some of this increase was no doubt the result of the more vigilant pursuit of the parents of out-of-wedlock children, initiated by the Guardians during the late 1810s and early 1820s. Concerns over the increasing cost of supporting poor children led the Guardians to document cases of illegitimacy more carefully. Because Philadelphians were now more concerned about containing the costs of poor relief, we must cautiously interpret this increase in cases. Nevertheless, these figures demonstrate that Philadelphians continued to engage in nonmarital sexuality into the antebellum period and that the cultural assault on nonmarital sexuality had little effect on the behavior of those who participated in the expansive sexual culture of the city.[17]

Those who parented children out of wedlock in the 1820s were in most respects the same kinds of people who had done so earlier. The fathers were drawn from all classes, with roughly 50 percent from the middle and elite economic ranks and 50 percent from the lower classes (see Table 24). The racial composition of the group was close to that of the city as a whole, with slightly more than 14 percent of the cases involving African-Americans. As in

16. The database covering 1822–1825 was created from case files for all those appearing in court and guardians records (957 cases). The 1826 figure was derived from the Guardians of the Poor, board of managers' published reports (269 cases). The analysis that follows is based on the four-year sample 1822–1825 of 957 cases histories.

17. Throughout this period the Board of Guardians was continually passing resolutions requiring better record keeping by each Guardian, stipulating the exact information required and ordering that books be bought to keep such records. This endless reissuing of procedural orders suggests that actually getting each Guardian to keep complete records was a struggle during the 1810s. By the early 1820s, however, record keeping appears to have been well established. These books have survived and provide a comprehensive look at how this system functioned.

(The record books concerning bastardy were the board's general minutes book; each Guardian's pauper book, which listed his own pensioners; the Committee upon Bastardy's book; the solicitor's docket book, with his list of cases; and a separate Bond Book, which recorded bonds posted. Cases of bastardy in the almshouse were recorded in DOD and the almshouse birth register. Bastardy cases appear in each of these

the 1790s and 1810s, African-Americans were the most likely group to be sent to the almshouse to receive assistance.[18]

The mothers also represented all classes and segments of the female population, except the elite. Some were from the female working lower classes, women who were whitewashers and servants. A few of the mothers had more profitable occupations, including mantua and bonnet makers, and still others were widows with occupations such as boardinghouse keeper, milliner, florist, and grocer. Despite the range of occupational classes, the exact class composition of the mothers is impossible to determine. They were not, however, drawn primarily from the poor. Of the 957 women, only 213 are known to have given birth in the almshouse, where their names and the circumstances of their children's births were recorded in the birth register and admissions log. The almshouse medical ward was the only facility that admitted poor unmarried women for childbirth. Many of these women, 22 percent of the mothers of illegitimate children during this era, came from the ranks of the destitute. But the other 744 women had enough resources to stay out of the almshouse during their confinement.[19] Like the women from the earlier eras, those who bore illegitimate children in the 1820s began establishing the father's identity

------

sources, but any given case does not appear in each one. Some cases were kept relatively secret, appearing only in the bond book without ever being mentioned by the father's name in the general meeting minutes and not appearing in the bastardy committee books.)

18. In 1820 African-Americans comprised 10.7 percent of the city's population. From 1822 through 1825, 14.4 percent of the documented cases of bastardy involved African-Americans (138 cases). During the 1820s the overwhelming majority of cases involving people of color were between a black woman and a black man, at 13 percent. Only 1.5 percent were cross-racial cases, involving fourteen couples: five of African-American men and white women, and nine of African-American women and white men. Population figures are from the 1820 federal census as reported by Nash, *Forging Freedom*, table 5, 143. Nash notes that the census figure might have underrepresented African-American men because many of them were mariners and were often absent from the city. From 1822 through 1825, African-Americans comprised 32 percent of the almshouse cases but only 7.6 percent of the out-relief cases.

19. Information on occupations and class was available for only a few women, not enough to be statistically significant. The exact class breakdown remains unknown.

Restrictions on reimbursement for lying-in expenses during this era severely limited the ability of poor unmarried women to use public funds for lying-in expenses incurred outside the almshouse. These changes in procedures will be discussed below. Poor married women could turn to the Pennsylvania Hospital.

and securing mandatory child support before the birth of the child: in the out-relief cases where the timing of a the woman's request can be established, 73 percent did.[20]

While the biographical profile of the parents of illegitimate children in the 1820s remained the same, the cultural context had been radically altered. Bastardy had receded from the cultural landscape as prostitution came to dominate the public discourse on illicit sex. Bastardy within the community was no longer acknowledged in humorous anecdotes and tall tales in popular print. The lives of those bearing children out of wedlock now appeared primarily in the "true crime" pamphlets, which were tremendously popular in the early nineteenth century. True crime pamphlets, especially murder stories, were the staple fare of popular print culture in Philadelphia from the American Revolution until the invention of the penny press in the 1830s.[21]

Women engaging in relationships that produced illegitimate children were now represented as gender deviants who lived in a world of extreme danger. Anna Ayer, for example, gained notoriety as the victim of Daniel Davis Farmer, who murdered her in 1821 for falsely naming him as the father of her illegitimate child. She was joined at the end of the decade by Ursula Newman,

20. Between 1822 and 1825, 73 percent of the nonalmshouse cases were initiated before the birth of the child, and 27 percent after the birth. Information necessary was available in 39 percent of the 805 out-relief cases. Almshouse cases were excluded from this analysis because almshouse cases were usually initiated before the birth because of economic necessity. See Table A.1.

21. This discussion of crime pamphlet literature is based on an analysis of the true crime murder pamphlets printed from 1750 to 1830. In Philadelphia, crime pamphlets became especially popular from 1790 on, as seen in the proliferation of them. Many accounts went through several printings and were picked up and reprinted in other cities. Produced cheaply for a popular audience, their readership extended beyond the coarser classes. Elizabeth Drinker noted reading several of them in her diary. See, for example, *Execution of La Croix, Berrouse, and Baker for Piracy: The Last Words and Dying Confessions of the Three Pirates Who Were Executed This Day* (Philadelphia, 1800) and *Report of the Trial of Jason Fairbanks on an Indictment of Murder of Miss Elizabeth Fales* (Boston, 1801). See Elaine Forman Crane, ed., *The Diary of Elizabeth Drinker* (Boston, 1991), II, 1369, 1604 (May 13, 1800, Jan. 20, 1802).

The penny press refers to cheap, mass-produced newspapers made possible by technological developments in printing in the 1830s that increased the speed of production and lowered costs. For an example of the impact on reporting of sex crimes, see Patricia Cline Cohen, *The Murder of Helen Jewett: The Life and Death of a Prostitute in Nineteenth-Century New York* (New York, 1998).

murdered by her lover for refusing to enter into a traditional marriage and legitimate their child. In the nineteenth century, bastardy and independent female sexuality led to tragic early deaths for the women in popular print.[22]

The cultural tales about bastardy no longer depicted assertive women and responsible men as they had in the 1760s. Now the stories told women not to submit to the sexual entreaties of men and not to expect that the larger society would support them in their attempts to hold men responsible for their sexual actions. This shifting interpretation was exemplified by the sensationalized life of Elizabeth Wilson, a bastard-bearing woman executed for infanticide in 1786. Elizabeth's story was told and retold for the next forty years, changing shape to fit shifting cultural understandings of the gendered responsibility for sexual transgression.[23]

Elizabeth Wilson was born into a reputable, economically secure Chester County family. As an adult she moved to Philadelphia, where she lived as an independent single woman and bore three illegitimate children in unremarkable fashion. But in 1784, when she conceived twins at the age of twenty-seven, her life took a tragic turn. The father of the children had promised to marry her. Then she revealed her pregnancy to him, and he confessed that he was already married and promised to provide for her lying-in expenses and support the children. But, after the children were born, he did not provide support. When Elizabeth sought him out six weeks after the births and threatened to go to the Guardians of the Poor, he murdered them in a secluded area outside the city. Elizabeth was tried, convicted, and executed for their murder.

22. *The Life and Confessions of Daniel Davis Farmer, Who Was Executed at Amherst N.H. on the Third Day of January 1822, for the Murder of the Widow Anna Ayer . . .* (Amherst, N.H., 1822). Richard Johnson was a printer who lived with Ursula Newman in Philadelphia during the mid-1820s. In 1827 she gave birth to a child fathered by Johnson, and the couple removed to New York three months later. The motives attached to Johnson's actions were his "desire to claim them as his wife and child" and the "frustration of his affectionate design" (quotes from *Trial of Richard Johnson*). The story generated at least three pamphlets: *Trial of Richard Johnson for the Murder of Mrs. Ursula Newman on the Twentieth of November, 1828* (New York, 1829); *A Correct Copy of the Trial, Conviction, and Sentence of Richard Johnson . . .* (New York, 1829); *Execution of Richard Johnson . . .* (n.p., n.d.).

23. Two distinct versions of Elizabeth Wilson's story were published, the first in the late 1780s and the second in the 1820s. Despite many changes in the narratives, including a change in her name, the later story was clearly modeled after Elizabeth Wilson's life. Several distinguishing "facts" remain in the narrative that identify it as Elizabeth's life.

The tragedy of Elizabeth's life was compounded by the fact that she was executed despite a stay of execution based on suspicions about the father's role; it arrived minutes too late.[24]

Elizabeth Wilson's experiences were immediately seized upon by local printers and memorialized in a number of pamphlets. While most of these accounts presented the biographical information related above, they also presented her as a tragic victim of seduction and betrayal. Hers was the most sensational murder case in Philadelphia during the 1780s and 1790s. In 1786, the year she died, pamphlets were printed in Philadelphia and Carlisle in Pennsylvania, Hartford and Middletown in Connecticut, New York, and Boston. A broadside poem was printed in Boston as a warning to other young women, and several Boston periodicals published her story. The subject in each of these was not the independent woman living at a tavern inn in Philadelphia who had chosen to leave the country for the varied sexual opportunities in the city, but was instead a repentant sexual victim. Elizabeth Wilson became a symbol of what fornication and bastardy would lead to. That she, and not the murdering father of the children, did in fact hang for their murder made the lessons of female responsibility for sexual transgression all the more powerful.[25]

In 1820 Elizabeth's story was resurrected and refashioned to conform to the era's cultural understanding of total female responsibility for sexual transgression. A new pamphlet saw two successive printings. The Elizabeth Wilson of this story, renamed "Harriot," had none of the sordid history of her predecessor. More important, her paramour, the father and murderer of the children, disappeared from the narrative. The tragic victim of seduction, Harriot was an innocent virgin when seduced at the age of eighteen under a promise of marriage. Abandoned by her seducer, she decided to kill her baby "to avoid

24. The details of Elizabeth Wilson's life are recounted in the autobiography of Charles Biddle, who sat on the executive council when Elizabeth Wilson's pardon was granted: *Autobiography of Charles Biddle, Vice-President of the Supreme Executive Council of Pennsylvania, 1745–1821* (Philadelphia, 1883), 199–202. See also Oyer and Terminer Docket for Chester County, June, October 1785, PSA; Henry Graham Ashmead, *Historical Sketch of Chester, on Delaware* (Chester, Pa., 1883), 54, 154. The earlier pamphlets also contained accurate biographical details; see *A Faithful Narrative of Elizabeth Wilson, Who Was Executed at Chester, January Third, 1786, Charged with the Murder of Her Twin Infants* (Philadelphia, 1786).

25. Each of the pamphlets was entitled *A Faithful Narrative of Elizabeth Wilson: A Dying Elegy* (Boston, 1786), broadside; "A Faithful Narrative of Elizabeth Wilson," *Boston Magazine*, III (1786), 217, and *Worcester Magazine*, I (1786), 44–46.

the disgrace that her imprudent connexion was likely to produce." Her deed was quickly discovered, and she was taken to trial. Unlike Elizabeth, who maintained her innocence to the end, Harriot was the model penitent, never denying her action and agonizing over the grief she had brought to her parents and family. Resigned and submissive, she approached the gallows and was turned off:

> After she had been suspended nearly a minute, her hands were twice evenly and gently raised, and gradually let to fall without the least appearance of convulsive or involuntary motion, in a manner which could hardly be mistaken, when interpreted, as designed to signify consent and resignation. . . . Her whole conduct evidently showed, from this temper of mind, a composed, and even cheerful submission to the views and will of heaven; a modest unaffected submission entirely becoming her age, her sex and situation.

Harriot's pardon, like Elizabeth's, came too late in the hands of her crestfallen brother. But Harriot's pardon arrived with no hint of injustice. She, not the father, in this story had murdered the child. By 1820 responsibility for sexual transgression had been gendered completely female. The father has been eliminated from the story, because his actions were unimportant. Responsibility for maintaining sexual continence lay in Harriot's hands. Had she remained "a chaste and virtuous woman," nothing any man could have done would have harmed her.[26]

It is not surprising that these transformations in the cultural understanding of sexuality affected the administration of the system of child support for illegitimate children. By the 1820s the gendering of responsibility for sexual transgression and the constructions of male and female sexuality embodied in

26. *The Victim of Seduction! Some Interesting Particulars of the Life and Untimely Fate of Miss Harriot Wilson, Who Was Publicly Executed in the State of Pennsylvania in the Year 1802, for the Murder of Her Infant Child* (Boston, n.d.). This pamphlet and another slightly different version by the same printer are held at the American Antiquarian Society. The 1802 date of publication attributed to them was based on the execution date in the pamphlet title. This date is fictional. I have concluded that the date of publication was in the early 1820s because this is when J. Wilkey engaged in publishing in Boston.

Merril D. Smith has analyzed the implications of Elizabeth Wilson's story on motherhood: " 'Unnatural Mothers': Infanticide, Motherhood, and Class in the mid-Atlantic, 1730–1830," in Christine Daniels and Michael V. Kennedy, eds., *Over the Threshold: Intimate Violence in Early America* (New York, 1999), 173–184.

representations of nonmarital sexuality had an effect on the treatment of the men and women who parented illegitimate children in Philadelphia. The law remained the same, but its administration now reflected and reinforced greater male sexual privilege and heightened female sexual responsibility.

The men who fathered illegitimate children in the 1820s exhibited a new, defiant attitude toward the system that sought to hold them financially responsible for their offspring. Unlike the men of their fathers' generation of the 1790s, these men often fought the charges brought against them. One-third of the fathers resisted the mothers' claims of their paternity. Unlike those in the court records of the 1790s, these men did not quickly post bond to settle the case with the Guardians of the Poor, but took their cases to trial. During the 1820s a full 22 percent of the fathers resisted paternity to the full extent the law allowed; in the 1790s only 2 percent of men had done so. Others appealed their cases to the Guardians themselves, requesting a special committee be appointed to investigate the woman's claims. The work of these committees resembled trials. Witnesses were called, and testimony was given. When the credibility of a woman's story was seriously undermined, the committee would recommend that the Guardians abandon their prosecution, and the solicitor would be told to discontinue prosecution of the case. But most women, it appears, told the truth. There were only twenty-one cases, from 1822 through 1825, where the paternity claims were abandoned because the woman's story did not hold up.[27]

In the 1820s the distinction collapsed between the two populations of women bearing illegitimate children, those receiving mandatory child support from the fathers and those relying on the almshouse. The practice begun in 1810 of treating some women entitled to out-relief like almshouse paupers was fully implemented: all women pregnant with bastard offspring came to be treated as the poor, undeserving, licentious rabble. In the 1790s class and race had marked women for separate treatment: poor women whose sexual partners were indigent and women of color were forced to rely on the almshouse for meager support. White women who had some resources and those

27. Between 1822 and 1825, of 957 cases, 295 resisted paternity, 265 men pursued their cases in court, and 213 sustained their case in court beyond the initial arrest. They posted bond to appear at court or remained in jail rather than posted bond with the Guardians to secure child support payments. They appear in the trial court dockets and in the Guardians of the Poor solicitor's docket for trial. The dispositions of many of these cases do not appear in the record. Thirty more men resisted paternity only within the Guardians' own systems, requesting special investigating committees.

pregnant by men of means were a separate group and used the Guardians' administration of mandatory paternal child support outside the almshouse. But in the 1820s more and more women pregnant by men of means were treated like their poorer sisters. In the 1790s only 2 percent of the out-relief paternal support cases ever crossed over into the almshouse population, but 23 percent of the total bastardy cases in the early 1820s moved from being out-relief cases (of mandatory paternal child support) to almshouse cases. The mothers in these cases were entitled to child support from men well equipped to provide it. But, because the fathers fought paternity and the Guardians refused to support the mother and child during the legal dispute over it, the mother was denied aid and forced into the almshouse.

The assumption of responsibility for bastardy was moving from men to women. The blending of these two populations of pregnant women, based on class and race in the eighteenth century, into one, based on gender, demonstrates the importance that female sexual behavior and adherence to female sexual purity had assumed. This merging of the two groups of women bearing bastard offspring simultaneously labeled the sexually deviant actor as poor. As more women were funneled into the almshouse because of their nonmarital sexual behavior, the public face of illicit sex became an attribute of the poorer classes, even when the men involved were well-to-do and middle-class.

By the 1820s reputable men were trying to keep their nonmarital progeny, and the illicit sexual behavior that begot them, secret, and the Guardians often accommodated them. The Guardians implemented a class-based double standard on personal privacy. Those men who commuted their cases by paying a one-time lump sum for the support of their child were not identified in the Guardians' records. The practice of obscuring the identities of elite and middle-class men was codified in the Standing Resolutions of the Guardians of the Poor in 1821:

> That in every case of Bastardy reported by a Guardian to this Board, *when the father has not commuted or bonded it the name of the father,* his occupation, late residence, age, colour, and other particulars, so far as can be obtained, shall be reported and entered on the minutes.

When cases were bonded, the father's identity, his occupation, and the identity of his surety were recorded in the Bond Book. Only those with the funds to commute their case entirely remained anonymous.[28]

28. *By-Laws and Standing Resolutions of the Guardians of the Poor* (Philadelphia, 1821), 11 (emphasis mine). During the 1820s the standard fee to commute a case of

The Guardians took other steps to protect the reputations of the men who shared their class. When children were admitted to the Children's Asylum, created in 1820 specifically for the care of illegitimate children, the same precautions applied:

That all orders for sending children to the Asylum shall specify the name and age of the child, and *as far as can be communicated with propriety, the names of the parents of such children.*[29]

The Guardians were always careful to reiterate the exclusion for commuted cases when they gave instructions for record keeping at their weekly meetings. In 1822, for instance, they instructed their agent to enter every day in his case book "the name, occupation, and place of residence of every person by them arrested on a charge of Fornication and Bastardy (Commuted cases excepted)." By establishing systems to hide the sexual indiscretions committed by men of secure economic standing, the Guardians were institutionalizing the facade of a licentious sexuality of the rabble and of the sexual rectitude of the middle class. This created the appearance of the sexual culture the middle class expected to see.[30]

Other institutions sprang up to accommodate the desire of men of means to avoid public exposure as the fathers of children born of illicit unions. Flora Cox ran a private nursery for mulatto illegitimate children during the 1820s. As the Guardians described it, she kept "a house for Boarding Bastard Children, whose mothers are black and fathers white, and names kept in the back ground." Illegitimate children had long been put out to nurse with women of the lower classes for financial compensation, and the Guardians often made child support payments to them for their care. But the presence of Flora Cox's institution, known for its discretion, highlights the changed social context of both nonmarital sexual behavior of men of means and cross-racial unions.[31]

———
bastardy was three hundred dollars, well beyond the means of the working men of the city.

Evidence of these omissions of fathers' identities is scattered throughout the records. See, for example, GPM: July 30, 1822, case of Ann Nutter; July 14, 21, Aug. 11, Sept. 1, 1824, case of Eliza Caldwell; Dec. 21, 1825, case of M——.

29. *By-Laws and Standing Resolutions of the Guardians of the Poor,* 9 (emphasis mine). The Children's Asylum was available for all poor children. But, when the Guardians developed the proposal for it, they envisioned it as an alternative to out-door support for the growing number of illegitimate children. See GPM, Feb. 20, Mar. 2, 1820.

30. GPM, Sept. 17, 1822.

31. GPM, May 4, 1825.

PLATE 15. *"Miss Chloe."* Plate 4 from *Edward Clay,* Life in Philadelphia
(Philadelphia, 1829). Courtesy The Library Company of Philadelphia

By 1820 racial prejudice against African-Americans was more openly displayed in Philadelphia, and African-Americans found the city increasingly hostile. Caricatures of African-Americans such as Edward Clay's demonstrated the growing resentment many whites harbored against them. As the caption to *Miss Chloe* states, African-Americans were perceived to aspire to social and economic positions beyond those many whites wished to grant them (see Plate 15). Resentment increased as the semibondage of long-term indentures expired and African-Americans came to compete at the bottom end of the wage-labor system. The fact that the majority of the city's African-Americans had, by 1820, established independent households and no longer lived in the houses of white masters or employers only intensified whites' anxiety about their ability to maintain superiority over them. Slanderous remarks about African-Americans' licentiousness shored up the otherwise receding boundaries between whites and blacks. The Guardians of the Poor embraced this racial bias. Writing in his personal docket book of Guardians' cases, John M. Scott, their solicitor, revealed the assumptions that now guided the board's treatment of cross-racial cases:

Memo: Finly [the reputed father] is a white lad—and she an ugly black— querie if it is not a false charge.[32]

During the early 1820s the proportion of cross-racial bastardy cases adjudicated by the Guardians dropped to only 1.5 percent, down from 5 percent in the 1790s. African-American women who came to the Guardians for assistance in securing child support from the white fathers now faced a hostile reception. From 1822 through 1825 only nine women brought such cases, and only two of these succeeded in securing child support payments from the father.[33]

32. Nash, *Forging Freedom*, 177–183; GPSD, Mayor's Court, September session, 1823, case of Margaret Stevenson (the mother in this case died in the almshouse before this case could go forward). Nash characterizes the period 1805–1820 as the era when Philadelphians engaged in "establishing the color line." The contrast in treatment by the Guardians of the Poor of African-American women whose partners were white men provides additional support for his periodization.

By 1820 approximately 75 percent of the city's free blacks lived in independent households (Gary B. Nash and Jean R. Soderlund, *Freedom by Degrees: Emancipation in Philadelphia and Its Aftermath* [New York, 1991], 161).

33. Of these nine cases, six of the reputed fathers disputed their paternity by requesting a committee to investigate and hold a hearing on their case (in only one did the Guardians decide in favor of the mother's claims and pursue the case, Ann Mintas case, below). In two cases the Guardians took the regular course of action, without

The men named as the fathers generally denied their paternity and fought the cases. Charles Remington and Daniel Davis, for instance, each requested a committee to investigate the charges and hired lawyers to represent them at the Guardians' hearings. In each case the committee found that the woman had not supported the charges, and they instructed the solicitor not to prosecute it. In contrast to their responses in contested cases in which both parties were white, the Guardians did not explain why they decided in favor of the father. Perhaps the cross-racial nature of these cases was explanation enough.[34]

Lavinia Smith failed to secure child support from Philadelphia merchant Daniel C. Ellis despite the Guardians' conclusion that he had fathered the child:

> The committee in the case of Daniel C. Ellis . . . report: that from the fact of the accused being a respectable married man, with a family of children, and the accused a coloured woman, they have been anxious to afford him every opportunity, in their power of clearing himself, from a charge of so serious a character—They regret to say that he has not been successful. They are therefore of opinion that the Case should be permitted to take the usual course.

When this case came to court two months later, the Guardians ordered the solicitor not to prosecute, voting unanimously. The record does not reveal why they abandoned this case, but it does demonstrate that they were relieved to do so.[35]

---

holding a special courtlike hearing (in one the father, a lower-class carter, gave bond for the support of his child; in the other the father appealed the Guardians' determination of paternity, taking his case to the Mayor's Court, where he was found not guilty). In the final case the mother and child died in the almshouse before any action was taken by the Guardians.

34. Charles Remington was a well-established lumber merchant of elite economic standing. Daniel Davis's occupation is unknown, but he could not have been below the middling classes, because he hired George M. Dallas, a prestigious lawyer, to represent him. Case of Juliana Woodley and Daniel Davis: GPSD, June session, 1825; GPM, Sept. 14, Oct. 5, 1825, June 1, 1826. Case of Ann Thomas and Charles Remington: GPM, Jan. 5, 19, 1825; GPCB, Jan. 19, 1825.

35. GPM, Sept. 28, 1825. There are no indications that the usual causes for abandoning a prosecution existed in this case. Neither the child nor the mother had died, the father had not commuted the case, nor had he bonded it to secure child support. If evidence emerged to discredit Lavinia's story, the Guardians made no mention of it. They might simply have been unable to face supporting her in court. The details of this case are in GPM, Sept. 28, 1824, Sept. 7, Oct. 26, Dec. 14, 1825; GPCB, Oct. 26, 1825; GPSD, December session, 1825.

The reason Mary Hawkins succeeded in her claims was apparent. Mary Hawkins obtained support from John Lyons because, despite his race, he did not have the class standing to command the Guardians' support. Lyons was a carter who lived on Dock Street. Mary lived around the corner on Front Street in 1825 when they had their child. When the Guardians set the case for trial in the Mayor's Court, John quickly posted bond, secured by his friend and neighbor George Beaty, who kept a tavern in the neighborhood. John, Mary, and George were all members of the lower-class waterfront community, and their movement through the Guardians' adjudication of child support was swift and conclusive.[36]

The racial prejudice and class bias of the Guardians made this system arduous for African-American women whose sexual experiences crossed racial boundaries. The Guardians could not have believed that such sexual unions did not take place, but they were extremely reluctant to facilitate public acknowledgment of this behavior by supporting African-American women's paternity claims. The law, however, did still give these women a right to pursue such support, and occasionally they were successful. Ann Mintas was the only African-American woman to secure child support from an elite white man during the early 1820s. What had been possible in the 1790s was now extremely rare.

Mintas initiated her paternity claim against Thomas Morrell, a member of Philadelphia's merchant elite, when she was five months pregnant. Morrell fought her claims. In February, just weeks after the child was born, the Guardians made their report:

> The committee report . . . that they have given the accused a full and fair opportunity to be heard in his defence. From the fact that Mr. Morrell is a married Man, with a family of children and that his accuser is a coloured woman, in no wise prepossessing in her appearance, who has already had at least five Bastard Children, it would have given the Committee great pleasure to be able to pronounce him innocent of the Charge. He having, however, produced no testimony whatever, they are compelled to recommend that the Case be permitted to take the usual Course.

The committee went on to say that they were willing to let the case go forward because they believed, as Morrell did, that he would be cleared in a jury trial.

36. Case of Mary Hawkins and John Lyons: GPSD, September session, 1825; Guardians of the Poor, Bond Book, Sept. 25, 1825, CCAP; GPM, Sept. 28, 1825; GPCB, Sept. 28, 1825.

The case, however, never went to trial. During the March session Morrell entered into an agreement to pay child support, and the state's attorney general dropped its prosecution. Morrell, however, remained noncompliant. By the following fall he had still failed to make the required payments, and the Guardians were forced to execute the bond against him to collect their funds.[37]

For African-American women, legal recourse that had been accessible in the 1790s was now almost always closed to them. Their actions, seen in this light, take on added significance. They took the initiative to hold white men accountable for their sexual activities during a period of increasing racial tension in Philadelphia. The early hopeful days of freedom for Philadelphia's free black community were coming to an end, but some courageous women, like Ann Mintas, refused to accept the changes without a fight.[38]

While the Guardians were adjudicating bastardy in ways that accommodated middle-class and elite men, they were simultaneously implementing policies that inflicted a greater hardship on poor women. In 1821 they passed a resolution to require all poor women to give birth in the almshouse. Women pregnant by men who had not commuted the case or bonded it before the birth of the child were to be sent to the almshouse. If a woman refused to go, the Guardian in charge of the case was "to inform the person or persons where she may reside, that the board will not make any allowance for her lying-in expenses." Two years later they denied these same women access to the almshouse for childbirth unless they had already sworn to the paternity of their child before an alderman or justice of the peace.[39]

In 1820 the Guardians had begun discussing severely limiting the weekly cash payments for women whose illegitimate children relied on public support. As a small step in this direction in 1814, they limited public assistance to

37. GPM, Feb. 4, 1824. Case of Ann Mintas and Thomas Morrell: GPSD, September session, 1823; GPCB, Feb. 4, 1824; GPM, Feb. 4, Nov. 3, 1824; Guardians of the Poor, Bond Book, Mar. 31, 1824.

38. One other woman stood out in her bold actions to hold a white man accountable for his sexual conduct. Ann Hains prosecuted her case against Isaac Brooks herself, without the Guardians' aid, in 1823 and obtained a conviction in Mayor's Court. Ann's place of legal settlement was Lancaster. When she approached the Guardians for assistance during her pregnancy, they had her removed there. She, however, returned to Philadelphia, gave birth there, and then pursued her suit against Brooks. Case of Ann Hains and Isaac Brooks: MCD, June 19, 1823; GPSD, June session, 1823; GPM, June 3, 10, July 22, 1823.

39. By-Laws and Standing Resolutions of the Guardians of the Poor, 6; GPM, June 17, 24, Oct. 15, 1823.

bastard children over age three, placed with nurses, to fifty cents a week. In 1821 they universalized this new, two-tiered system of child support. Women whose children were fathered by poor men unable to contribute to their support were now limited to payments of twenty-five cents a week. Mothers of commuted or bonded cases received between fifty cents and two dollars a week. Mothers who objected to these reductions in child support were told that they could accept the lower payments or have their child sent to the new Children's Asylum.[40]

During the 1820s the increased vigilance of the Guardians also made their new system more intrusive. Compared to their predecessors, the Guardians of the 1820s were less willing to wait for cases to come to them. They tried to discover pregnant women whose children might become financial burdens to the city and often sought them out. Establishing paternity, more easily accomplished while a woman was pregnant, would allow them to assign financial responsibility to a particular member of the community, lest the children, when paternity was not established, become public charges down the road.[41]

In this environment some women began to resist the Guardians' intervention. They "absconded" with their babies after leaving the almshouse, failed to appear in court, or refused to cooperate with the Guardians' investigations. Some women did so because they were reluctant to appear in court, like Eliza Allen, who refused to come to court to establish the facts of her illicit connection with Alexander Armor. Her mother informed John Scott, the Guardians' solicitor, that she simply "won't come to court." Elizabeth Jenkins's mother refused to permit her daughter to appear in court and told Guardian Fitler this herself. She assured him that her daughter's child would not become chargeable to the city, and the case was dropped. These women were unwilling to assume the burden of appearing in court. The increased resistance by men to accepting paternity within this system meant that more women had to publicly testify to their nonmarital sexual behavior to secure child support. The system that had in the past required them only to swear an oath of paternity before a

40. GPM, Sept. 1, 1814, Feb. 15, 1820; *By-Laws and Standing Resolutions of the Guardians of the Poor,* 9. In practice, during the early 1820s, not all Guardians enforced these new financial restrictions; many continued making the payment they had always made to the women in their districts. New cases were more likely to have the lower payments enforced. Individual Guardians enforced these rules based on their own sense of fairness, and many did not fully embrace the restrictions. As the composition of the Guardians changed in the middle of the decade, these limitations were enforced more rigorously.

41. See, for example, GPM, Jan. 14, June 9, 1824.

justice of the peace now increasingly required a public trial. In this era when the quintessential attribute of middle-class womanhood was modesty, some women relinquished their right to child support in exchange for maintaining their privacy.[42]

The majority of women who refused to cooperate with the Guardians' intervention refused because of the hardships brought to bear upon them and their sexual partners. The system had always placed a greater hardship upon the men and women of the lower classes. The standard procedure of issuing an arrest warrant and holding a man in jail until he posted bond meant that poor men often remained imprisoned for an extended period. Not until the Guardians were convinced of a man's insolvency and complete lack of resources would they abandon their financial quest and have him released. Nothing new in these procedures arose during the 1820s. But, in the past, it had been easier to shield one's lover from detection and simply stay out of the system. The increased vigilance over bastardy cases now meant that couples from the lower classes who made amicable arrangements were more often pursued by the Guardians. When William Morrison, for example, was imprisoned for bastardy in 1823, his partner appealed to the Guardians to drop the case. Maria Hicks maintained that she would support their child and would never prosecute the case. In another instance an African-American couple took similar action. When Jeremiah Frisby sat in jail unable to post bond for his illegitimate child, the mother gave her own bond, secured by two "coloured Men as Sureties" to secure his release. We do not know the exact nature of the relationships in many of the cases where women resisted the Guardians' intervention, but for some couples the assistance of the Guardians was not welcome. Hannah Park and William Waley made this clear when they successfully circumvented the Guardians' intervention and simply ran off together.[43]

42. See, for example, women who resisted the Guardians' intervention: Ann Huddle, GPSD, March session, 1825; Margaret Carson, GPSD, September session, 1825; Eliza Painter, GPSD, June session, 1825; Hannah Williams, GPSD, September session, 1822; Rachel Hawkins, GPSD, March session, 1824; Mary Barry, GPM, Feb. 25, Mar. 11, Oct. 7, 1823; Eliza Allen, GPSD, September session, 1825. Mrs. Jenkins must have had the resources to support her grandchild, or the Guardians would probably not have so readily acquiesced (GPSD, June session, 1825).

43. The Guardians maintained a Prison Committee to explore the circumstances of such cases and process the requests of poor men in jail appealing for their release. Case of Maria Hicks and William Morrison: GPM, May 20, 26, June 24, Oct. 15, 1823; GPSD, June session, 1823; PFT, May 16, 1823. Jeremiah Frisby: GPM, Mar. 1, 1826. Hannah

Despite the policies of the Guardians restricting the options of poor women, the law still guaranteed women who bore illegitimate children support, and hundreds of women still asserted their rights to claim it. Even when the character of the woman was objectionable, the Guardians were under the legal obligation to provide her with child support. Such was the case of Eliza Johnson, who ran a brothel in the city. Eliza had given birth to a daughter in 1822, and the case was commuted by the father. In 1825 the Guardians attempted to have the child placed in the Children's Asylum, but Eliza refused:

> The mother is an indifferent Character, and it is firmly believed keeps a house of ill fame. But she is entitled by Law to something. It is suggested whether she should not [sic] have as Small an allowance as possible. She refuses to send the Child to the Asylum.

Despite their objections, the Guardians continued to make payments to her.[44]

The actions of the Guardians of the Poor were part of a broad attack on the autonomy of the lower classes. Philadelphians, like Europeans, had a growing disdain for the poor and a desire to force them to acquiesce to middle-class standards of industry and morality. In Britain, western Europe, and the urban centers of the United States, new disciplinary regimes were instituted in the early nineteenth century to support the development of the modern industrial state. Reformers established a host of institutions to discipline and control the lower classes. In Philadelphia, sexual behavior would be an important justification for adopting punitive disciplinary strategies to control the rabble.[45]

Park: GPSD, September session, 1823. The cases that appeared only on the solicitor's docket were most likely to be ones where the woman resisted the Guardians' efforts. There is no record of these women's soliciting the Guardians' intervention in the standard ways, through appealing to their district Guardian or appearing before the board.

44. GPCB, Case Book, Mar. 16, 1825.

45. Michel Foucault first explored the centrality of the development of disciplinary regimes to the establishment of the modern state in *Discipline and Punish: The Birth of the Prison*. Michael Meranze reveals how these processes were applied in early national Philadelphia in *Laboratories of Virtue: Punishment, Revolution, and Authority in Phila-delphia, 1760–1835* (Chapel Hill, N.C., 1996). Christine Stansell explores the role sexuality played in regulating the lower classes in antebellum New York, in *City of Women: Sex and Class in New York, 1789–1860* (Urbana, Ill., 1982). See also Anna Clark, *The Struggle for the Breeches: Gender and the Making of the British Working Class* (Berkeley, Calif., 1995); Ruth Richardson, *Death, Dissection, and the Destitute* (Chicago, 1987).

The founding of the Children's Asylum to control the development of working-class children, the regimented discipline of the Magdalen Asylum inmates, and the move from public corporal punishment to secluded incarceration were all part of this attempt to discipline the lower classes and, more important, to single out their cultural practices—from sexual behavior to economic habits—as illegitimate and deviant. As the second decade of the nineteenth century came to a close, leading Philadelphia politicians and philanthropists turned their attention to poverty and morality, which they increasingly saw as inextricably linked. By the late 1810s and early 1820s, the Guardians came under outside pressure to reduce the cost of poor relief. The number of Philadelphians receiving poor relief had steadily increased through the 1810s, and the poor tax increased accordingly. But the economic dislocations produced by the War of 1812 and the Panic of 1819 made some resent the price of aiding the poor. In 1817 a group of well-to-do Philadelphians led by the wealthy philanthropist Robert Vaux launched an investigation into poverty in the city, and their published report explained that poverty was the result of a moral failing in the individual. Politicians in many major United States cities and the national government of England made investigations that led to similar findings between 1817 and 1820. Investigations of poverty that laid blame on the "lazy" laboring classes were part of an assault on the laboring classes in defense of the capitalist transformations of the economy.[46]

In 1820, the Guardians remained dominated by men of middling economic status with closer ties to the difficulties of the working poor in the expanding, volatile industrial economy. Most of these men worked as a body to fend off the attacks on the system of poor relief. In the late 1810s the Guardians had responded to the pressure to reduce the costs of poor relief by more carefully monitoring out-relief, but the board left it up to individual Guardians to be as frugal as they saw fit, and the legislature took no action to fundamentally alter the poor laws. Forcing pregnant poor women into the almshouse and reducing the instances when women bearing bastard children received public support in cash payments were steps the Guardians felt they could take without harming those they perceived as the deserving poor. But, despite their interest in defending the working poor, the Guardians were blind to the gender implications and sexual politics of their policies. Poor women bearing bastards were fair targets.

46. For an analysis of the poor law reforms in England as an attack on family formation among the working classes and plebeian cultural traditions, see Clark, *The Struggle for the Breeches*, 187–196.

The modifications by the Guardians in their adjudication of child support during the late 1810s and early 1820s were only symptoms of a larger problem. This system had grown increasingly incompatible with the cultural understandings of male and female sexuality, appropriate gendered behavior, and notions of public propriety. It granted too much power to sexually active women and supported unacceptable levels of agency among women who bore bastard children. Yet the reconstruction of sexuality, the cultural assault on nonmarital sexual practices, and the reform efforts of benevolent organizations had failed to transform the sexual habits of those who embraced expansive nonmarital sexual lifestyles. Many Philadelphians refused to restrict their sexual behavior to marriage. White men from the elite and middle classes continued to perceive sexual access to women below their social position as an important masculine prerogative. In the face of this continuing resistance, the political and economic elite now turned to more punitive measures to compel conformity or to drive evidence of nonmarital sexuality out of the public domain.

Attacking the system of child support for the mothers of illegitimate children was at the heart of this new campaign to undermine female nonmarital sexuality and focus public attention on the illicit sexuality of women and the lower classes. It was also the path that would be used to undermine poor relief and dismantle the traditional responsibility of the community toward its poor members. During the 1820s many of the Guardians sought to dismantle the bastardy system by making changes internally within the the existing poor laws.

But the Guardians and the Philadelphia community at large were conflicted about how punitive the system should become. During the early 1820s the members of the Board of Guardians divided into factions on whether they should simply limit the payments to the mothers of indigent illegitimate children or eliminate them entirely and compel these women to give up their children to the Children's Asylum. These divisions took on added importance because they coincided with a shift in the balance of power on the board that was representative of the politics of the city at large. In 1820, for the first time, the Guardians from the districts (Southwark, Northern Liberties, Moyamensing, Spring Garden, Kensington, Richmond, and Penn District) became the numerical majority, surpassing those from the city proper. At the same time, the economic development of the city led to greater residential segregation based on economic status. The districts became the areas with greater concentrations of the working classes and poorer laborers. The district Guardians tended to be political representatives of their communities, middle-class,

Democratic-Republican, and sympathetic to the needs of the working poor. The city Guardians were better off and tended to be Federalists. Early in the 1820s the majority faction increased the use of out-relief, particularly to poor families, exacerbating the tensions between the two factions. During 1824 and 1825, members of the board repeatedly raised the resolution to eliminate all out-relief for illegitimate children above the age of eighteen months. Each time the resolution was voted down by the majority faction.[47]

Beginning in 1825 the economy improved, and employment opportunities for the working poor and business ventures for the rich alleviated the economic imperatives to poor law reform. But the attack on poor relief had taken on a life of its own. Despite economic improvements, the assault on poor relief increased. By the end of 1825 the center-city Guardians pushing for fundamental transformations of the system turned their efforts outward and began a campaign to encourage public support of a legal reform of the poor laws. Wealthy Philadelphia Federalist William M. Meredith developed the case against out-relief, criticizing Philadelphia's system and presenting his report to the legislature. Meredith's report argued that aid only made the poor dependent and slothful and increased their numbers. The numbers of poor and the cost to the public could be reduced only by forcing them to adopt the habits of industry and sobriety. Reforming the poor through compulsory, institutionalized work programs became a symbol of the virtues of economic development and a test of political might.[48]

In 1826 the Guardians, responding to Meredith's report, set up a committee to study the poor laws of other major cities, the four members being all wealthy, city-center Guardians. In June 1827, after visiting Baltimore, New York, Providence, Boston, and Salem, the committee concluded that the poor relief system of Philadelphia was by far the most costly and was an inducement "to idleness and crime," owing to the practice of supplying the poor with outdoor relief, or relief "in their own families."[49]

The Guardians' report maintained that the Philadelphia practice of outdoor relief "in the cases of Bastardy" was "one of the most odious features in the whole system, in as much as it is an encouragement to vice, and offers a

47. GPM, Oct. 6, 1824, Feb. 25, June 3, July 6, 1825.

48. Clement, *Welfare and the Poor,* 50–56; GPM, 1820–1828. Comments regarding reform run throughout the minutes during these years.

49. *Report of the Committee Appointed by the Board of Guardians of the Poor of the City and Districts of Philadelphia to Visit the Cities of Baltimore, New-York, Providence, Boston, and Salem* (Philadelphia, 1827), 24.

premium for prostitution." They attacked the system of child support as "an inducement to a departure from virtue."

> And if the extending relief to all cases of this nature that come under their notice, if paying a regular stipend from the public purse, whenever the female cannot find a profitable father for her offspring, be not affording countenance and encouragement, then are your committee ignorant of the meaning of words, and incapable of estimating the moral consequences of things.[50]

By prohibiting outdoor support, other cities had reduced or eliminated the number of bastardy cases handled by public relief. Throughout their report the Guardians attacked the Philadelphia system of child support for illegitimate children by highlighting the treatment of bastardy in other cities. In Baltimore, for instance, the mothers of illegitimate children were responsible for their support and were required to reimburse the city for the expenses incurred in the almshouse. In Boston and Salem no support whatsoever was supplied to the mothers of illegitimate children unless first obtained from the fathers. In New York, when the father was unable to provide support and the woman could not support the child herself, she remained in the almshouse: no outdoor relief was available.[51]

Not only did Philadelphia's system stand out as the most liberal, but, according to the report, it supported unseemly behavior in the city's lower-class women. In contrast to the cities that treated the mothers of illegitimate children with "restraint, reproof, and punishment," Philadelphia encouraged an assertive independence in them.

> Let any one whose convictions on this point are not sufficiently clear, attend at this room on the day when the committee on bastardy pay the weekly allowances to their pensioners, and mark the unblushing effrontery, that some of them exhibit. The thanklessness with which they receive their allotted stipend; the insolence with which they demand a further supply, arrogantly exacting as a *right,* what ought never to have been granted, even as a charity.[52]

50. Ibid., 29.

51. The report stated that the number of bastardy cases supported by the public for the previous year had been 0 in Baltimore, 80 or 90 in New York, 9 or 10 in Boston, and in Salem 2 or 3. In Philadelphia it had been 269. Ibid.

52. Ibid.

The Guardians who authored this report, and the full board that ratified it and put it to print, had fastened upon bastardy as a target of reform and a symbol of the ills of the existing system. It was the issue they believed would energize public support for their proposed reforms and weaken their opposition on the Board of Guardians.

The actions of the Guardians led, in the summer of 1827, to a community-wide commission to study poor law reform. This committee quickly issued its report, which endorsed the findings of the Guardians and added some concrete suggestions of its own. *The Report of the Committee Appointed at a Town Meeting of the Citizens of the City and County* had found another weak link in the system. All support of paupers, they concurred, should now be confined to institutional settings. But, for the system to be most beneficial to poor children and most cost-effective for the community, the Guardians must have the power to put children out to service when they reached the age of indenture. The committee found that the parents of poor children often withdrew them from the Children's Asylum right before they reached the age to be bound out. These children were thus "returned to the haunts of poverty and vice from which they were taken, and thus the benevolent purposes of the institution are defeated and the public funds uselessly expended."[53]

By attacking the support for children born out of wedlock, these reformers hoped not only to popularize their reform movement but also to rein in the small amount of sexual autonomy this system now allowed women. The poor laws passed in 1828 did just that. Under the new poor law, public relief for illegitimate children was limited to institutional care in the almshouse or Children's Asylum. No public money could be used for outside support. The Guardians would still administer the adjudication of paternal support, but cash disbursements would be limited to what money could be collected from the father. Under this system the Guardians' financial motivation for advocating the mother's right to collect child support from the father was severely limited: the community would no longer provide child support if the father shirked his responsibility. The Guardians of the Poor thus ceased their vigilant pursuit of the fathers.[54]

53. *Report of the Committee Appointed at a Town Meeting of the Citizens of the City and County of Philadelphia on the Twenty-third of July 1827, to Consider the Subject of the Pauper System of the City and Districts, and to Report Remedies for Its Defects* (Philadelphia, 1827), 30.

54. The new law stipulated that babies under the age of eighteen months could still

But the most punitive aspect of these changes was that children who had been supported in public institutions could not be discharged unless the expenses incurred for their support had been refunded to the Guardians. If the parents were unable to do so, the Guardians now had the authority to put these children out to service, against their parents' objections, to repay the debt. Placing a child in the almshouse or Children's Asylum now meant that the mother stood to lose custody of that child indefinitely, unless her own financial circumstances changed dramatically and enabled her to support the child and repay the debt. For women who bore children out of wedlock in the 1820s, the likelihood of such upward economic mobility was extremely small. Women in Philadelphia would now bear the moral and financial burdens of nonmarital sexual behavior.[55]

Poor law reforms in the United States, like those taking place in Britain, were designed to make programs to relieve poverty so punitive that people would refuse to use them. Institutional settings mimicking insane asylums and prisons culturally ascribed criminality to poverty. They also granted greater control over those inside through regimes of discipline, and over those outside, it was hoped, by cultivating the desire to remain free of the institutions' grasp. For women bearing illegitimate children in antebellum Philadelphia, the difficulty of extracting a child from the Children's Asylum would certainly serve such a purpose. Just as the English Anatomy Act, also enacted in 1828, discouraged the use of the workhouse by granting control of the bodies of those who died there to the state for use in anatomical dissection, the Philadelphia Guardians took legal control of the children who passed through the Asylum's doors. Philadelphia enacted its poor law reforms in 1828, the same year as the Anatomy Act and a few years before England completed its poor law reforms in 1834. On the issue of out-relief, Philadelphia's poor law reforms were more severe, since the English reforms left some out-relief intact. The impetus for poor law reforms in both countries lay in the conflicts over workers' rights in the emerging capitalist order and in the desire to shore up the patriarchal family by forcing working-class women into dependent relationships with men by eliminating the option of self-support supple-

---

be cared for by their mothers. *An Act for the Relief and Employment of the Poor of the City of Philadelphia, the District of Southwark, and the Townships of the Northern Liberties and Penn* (Philadelphia, 1828), passed into law March 1828.

55. Ibid.

mented by poor relief. In Philadelphia the main recipients of out-relief in the 1820s were single women who headed their own households.[56]

But there were significant differences between England and Philadelphia, as in the treatment of bastardy and the aims of reformers in attacking out-relief. In England the poor law reforms were aimed at undermining the ability of poor working people to establish families, in order to limit the poor population. Intervention by authorities in bastardy cases, English reformers believed, had induced poor men and women to marry, thereby creating more poor offspring. Institutionalizing poor relief would separate existing families, and shifting responsibility for bastardy to women would discourage family formation. In Philadelphia, the move to institutionalize poor relief was also an attack on family formation among the poorest classes, as well as also an attack on independent women. Eliminating outdoor relief removed a fundamental tool poor families and single women had used for economic survival. But Philadelphia officials and the system of adjudicating bastardy had not encouraged marriage as a solution to bastardy, and few documented cases of bastardy led to multiple births. Bastardy was important in the poor law reform efforts in Philadelphia because it was the issue that bridged the two competing political and economic factions. By the mid-1820s members of both the city's upper-class political leadership and the districts' middle-class Guardians saw independent female sexuality as a threat to good order, morality, masculine political authority, and male sexual prerogatives. While the district Guardians and the city leadership differed on the culpability of the working poor for their poverty, they agreed on the immorality of overtly sexual women. Middle-class district Guardians were not interested in being associated with the licentious sexuality publicly acknowledged by bastardy and so supported the changes to the system of publicly adjudicated bastardy. In doing so they lost the battle to save out-relief for those they deemed the worthy poor.

The final stage in the bifurcation of sexuality had been accomplished. Philadelphians had transformed the relationship between the state and the members of the community who practiced nonmarital sexuality to reflect the cultural beliefs held by many of its elite and middle-class citizens. The poor laws embodied the gendered constructions of sexuality that asserted that women were naturally sexually restrained and men naturally carnal. They also codified their belief in two opposing sexualities: the dominant and public version of

56. Richardson, *Death, Dissection, and the Destitute*, 149, 192; Clement, *Welfare and the Poor*, 70, 75–76.

virtuous women and virile men, and a lustful, uncontrollable sexuality of the rabble. The dismantling of the bastardy child support system created the social appearance of this reality by masking male sexual privilege and codifying the sexual vulnerability of nonelite women.

This was how white upper- and middle-class men exercised sexual dominance in antebellum Philadelphia. The fact that nonmarital sexual behavior continued to exist but was portrayed as residing amid the rabble made it possible to sexually exploit not only the lower classes but also any women who could be construed to belong to the rabble. In the early years of the new nation, Philadelphians had begun this process by embracing racialized notions of sexuality, attributing an inherent licentious sexuality to African-Americans, and gradually extending the association to poor white women, then to all women who exhibited an active or independent sexuality outside marriage. By the 1820s all women who engaged in nonmarital sexuality fitted this description. The construction of nineteenth-century notions of virtuous middle-class womanhood were built in opposition to such a construction and depended upon it. Upper- and middle-class Philadelphians had embraced a new moral code, which narrowed the range of acceptable practices in sexual behavior and family formation. Now middle-class men were allowed to engage in nonmarital sexuality in parallel lives that never intersected with their lives as respectable family men, middle-class women were allowed no sexual experiences outside courtship and marriage, and lower-class men and women and people of color paid a price for their nonmarital sexual transgressions that was extracted from their children.

At the same time, the broad range of cultural traditions that had operated within the eighteenth-century city were excluded from the dominant discourse on gender and sexuality. The ethnic traditions that allowed out-of-wedlock sexual behavior and the lower-class practices of serial nonmarital monogamy became stigmatized. Prostitutes were marginalized, and the economic and sexual independence some women attained was obscured in popular culture. While these forms of sexual behavior continued to be practiced in Philadelphia, they had been driven out of public view.

The ascendancy of the white middle-class construction of sexuality in the 1820s was accomplished, in part, by the bifurcation of sexuality. Within this construction, the nature of a woman's sexuality depended on her position in a society stratified by race and class. The acceptance of this new, bifurcated version of female sexuality by middle-class women shored up their social position by differentiating them from women of color and the lower classes and was essential to the establishment of the cultural hegemony of the nineteenth-century middle-class gender system. Attributing sexual "licentiousness" to the rabble reinforced the social divisions between elite and middle-class whites on the one side and the rest of the community on the other. During this era, when the creation of the first modern republic brought Americans closer together as political citizens and the abolition of slavery recognized the basic shared humanity of blacks and whites, the creation of a two-tiered sexual system reestablished traditional social divisions based on race, class, and gender.

By constructing a normative sexuality associated with the white elite and middle classes and a deviant, oversexed sexuality of the rabble, Philadelphians fused perceptions of illegitimate sexuality onto the bodies of African-Americans and lower-class whites. This not only naturalized racial and class-based "difference" between Philadelphians but also naturalized the inferior economic and political positions blacks and lower-class whites held in the antebellum city. For, if only the women of the rabble were purposefully licentious, and their children illegitimate, then their communities themselves must be responsible for their own hardships and failures.

Philadelphians had traveled far from the days when its men read "The Half-Joe Changed" in the London-Coffee House and joked about being called to task for their sexual exploits. They had left behind the era when the independent sexuality of their women was left unpoliced and their community openly engaged in struggles over the patriarchal prerogatives of husbands, embodied in the actions of eloping wives, adulterous women, and women who established sexual liaisons outside marriage. The debates over the nature of female sexuality and the extent of female agency, aired through competing discourses in the words of the public presses and the deeds of Philadelphia women, had been silenced. The open discussion of a range of possibilities in gender relations, sexual behavior, and distribution of power was curtailed by narrowing the sexual scripts presented in the public print culture and changing the public policy on nonmarital sexual behavior to penalize and publicize only women and the lower classes and to obscure the participation of elite and middle-class men.

Philadelphians had faced the problems and embraced the possibilities of creating a modern state in a new, enlightened world. The society they crafted allowed them to break with the past to create a modern republic and yet maintain fundamental hierarchical social relations between men and women, whites and blacks, and elites and the lower classes. Creating a new gender system consistent with an Enlightenment liberal worldview had played an important role in this work. Philadelphians had abandoned their mid-eighteenth-century notions of gender as a fluid continuum enacted through performances and crafted a new understanding of gender consisting of rigidly dichotomous male and female beings, whose fundamental differences were made evident through sexuality. The primary mechanism used to establish the new basis of gender was enhancing the importance of the sexual character of the individual. In creating highly gendered sexualities, female sexuality had become a core attribute distinguishing and defining women. In Philadelphia this had two parts. First, during the mid-eighteenth century, the distinctions between male and female sexualities were accentuated, creating a belief that male sexuality was dynamic and malleable and open to influence by the individual through the use of reason. Female sexuality was constructed in opposition to this male model by emphasizing the inherent and fixed nature of female sexuality. In the early new nation the second step was to refashion the attributes of female sexuality to oppose the licentiousness culturally ascribed to African-American women and women of the lower classes. The new attributes of female sexuality were moderate desire, inherent sexual reserve, and a natural inclination to chastity and sexual constancy. Female sexuality remained inherent, static, and fixed and was therefore essentialized. Actively seeking sexual fulfillment, exhibiting unbridled sexual desire, and embracing sexual relationships outside courtship and marriage had become deviant for women. By 1820 sexual character had become a defining aspect of the female individual, and sexual temperament was recognized as a central attribute of the individual self. In creating deviant sexuality, sexuality itself had become a useful concept for deploying power.[1]

For women, embracing this conceptualization of the female self became the springboard for nineteenth-century moral reform and political activism. But it also foreclosed the possibility of building women's place in society based on her equality with men. It would take another hundred years for women's rights to be advocated from the premise of her equality and her essential human likeness to man. Acceptance of this new model of gender, grounded in sexuality, came with another price as well. It divided women by denigrating the sexual character of working-class women and women of color and enhancing the position of middle-class, mostly white women at the expense of other women, creating a division that persisted through much of the nineteenth and twentieth centuries.

The early years of the new nation also set in motion important components of modern race relations among free people. The simultaneous abolition of slavery and creation of the Republic made Philadelphia one of the first places to negotiate race relations. But in early national Philadelphia racialized understandings of sexuality were used to reconstruct the basis of racial domination by white Philadelphians. Here the promotion of distinct sexualities for whites and blacks reaffirmed a racial hierarchy that most white Philadelphians were committed to, despite their objections to slavery. Perhaps if slavery had been abolished nationwide, things could have been different. But early national Philadelphia developed within a broader slave society. Dismantling slavery did not shield white Philadelphians from the fears and anxieties of racial warfare that were generated by the United States' steadfast commitment to slavery. In the early nineteenth century, racial hatred became a way to pit members of the

1. In this respect early national Philadelphians fitted the pattern of development Michel Foucault suggested was the impetus for the birth of the concept of sexuality. *The History of Sexuality*, I, *An Introduction*, trans. Robert Hurley (New York, 1978).

lower classes against one another, as each struggled to survive the economic hardships of wage-labor capitalism. In this environment, attacking the sexual morality of the city's free African-Americans and promoting beliefs in their natural licentiousness became fundamental to race relations. In so doing, Philadelphians began pathologizing the intimate relations and family formation of free African-Americans, which has continued as an important strand of racial hatred to this day.

The impetus to research and write this book began as I participated in contemporary political struggles in the years before I undertook the professional training to become a historian. It was born of my experiences working with other women struggling to find ways to address the interwoven strands of racial, gender, and economic oppression evident in the sexual subordination of women in the contemporary United States. It is my hope that this book has shed some light on the ways that privilege and oppression of specific groups of women were created in relationship to one another and were also part of the overall societal interest in limiting the range of opportunities for all women. I hope it will encourage us to think twice when we hear the contemporary rhetoric demonizing "the welfare mother" or the "pathology" of single parenthood and to consider what purposes these derogatory appellations serve and what interests they protect. Finally, I hope this book allows us to remember a time in American history when, in Philadelphia on the eve of our nation's founding, families were created in a wide variety of forms, born of a broad spectrum of beliefs, and the responsibility for children born "legitimate" or "illegitimate" belonged to the community in which they lived and was understood as part of the expression of a belief in collective social responsibility.

APPENDIX

Class was determined by locating individuals in tax records and city directories and by internal evidence on occupation and wealth within the records of the Guardians of the Poor, Pennsylvania Divorce Papers, and Prisoners for Trial Docket. I adopted the system of categorizing class by occupation developed by Billy G. Smith and followed Stuart M. Blumin's analysis of class formation. Smith and Blumin differ on their classification of lower-paid skilled trades. I followed Smith's system and classified shoemakers as lower-class. Smith, *The "Lower Sort": Philadelphia's Laboring People, 1750–1800* (Ithaca, N.Y., 1990); Blumin, *The Emergence of the Middle Class: Social Experience in the American City, 1760–1900* (Cambridge, 1989).

Sources

Tax Records. "Taxables in the City of Philadelphia, 1756," *Pennsylvania Genealogical Magazine*, XXII (1961), 3–41; Philadelphia Tax Lists for 1772, 1780, 1789, 1798; Philadelphia Constable Returns for 1775; computerized data provided by Billy G. Smith.

City Directories for 1790s. Clement Biddle, *The Philadelphia Directory* (Philadelphia, 1791); Edmund Hogan, *The Prospect of Philadelphia . . .* (Philadelphia, 1795); Thomas Stephens, *Stephens's Philadelphia Directory, for 1796 . . .* (Philadelphia, 1796); *The New Trade Directory, for Philadelphia, Anno 1800 . . .* (Philadelphia, 1799); Cornelius William Stafford, *The Philadelphia Directory, for 1799 . . .* (Philadelphia, 1799); Cornelius William Stafford, *The Philadelphia Directory, for 1800 . . .* (Philadelphia, 1800).

City Directories for 1820s. John Adams Paxton, *The Philadelphia Directory and Register, for 1819 . . .* (Philadelphia, [1819]); Edward Whitely, *The Philadelphia Directory and Register for 1820* (Philadelphia, 1820); Edward Whitely, *Whitley's Annual Philadelphia Directory* (Philadelphia, 1822); Robert DeSilver, *The Philadelphia Index; or, Directory for 1823* (Philadelphia, 1823); Thomas Wilson, ed., *The Philadelphia Directory and Stranger's Guide, for 1825 . . .* (Philadelphia, 1825); Robert DeSilver, *Desilver's Philadelphia Directory and Stranger's Guide, 1830 . . .* (Philadelphia, 1830).

Bastardy cases were culled from the court records and Guardians of the Poor records for each era to make a comprehensive database for each period.

1767–1776. This figure was derived by taking the totals for five years of complete records by the Overseers of the Poor (1767–1769, 1775, 1776) and court records and doubling the five-year figure. The extant court records for this decade show a six-year gap in the Mayor's Court records (1771–1776). Two cases were added to the five-year total, to compensate for these missing records, based on the frequency of bastardy cases in the Mayor's Courts from 1760 to 1770. Overseers of the Poor records: OPM, Bonds, 1755–1787; Philadelphia Almshouse Ledger, 1767–1768, HSP.

Court records: MCD; QSD (Philadelphia cases), HSP; Philadelphia Grand Jury Presentments, and Miscellaneous Court Records, 1716–1786, HSP; Eastern District, Philadelphia County, Court of Oyer and Terminer, Dockets and Case Files, 1757–1759, 1763, 1765, 1767–1776, 1778, 1782, PSA, 1799–1830, HSP.

Extant Church disciplinary records contributed 10 cases to this decadal figure: PWMM; Scots Presbyterian Church, Session Minutes, 1758–1821, PHS; Second Presbyterian Church, Session Minutes, 1750–1830, PHS; First Baptist Church Minutes, HSP.

1790s. Full records survive for both the Guardians of the Poor and the city courts. Guardians of the Poor Minutes (GPM) and Bond Book were each used for all ten years; in the Almshouse Daily Occurrence Docket (DOD), which recorded almshouse bastardy cases, a sample of three and one-quarter years was multiplied to get the ten-year figure (1790, 1793, 1796, one-fourth of 1798); and the court records were used for all ten years: PFT, MCD, QSD (Philadelphia cases only). Extant Oyer and Terminer Case Files were used for 1795–1799 to contribute the few bastardy infanticide cases, and evidence of bastardy was extracted from the Philadelphia cases in PDP, 1790–1799.

1805–1814. The same records were used as in the 1790s. All the court records were used completely for all ten years. For the Guardians of the Poor it was necessary to estimate the number of cases appearing in GPM from 1806 though 1814 because the record was abbreviated during those years, and bastardy cases could not be conclusively distinguished from other forms of support. This estimate was arrived at by establishing the proportion of cases that appeared only in the Minute Book in 1805 (55 percent) and calculating the same proportion in relationship to the cases found in the Guardians Bond Book and in the court records for each of the missing years. This estimate added 835 cases for the missing nine years of GPM. In 1805, 55 percent of out-relief cases appeared only in GPM, and in 1822 that figure was 56 percent. Because the proportion of GPM-only cases remained unchanged at the next year for which full data were obtained (1822), it was deemed an acceptable figure for the multiplier used. A four-year sample (1805, 1810, 1812, 1813) of the DOD was used to compute a ten-year figure to establish the almshouse cases.

1822–1826. The Guardians' records were used in full, as were the court records for 1822–1825. The 1826 case number of 269 was taken from the Guardians published year-end report for 1826. The Guardians of the Poor records for 1822–1825 were GPCB Bond Book, GPM, Bastardy Bond Papers, GPSD. Almshouse cases were established by using two sample years, 1822 and 1825, from DOD, multiplied to get five-year figure. The Almshouse Register of Births, 1808–1830, CCAP, was also used, although it contributed few new cases to the database. Court records were the same as in previous decades: PFT; MCD; QSD (Philadelphia cases only); Records of the Office of the Secretary of the Commonwealth, Extradition Papers, 1822–1826, PSA; Oyer and Terminer Dockets and Case Files, 1822–1826, HSP (Philadelphia cases only). The 1826 figure was taken from Guardians of the Poor, *Report of the Committee Appointed . . . to Visit the Cities . . .* (Philadelphia, 1827).

MOTHERS' REQUESTS FOR OUT-RELIEF BASTARDY CHILD SUPPORT

Table A.1. Bastardy Cases: Timing of Mother's Request for Out-Relief

Timing of Request	1750–1779 No.	%	1790–1799 No.	%	1805 No.	%	1822–1825 No.	%
Before birth	78	60	101	73	32	67	233	73
After birth	53	40	38	27	16	33	84	27
Total	131	100	139	100	48	100	317	100

Notes: Totals represent number of cases for which information was available. Overall number of cases: 1750–1799: 165; 1790–1799: 508; 1805: 120; 1822–1825: 805.

Cases where the mother was admitted to the almshouse before the birth of her child have been excluded from consideration here for all eras except the pre-Revolutionary. From 1790 on, the Almshouse Daily Occurrence Docket (DOD) records bastardy cases of women who used the almshouse to give birth. All of these women entered the system before the birth of their child, but use of the almshouse, in many cases, indicated the poverty of the mother and father and did not necessarily reflect the mother's lack of confidence in the father or a judgment on the relationship with him. Almshouse bastardy cases represented about 28 percent of the cases throughout this half-century. See Table 14, above.

In 1750–1780, 15 women entered the almshouse sometime during their pregnancy. At least one-third of them stayed there only long enough for the Overseers to secure a bond from the father. The data cannot establish how many of the remaining ten women were forced to give birth in the almshouse because of their poverty and the poverty of the father of their child.

Because we have no comparable record from the almshouse in the pre-Revolutionary era, we cannot know how many of the women who entered the almshouse were poor and stayed there through the birth.

SEXUAL TRANSGRESSIONS

Table A.2. Sexual Transgression: Summary, 1750–1814

Offense	1750– 1779	1790– 1799	1805– 1814
Adultery and bigamy	9	115	145
Bastardy	165	711	2,193
Prostitution	4	53	220
Miscellaneous	86	30	80
Total	264	909	2,638

Sources:

1750–1779: OP, Bonds, 1755–1779; OPM, 1768–1779; Overseers of the Poor, Philadelphia Almshouse Ledger, 1767–1768, HSP; Overseers of the Poor, Miscellaneous Papers, 1750–1751, HSP; MCD, 1759–1771, 1779; QSD, 1753–1779 (Philadelphia cases); Court of Oyer and Terminer, Eastern District, Philadelphia County, Dockets and Case Files, 1757–1759, 1763, 1765, 1767–1776, 1778; Philadelphia County Records, Grand Jury Presentments and Miscellaneous Court Records, 1750–1779, HSP. Church disciplinary records, 1750–1779: PWMM, 1760–1779; First Presbyterian Church, Minutes, 1750–1772, PHS; Scots Presbyterian Church, Session Minutes, 1768–1779, PHS; Second Presbyterian Church, Session Minutes, 1750–1779, PHS; First Baptist Church Minutes, 1757–1779, HSP.

1790–1799: PFT, 1790–1799; MCD, 1790–1799; QSD, 1790–1799 (Philadelphia cases); GPM, 1790–1799; Guardians of the Poor, Bond Book, 1798–1799, CCAP;

DOD, 1790–1799; Court of Oyer and Terminer, Dockets and Case Files, 1795–1799; PDP (Philadelphia cases), 1790–1799.

1805–1814: PFT, 1805–1814; MCD, 1805–1814; QSD (Philadelphia cases), 1805–1814; GPM, 1805 (3 months); Guardians of the Poor, Bond Book, 1805–1814; DOD, 1805–1814; Court of Oyer and Terminer, Dockets and Case Files, 1805–1814; PDP (Philadelphia cases), 1805–1814.

Table A.3. Sexual Transgression, 1750–1779

Offense	Subtotal	Total
Bastardy		165
Simple bastardy	156	
Bastardy and infanticide	7	
Bastardy and child abandonment	2	
Adultery		5
Bigamy		4
Keeping a bawdyhouse		2
Abduction for prostitution		1
Luring (prostitution)		1
Fornication		15
Premarital sex[a]		22
Marrying outside meeting[a]		13
Consanguineous Marriage[a]		2
Rape		4
Disorderly house		12
Keeping bad company		8
Miscellaneous infractions		
Improper conduct		10
Grand total		264

[a] This transgression was recorded in Quaker Minutes only.

Sources: See Table A.2.

Table A.4. Sexual Transgression, 1790–1799

Offense	Subtotal	Total
Adultery and bigamy		115
Simple adultery	82	
Adultery with venereal disease and prostitute	2	
Adultery with venereal disease	5	
Adultery with prostitute	5	
Bigamy	21	
Bastardy		711
Simple bastardy	700	
Bastardy with adultery	8	
Bastardy and child abandonment	2	
Bastardy with infanticide	1	
Prostitution		53
Keeping a bawdyhouse (27 houses)	34	
Fornication in a bawdyhouse	9	
Street prostitution	10	
Other sexual offenses		30
Cohabitation with absconded servant	1	
Cohabitation, woman with woman	1	
Cross-dressing	1	
Exposure	1	
Fornication	7	
Lewdness (men)	3	
Public fornication	2	
Rape, simple	5	
Rape, aiding and abetting	2	
Rape, attempted	5	
Seduction	1	
Sexual abduction	1	
Grand total		909

Notes: Each offense is counted only once, although it might have involved several transgressions. For instance, bastardy that was committed during marriage is counted only under bastardy (bastardy with adultery).

Divorce suits were often filed years after a couple separated. The date of the sexual infraction determines inclusion in this table.

Sources: See Table A.2.

Table A.5. Sexual Transgression, 1805–1814

Offense	Subtotal	Total
Adultery and bigamy		145
Simple adultery	97	
Adultery with venereal disease	1	
Sexual fraternization[a]	13	
Bigamy	34	
Bastardy		2,193
Simple bastardy	1,340	
Bastardy and child abandonment	1	
Bastard murder	17	
Bastardy[b]	835	
Prostitution		220
Keeping a bawdyhouse (118 houses)	147	
Fornication in a bawdyhouse	8	
Street prostitution	65	
Other sexual offenses		80
Bestiality	1	
Bawdy language	1	
Cross-dressing	1	
Exposure	3	
Fornication	32	
Incest	1	
Infant abandonment	1	
Infanticide	4	
Infanticide, attempted	1	
Lewdness (men)	3	
Licentious conduct (women)	1	
Public fornication	2	
Rape	14	
Rape, attempted	5	
Scandalous behavior	3	
Seduction	1	
Sexual assault	1	
Sexual fraternization[a]	2	
Sexual abduction	1	

Table A.5. continued

Offense	Subtotal	Total
Sexual abduction, attempted	1	
Sodomy	1	
Grand total		2,638

[a] Sexual fraternization: usually a woman charged with harboring another's husband, when the wife brought the charge (12 of those, plus 1 woman harboring underage son, 1 man harboring another's wife, 1 man with a master's female servant).

[b] The Guardians of the Poor Minutes are abbreviated during this decade. An estimate was used to established the cases of bastardy recorded in the minutes. See the explanation above in "Bastardy Totals."

Notes: Each offense is counted only once, although it might have involved several transgressions.

Divorce suits were often filed years after a couple separated. The date of the sexual infraction determines inclusion in this table.

Sources: See Table A.2.

MANUSCRIPT SOURCES

Overseers of the Poor
Bonds of Indemnity, 1755–1787, HSP.
Minutes, 1768–1787, CCAP.
Miscellaneous Papers, 1750–1751, HSP.
Philadelphia Almshouse Ledger, 1767–1768, HSP.
The Poor's Day Book for 1739, Simon Gratz Collection, HSP.

Guardians of the Poor
Almshouse Black Book, 1810–1814, CCAP.
Almshouse Daily Occurrence Docket, 1789–1825, CCAP.
Almshouse Hospital Register of Births, 1808–1830, CCAP.
Almshouse Syphilis Ledger, 1808–1812, CCAP.
Applications to Remove Children from the Asylum, 1826–1829, CCAP.
Bastardy Bond Papers, 1811–1825, CCAP.
Bond Book, 1799–1827, CCAP.
Cases Referred to the Committee upon Bastardy, 1821–1826, CCAP.
Committee on the Children's Asylum, 1820–1830, CCAP.
Indenture Papers and Bonds, 1794–1830, CCAP.
Letter Book, 1823–1829, HSP.
Minutes, 1788–1830, CCAP.
Paupers Lists, 1821–1829 (17 volumes), CCAP.
Solicitors Docket, 1822–1828, John M. Scott, Solicitor, HSP.

Court Records
Ancient Records of Philadelphia, 1702–1790, Wallace Collection, HSP.
Court of Oyer and Terminer, Eastern District, Philadelphia County, Dockets and Case
    Files, 1799–1830, Pennsylvania Court Records, HSP.
Court of Oyer and Terminer, Philadelphia County, Grand Jury Inquest, 1817, HSP.
Court of Oyer and Terminer, Eastern District, Philadelphia County, Dockets and Case
    Files, 1757–1759, 1763, 1765, 1767–1776, 1778, 1782, PSA.
Court of Quarter Sessions, Philadelphia County, Docket, 1753–1785, HSP.
Court of Quarter Sessions, Philadelphia County, Docket, 1786–1830, CCAP.
Mayor's Court, Docket, 1759–1771, HSP.
Mayor's Court, Docket, 1779–1830, CCAP.
Narratives in Slander, Philadelphia District Court, 1810–1818, CCAP.
Pennsylvania Supreme Court, Convicts Sentencing Docket, 1804–1810, CCAP.
Pennsylvania Supreme Court, Pennsylvania Divorce Papers, 1785–1815, PSA.

Philadelphia County Records, Grand Jury Presentments and Miscellaneous Court
Records, 1716–1786, HSP.

Prisoners for Trial, Philadelphia County Prison, Docket, 1790–1830, CCAP.

Records of the Office of the Secretary of the Commonwealth, Extradition Papers, 1794–
1829, PSA.

Vagrancy Docket, 1790–1797, and 1805–1814, CCAP.

Church Records

Fifth Presbyterian Church, Session Minutes, 1816–1830, PHS.

First Baptist Church, Minutes, 1757–1779, HSP.

First Presbyterian Church, Minutes, 1750–1772; Session Minutes, 1807–1830; Minutes of
Trustees 1796–1825, PHS.

Fourth Presbyterian Church, Session Minutes, 1802–1830, PHS.

Kensington First Presbyterian Church, Session Minutes, 1814–1830, PHS.

Mother Bethel African Methodist Episcopal Church, Minutes and Trial Book, 1822–1825,
HSP.

Old Swedes (Gloria Dei) Church, Baptisms and Marriages, vols. I –IV, 1750–1825, HSP.

Scots Presbyterian Church, Session Minutes, 1758–1821, PHS.

Second Presbyterian Church, Session Minutes, 1750–1830, PHS.

Society of Friends, Philadelphia Men's Monthly Meeting, Minutes, 1760–1762, FHL.

Society of Friends, Philadelphia Women's Monthly Meeting, Minutes, 1760–1779, FHL.

Other Manuscripts

Bradford, Thomas. Day Book of Bradford's Circulating Library, 1771–1772, HSP.

Bradford, Thomas and William. Invoice Book, 1767–1769, HSP.

Bradford, Thomas and William. Inventory Book, November 14, 1767, HSP.

Magdalen Society of Philadelphia. Minutes of the Board of Managers, 1800–1825, HSP.

Managers of the Poor of the Township of Germantown. Minutes, 1809–1822,
Germantown Historical Society.

Pennsylvania Abolition Society. Acting Committee Minutes, 1798–1804; Committee for
Improving the Conditions of Free Blacks, Minutes, 1790, HSP.

Philadelphia Society for Alleviating the Miseries of Public Prisons. Minutes of the Acting
Committee, 1798–1807, HSP.

Philadelphia Tax Lists for 1772, 1780, 1789, 1798; Philadelphia Constable Returns for 1775,
computerized data Provided by Billy Smith. Originals at HSP.

[Wilson, James ?]. Account Book and Diary, APS.

ACKNOWLEDGMENTS

This book began as a research paper in Pat Cohen's seminar at the University of California at Santa Barbara well more than a decade ago, grew into a dissertation at Yale University under the direction of Nancy Cott, and then morphed into the book it is during my first years on the faculty at the University of Maryland. It has undergone such a prolonged gestation that I have whole generations of friends and colleagues to thank. It is with great joy that I turn, finally, to this task.

I am deeply grateful to the cadre of scholars who supported my intellectual development as a graduate student. Each of them in their own way took me in, greeting me as a fellow scholar, and provided the support necessary to make that assumption a reality. A wonderful dissertation committee, Nancy Cott, John Demos, and Jon Butler, always showed nothing but enthusiasm for this project. My thanks to Nancy Cott, who gave me the free rein I needed to develop my ideas but shared her astute insights each and every time I sought advice; to John Demos, whose puzzled inquiries often forced me to clarify my arguments and taught me much about graduate teaching in the process; and to Jon Butler, who was never surprised by what I proposed to write and shared that crucial and sage advice, "Just keep writing." Bill Cronon also deserves thanks for his part in fostering an environment of intellectual creativity during my first years at Yale. I owe a special debt of gratitude to Pat Cohen, my first mentor and longtime friend. It is a pleasure to thank her for her intellectual insights, her candor, and her never-ending support.

Many friends and colleagues have discussed this work and shared their ideas with me. For their emotional and intellectual support I thank Stacy Robertson, Ula Taylor, Rachel Casas, Cara Anzilotti (who first suggested Philadelphia as the site for this study), Jill Lepore, Becky Tannenbaum, Jonathan Halloway, Demaris Lugo, and the late Markie Rath. Thanks also to Colleen O'Neill, who shared the path from political activism to graduate school and on into the academy; and to David Reichart for making much of the research possible by opening his home to me in Philadelphia. Thank you each for your intellectual contributions and friendship during my years in Santa Barbara and New Haven. Many of my colleagues at the University of Maryland have shared their insights with me. I am especially grateful to Ira Berlin, Emory Evans, Elsa Barkley-Brown, Robyn Muncy, and Leslie Rowland for their support of my scholarship. Special thanks to Shelley Sperry for careful reading of and editorial assistance on an earlier draft of the manuscript.

Several scholars read parts of the manuscript as it made its way into scholarly conferences and offered their formal comments for my consideration. Thanks to Herman Bennett, Kathleen Brown, Patricia Cohen, Richard Godbeer, and Susan Klepp for their responses and critiques. Thanks also to conference participants who shared their ideas and reactions to my work. And many thanks to Billy Smith, who shared his computerized data of Philadelphia tax lists with me, making the class analysis of the subjects in the study much less arduous. Finally, thanks to the two anonymous readers who read the entire manuscript for the Institute and offered their detailed critique of the book as it took its final form.

To the archivists and staff members of the libraries I utilized, a special thanks, for without their work our histories could not be written: American Antiquarian Society; City and County Archives of Philadelphia; Friends Historical Library, Swarthmore; Germantown Historical Society; Historical Society of Pennsylvania; Library Company of Philadelphia; Library of Congress; Presbyterian Historical Society; American Philosophical Society; Pennsylvania State Archives; Sterling Library, Yale University, especially the staff of the microtext room; and the University of Maryland's McKeldin Library. I am deeply grateful for your patience pulling box after box of dusty old documents, for leading me to sources new to me, and for working to protect these treasures by advocating for public support of the archives.

I have been fortunate to enjoy financial support for this project throughout its long gestation. Financial support for the research and writing of the dissertation was provided by the Library Company of Philadelphia; the Kate B. and Hall J. Peterson Fellowship at the American Antiquarian Society; the Andrew W. Mellon Foundation; the Pew Program in Religion and American History; and the Robert M. Leyland Dissertation Fellowship in Humanities at Yale University. Expansion and revision of the manuscript were supported by a year at the Omohundro Institute of Early American History and Culture as an Andrew W. Mellon postdoctoral fellow. This gave me needed time away from the day-to-day duties of the university to think, research, and write. Thanks to all those at the Institute who made me welcome and gave me the space to work, especially the always-smiling faces of Beverly Smith and Sally Mason. The Department of History at the University of Maryland sponsored a semester's leave from teaching, providing time to write and revise, and the Graduate Research Board at the University of Maryland provided summer research funds to finish the research. I am grateful for the support provided at every step of the way and hope the finished product justifies the faith these funders extended to me and to the idea of this project.

I want to extend a special thanks to Ron Hoffman and Fredrika J. Teute at the Institute. Ron became a supporter of this project early on and has always shown nothing but enthusiasm for it and encouragement for me as its author. Fredrika too has been a longtime advocate of this book, asking tough questions and applying her probing analytical skills to the manuscript but also demonstrating her faith that I would write the book envisioned. Together they have made a fine team, the yin and yang of the Institute, and I have benefited from working with them. The last to make his contribution is Gil Kelly, who has worked arduously to copy-edit the book. His commitment to making this the best book possible is unsurpassable. Here, Gil, is the last bit you need to copy-edit. My heartfelt thanks for your skill and dedication!

Another set of institutions deserves my deep thanks, the Edith B. Jackson childcare center in New Haven and the Kensington Forest Glen Children's Center in Silver Spring.

The EBJ and KFGCC staffs provided the tender and stimulating care of my children that allowed me the peace of mind to write. In another era a woman like myself would have had to choose between writing such a book and caring for her infant children. I have been blessed to live a life where I could do both, owing to the commitment of other women like Ellen Burnstein, Georgette Telescus, Gailie Bird Miller, and Jackie Howell.

The greatest thanks, and appreciation, I owe are to my family. You have been the wellspring of my strength, helping in myriad ways in the creation of this book. To all the Bergs, especially Lorraine and Roger, thanks for never giving up on asking how the book was coming, and then letting me move on to other topics! To my brother, John, thanks for those early lessons in argumentation taught at the family dinner table. Thanks to my sister, Claudia, the artist, who drew the delightful bawdyhouse maps, and together with my brother-in-law Loel and nephew David provided consistent support and much-needed retreats and diversions. To Andrew and Eve, thanks for graciously tolerating the intrusions this book has made into your young lives and bringing more joy into my life than you can imagine. To Steve, thanks for being there in every imaginable way, from before either of us ever imagined a book and now into life after the book.

Above all, I want to express my gratitude to my parents. I dedicate this book to my father, Neil Lyons, for a lifetime of guidance, encouragement, and fatherly devotion and to the memory of my mother, Beverly Lyons, whose keen intellect and tenacious spirit continue to encourage and sustain me.

Connoisseur, 137, 138–139, 144, 148

Constitution: of Pennsylvania, 209; of New Jersey, 238–239; of the United States, 238–239, 291

Contraceptives, 189

Corydon and Phillis (Cunningham), 294–295

Cox, Flora, 375

Craigie, Andrew, 85, 92

Cross-racial sex: instances of, 11, 56, 68, 88–91, 193–197, 199, 224, 266–269, 277n. 57, 356–357, 364n. 12, 368n. 18, 375, 377–380; law on, 88–89, 91, 195n. 17; in popular culture, 103; views on, 218, 224, 230–232, 356–357, 377

Cry, The, 149

Cuckoldry. *See* Adultery

Customary sexual practices: of the Welsh, 72; of the Scots, 72; of the English, 72–73

Davidson, Cathy, 317

Dempsey, Sarah, 268

Descartes, René, 154

Devil upon Crutches, 137, 141, 144–145, 148

Disappointment; or, The Force of Credulity, The (Forrest), 106–107

Divorce, 8, 17, 18n. 4, 56n. 68, 177n. 78, 199–207, 270–274; from bed and board, 18n. 4; in Scotland, 28; law on, 199–200, 200n. 24, 201, 204, 270n. 43, 285n. 67; and length of marriage, 205; and class, 207–208; in New England, 270. *See also* Runaway wife advertisements; Self-divorce

Domestic violence, 45–52, 275–276; in popular culture, 41–42; legal recourse in, 46–49, 48n. 55; customary extralegal policing of, 49–50; and limits on force, 51–52

Drinker, Elizabeth: on infanticide, 95; on servant's sexual behavior, 187, 199, 222–223; on bastardy, 199; on prostitution, 199, 323, 341; on African-Americans, 212; on crime pamphlets, 369n. 21

Dunbar, Rebecca, 20, 179

Dunlap, William, 117n. 2, 119–120

Dwire, Catharine, 109–110

Dwire, Peter, 109–110

Edward the Fourth's Amours, 131

Elizabeth ("mulatto Elizabeth"), 96, 100

English Anatomy Act (1828), 389

English Rogue, The, 131, 133–136

Enlightenment, 1–3, 151, 154, 157, 160, 163–164, 166, 175, 287–288; and political philosophy, 2, 183–185, 239–244; and women's status, 2–4, 163–164, 181, 184, 239, 288n. 71, 393–394; and gender relations, 289–290; Scottish, 289n. 71, 290. *See also* Citizenship; Republicanism

Eve (biblical), 157–158

Everyone Has His Fault (Inchbald), 287

Evitt, William, 145

Fair Adulteress, 148

Fanny; or, The Happy Repentant, 148

Farmer, Daniel Davis, 369

Father Abraham's Almanack, 116, 117n. 2, 119–120, 173

Female Council; or, The Moot-Point of Matrimony, 173–175

Female Policy Detected (Ward), 298–300

Female sexuality: construction of, 3–4, 155–159, 163–169, 171, 251–252, 286–307, 312–318, 390–392

Feme covert, 29, 52, 237–240

Feme sole trader status, 30n. 23

First Presbyterian Church, 85

Fortunate Footman, 148

Francis, Tench, 132

Franklin, Benjamin, 19, 37, 38–40, 39n. 39, 117n. 2, 126, 131; and *Miss Polly,* 81–82

French Revolution, 2, 183–184, 287
French Rogue, 133

Gender: early modern understanding of, 2, 151–153; and one-body model of anatomy, 2, 151–153, 155–156, 393; as binary opposites, 2–4, 153, 309, 393–394; as constructed through sexuality, 2, 4, 289–307, 309–311; and sexual responsibility, 4–5, 295–297, 352–354, 360, 370–374, 388–389; defined, 9; and poor relief, 384–390
Gender culture: of Philadelphia, 6, 11–12, 36, 42–43, 58, 244, 288; of New England, 6; of the Chesapeake, 6
Gloria Dei church, 18, 217
Goggin, John, 11–13, 18n. 4, 56
Gradual Abolition Act (1780), 23, 184, 195n. 17, 209–210, 215, 265
Great Awakening, 131, 132n. 19. *See also* Religious revivals
Greensickness (chlorosis), 158
Guardians of the Poor. *See* Overseers of the Poor
Guermeteau, Julie, 277, 288

Haitian Revolution (San Domingue), 2, 183–184; refugees of, in Philadelphia, 195, 212, 359
"Half-Joe Changed, The," 59–60, 393
Hall, David, 109, 117n. 2, 135, 146n. 38
Hamilton, Alexander, 201n. 26
Hardwicke Marriage Act (England), 17n. 3, 35, 35n. 32
Hay, Rev. John, 190, 202
Hilliad Magna: Being the Life and Adventures of Moll Placket-Hole, 104–106
Histories of Some of the Penitents, The, 323
History of Sally Sable, The, 149
Hogarth, William, 127, 140–141
Husband, The, 149

Illegitimacy, 64. *See also* Almshouse: and bastardy; Bastardy
Illustrious French Lovers, 138
Indentured servants: and bastardy, 90–92, 361–362; and sex commerce, 110–112; policing sexual behavior of, 214–216; and resistance, 216; and marriage, 217–218; as witnesses to adultery, 232–235, 271–273; as children of slaves, 265; as bastard children, 389
Indescreet Jewels, The (Les bijoux indiscrets), (Diderot), 131
Infanticide: and legal prosecution, 95, 99; in popular print, 99; in New England, 100
"Inscription for the Tomb of an Unfortunate Prostitute, An," 313–314
Invisible Spy, The (Haywood), 138,
Irish Rogue, The, 133

Jefferson, Thomas, 227, 230, 289
Jones, Absalom, 357
Jones, Griffith, 280–281
Joyce, John, 216, 358

Lacy, Elizabeth, 93–94
Laqueur, Thomas, 151
Laws: on adultery, 18n. 4, 285n. 67; on marriage, 28, 35–36, 36n. 34, 218n. 54; on bastardy, 77–78, 90–91, 388–389, 389n. 54; on cross-racial sex, 88–89, 91, 195n. 17; on infanticide, 96, 97n. 44; on divorce, 177n. 78, 199–201, 200n. 24, 204, 270n. 43, 285n. 67; on vagrancy, 198n. 22, 214n. 47; on masked balls, 342–343; for racial discrimination, 355; on poor relief, 388–389. *See also* Legal prosecution; Legal standards
Legal prosecution, 198; and domestic violence, 46–49, 48n. 55; and bastardy, 76–79, 80–81, 196–197, 267, 360, 379, 380n. 28, 381–382; and infanticide, 95–

Public sphere: and print culture, 18–19, 58, 150–151, 291–292, 393

Quakers. *See* Society of Friends

Race: and the construction of sexuality, 4–5, 86, 230–232, 356–357, 391–394; construction of, 88–89, 356; biological theories of, 229–230; environmental theories of, 229–232; relations, 355–359, 377, 394–395. *See also* Cross-racial sex

Rape, 197, 251, 251n. 14, 253, 270n. 42; in popular culture, 138, 142; as political metaphor, 297–298

Reform: of prostitutes, 323–333, 348–353; of mentally ill, 324; of penal system, 324, 335, 336n. 20; of the poor, 324, 383–384; of poor relief, 384–390; of public policy on bastardy, 384–390

Religious revivals, 296n. 82; and women, 291, 394; and reform of prostitution, 310, 321–323, 333; and reform of African-Americans, 357–358. *See also* Great Awakening

Republicanism: and women's political status, 3, 184, 237–244, 286–288, 290–291, 305–307; and sexuality, 188, 209–210, 223, 225–229, 286–291, 305–307, 392–394; and slavery, 229; and race, 229–232; and gender relations, 290–291

Ristiur, Justina, 186–188, 270, 287, 305

Rivington, James, 130, 136–137

Rousseau, Jean-Jacques, 238–239, 242

Rowlandson, Thomas, 301

Runaway husband advertisements, 177–178

Runaway wife advertisements: number of, 15; geographic location of, 15n. 1; and false allegations, 19–21; and wives' responses, 21–22, 43–48, 50–54, 179–

181; and class, 22–23; and ethnicity, 23. *See also* Self-divorce

Rush, Benjamin: on bastardy, 190–192; on lower classes, 223, 228–229, 353; on republicanism and sexual virtue, 226–229, 289, 305; on African-Americans, 229–231; on male sexuality, 245, 293, 352–353; on print in public sphere, 291–292; on female sexuality, 293; as reformer, 323–324; on sexual appetite, 352–353

Rush, Benjamin (distiller), 200–201

Sappho, 149, 150n. 42

School of Woman; or, Memoirs of Constantia, The (Génard), 133n. 20

School of Women (L'académie des dames) (Chorier), 133n. 20

Scientific rationalism. *See* Enlightenment

Scots Presbyterian Church, 86–87, 191

Scott, John M., 377, 381

Second Presbyterian Church, 85–86, 329

Secret Memoirs of the Duke and Dutchess of Orleans, The, 132

Select Trials at . . . the Old-Baily, 141–143

Self-divorce, 8, 11, 14–15, 171; and reconciliation, 15n. 1; in England, 16–17, 28; and financial obligations, 17–18; and just cause, 18, 21, 24–26, 43–47, 52–55, 175–176, 178; and wives' sexual independence, 25–26, 26n. 16, 54–58, 171, 175–178, 187–188; and property, 26–29, 46; and subsequent legal divorce, 56, 56n. 68, 56n. 69; and sensibility, 175–176; no-fault, 176–177; as political metaphor, 237. *See also* Runaway wife advertisements

Sentimental Journey through France and Italy (Sterne), 299–302

Sex: defined, 9

Sex commerce. *See* Bawdyhouses; Magdalens; Prostitution

Sex diarists, 248–254, 269; and views on

male sexuality, 249–252; and views on female sexuality, 251–252

Sexual coercion, 252–253, 269–270. *See also* Rape

Sexual culture, 72–73, 94–95, 117–118, 181, 185, 188, 195, 200, 208–209, 235–236, 309, 390–392

Sexuality: and construction of deviancy, 4, 309–311, 352–353, 369–372, 374, 390–395; and construction of racial difference, 5, 86, 88–89, 230–232, 356–357, 391–392, 394–395; and construction of normality, 5, 309–311, 390–392; defined, 9; and identity, 9, 393–394; and one-body model, 151–153, 160; as gendered binary opposites, 153, 304–307, 390; and Enlightenment thought, 154, 157, 160–164, 166, 175, 181, 188, 288–287; and biblical traditions, 157–158; perceptions of, of lower classes, 218, 221–224, 228–229, 260–261, 390–392; and construction of male citizen, 244–245, 290–291; and construction of gender difference, 289–307, 309; bifurcation of, 310–311, 333–335, 345–354, 375, 390–392; in medical discourse, 352–353. *See also* Class: and construction of sexuality; Female sexuality: construction of; Male sexuality: construction of; Male sexual privilege; Republicanism: and sexuality; Women: and sexual independence

Sexual slander, 103, 119n. 3; and race, 356–357, 377

Sisters; or, The History of Lucy and Caroline Sanson, The, 140–141

Slavery, 23, 88–89, 265, 358–359, 394; abolition of, 5, 91, 184, 209–210; resistance to, 89, 184; and semifree status, 184, 210n. 39, 265, 358–359

Slaves of Algiers (Rowson), 287

Society of Friends: and equalitarian marriage, 35; and bastardy, 83–85, 94; and premarital pregnancy, 85

Stevenson, Mary Ann, 331

Studham, John, 11–13

Theater, 61, 106, 284, 287

Thompson, E. P., 50

Turkish Spy, The, 148

Union Library Company, 143

Unmarried women: as heads of households, 32; as voters, 239

"Upon the Author of the Play Call'd Sodom" (Oldham), 132

Upper classes: and self-divorce, 23; and bastardy, 69–70, 206–207, 367, 374–380; and adultery, 206–208, 232–235; and nonmarital sex, 235

Vagrancy, 198n. 22, 214n. 47, 339–340

Vaughan, Mary, 77–78

Vaux, Robert, 384

Venereal disease, 112–114, 247, 253–255, 262–263, 327n. 8, 339–340, 343–345

Venus in the Cloister (Barrin), 131

Vindication of the Rights of Woman, A (Wollstonecraft), 242

Virtuous Orphans, 148, 149

Wallace, Mary, 96–97

White, Rev. William, 323, 351

Whites: and racial animosity, 355–356, 377–380

Wife sale, 16, 17n. 3, 222

Wilson, Elizabeth, 370–372

Wilson, James, 249n. 13

Wister, William, 235

Wo and a Warning; or, The Three Cruel Mothers, A, 99

Wollstonecraft, Mary, 238, 242–244, 287–288; *A Vindication of the Rights of Woman,* 242

Women: and sexual independence, 3, 25–26, 26n. 16, 54–58, 175–178, 181, 244, 256, 270–288, 305–307, 309, 318, 331, 387, 390, 393; economic roles of, 30–33, 113, 210–211, 284, 286, 320–321; as mothers, 62, 77–78, 91–95, 191, 259–261, 263–266, 277, 362–366, 368, 378–379, 380n. 38, 382; as readers, 147, 149–151, 149n. 41; political status of, 184, 237–244, 290–291, 305–307; and the franchise, 237–238; and education, 238, 240–244; and sexual autonomy, 256, 270–277, 317, 388; in prostitution, 323, 326, 328–333, 344, 348, 383; as moral reformers, 394. *See also* Female sexuality: construction of; Married women; Unmarried women

Yellow fever epidemic (1793), 223
York, John, 193–195, 216
Young Ladies' Academy of Philadelphia, 243